風口浪尖的歲月
Life on the Cusp

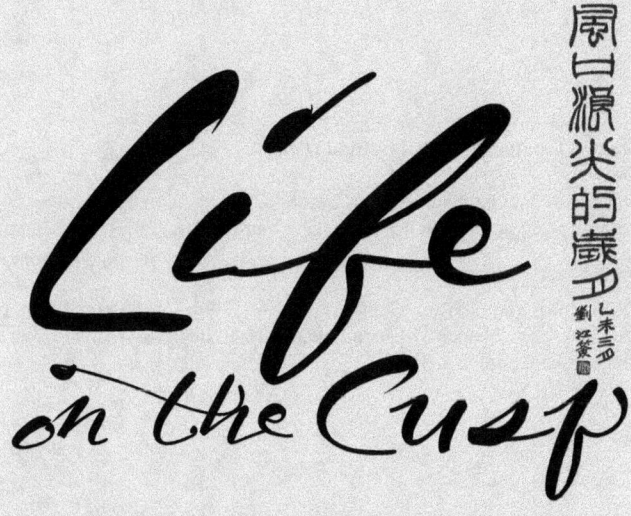

Weimin Wu

Fermilab

Translated by
Harry Tong • Candice Yuxi Wang

Cover calligraphy by Jiang Liu, Executive Director, Xilingyinshe

NEW JERSEY • LONDON • SINGAPORE • BEIJING • SHANGHAI • HONG KONG • TAIPEI • CHENNAI • TOKYO

Published by

World Scientific Publishing Co. Pte. Ltd.

5 Toh Tuck Link, Singapore 596224

USA office: 27 Warren Street, Suite 401-402, Hackensack, NJ 07601

UK office: 57 Shelton Street, Covent Garden, London WC2H 9HE

Library of Congress Cataloging-in-Publication Data
Wu, Weimin, 1943–
 [Feng kou lang jian de sui yue. English]
 Life on the cusp / written by Weimin Wu, Fermilab ; translated by Harry Tong, Candice Wang.
   pages cm
 In English.
 ISBN 978-9814630016 (hardcover : alk paper) | ISBN 978-9814651356 (pbk. : alk paper)
 1. Wu, Weimin, 1943– 2. Physicists--China--Biography. 3. Physicists--United States--Biography.
4. Chinese Americans--Biography. I. Title.
 QC16.W84W8413 2016
 530.092--dc23
 [B]
                              2015032207

British Library Cataloguing-in-Publication Data
A catalogue record for this book is available from the British Library.

Copyright © 2016 by World Scientific Publishing Co. Pte. Ltd.

All rights reserved. This book, or parts thereof, may not be reproduced in any form or by any means, electronic or mechanical, including photocopying, recording or any information storage and retrieval system now known or to be invented, without written permission from the publisher.

For photocopying of material in this volume, please pay a copying fee through the Copyright Clearance Center, Inc., 222 Rosewood Drive, Danvers, MA 01923, USA. In this case permission to photocopy is not required from the publisher.

Desk Editor: Shreya Gopi

Typeset by Stallion Press
Email: enquiries@stallionpress.com

Foreword

by Professor K. K. Phua

I have known Weimin for nearly thirty years since I first met him in 1984. The first time we met was at a photography competition in Geneva, Switzerland. His pictures won the first prize at that time, so I first thought that he was a professional photographer. Later, after talking with him, I learned that photography was just his hobby, whereas nuclear physics was his real profession. That really amazed me: it's rare to come across a physicist who could shoot such professional pictures. Later I found out that he had a lot of interests in life, and excelled in all of them, including photography. He is truly a multi-talented scientist.

Weimin and I have kept in contact ever since we met at Geneva, exchanging thoughts and ideas in physics research, and I was lucky enough to have invited him to work in my office in New Jersey, USA. He has an active and creative mind, and has always been rigorous with his scientific research. Such a well-rounded, talented person is a rarity, and it all has to do with the excellent education he received from his family and his own rich life experiences.

Weimin's life is unique and legendary. He participated in the making of the first atom bomb, and in the launch of the first artificial satellite of China, and was listed as the first person to send out an e-mail message in the Internet history of China. This autobiography records his rich, colorful, and eventful life with lively writing and precious pictures. For those who have not lived through that period of Chinese history, this book helps them to understand and feel the social environment of that time. At the same time, the rich emotional life of Weimin adds spice to his autobiography, with details rivaling stories in novels and movies! He wrote the book in a true to life way, with no undue embellishments. He presents his truest self to the readers. In the last chapter, Weimin analyzes his life experiences in both China and America, advancing the "convergence" theory of social development, which may capture the imagination of the readers.

At the time of publishing *Life on the Cusp*, I would like to offer my sincere thanks and congratulations to Weimin Wu.

Professor K. K. Phua

Director of the Institute of Advanced Studies of Nanyang Technological University, Singapore

Fellow of the American Physics Society

Foreword

By Professor Minghan Ye

I got to know Weimin in 1979, but the story really started from the end of 1953, when China began the construction of an electrostatic accelerator with an energy of 700 KeV. Chinese scientists learned from the journal *Review of Scientific Instruments* that Brookhaven National Laboratory of the United States had built a high energy accelerator called Cosmotron that can produce protons with an energy at 3 GeV. Upon hearing the news, we were all very excited, and Prof. Ganchang Wang was among the most excited. Although this was not a Chinese accomplishment, it was a major step ahead in experimental nuclear physics for the world. At that time, we had just gotten started in the game, but we had faith that we would catch up with the tide of world scientific development.

Time passed by all too quickly, and high energy particle physics developed on the foundation laid by high energy nuclear physics. The Institute of High Energy Physics in China was founded in 1973. An experimental base for high energy particle physics was established and talents were sought from over all the country. As luck would have it, Weimin joined the Institute of High Energy Physics. At that time, I was focused on developing a detector for high energy physics research, and was not in charge of recruiting, but I was excited to see the number of personnel increasing by the day. In order to carry out high energy physics experiments successfully and construct the accelerator and detectors, China attempted to train researchers by sending them abroad to participate in high energy physics experiments to get practical experiences. In 1979, thanks to the effort of Prof. T.D. Lee, which persuaded national leaders of China, as well as the generosity of leading scientists in America, the Institute of High Energy Physics sent more than 30 physicists to American research institutes and universities to join their high energy experiment groups. At the same time, three scholars were sent to the European Organization for Nuclear Research (CERN) based in Switzerland to join the CDHS group. Weimin was one of the three. By that time, I had gotten to know his name but not his background. I was appointed as the Director of Department One of Physics, responsible for the development of the Beijing Spectrometer. When it came to selecting staff members for the Beijing Spectrometer from the original members of Department One of Physics, I preferred volunteering. At the same time I also encouraged some scientists of other groups to join Department One of Physics. Someone told me that Weimin was very good. One day, I happened to catch Weimin walking on stairs, so without a second thought I invited him to join the work on the Beijing Spectrometer. He declined, and said that he was now busy with the work in the ALEPH group, which could not be finished in a short time. I felt that what he said made sense, so I did not insist.

In 1983, Weimin met with me to discuss China's participation in the ALEPH research group, when I was the Director of Department One of Physics. I said, "you need to combine the work of the Beijing Spectrometer with the ALEPH cooperation effort, and only this way can the ALEPH cooperation be incorporated into the main agenda of the Institute of High Energy Physics." When I said this, I was thinking that constructing the Beijing Electron-Positron Collider and developing the Beijing Spectrometer were the top priority tasks at the Institute of High Energy Physics, and therefore needed all the talents that could be found. At the same time, some effort should be spent on building up a team for analyzing high energy physics experiments in China and obtaining the analysis software that we needed urgently from abroad.

I think it was in 1984 that Weimin made a presentation about his work at the ALEPH group, and mentioned some issues related to software development. He said, "A software developer should make public his ideas to his group members all the time, share his thinking process with everyone, and make progress through cooperation; he cannot work alone by himself when he has some good ideas, and he should not be afraid that others will steal his ideas." I appreciated his attitude very much.

In 1986, when the Department One of Physics adjusted the makeup of its leadership, I felt that the manpower input on the application software for the Beijing Spectrometer should be strengthened.

I proposed that Weimin be appointed as the vice director in charge of software development. There were different opinions at the meeting regarding the appointment. However, I insisted on my choice and others stopped objecting, so the proposal was considered accepted. Later, it was described in the institute communiqué that "at the insistence of the Director Minghan Ye, the proposal for appointing Weimin Wu as the Vice Director of Department One of Physics was accepted." I was surprised after reading the communiqué. At the institute meeting, all staff members spoke freely, once any resolution was made, the communiqué would simply report the resolution, and had never before reported the discussion process, or if there were any dissenting opinions. The writing of this communiqué made me wonder why it was so written. Was it about making a footnote for responsibilities for future problems? I thought I would not worry too much; whatever I did, I should take responsibility. By October 1988, the Beijing Spectrometer was completed according to schedule, Weimin made his contributions, proving that my insistence was correct. Before that, many kind-hearted people worried about the construction speed of the Beijing Spectrometer, and were afraid that the progress of the software could not follow that of the hardware, resulting in a situation where after the completion of the hardware of the detector, data could not be taken, or once the data was taken, analysis could not be performed on it. We were all very happy that as soon as the Beijing Electron-Positron Collider was in operation, the Beijing Spectrometer recorded the data, which was analyzed to show that there were collisions of electrons and positrons.

From May to June of 1989, China went through a big shock of historical events. I lived in Zhongguan Village in the suburbs, and Weimin lived on Yuquan Road near downtown. I did not know about his activities, especially about how he made many videotapes of what happened at the Tiananmen Square protest. In July of the same year, I was invited to visit the Japanese High Energy Physics Research Institute (KEK), and joined the experiments of the AMY group. Only in Japan did I learn that he was in Switzerland to take part in the work of the ALEPH group. I thought it was just a simple scholarly visit. In 1990, Weimin helped organize the 25th International High Energy Physics Conference, and he made a special trip to Japan to carry out the liaison work. I met him in Japan, and learned about his activities in 1989.

Only in 1994, when I read *The Stormy Fifty Years* by Weimin, did I learn that Weimin had grown up in Shanghai. I had also grown up in Shanghai, and we shared much of the same environment in our youth, so I was very interested in his formative years. I felt that our generation had gone through various kinds of "movements" since 1949, especially the unprecedented Cultural Revolution. Such experiences are hard to comprehend for the following generations. How did it all happen? It is great that such a life story is written up for posterity.

I joined the Chinese Academy of Sciences as soon as I graduated from college, and worked there until retirement, quite a routine and predictable life. The life story of Weimin is much more rich and colorful. In short, he was selected to study in the Soviet Union, became a graduate student after taking examinations, was banished to the poorest countryside to join the peasants, almost died of illness, had confused thinking at the beginning of the Cultural Revolution, participated in the construction of the atom bomb, analyzed data gathered by the first artificial satellite, was transferred to do research in high energy physics, joined an international research effort, sent out the first international e-mail message from China during the process, measured the first bunch of J/psi particles recorded by the Beijing Spectrometer, witnessed the Beijing Protest Movement of 1989, and was forced out of China to work on high energy physics abroad. So many things happened to him in one lifetime.

Weimin wrote down his life story with a truthful spirit, describing his experiences with associated inner feelings in candid detail. After so much suffering, he has kept his untarnished heart! Let us understand him, and let more readers know about an era that we experienced, drawing inspiration from reading his wonderful life stories.

Professor Minghan Ye
Scientific Director, China Center of Advanced Science and Technology
Member, Chinese Academy of Engineering
Former Director of the Institute of High Energy Physics, Chinese Academy of Sciences

Prologue

I did not accomplish historical feats that shaped the landscape of modern Chinese science and technology, nor am I a scientific star of household fame. What compelled me to write this autobiography?

My father Benhao Wu was born in the year of Xinhai Revolution, the 1911 revolution that overthrew China's last imperial dynasty, the Qing Dynasty. My mother Xi Luo was born in the year of the founding of the Communist Party of China, 1921. I was born in the midst of the Sino-Japanese war, 1943. Perhaps it was those historical events in modern China that imbued the lives of my family members and myself with political overtones. If life has one hundred flavors to offer, I must have tried ninety-nine of them; if one hundred persons have one hundred life stories to tell, then my own life may have touched them all. The seventy years of life at the vortex of history showed me a unique life path, with some parts like thorny country roads and other parts like the German autobahns for speed driving, aided by the light of a bright sun. My life has left a series of indelible footsteps in the history of China's scientific and technological development. The story of my life unfolded like a scroll of history in a unique way.

First, regarding my career. I was personally involved in the making of the first atom bomb in China, as one of the youngest members of the 58-member team, at the tender age of seventeen. I participated in the data analysis of the first Chinese satellite, as well as the construction of the first Electron-Positron collider. The email message that I sent out from Beijing to Switzerland on August 25th, 1986, was recognized as the first one in the history of the Internet in China. I was a member of the research team that observed the first J/Psi particle on a recorder located in Beijing. I played an important role in using the CMS detector to discover the Higgs particle in 2012. It is a marvel how one person got involved in all those fields of research that appeared to be totally unrelated: the atom bomb, the artificial satellite, the Electron-Positron collider, and the Internet. Such a confluence of events associated with one person may occur only once in the world, a unique product of a Chinese society undergoing momentous changes at a special point in history.

While I had a remarkable scientific career, the jobs that I had along the way may sound farcical. I worked as a laborer who constructed houses, loaded up freight trains, and created tunnels using high explosives; I also worked as a farm hand who tended sheep, fed the pigs, and collected dung. It is difficult to reconcile these kinds of jobs with my career at the scientific frontiers in China and in the world, which makes my autobiography one-of-a-kind.

It may be interesting to use the houses I lived in as landmarks to describe my life. My birthplace in Shanghai was a small building located on a lane with a stone door entry. It had an attic that housed my entire family. I remember sleeping while holding the bound feet of my grandmother. Later we moved to a house with a garden, where I got to use running water for the very first time. As my mother changed jobs, we moved to a beige-colored building located on Julu Road. My younger brother once published a touching article describing life in this building. However, he missed an important event that occurred near this building: the farmer's market located on Julu Road once served as a showcase for the visit of the American President Nixon to China. I bore personal witness to that unforgettable historical event. After 1966, China went through a period of tumultuous changes. Those were years of calamity for my family. We lost the cozy beige building that we called home. My brothers and sisters were banished to various corners of China. Afterwards, it was hard to imagine the kinds of places that I had stayed in: raw caves fit for primitive man, Yaodong (cave houses) that were just a little more furnished than simple caves, and constructions made with unbaked earth bricks or metal sheets. I also lived in flimsy houses with thatched roofs, in buffalo sheds, in camps, in Mongolian style yurts, and in barracks. Hardest to imagine is such a cave, with a single bed made of bricks to accommodate an entire family plus myself. One tombstone for the ancestors stood at the end of the cave. There were rats running around every night, sometimes climbing on top of my body. After my return to Beijing, I first slept in a big classroom, and then moved to a simple building with only one shared toilet per floor. Lately, when I lie down on a big bed with a mattress, gazing into the high ceiling in my big house and searching in the depths of my memory, I often come up with nightmarish scenes of the past that feel so unreal.

For some seventy years, I experienced dramatic changes of fortune. At sixteen, I was granted a visit to the Huairen Hall of Zhongnanhai Palace as a representative of Shanghai students with high academic achievements, where I was received by and photographed with the late Chairman Mao and other Chinese national leaders at the time. Half a century later in Chicago, I had a similar meeting with President Hu Jintao and other Chinese national leaders, as a representative of the local Chinese community. During the time when I was at the Institute of High Energy Physics, I met with Deng Xiaoping and other national and party leaders of China. Those might be experiences of pride and moments of personal glory. However, during the movement against bourgeois-liberalism, I was targeted as a figure of dishonor for public humiliation.

At the beginning of the Cultural Revolution, I was among some fervent advocates who believed in the downfall of those bureaucrats and party functionaries who lorded over the common people. I repeatedly gave a speech titled "From the October Revolution in Russia to the January Revolution in China", first to audiences from the city of Lanzhou, and then to people all over the Province of Gansu, totaling over one hundred thousand. I was promoted to the top echelon of Lanzhou University administration as a representative for the people. However, towards the end of the Cultural Revolution, my parents and other members of my family all suffered from political persecution from the Gang of Four, as the country sank deep into economical and political chaos, with people struggling for basic subsistence everywhere. I began to take up a stance against the Gang of Four, and was eventually branded as a counter-revolutionary. The period from 1983 to 1988 were the golden years of my life, which happened to be when China was most open politically. I published a collection of articles under the title "Another Look at Capitalism", and made related speeches in numerous places. During this period, I made friends with Minghan Ye, Zhipeng Zheng, Hesheng Chen and others. Each of those named friends served in turn as the director of the Institute of High Energy Physics in Beijing. They helped me with my research work and with my personal life. However, those good times were short-lived. First came the movement against bourgeois-liberalism, followed by the famous Tiananmen Square protest. I got personally involved in the Tiananmen Square protest in 1989, and made lengthy video recordings of the student demonstrations, which quickly brought me personal misfortune, culminating in my escape from China. Over the next three years, I was not only fired from the Institute of High Energy Physics, but was also denied passport renewal by the Chinese consulate, rendering me technically stateless. Then I immigrated to the United States of America, becoming an American citizen in due course. History turned a new page, and China changed beyond imagination. China's GDP became the second highest in the world, indicating that the Chinese people had finally risen up for real. "The scientific concept of development" was written into the official charters of the Chinese Communist Party. I made my personal contributions to the promotion of friendship and cooperation between China and America. During my twenty years of living in America, I experienced the vicissitudes of life too, which made me have a deeper understanding of the true nature of American society. Those years of my life taught me one thing: people of different countries and cultures must learn from each other, to converge on a path that leads to a more harmonious and prosperous tomorrow.

Admittedly, I am a lucky man overall. At some key points of my life, even moments of adversity, I always had help from worthy persons of courage and compassion, most of whom happened to be women. In 1966, when I was banished to the remote mountain region of Yinjia, one of my legs was bitten by a dog, resulting in a life-threatening infection. It was the attentive care of an old country woman that helped me recover eventually. In 1964, I was doing "Four Clears" in the countryside, a sort of political activity that all college students had to do under Chairman Mao's instruction at that time, when it was time for my entrance examination to graduate schools. The team leader for Four Clears, Liying Mi, gave me special permission to return to Shanghai to take part in the examination without permission from a Fudan party leader. In 1989, I left China, and it was a woman from the Science Academy of China who gave me authorization papers at the last minute to leave the country. Professor Saulan Wu provided recommendations to help me find a job at Fermilab in the United States. If not for my "luck with ladies", it would be hard to imagine where I would have wound up in life. I also had a rich emotional life. My first love was full of emotional turmoil. My novel *The Shadow of First Love* came close to being made into a movie, but was aborted due to my sudden departure from China. I went through two marriages. The first was with Hengbao, the daughter of a high-ranking People's Liberation Army official. Her father was a General at the founding of the People's Republic of China. It was Hengbao who saved me from some disastrous circumstances of the Cultural Revolution. Later, I divorced her, and I was called "Shimei Chen", a notorious wife deserter in Ancient China with the reputation of Don Juan. Perhaps I deserved the label. My second marriage was to a woman of entirely different character, Li Liu. To say that one of them came from Mars and the other from Venus would not be an exaggeration. The first one never ventured into a shop for cosmetics, and the other would never go anywhere without first spending at least half an hour in front of a mirror. Like all bad husbands, I had several extramarital affairs. The love letters that I wrote to my girlfriends were charged with emotion. I am not seeking defense of my personal indiscretions. I only wish to say that it was just what happened in the real world, a reflection of the social mores of the time.

During my life, I was lucky to get to know many great men, including the Nobel Prize winners Jack Steinberger, C N Yang, T D Lee, Samuel CC Ting and others. Jack Steinberger's personal charisma influenced my life immeasurably. I also had the good fortune of making friends with many persons of accomplishments, including K. K. Phua, Saulan Wu, Zeng Fan, the Zhou Brothers, Xiaohui Ma, etc. Furthermore, there were many not-so-well-known friends whose lives and work have enlightened me. I will always cherish these names: Paolo Palazzi, Erna and Reinhold Hohbach, Sally Alderson and Bill Bardeen. I will not tell stories about them which are already in the public knowledge, but I will talk about my personal interactions with them, the anecdotes that were especially memorable. Their characters and personal charms brightened my life.

Lastly, I have to mention my brothers and sisters. My elder sister Fumin Wu is a journalist. Her reporting influenced many events in China from the sixties onwards. My younger sister Xiaomin Wu was one of the pioneers in the Special Economic Zone of the city of Shenzhen. She was one of the first journalists who visited the United States from China. Xiaomin was among the earliest persons to be recognized with honorary citizenship by the US government. My second younger brother Xinmin Wu was a participant in the "ping-pong diplomacy" between China and America, and his picture with Glenn L. Cowan appeared frequently in books and newspapers tracing the diplomatic history of these two countries. My other two brothers, Jimin Wu and Minmin Wu, both worked for television networks as reporters. Minmin Wu was the first Chinese person to work for NHK in Japan. They are all prolific writers. Their accomplishments serve as a source of inspiration throughout my life.

I hope that my story will take my readers on a journey to explore the inner workings of true history, helping them achieve a deeper insight that may serve as inspiration for making history of their own.

Preface to the English Edition

The publication of the Chinese version of my autobiography generated many positive comments from various readers. A glowing review of the book was presented with comments from semi-official sources such as the former Director of the Institute of High Energy Physics in Beijing, Zhipeng Zheng, as well as from a "liberal activist", Mr. Wu Gong, the author of "The Elf of the Universe", who was jailed for his activities during the Tiananmen Square event around June 4th, 1989. Reviewers for my book included Professor Wei Shu Hou from the National University of Taiwan, Li Zhang, a famous medical doctor from the United States, and Dr Enhai Wang from the Internet Information Center of the Chinese Academy of Science. Dr Wang personally led a group that confirmed after much research that a 1986 email I sent out of China was the first such event listed in Chinese Internet history. One comment went like this: "We all live in the stream of history. A person's life is a special representation of history. The life of Weimin Wu bore witness to seventy years of Chinese history, with sweat, tears and blood, and with pride and humility." According to another comment, "This is the sort of good book that has not been seen for a long time: truthful, rich in content, moving, thoughtful, plain and straightforward in style, and very readable." One commentator said, "From China in the East, and America in the West, from a premature infant who hung on to life by a thread, to a prolific physicist, what did it take to make a physicist of Chinese origin? *Life on the Cusp* traced a life that is legendary and brilliant." Another said, "I have not read anything all day long for a long time ... I started to read the first page of this book after supper on a weekend. I just could not stop reading, and read through it in one go, and finished it at day-break. What an autobiography! The only feeling after reading was just one word — striking!" Yet another continued: "The language of your autobiography is plain, almost colloquial. Reading it felt like when, on a quiet night, we sit around a burning camp fire, with me sitting opposite to you, listening attentively to an old man of wisdom speaking about his experiences and thoughts. Although this old man experienced the ups and downs of life, he spoke with a measured tone, with not a hint of personal emotion or bitterness, expressing his love of life and his attachment to his motherland."

All this feedback encouraged me to translate this book into English, making it accessible to more readers around the world. I am indeed a man with exceptional experiences. I was involved in several most important scientific and technological achievements in China, such as the making of the first atom bomb, the launch of the first artificial satellite, the construction and operation of the first electron-positron collider, and the establishment of the first Internet line in China. It is not that I have great personal talents, but fate gave me amazing opportunities. I must have been the only one with such experiences in China, I think. I was the last group of Chinese students selected to go to the Soviet Union to study and the last group of graduate students before the Cultural Revolution. After the Cultural Revolution, I was among the first wave of Chinese scientists who went abroad to study. I basically caught the first and last bus of history, thus shaping my unprecedented and unique life path.

I lived in China for several decades, experiencing the full spectrum of personal glory and humiliation. The bright moments include a reception by the former national leader Mao Zedong and shaking hands with the paramount leader Deng Xiaoping; the dark moments include being criticized for "bourgeois liberalization", almost landing in jail, being expelled by the Institute of High Energy Physics, and my Chinese passport being rendered invalid by the Chinese Consulate General in Chicago. When I was at the highest point of my career in China, the Tiananmen Square protest of 1989 changed the later half of my life completely. What I personally experienced and witnessed during the Tiananmen Square protest made me escape from China. I originally intended to go abroad to avoid the political persecutions of that time. I unexpectedly migrated to the States, eventually becoming an American citizen. There are no rights or wrongs in life, but only the persistence after choices are made, going on with no regrets, expecting everything to become right. America is a great country, a melting pot of many races. She gave people all over the world justice and opportunities to compete freely. This has been the basic tenet for the founding of the nation. However, China and America had been at odds for so many years, it was understandable that my experience in China attracted the attention of relevant authorities in America. How can one imagine that I participated in the research that led to the Chinese atom bomb, when I was just a freshman in college? Or that I was still building houses, loading freight trains, digging manure and raising pigs several months before I got involved in the launch of the first artificial satellite of China? A worthy point of my autobiography is the factual description of historical events.

My emotional life, just like my work life, was full of surprises and complications. My first love was full of bitterness, and it sadly ended before it even started to bloom fully. My short novel, *The Shadow of First Fove*, is included in this book as the fourth chapter. It tells about this true story. Later, I married the daughter of a founding general of the Chinese Army. It happened during the stormy years of the Cultural Revolution, but the union of a "Five Red Types" like her, and a "Five Black Categories" like me, became almost an impossible match. Later, during those years of reform and opening-up, I fell in love with a Chinese student in Europe. We were forced to go our separate ways because of the Tiananmen Square protest. Last, I married a Chinese herbal doctor, beginning a new happy life. Those four outstanding females, like four different flowers from spring, summer, fall and winter, brightened up my life. They brought me inspiration, passion, courage and the motivation to overcome any difficulties. My stories with them are an epitome of Chinese history at the time.

I lived in China for over three decades, and I also lived in the West, including Europe and America, for over three decades. To many British, German, Italian, French, American, Polish and Russian friends, I was the first Chinese they personally knew. They were also the first group of foreigners known to me. Whether reality goes like "fragrance was lost after being smelled for too long", or "stench could not be smelled after a while", the first impression turned out to be the most true. I honestly describe our true feelings and cultural clashes in my autobiography. Even after living in the States for several decades, when I mentioned many stories related to China's past and present to some American friends, they appeared to have never heard of anything like that. I believe my book will deepen the mutual understanding among people of different nations, engaging the interest of many Western readers.

My seventy years of life on the cusp made me believe more strongly than ever in the idea that the political systems and lifestyles of different countries in the world are converging. China declared in 1949 that the Chinese people had stood up. However, even though China acquired atom bombs and missiles along the way, the country had merely gained a certain sense of security. The Chinese people had not really stood up. In 1987, I passed through Hong Kong for the first time, and went shopping downtown. The shopkeepers were lukewarm towards me on hearing my Mandarin accent. I could not blame them for being snobbish. I had less than one hundred bucks in my pocket, what could I buy with that? Only after I started to speak English did the shopkeepers warm up to me with broad smiles. Now, whenever Chinese leaders visit foreign lands, they get grand receptions wherever they go. Why? International relationships are not about romance, nor about ideals. They are the results of calculations based on various national interests, a stark reflection of current reality. With business orders measured in the tens of billions of dollars, it is hard for businesses and national leaders for foreign powers not to take each other seriously. There is no comparison between China now and China thirty years earlier, with changes brought about entirely by the process of reform and opening-up of the country.

What exactly is reform and opening-up? Frankly speaking, reform is about the fact that decades of political practice demonstrated that a system would not work with focus on class struggles, using the will of political leaders as the guiding principles, and using the "big pot" way of wealth distribution that would kill workers' enterprising spirit. Only after adopting an economic system that had been developed for several hundreds of years, perfected by market practice, was China finally committed to a path of rapid economic development. Opening-up means that decades of experiment in China had shown that thinking of China as the center of "world revolution", was arrogant, inward-looking, and narrow-minded, and had disastrous consequences for both the country and the people. The right way for the Chinese people to stand up was to go beyond national boundaries, to integrate into the international community, to learn humbly, to form complementary relationships, to actively exchange goods and services, and to become a large responsible nation. As a scientist, I made many presentations at large and small international scholarly conferences. In June of 1987, under the direction of Director Minghan Ye, I made a presentation about the Beijing Electron-Position Collider at the annual meeting of European high-energy physics in Uppsala in Sweden. This presentation made me feel that the Chinese people had indeed stood up. I pointed out that the Electron-Positron Collider (LEP) at the European Nuclear Research Center (CERN) had a circumference of 27 kilometers, whereas the Beijing Electron-Positron Collider (BEPC) had a circumference of only several hundred meters. However, these two colliders were all little brothers compared to the earth. Most importantly, the fact that China had an Electron-Positron collider indicated that China had since become a member of the international big family of high-energy physics. At this moment, the audience stood up applauding, and the applause lasted several minutes. At that moment, I truly felt from my heart that only reform and opening-up can make the Chinese people stand up for real. The applause was the trumpet that sounded the entry of Chinese High Energy Physics.

My participation in high-energy physics research, and in the establishment of the Internet in China, got much more recognition than my research on the atom bomb and guided missiles. It showed that China was in step with the rest of the world on the path to explore the secrets of the universe, and in information exchanges with the international society. Indeed, I felt that China needed to declare in fact that reform and opening-up meant revising the dated theories of Karl Marx and others. "Revisionism" demonized the word "revision". The doctrine of Marx was that capitalism created wealth, and at the same created the proletariat grave-digger. When it came to Lenin, imperialism became the highest stage of capitalism, leading necessarily to war and to destruction, and the bourgeois became their own grave-diggers. These two prophecies differed much from the realities of historical development later, because when the proletarians were about to dig graves, capitalism reformed, resulting in welfare states. After the imperialists fought against each other, they realized that their problems could be solved without a fight. The result was the European Union. These two kinds of differences were the results of self-adapting powers of capitalism, and yet Marx's prophecy declared that the capitalism was beyond adaptation.

Furthermore, the capitalist system was "revising" itself constantly. Even inside a capitalist country, there are constant changes in the degree of nationalization and privatization, to search for an optimal point between development and justice. Why can China not "revise" some theories of its own communist patron deities? Recently, I found an article in the *Wall Street Journal* promoting a textbook titled "Thinking about Capitalism." Note the present sense of the word "thinking". This book presented a collection of statements of the last three hundred years from the founding fathers of capitalist theories to the current capitalist theoreticians about the birth, development and evolution of capitalism. I believe ever more firmly in the idea of converging social systems, which is what my book tries to explain. Every country in the world is undergoing development. In today's trend of global integration, no two countries follow two entirely non-interfering parallel paths of development. It is my belief that if we all look at the world using equality, respect and love, show appreciation, tolerance and mutual learning when looking at different civilizations, and promote mutual understanding and appreciation, through constant exchanges, adjustment, learning, revisions … this will converge to make a bright future for humankind, and the planet that we call home will become ever more beautiful.

Lastly, I am grateful for the warm support of Dr. K. K. Phua, President of World Scientific Publishing Company. Dr. Phua personally wrote a Foreword for my book. I must also thank the Science Director of the China Center of Advanced Science and Technology, former Director of the Institute of High Energy Physics, Professor Minghan Ye. He is a good friend and a mentor in my life. I also thank Nobel Laureate Jack Steinberger, who showed me what it is to be a true scientist. He transformed the latter half of my life.

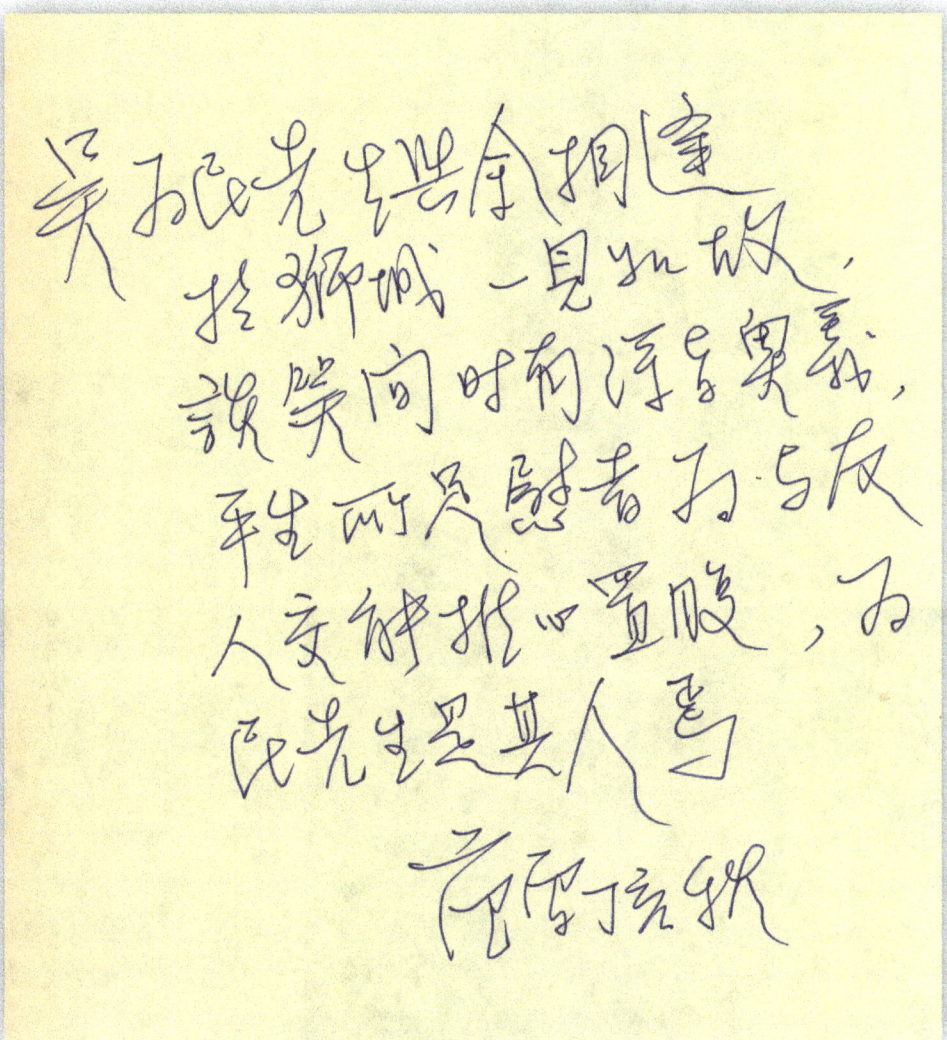

> My first encounter with Mr. Weimin Wu at the Lion City of Singapore resembled a reunion with a longtime friend. Words of profound wisdom flowed at the meeting of great minds. It is a pleasure to have a bosom friend in my life, a precious companion rare to find. Weimin is such a cherished friend indeed.
>
> Fan Zeng, fall of the Year Dinghai.

❶–❼ Weimin Wu's standard photos taken in his days as a student: from elementary school, to middle school, high school, university, all the way to graduate school
❽ Studying in a dormitory at Fudan University
❾ Working with a handheld computer at Lanzhou University, Office of Graduate Studies
❿ In front of a dormitory building at Fudan University
⓫ April 1960, attended conference in Beijing and met with Mao Zedong. Pictured at Tiananmen Square
⓬ While attending Fudan University, pictured at Shanghai People's Park
⓭ While attending Fudan University, pictured at Shanghai Fuxing Park

⑭ During high school, pictured with classmates in the historic bund district of Shanghai
⑮ Youthful high school years
⑯ Trip to Suzhou during high school

❶ 1961, "Students for studying in the Soviet Union", "zero class" of the Department of Atomic Energy at Fudan University
❷ 1965, graduation picture of class No. 3 of Nuclear Physics at Fudan University
❸ 1967, four graduate students at Lanzhou University, Department of Modern Physics in Nanjing during the Cultural Revolution Red Guards rallies
❹ Arrival at Harbin during the Cultural Revolution Red Guards rallies
❺ Arrival at Mount Huangshan during the Cultural Revolution Red Guards rallies
❻ Return to Fudan University during the Cultural Revolution

Pictures of my Parents in Early Years

❼ Mother and father in Shanghai in the late-1940s
❽ Father at Shanghai Fuxing Park in the mid-1950s
❾ Mother and father at Shanghai People's Park in 1959
❿ Father in the house on Julu Road in Shanghai in the early-1960s
⓫ Mother in the house on Julu Road in Shanghai in the early-1960s
⓬ 1975, parents with former colleague Jihua Wang from Zhonghua Workers Part-time School in Shanghai
⓭ Grandparents on the top-floor balcony in the house on Julu Road in Shanghai in the 1970s
⓮ Aged parents in Shanghai, 1980s

Early Family Pictures
1. Sister Fumin and I in Shanghai, late-1940s
2. Sister Fumin, Brother Jimin, and I at Shanghai Fuxing Park, 1950s
3. 1959, the first ever family photo taken at Shanghai People's Park
4. 1969, the six siblings on the balcony of No. 64 on Julu Road
5. Grandson Wei Wu and granddaughter Chen Wu with their grandparents at the house on Julu Road, 1970s

❻ 1987, mother's funeral
❼ 1987, at the mourning hall at No. 64 on Julu Road
❽ 1984, parents with their three grandchildren, Wei Wu, Chen Wu, and Yuanxing Wu
❾ 1985, the last family picture with all six siblings taken when both parents were alive

The entire Wu family at Hanshan Temple in Suzhou after paying respects to parents' graves

The Wu Siblings Going International

1. 1971, brother Xinmin Wu with American ping-pong player Cohen, a classic in Sino-America ping-pong diplomacy
2. 1989, former Japanese ambassador in China Yosuke Nakae met with brother Minmin and I
3. 1987, I gave a presentation at the annual European conference of high-energy physics at Uppsala, Sweden
4. 1995, sister Fumin attended the NGO Forum on Women in Huairou, China, representing Chinese women
5. July 7, 1988, sister Xiaomin was given the award of Honorary Citizen by the city of Harris, USA
6. 2012, daughter Yuanxing attended the entrepreneurial conference at the White House, pictured with Vice President Biden
7. 2012, daughter Yvonne won the President's Education Award

The Wu Siblings after Reform and Opening up

❶ Six siblings reunited, early-1980s
❷ Six siblings reunited, mid-1980s
❸ Six siblings reunited, late-1980s. I was the photographer
❹ 2002, a child was born into the fourth generation in the Wu family
❺ 2005, siblings reunited
❻ Fumin, Jimin, and I attended Fudan University's centennial celebration as alumni
❼ Brother Jimin interviewed at the Chinese satellite launch site
❽ June 2011, I gave a presentation at Fudan University's Inspiration Forum. I used to be a faithful audience at this forum.

Mother and Father, Rest in Peace

❾ The hospital where mother passed away in 1987 used to be a church. Now it has been changed back into a church. Minmin was photographed there.

❿ Father was the first among Chinese people to donate their bodies to medical research after death. The government set up a memorial for them with their names on it. The children and grandchildren paid our respects there.

⓫ Wife and daughter pushed me on a walk in Fushou Garden when I was wheelchair-bound due to gout.

Leaving China

1. 1988, Hengbao, Yuanxing, and I in the tiny apartment at IHEP. The thought of leaving China had never crossed my mind then
2. 1990, Hengbao and Yuanxing reunited with me at the Zurich airport after overcoming various obstacles
3. 1990, our family of three in front of our apartment building at Geneva
4. April 1990, I took a picture with my daughter at Lake Lemon before leaving Geneva for America

Immigrating to the United States
- ❺ The family in front of our first house in America
- ❻ Sister Fumin visited our home in America; Yuanxing's classmates' signatures in congratulations of her green card were hanging on the wall
- ❼ Sister Xiaomin visited us at our first house. I had bought my daughter a piano by then
- ❽ Reuniting with sister Xiaomin in America
- ❾ All kinds of feelings arose in my heart as I stood in front of the Statue of Liberty on my fiftieth birthday, having immigrated to the United States

ALEPH Collaboration and Beijing Spectrometer
❶ My office when I first went to CERN as a Tsung-Dao Lee Scholar
❷ CDHS and ALEPH teams often held parties together; we had close relationships among colleagues
❸ Beijing spectrometer coil was delivered to the site
❹ The Beijing spectrometer and I
❺ I always organized the Beijing ALEPH annual banquet
❻ 1960, I almost studied abroad at University of Moscow. After a quarter of a century, I finally visited the University.

What a Wonderful Life!

❼ Visiting the U.S. Morton Arboretum with ALEPH colleague Zhigang Li, who was later promoted to be the General Secretary of the Chinese Academy of Sciences

❽ Visiting the Alps with "Xiao Ju": I looked like a giant standing on the giant mountain

❾ Singing in the Yellow River Cantata at Chicago Symphony Hall in 2005 in celebration of the sixtieth anniversary of victory in WWII

❿ The mysterious rainbow above my house that appeared on the day I submitted the separation agreement

⓫ Rarely seen rainbow at the Death Valley

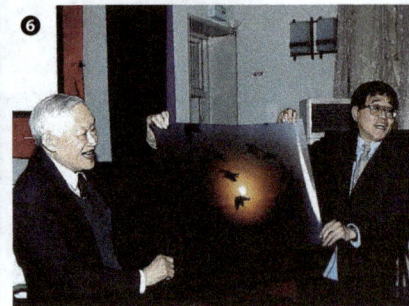

Some Important Meetings

❶ National People's Congress Vice Chairman Jici Yan, Chinese Academy of Sciences Director Guangzhao Zhou, and IHEP Director Minghan Ye listened to my presentation before meeting with Professor Steinberger

❷ Chinese Academy of Sciences Director Guangzhou Zhou, Chen-Ning Yang, Steinberger and I at Steinberger's sixty-fifth birthday celebration

❸ 1984, meeting with Professor Chen-Ning Yang at Leipzig High-Energy Physics Conference

❹ 1998, Professor Steinberger and Lederman who shared the Nobel Prize visited my house

❺ Meeting with Professor Tsung-Dao Lee at Fermilab

❻ I gave a photo I took to Professor Minghan Ye as a present for his eightieth birthday

❼ 1996, Steinberger came to my house when on a visit to Fermilab. It was the first time we saw each other since I moved to America

❽ 1992, the Chinese delegation led by IHEP director Zhipeng Zheng visited the Morton Arboretum behind my house on a trip to Fermilab

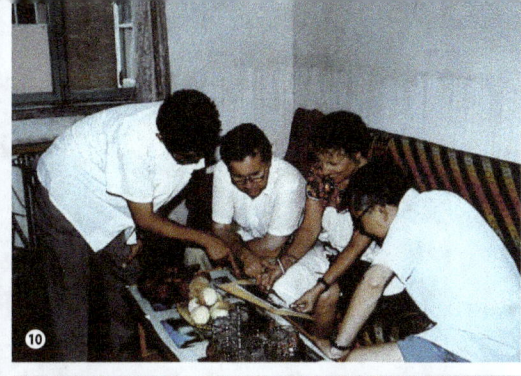

Some Important Meetings
- ⑨ 1988, I hosted U.S. Department of Energy's Director of high-energy physics O'Fallon on his visit to IHEP
- ⑩ Italy Academy of Nuclear Science director Cabbibo visited my tiny home on his trip to IHEP
- ⑪ July 19, 2008 was my sixty-fifth birthday. IHEP director Hesheng Chen invited Chinese Academy of Sciences Secretary General Zhigang Li, Professor Minghan Ye, and me to visit BEPC/BES
- ⑫ 2007, IHEP director Hesheng Chen and I met with World Scientific Publishing Co. CEO Dr. K. K. Phua
- ⑬ Dr. Phua with Professor Saulan Wu and I
- ⑭ American Physical Society's Friedman and I
- ⑮ Professor Dajun Wu, his wife Professor Saolan Wu, and I

With Great Contemporary Artists
❶ The amazing Chinese painting master Fen Zhen and I
❷ Visiting Fermilab with modern art masters the Zhou Brothers
❸ Erhu Angel Xiaohui Ma and I after her successful performance in Chicago

I helped organize several important meetings with the Chinese Academy of Sciences and Institute of High-Energy Physics
- ❹ Chinese Academy of Sciences Director Guangzhao Zhou visited CERN and signed a collaboration agreement that put ALEPH collaboration on the same plane as L3 collaboration
- ❺ IHEP Director Minghan Ye visited CERN, officially establishing ALEPH collaboration
- ❻ IHEP Director Hesheng Chen visited Fermilab, officially establishing CMS collaboration

Life and Work in Peace

❶ Daughter Yuanxing became a lawyer after attending law school
❷ Younger daughter Yvonne loves art and has often won awards for her work
❸ I enjoyed the beauty of nature after retiring from Fermilab (photographed by Yvonne Wu)
❹ Wife Li Liu is a doctor of Chinese medicine; she runs a Chinese medicine clinic

❺ I received a special birthday gift on my seventieth birthday — an oil portrait painted by my beloved daughter Yvonne

❻ 2009, I gave an introduction in the control center on the Chicago Chinese Consulate delegation's visit to Fermilab
❼ March 16, 2013, Chicago Chinese Consulate General Weiping Zhao and wife held a banquet at their residence for renowned Chinese scientists in the Chicago area. Two other scientists, my wife and I were invited
❽ 2011, Chairman Hu Jintao met with Chinese representatives in Chicago during his visit to the United States; I attended the meeting upon invitation

❶ National Taiwan University Professor Wei-Shu Hou and I
❷ National Taiwan University Professor Yee Bob Hsiung and I
❸ Meeting Dr. Enhai Wang from the China Internet Network Information Center for the first time in Beijing
❹ IHEP Director Yifang Wang, Chinese Academy of Sciences General Secretary Zhigang Li, Academician Hesheng Chen, and others at my seventieth birthday celebration
❺ Group picture taken at my birthday party hosted by IHEP director Yifang Wang
❻ Group picture taken at IHEP Dongguan Branch director Yuanbo Chen's banquet for my sister Xiaomin and I
❼ The Fu Sinian Bell at National Taiwan University
❽ Misty dawn at the national treasure in Taiwan — Sun Moon Lake

About the Author

Weimin Wu, a famous Chinese American physicist, was born in 1943, Shanghai, China.

Weimin Wu received a Bachelor's degree from the Department of Atomic Energy at Fudan University, and a graduate degree from the Department of Modern Physics at Lanzhou University, China. He joined the Institute of High Energy Physics of the Chinese Academy of Sciences in 1979, engaging in research in high energy physics, and becoming the Chinese team leader of the ALEPH international collaboration (ALEPH was a particle detector on the Large Electron-Positron collider (LEP)). In 1986, Weimin Wu became the Deputy Director of the Beijing Spectrometer (BES) for the Beijing Electron-Positron Collider (BEPC).

After immigrating to the United States, Wu became a physicist at the Fermi National Laboratory, participating in the search for the Higgs particle and other research work. Lately, he visits China frequently to take part in research and educational activities, promoting international collaboration and exchanges between America and China.

Wu is not only prolific in his scientific research work, but is also accomplished in the arts and humanities. He has published numerous plays and novels, and in particular, a photography collection titled "The Beauty of Physics". Wu's photo "Fly Me to the Sun" advanced to the semi-finalist round in the International Open Amateur Photography Contest. Wu has been nominated to join the International Society of Amateur Photographers' Hall of Fame.

About the Translators

Dr Harry Tong, born in Hunan, China, received a PhD in structural biology from Sydney University, Australia in 1991. While in Australia between 1984 and 1991, Dr Tong also obtained certification as a professional interpreter and translator of the Mandarin and English languages. Dr Tong has published widely in both English and Chinese with his research work in structural biology and information science in Sydney University of Australia, University of British Columbia, McMaster University of Canada, in the Netherlands Cancer Institute, and in Argonne National Laboratory, USA.

Ms Candice Yuxi Wang, born in Beijing, China in 1996, started attending boarding school in the United States at age 14. While studying at St. Mark's School, MA, Ms Wang was inducted into the Cum Laude Society for academic excellence. Ms Wang has had translation experience in the fields of arts and cultural exchange. Ms Wang attends Pomona College in Claremont, California. She is a member of the class of 2019 and she anticipates to concentrate in Religious Studies and Neuroscience.

Calligraphy on Cover

The calligraphy of the book title on the cover was done by Jiang Liu, Executive Director of Xilingyinshe, Hangzhou, China. Jiang Liu, born in 1926 in Wanzhou, Chongqing, is a Professor at the China Academy of Art. He also serves as the Director of China Seal Museum, Hangzhou, and the Executive Director of Xilingyinshe (Xiling Seal Engraver's Society). Established in 1904 (the 30th year of the reign of Emperor Guangxu in the Qing Dynasty), Xiling Seal Engraver's Society is a society of literati and artists with the longest history among those still existing in China and is also China's first professional academic organization specializing in stone seal carving.

Contents

Foreword by Professor K.K. Phua   v
Foreword by Professor Minghan Ye   vii
Prologue   xi
Preface to the English Edition   xvii
Inscription by Zeng Fan   xxiii
Pictures   xxiv
About the Author   xlv
About the Translators   xlvi
Calligraphy on Cover   xlvi

Chapter 1	A Premature Infant	1
Chapter 2	Wandering Years	9
Chapter 3	Prime Time	17
Chapter 4	The Shadow of First Love	35
Chapter 5	Decade of Calamity	59
Chapter 6	Pinnacle of Life	87
Chapter 7	A Turning Point in History	153
Chapter 8	Immigrating to the United States	179
Chapter 9	Energy Frontier	201
Chapter 10	Treasure Island Taiwan	245
Chapter 11	Convergence of Civilizations	265

Epilogue by Weimin Wu   283
Book Reviews (Chinese Edition)   287
Translator's Note   325

Chapter One

A Premature Infant

On July 19, 1943, a boy was prematurely born in an old-fashioned *Shikumen* — a historical building at Yangjia Lane, Wenlan Circle 39, Julu Road, Shanghai. He had breaths and pulses, but did not know how to cry, nor suckle milk from his mother, and remained motionless, as though dead. That was me. My father's name was Benhao Wu, and my mother's name was Xi Luo. They gave me a name, Huimin, meaning "giving to the people". Upon graduation from primary school, my name was changed to Weimin, meaning "serving the people".

At that time, China was in dire straits. Japan occupied over half of China, including Shanghai. My mother gave birth to me prematurely while escaping from the military police after she took part in an anti-Japanese demonstration. As the saying goes, "Seven months lives but not eight". A doctor gave me an injection, and three days later, I started to cry while lying down on a bamboo mat. My mother laughed after much despair, and hugged me tightly to her bosom. Thus, my young life came to this world two months too early. Perhaps it was the hot summer of Shanghai like a natural heat incubator that protected me. No matter what, this was a miracle, because even with modern medical equipment and intensive care, the chance of having a healthy baby at 28 weeks is only fifty-fifty, and the death rate is still above ten per cent. The rest that survive would grow up with various health issues, especially with their eyes, ears, hearts and lungs. Therefore, I feel very grateful to the kindness of the heavens, which has allowed me to live a healthy life for over 70 years. There is an old folk saying: "Out of 10 persons born in the year of the goat, nine of them fall short." It means that a person born in the year of the goat usually does not have much luck in his or her life. As a person born in the year of the goat, I'm not sure about my own luck. I have lived my whole life on the cusp of historical events in China, full of ups and downs.

My paternal grandparents both died before I came to this world. I grew up hearing about them from my father: Grandpa was a scholar of the late Qing dynasty, but he became a shoemaker after the 1911 Revolution that overthrew the Qing dynasty. My father was born in 1911. When he was 13, he moved from Ningbo to Shanghai. He was at first an apprentice in a printing shop, and then an intern at Siming Bank. When he was 30, he was promoted to Siming Bank's Accounting Chief Officer and became the Principal of the Chinese Workers' Part-Time School. The apprentices of those times worked and lived like cattle. Besides his professional work, my father had to do housework for the boss as well. Strenuous work and childhood hardship built his strong character. With a steadfast will, he used the spare time between type setting and the internship at the bank to learn to read and write, studied the classics of Ancient China, and mastered accounting. Thus, he rose from being the child of a poor family to a high-ranking clerk with some social standing. My father repeatedly told me the story of how, when he was a child, he asked a barber to cut off a pus-filled bump on his head with a pair of scissors in one go, all in the absence of any proper medical treatment. His childhood hardship, and his efforts at self-improvement, all strengthened his will. That was why, later during the Cultural Revolution, in the face of persecution, torture, imprisonment, and beatings, he spilled blood but shed no tears, and would not bow his head even with broken bones. His extensive knowledge, charming calligraphy, and his expertise in Chinese history and folk stories influenced my sisters and brothers tremendously. His mastery of the abacus was exemplary, and he could work with both hands at the same time. My mother told me that when my father was an accountant at the bank, he never made any mistakes. Even when one cent was missing, he would re-calculate everything until things were set straight. That was how he rose from being an intern to becoming the Chief Accountant in 10 years.

My mother's life experiences were somewhat different. She was born in 1921, the year the Communist Party of China was founded. My maternal grandfather, Changlin Luo, was among the first group of workers to work at the running water plant of Shanghai. He was so proficient that he was called the "living map" of the underground water distribution lines of Shanghai. My maternal grandmother, Lindi Zheng, like my maternal grandfather, was completely illiterate. After graduating from primary school, my mother was no longer allowed to continue her education. One of the main reasons was the financial difficulty of the family. A Japanese bomb destroyed my maternal grandfather's house, which cost half of his life's savings. Once, the Shanghai running water plant was shut down, and my maternal grandfather lost his job. Under those circumstances, it was really difficult to send my mother to school. Another reason was the Chinese tradition of favoring sons over daughters. My maternal grandfather thought that graduating from primary school was good enough for a girl. However, my mother's strong desire to study put her in conflict with my maternal grandfather. Once, in anger, my maternal grandfather kicked my mother down a staircase. Nevertheless, he eventually respected the will of my mother, and she graduated from high school with excellent grades. My father and my mother got to know each other at the Chinese Workers' Part-Time School. The family background of poverty and the aggression of the Japanese made them sympathize with the Chinese communist party. The Chinese Workers' Part-Time School was actually an outlying organization of the communist party. The founder of the school was Yanpei Huang, a famous figure in China. My father, who was a teacher in the beginning, subsequently became the principal. My mother was a student at first, but then joined the faculty. They were formally introduced to each other by the communist party member Jun Cheng, and got married in 1939. A year later, my elder sister was born. My parents named her Fumin, meaning "the revival of the nation". At that time, the Chinese nation was at a most critical time in history. To revive the nation and save China from Japanese aggression were the common goals of Chinese people all over the country. My parents' enthusiasm for the anti-Japanese movement and support for the communist party were beyond comparison. They wrote many articles personally, inscribed them on metal sheets, and printed them out as pamphlets. They also taught workers to read and write anti-Japanese materials. The bedroom for their wedding night was actually used for sheltering a communist party member, Jun Yi Mao, who was to join the New Fourth Army. During that period, the Chinese Workers' Part-Time School trained group after group of educated youth to serve the purpose of the anti-Japanese movement. Many among them became high-ranking officials after the founding of the People's Republic of China. My father even used his position as the

Chief Accountant at Siming Bank, a position with considerable social standing, to organize the shipping of medicines and other needed materials to the New Fourth Army in North Jiangsu province from Shanghai, at the risk of his own life. My mother, besides working at the Lisheng Rubber Factory, devoted herself to performing, selling and collecting donations for the anti-Japanese movement. She starred in well-known plays such as *Drop Your Whips* and *Thunderstorm*. The Lan Xin Theater, now the Shanghai People's Art Theater, was a top theater in the French Concession of Shanghai. My mother often showed me her play shots of when she performed at the Lan Xin Theater. Unfortunately, all those pictures were destroyed during the period of time when wearing a *Cheongsam (Qipao)* dress was considered part of "feudalism, capitalism and revisionism". Soon after the Anti-Japanese war was won, the civil war broke out, resulting in hyperinflation and extreme hardship in people's lives. My father contracted tuberculosis, and my mother gradually took over the burden of paying for the expensive medicines and day-to-day living. At that time, the Lisheng Rubber Factory where my mother worked was on the verge of bankruptcy, and used unsold rubber bends or shares as substitutes for wages. Gradually, my mother accumulated many shares, becoming one of the principal shareholders. In her eyes, the Factory became her own, and her talents for operation and management came into play. She got a loan through my father's connection with Siming Bank to improve the management. In two short years, the Lisheng Rubber Factory came out of insolvency, and the shares started to make money. She used the money to buy a gray fur coat. However, once the People's Republic of China was founded, those shares and her fur coat became the evidence for her to be labelled a "capitalist", bringing her many misfortunes. Although later my mother became the first Vice-Director for the Shanghai Watch Factory, making full use of her management talents, the label of being in the exploiting class followed her throughout her life until she passed away.

After I recovered from near death, I could only sleep in a baby's crib all day long to the point that my head became flattened. It was because of my father's illness, and the fact that my mother was busy with her work, and with various kinds of progressive activities. My maternal grandmother took care of me. When I was four, my younger brother Jimin was born.

My maternal grandmother needed to take care of him, so I was sent to school. I did not know how to put on or take off normal trousers by myself, so I had to wear "open trousers", exposing my private parts when I went to school. Luckily, the school was not far from home, and could be reached by going out of our lane, turning left, and walking two hundred meters. That was Tongyi Primary School. As a prematurely born child, short and small, wearing "open trousers", it was no surprise that I got bullied a lot by my schoolmates. I often complained about my plight to my maternal grandmother. When she told me stories, though, I would forget all my grievances. I slept in the same bed as my maternal grandmother from early childhood. She was a woman from the late Qing dynasty, and had small, bound feet. Every night, I slept holding her small feet, until I was sent to board at the Changqiao Village Primary School.

The stone hedged *Shikumen* house we lived in had an enclosed yard with a well in the middle. All the water we needed came out of the well. From a young age, I learned to draw well water, an activity involving some physics principles. In order to draw water, a piece of rope must be used to make a few turns with a bucket, subsequently plunging the bucket into water with the opening of the bucket pointed downwards. After the bucket was half full with water, the weight of the water would allow it to sink below the water surface. Once the bucket was filled up this way, it was drawn up the well. The water from the bucket was poured into a big water container, with some alum added. The water would become clear the next day. Actually, what I described is rather superficial. A true genius would deduce important principles from the workings of a simple bucket. Isaac Newton did an experiment with a bucket filled with water, tied to a long piece of soft rope. He twisted the rope several times but held it tight. The bucket remained still, and the water inside it was also still and flat. He suddenly released his hand, and the rope started to turn, making the bucket turn with it. Initially, the water inside did not turn, only the bucket. There was relatively little movement of the water against the bucket. Gradually, the water started to follow the bucket. In the end, water moved along with the bucket, and they were motionless relative to each other. However, the water surface would curve in at the center, remaining higher near the side of the bucket. Thus Newton would ask, "Why is the water surface flat sometimes, and curved at other times?" He offered some explanations, as did Ernst

Mach and Albert Einstein many years later. The "Newton's Bucket" experiment lasted over four hundred years, involving the design of gyroscopes and the relativity theory, and inspiring new theoretical models. Look! This is the difference between ordinary folks like myself and true geniuses.

The residents of Shanghai woke up early. Before dawn, carts would come to take away the waste matter. Every household would take out the barrels they used as lavatories, and used brushes made of bamboo to clean them out. The barrels were lined up with seashells, and the sound of tens of families brushing them is unforgettable for a life time. However, the rich and the influential citizens of Shanghai slept very late. Two streets away, there was the Four-Sister Dancing Club, where parties went on every night until dawn.

My parents did many things for the communist party, and contributed a lot of money. Strangely, it became a source of trouble later. During the Cultural Revolution, they would be asked: "You were so close to the communist party, why didn't you join yourselves?" "You sent so many people to the New Fourth Army, why didn't you go yourselves?" Especially obnoxious was the case with a communist party member, who was arrested by the Nationalist Party authorities. My father used his own gold bars to bribe some officials to rescue him from jail. However, the party member wrote up a repentance letter, saying that he was "young and naïve", "misguided to the wrong side" and such. Later, all these became evidence that my father was a traitor and a secret agent. Such "historical" problems tortured my parents for many decades. They wrote countless "self-criticism letters" whenever there was a political movement. However, they were never cleared completely, but were persecuted repeatedly. My parents risked their own lives to work for the revolution, contributing their money and time while neglecting the education of their own children. Perhaps they would have been better off if they had done nothing of the sort to begin with?

Because I was born prematurely, one question intrigued me often. In the end, what difference does a premature birth make to the intelligence of a person? I researched various cases: from Pablo Picasso to Albert Einstein, from Mark Twain to Winston Churchill. All those famous people — a painter, a scientist, a writer, and a statesman — were born prematurely. So a premature birth does not necessarily have a negative effect on the development of intelligence. On the contrary, as some would say, a prematurely born child could be smarter than average, or just blossom later in life. In my opinion, the science behind such phenomena still needs to be researched more thoroughly. In fact, the problems associated with premature births intrigued many people other than myself. The June 2014 issue of *Time* included a cover story about premature babies. The picture of a prematurely born child on the cover, just the size of a palm, caught the eyes of many readers. At the end of the article, it was written that premature babies came out of the hospital, and bright sunny days and star-charmed nights awaited them at home. From that day of home coming, the hard work started for the parents. I remember that because of my premature birth, which gave me weak and sickly physical conditions, my mother took extra care of me. When the family stewed a chicken, my mother would carefully scoop a layer of oil floating above the broth to give to me to drink, just to get enough fat for growth. I would often joke to my friends that my high cholesterol level was caused by that layer of chicken oil that I drank in childhood. Nowadays, whenever my family makes chicken broth, I carefully take away that layer of floating oil before I give the broth to my daughter to drink. Oh, how times have changed. What remains unchanged is the "tender heart of the parents".

In 1949, another brother of mine, Xinmin, was born. My parents gave him his name to commemorate the founding of the new China with a new life, because *Xin* means "new"! Thus, the home became even more crowded. "Attic rooms" were built inside the bedrooms. The so-called "attic rooms" were just shelves erected inside a room so that family members could climb up and sleep in there. Of course, there was no space to stand up on such shelves. Soon, however, great changes were brought about in our lives.

Chapter Two

Wandering Years

After the liberation of Shanghai, my parents were treated favorably by the new regime because they had many friends who became high-ranking officials of the Communist Party, and because they had done a lot for the communists in the past. My mother got a job at the tax bureau of Shanghai. My whole family moved from the small, old fashioned *Shikumen*, a legacy building, to a beautiful villa with a garden, situated at 30 Yuyuan Road, Butterfly Village. This villa had two storeys, and we lived on the first floor with polished hardwood floors and an attached garage. There were two trees in the small garden; one was rosewood, and the other a loquat tree. When the rose tree bloomed, it filled the whole garden with fragrance. My favorite was the loquat. I would climb it to get the fruits, sometimes even before they became ripe. Since we did not own a car, we turned the garage into a storage room. This new residence had running water, flush toilets, and other modern amenities, and was beyond comparison with the old stone house. Naturally, we were full of gratitude to the Communist Party and to the liberation of Shanghai. My mother joined the Communist Party, and she gave up all her shares to the party, to show her determination to part with the exploiting class. However, the hat of the exploiting class still accompanied her throughout her life. My mother sent my sister and me to the "Long-Bridge Village" Primary School of Longhua District to get a more "revolutionary" education. Because it belonged to the countryside, it was more revolutionary as students there were children of either communist cadres or peasants. This was a boarding school, and on the weekends, my grandmother would take a bus to Xujiahui, and then take a bike ride to school, to bring us home. On Mondays, she would send us back to school again, and so on and so forth. There was only a small country road from the bus station to school. A hired bike rider would put a piece of wood on the back of the bike, with me and my sister sitting on either side of the wood, and my grandmother sitting on the bike stem at the front. So the bike took on four persons, shaking and bumping all the way. The fare was fifteen cents, and could buy at least three eggs. I have long forgotten what I learned at that school, but can never forget the mass meetings that the school took us to for "struggles against the landlords". The scenes of landlords tied up tightly and wearing high hats during such meetings often gave me nightmares for many years. I would ask repeatedly in my young mind, so this was the so-called "class struggle"?

Soon enough, such "class struggle" fell on my mother's head. The first political movement, began — the "Three-anti and Five-anti" campaigns. Although my brother and my sister were born one after another, the living standard of my family was still higher than the average due to the high salary of my grandfather. Someone reported that my mother was guilty of corruption, and she was imprisoned after being labeled a "big tiger". My elder sister was just 10 at the time, and was asked to persuade my mother to "confess" for lenient consideration. Later, several months of investigation found no evidence of corruption, and mother was released. At that time, we had no intention to ask for an apology, but thanked the "seeking truth from the facts" policy of the communist party.

After learning about "revolution" from the "Long-Bridge Village" Primary School for over a year, I was transferred to Zhenning Road Primary School, which was not far from home. On the way home from school, I would pass by a very small church. At that time, churches did not have a good reputation. They were considered hiding places for "imperialist spies" or hell for "eating human hearts and babies." To believe in God was not only considered a superstition, but also a sin against the people. After Pinmei Gong, the first Chinese Bishop of Shanghai, was arrested for counter-revolutionary activities, the school organized a trip to an exhibition at a church in Xujiawan. Those horrible pictures on display scared me to death. After that whenever I passed by the church and saw that cross, I would hold my breath, and walked away hurriedly. One day, when I went near the church, I saw something different. Its door was wide open, and two nuns dressed in white were standing there addressing the passersby, all smiles. I felt somewhat intrigued, and gathered enough courage to take a look inside for the first time. I saw some colorful windows gleaming, and heard waves of sound of singing and music. Those two nuns saw me looking their way, so they walked towards me and said: "Merry Christmas!" One of them handed me a paper bag, with half of a banana sticking out. I did not dare to take it, and was about to leave. Then I saw a boy taking a bag from a nun, and eating a banana right away. Suddenly, my hunger for the food package overcame me, so I took the bag from the nun, started to eat the banana, too. I walked away some steps, and found that besides some candies that I recognized, there was something dark inside the bag. I got suspicious, and walked back to return it to the nun. She laughed, and put that dark stuff into her own mouth. Then she put one piece inside my mouth. I ate it, and really liked the taste. From then on, I knew it was called chocolate. That particular day of the year was called Christmas. However, this episode became a secret that I would not even tell my mother: I had eaten something that a nun gave me, and it was called a chocolate.

During the summer vacation of that time, the school occasionally organized "bonfire parties." The children would sit around a pile of burning wood, eating bread and boiled eggs treated with tea leaves. When there was a bottle of soda, so much the better. Unfortunately, such activities were too few, and I spent the summer vacations mostly with grandfather. My grandfather was getting old, and he quit his job as a worker at the water plant, and took up a job as a security guard. A small house was used for the guard post. It had two rooms — an office on the outside, and a bedroom inside with a bed, where I slept with my grandfather. The water plant was located in the suburbs. There was a huge water treatment pool surrounded by grass and many trees. Besides the sound of water flowing, there was just the chirping of birds. I would catch crickets and gather bird eggs in the grass, trees, and rock crevices. Compared with the noisy city, the quietness of the place was unforgettable.

Later, my mother changed jobs. My entire family moved to a new apartment her new work unit assigned to her, at 64 Julu Road. This ship-shaped building became the home for the Wu brothers and sisters to grow up with. It was not beautiful like the house at Yuyuan Road, but it was our real home in memory. In this yellow building, I witnessed the joys and sorrows of the Wu family, where I bid farewell to our beloved maternal grandfather and grandmother, my father and mother for the last time. This was also the starting point for the Wu brothers and sisters on their eastward journeys to Japan, and westward trips to Lanzhou. It was the harbor and assembly place for us to go all directions to the wider world. At this building, I spent my school years from my last primary school, Julu Road Primary School, to middle school, high school, and all the way to graduating from Fudan University. Indeed, sixty years of life going on in the building was not just an epitome of the Wu family, it also reflects the tumultuous changes in China over the sixty years. Standing at the balcony, the Pudong building could be seen at the northeast side. At the ground level of this building was the Four-Sister dancing hall. To the southwest direction were the famous landmarks of Shanghai at that time: the French Tower, also called the Maoming Tower, and Jinjiang Hotel. That section of Julu Road was the largest outdoor farmer's market. A performance for former US president Nixon's visit to Shanghai took place in this Julu Road outdoor farmers' market. Now the yellow building has been demolished, with a high viaduct above its original location, which has been turned to a street garden, complete with birds and flowers. The French Tower and the Jinjiang Hotel are still well known in Shanghai, but are no longer its most conspicuous landmarks. My brother Minmin wrote an essay titled "The Yellow Building", that touched many readers. I also tightly link my own story with the yellow building.

Before middle school, my body had been weak all along, and short too. My test scores were not that good, either, and my parents worried for me. At that time, the education system of China was underdeveloped. A primary school education was universal, but only a small part of graduates could go on to middle school. Then there was a primary school graduate, Jianchun Xu, who volunteered to become a peasant, and was made a "model." Unlike years later, it was considered exceptional only if a college graduate volunteered to become a peasant. Fortunately, at that time there was the open competition policy for middle schools, with each school releasing and updating the numbers of admissions and applications in a timely fashion. My father took me from one school to another, and finally applied to a middle school called Qiwen, which did not even have a high school associated with it, making it a problem to continue to high school after graduation. However, my father felt that my scores could only allow me to enter such a school. Compared to my elder sister, I felt utterly shamed. She excelled in each subject, and went to the Shanghai Third

Girls School for middle school, and Xiangming School for high school. Both were well known schools in Shanghai. At that time, I was filled with low self-esteem.

The Qiwen School, later called the Twenty-Second School, was located at Xiangshan Road, opposite to the former residence of Sun Yat-Sen, and next to Fuxing Park. Xiangshan Road was a closed road with a round flower bed, and was a good place to learn to ride a bicycle. A major reason for me to learn to ride a bicycle was my father's stay at the Hongqiao Recovery Center due to illness, and visits by bus cost me several dimes weekly. So I was determined to learn to ride a bicycle. For fifteen cents, I rented a bicycle that would make noises everywhere except for the bell. With countless falls, I finally learned to ride. However, at that time my family could not afford to buy a bicycle, so I had to walk to the house of a classmate who lived on Tibet Road to borrow one. I rode to the hospital where my father was staying, and afterwards I would return the bicycle, and then walk home. I would spend an entire Sunday this way. I got very tired after my visiting trips, but I could never forget the way my father led me by the hand, going from one school to another, in search of a place that would be most likely to accept me. I knew my parents placed high hopes in me, and I vowed to study hard. However, things did not turn out that way. I filled my middle school time with various kinds of hobbies, and my grades did not improve much. From home to school, I would walk on the Huaihai Road, one of the busiest streets in Shanghai. There was a house belonging to a philatelic society called Weimin that I would pass by every day. The colorful stamps, banknotes, and all sorts of coins often made me pause. At that time, my mother gave each of us one Yuan (RMB) per month, to be spent at our own will. I would be very contented to spend five cents on an egg boiled with tea leaves, and a dime to watch a movie. Since I started to collect stamps, I had an extra spending. Later, I became more and more interested in philately, often staying for quite a few hours at Weimin's at a stretch. At last, I acquired all the issues of stamps in print since the founding of the People's Republic in 1949, each and every one of them. I remember a set of stamps called the "Broadcast Gymnastics," a total of 40, that I think might be the most distributed set of stamps in the world. To collect this set of stamps, especially the last one, I really spent a lot of time. There was one thing that I did that I often regret. I had a classmate, whose family owned many rubles from the Tsar period in Russia, with face values over tens of thousands, in large paper sizes and excellent quality. He gave me a lot, and my friends used them as raw materials for folding paper toys, such as frogs that could jump. By chance, I found that the Weimin Philatelic Society was buying those "fake notes" at five cents a piece. Thus, I unfolded the "fake notes" that were in the shapes of "frogs" and "airplanes", and turned them all into money. At that time I thought I had made over one Yuan from nothing, but now I regret it very much. However, at a time when five cents could buy a bowl of delicious vermicelli noodle soup with fried tofu, it was not surprising that I did it. Besides collecting stamps, I also played with crickets, practiced sericulture, harvested mulberry leaves, kept guinea pigs, and even raised a kind of "foreign bug" similar to bed bugs. These "foreign bugs" ate only walnuts, dates, and other nutritious food, and people would consume them as a highly prized nutritional supplement. While practising sericulture, it was very interesting for me to observe the whole life cycle of silkworms, from eggs hatching on a piece of cotton, to tiny silkworms that grew up by feeding on mulberry leaves, built up cocoons, and then became flying moths. My heart was really on my hobbies, so I could hardly keep up with my homework, and my test scores were always around 4 when 5 was the full score. When I graduated from middle school, it was a big problem whether I could make it to high school. At that time, the admission rate for high school was the lowest since the founding of the People's Republic of China. For a relatively good school, the admission rate was only one in five. Going to the countryside, becoming a factory worker, or staying home to study for another year, were the choices faced by many middle school graduates. My sister was one grade higher than me, and she already entered the famous Xiangming School, and she was among the best known top students in the whole school. For me, such good schools were simply beyond my reach. My father led me from one school to another, and finally settled with an "alley school" — Chengdu Second School. The so-called "lane" school did not have regular school buildings. The classrooms were very shabby, and the voice of a teacher in one classroom could be heard in another one. The school had no athletic field, and morning exercises were performed on the sidewalks of the street. Naturally, I was very reluctant to go to such a school. However, neither my parents nor I would risk the chance of not being able to pass the entrance examinations of other high schools, so I applied to the Chengdu Second School anyway. Finally, I passed the examinations. Even for a school of such poor conditions, the admission rate was only one in three. I did not feel that happy about the school, but celebrated my successful admission nevertheless. At least now I had made it to high school. Unexpectedly, after entering the high school, everything changed, perhaps by the will of God. I grew taller and stronger day by day, and I got top grades from the very beginning. My prime school time had started.

Chapter Three
Prime Time

3.1 Budding

I went to Chengdu Second School with some regrets. However, I soon discovered that the school had some exceptionally good teachers. There was an odd reason for this: it was difficult for teachers with so-called political problems to teach at the top tier schools. Thus, some excellent teachers were unexpectedly banished to work in kinds of "alley schools", including a "rightist" teacher for Physics, Zhipan Zheng, a "historical counter-revolutionary" teacher for algebra, Yunyuan Qiu, a history teacher Yixun Lin born in a capitalist family, and a "democratic party" teacher for biology, Bingbai Li. In my twenty years of student life, I had several dozens of teachers. Out of those whose names I can still recall, quite a few were from the Chengdu Second School. There were common features among those teachers: easy to understand, clear minded, thinking in the position of the students, talking with them on equal terms, and never suppressing their curiosity. Once, when learning about electric generators, I asked my teacher: "Can't we produce light if we put a small generator on the wheel of a bike?" He said: "You have a good idea, but it already exists, and it's called a mill lamp." Another time, the teacher was talking about bridges. The bridges built in ancient times were very tall, allowing boats to pass under them. However, it was difficult for modern vehicles to drive through. What could be done? I thought about it, and added two long tails to a bridge that that I drew. The teacher praised me, telling me, those were called bridge approaches that I had just re-invented. My history teacher Yixun Lin told us about how many dynasties in China started out being clean and fair, but became corrupt over time, so the common folks would revolt and change the dynasty. That was the historical cycle proposed by Yanpei Huang. All these teachings left me with unforgettable impressions for a life time. Regrettably, for the Chengdu Second School, the passing rate for college entrance examinations was not high, so its reputation was not great. It could not be blamed on the teachers. Because of its low admission standard, the students had rather low academic achievements. Later, I often talked about why Harvard University was so good, half of the reason was that it had a high selection threshold, and the quality of the students was excellent to start with. My opinion was inspired by my experience with Chengdu Second. In Chengdu Second, even political science teachers like Yucheng Zhu and Zhizhen Yu were very good in my opinion. They let me know that there were many respectable and adorable people in the communist party, but there were also many heinous elements. I will talk more about them later in the book.

My mother was one such adorable communist party member. She joined the party shortly after the liberation of Shanghai. It was said, because she joined the party a few days too late, she was not considered a "revolutionary cadre". However, she really was too "revolutionary." What I never quite understood was why the party itself always persecuted such a clean and selfless party member like her. The income from a limited number of shares for some short years would burden her with the label of being in the "exploiting class" for decades. After leaving the Internal Revenue Department, my mother was appointed the director at the Consumers Cooperative of Shanghai Luwan district. In this position, she managed thousands of small shops in Luwan district. The house we lived at on Julu Road was assigned by the Consumers Cooperative. The enamel on our bathtub came off because of long-time use. The property management offered to change the tub a few times. My mother declined, saying that our country was still poor, and many families still shared toilets, and we should not be given "special treatment". Our family occupied the fourth floor of 60, 62 and 64 Julu Road combined. It was relatively large, but because of the number of family members we had, it did not feel spacious. Nevertheless, my mother gave away some kiosk-like space to the neighbors to be used as kitchens. It was really a rare act in Shanghai, where every inch of space was precious. My family had a nanny called Aizhen Shao, who was a widow. Her son grew up with us until he graduated from middle school. At that time, my family had six children going to school at the same time, and the cost was considerable. According to policy at the time, my family was qualified for fee exemptions. However, my mother never applied for the fee exemptions, saying that a communist member should take the lead in relieving the burden of the state. She worked late often. When she came home, I would have fallen a sleep on a couch. My mother would then carry me to my bed. Later, my mother was appointed the vice director responsible for production at the Shanghai Watch Factory, utilizing her management talents to the fullest. The first watch of new China was manufactured with she in charge. However, none of my family members had a Shanghai brand watch while she worked at the watch factory. I believe that most communist party members were like this in the 1950s in China. I had another good impression with the communists because of father. My father was hospitalized for a long time. The cost of his hospital stay and surgery were very expensive, but it was all paid for by the state. So it was natural for my whole family to be grateful to the communist party. I got perfect grades for my first year of high school. My family members did not think much about it. At that time, my elder sister was at Xiangming High School, and my younger brother was at Shanghai High School, both being well-known top schools in Shanghai. Earning perfect scores from an "alley school" was no grand achievement. My pride was not satisfied, so I took part in many different kinds of competitions, including math competitions, winning many prizes in a row. There was a book that compiled all the entrance examination questions and math competition questions from 1936 to 1956 in the Soviet Union. I practiced all the test questions, not missing a single one. From then on, no test or competition questions could stop me. In addition, I read widely. The Shanghai Library was very close to my school. I was a frequent visitor there, going there almost every day after school. I read many literary masterpieces of the world during that time. My grades were so good that my teachers and classmates praised me as a "genius". I had perfect scores for all the subjects that I took throughout the high school years, earning fives out of five all the way.

    I did not only just have good grades, but performed like an "all-rounder." I reached the national standards for professional athletes in several sports, including sprinting, high jumping and basketball. I recited poetry in Russian, and sang at the Shanghai Children's Palace Chorus. When helping the school publish a blackboard poster, I would dictate to five or six schoolmates at the same time to transcribe several articles of different styles such as poems and essays, with no need for drafts. I remember that in order to give tribute to the tenth anniversary of the National Day, the school organized an exhibition. I designed an exhibit titled "The red sun rising from Shaoshan". The principle behind its working was actually simple: a movement detector would trigger the moving of the motor whenever a person got close to the exhibit. This little thing caused quite a sensation. It was advocated at that time to "leave no class brother behind," meaning giving help to those classmates with poor grades. I often spent time on weekends to give lectures to classmates who fell behind in their studies. As I was a student myself, I knew where the difficulties were, so I often got the work done with half the effort, and my classmates liked my lectures. For a time, I felt I was at the right time, in the right place, and with the right people, winning all kinds of praises and honors in succession, such as the "three good and five virtue student[1]," "heroic model," and "standard bearer and representative." The various kinds of awards that I received were too numerous to count. As a proverb goes, "with a man in bad luck, even drinking cold water would plug the teeth." On the other hand, "A man in luck just cannot stop the blessing of many good fortunes." Since I could sing, write, and articulate, I was made a pacesetter for various kinds of activities, giving speeches everywhere. Thus, I was a pacesetter first for my district, then for the city, then the whole country. Everything came in a rush, just like a dream. In reality, I did many silly, stupid things, such as "wiping out sparrows", "making steel in a big way" with crude home-made furnaces, and "digging deep into soils" — all slogans of the time. In order to "wipe out sparrows," I would reach into birds' nests in the middle of night with the help of a torchlight; to "make steel in a big way," we went to all kinds of households to take off the metal handles of doors and windows; to "dig deep into soil," we dug out the tombs of peasants' ancestors. Looking back, it was all so ludicrous and regrettable.

There was something that I cannot forget for a lifetime, and cannot understand to this day. At that time, the Shanghai West High School had

---

[1] A communist slogan describing the ideal student as being in good health, good at studies and good at work ("three good"), and possessing the five virtues of love for work, love for studies, love for people, love for science and love for public property.

a very talented student. I will call him Feng He (not his real name). He had a very big head and was called "Big Head He." He was in my grade. The difference between us was that he was at a top school well-known in Shanghai, whereas I was at an "Alley School." Whenever there was a math competition, I could never win the first place if he took part in it too. He was simply a genius who knew multiple foreign languages, including English, Russian, and Japanese. Later, he got accepted into the "Math Training Class" organized by the famous mathematician Professor Buqing Su at Fudan University. It was created for students gifted in mathematics. Coincidentally, I also entered Fudan Unversity, but I was at the class for students selected to study in the Soviet Union. Since we were at the same university, I knew of his later situation. After He entered Fudan, his academic performance slipped and he eventually graduated with some difficulty, becoming a teacher in a high school. In my opinion, he might have been too precocious, whereas I might be considered a late bloomer.

3.2 Seeing Chairman Mao

In 1960, I went to Beijing to join a conference as a representative for top students in Shanghai. Before we went, the state gave each of us a suit and a pair of cotton shoes. We stayed at the Xiyi Hotel. The bright and spacious suite with mattress beds felt a like a dream. April 23 was a sunny and memorable day, and the conference reached a climax. We rode in a big sedan, entering the Zhongnaihai compound from the Xinhua Gate. The sedan followed a zigzag path among the high red walls, and stopped at the Huairen Hall. The still water of a lake and the peaceful gardens within the compound left a deep impression with me. This was the new Forbidden City. We came to a little square, with camera pods and chairs for the leaders already set up. After taking pictures with us, Mao Zedong and other leaders walked around the square to see us face to face. When Mao walked in front of me, I could see the mole on his face clearly. We also attended a state banquet in the Great Hall. A huge red star embedded in the ceiling of the hall emitted beautiful bright light. In later years, I saw scenes from the Great Hall in movies or on TV numerous times, and the memory of over half a century ago has been kept vivid in my mind. On the same occasion, we also went up the Tiananmen Square viewing stand.

At that time, I really felt like the happiest person in the world. However, some inexplicable worries and misgivings have kept turning up in my mind over the years. We melted handles from windows and other scrap metals in a furnace, shaped them into pieces of nuggets, weighed them, and reported how much steel we made, just to reach the targeted number of 10,700,000 tons of steel. Was it the right thing to do? When the school organized for us to work in the countryside, our superiors asked us to "dig deep" beyond three feet. Sometimes, we dug out the tombs of the ancestors of the peasants. I thought, could the roots of the crops reach that deep? Was it necessary? I really liked my physics teacher Zhipan Zheng. I remember, once we went together to a factory to "work to support study." That was a factory for assembling valves. I asked Teacher Zheng if we could use a heavy ball to regulate the pressure of a sealed vessel. He replied, "You may be disappointed again. This technology is already in use." "However," he continued, "you need to keep asking questions, until nobody can find an answer except through your research, then you would have really invented or created something." It could be said that Zheng led the way for me to do research in physics. However, how could such a good teacher be a "rightist"? I once discussed these kinds of issues with my politics teachers Yucheng Zhu and Zhizhen Yu. They told me, "you are a standard bearer for our time. You need to keep in step with the party and Chairman Mao. Uphold the three red flags high." However, I could sense that they had the same feelings and doubts as I did.

I think that it is beneficial to get high school students to do a moderate amount of labor in factories or in the countryside. I grew up in the city, and had never seen stretches of yellow glistening flowers of vegetables and waves of wheat crop tumbling in the wind. The crisscrossing crop fields of southern China, the crowing of roosters in the morning, and the chorus of frogs and insects in the evening simply fascinated me. The squelching and hum of machinery in the factories, though a bit harsh, made me feel fresh. For the first time, I learned what it was like to be a worker or a peasant. I was still in a trance after having had the honor of seeing Chairman Mao, but at the same time I was puzzled by what was really going on. When I was eating from "a big pot of rice" that "tasted good but cost nothing" at a people's commune, a peasant told me that the rice was cooked from seeds intended for the next year, I was speechless with astonishment, and an ill feeling about the future filled my mind.

3.3 Key choices

Back from the conference in Beijing, it was time for the college entrance examination. Actually, before I went to Beijing, the high school administrators already told me that the school was going to "secure a place" for me to go to study at the Harbin Military Engineering Institute. To study at Harbin Military Engineering Institute was the dream of many young people at that time. This was comparable to the West Point Military Academy in the United States. Furthermore, all the costs of tuition and boarding were to be paid for by the state. Even more importantly, it did not need an entrance examination, but completely depended on the recommendation of selected high schools. To go or not to go, it became an important choice. At that time, my family had six children going to school, and the financial burden of education reached a peak. My parents at one time suggested that my elder sister apply to a Normal, a university to train teachers, because all the cost for Normal was to be paid by the state. However, my sister's grades were extremely good, and she published many articles in newspapers and magazines even when in junior high school. She simply loved journalism. Finally, my parents reached an agreement that if my elder sister could enter the Department of Journalism in Fudan University, they would let her go to Fudan, otherwise she would go to a teachers' college as a second choice. In the end, my sister passed the entrance examination to the Journalism Department of Fudan with excellent marks. At this key point, my parents encouraged me to apply for an ordinary college, and not to go to Harbin Military. Later, the school authorities realized my determination, and decided to select me to take part in the examination for students intending to study in the Soviet Union. This was different from a "secured place through recommendation," because I needed to succeed in the examination. In reality, there were too many children of high-ranking officials involved and the examination was just for show. For someone like myself born in an ordinary family, to win the competition through an examination was a real fight. To prepare for this examination, I went with little sleep and did not care much for regular meals either. Even when I was attending the conference in Beijing, I gave up many opportunities to see performances at the People's Hall, and studied in my hotel room. After returning to Shanghai, I had to make speeches everywhere about my Beijing trip, with no time for regular classes during the day time, forget studying for exams. I would often study and prepare for the exams until midnight, and then get up before dawn the next day. In order not to disturb others while they slept, I would sit on a toilet seat in a bathroom to read by myself. It could be said that for several months before the college entrance examination, I hardly stayed in the school. It was either going away to conferences or making speeches everywhere. As to preparing for the examination, it all depended on the evenings. I was rewarded for my effort. Finally, with top marks, I became a student designated for studying in the Soviet Union! That was a first in the history of Chengdu Second, causing a sensation in the whole school. Chengdu Second became noted because of my accomplishment. In a show room in the school, my personal history of achievements, pictures, and awards were on display permanently. I deliberately sought out Teachers Zheng and Qiu to express my thanks, and made an apology to Teacher Lin, who thought that I would certainly become a successful writer. Thus, I ended my high school life with admission to join a group of students bound for studying in the Soviet Union.

3.4 The fifty-eight squadron

The joy of being admitted to the group of students designated for studying in the Soviet Union soon gave way to a cloudy mood. I saw that others went to their universities and colleges to start their academic year, but after I got my acceptance letter I had heard no news whatsoever. We were kept in the dark about what was happening. I hang on until the beginning of October, when I got a letter of acceptance from the department of atomic energy of Fudan University. I was shocked for a moment. How did it change to Fudan University? I arrived at Fudan according to schedule. I attended a meeting held by the party secretary of Fudan University, Xiguang Yang, who was also an alternate party secretary of the city of Shanghai. Only then did I learn that the relationship between China and the Soviet Union had worsened, and that our group of students, all fifteen of us, could no longer go to the Soviet Union to study physics. The state decided not to disband the group, but formed a class for us, called the "zero" class, to take part in a top secret project coded "the fifty-eight squadron". During the daytime, we attended classes like the other four classes in the department of atomic energy. At night, we took part in the making of the atomic bomb. In reality, it was not that complicated to make an atom bomb. The difficulty lay with obtaining enriched uranium. It was known that in nature uranium existed mostly in the form of Uranium-238, with a tiny portion of Uranium-235. Only nuclear materials containing Uranium-235 in sufficiently high concentration could be used to make the bomb. There was very little difference between the two isotopes Uranium-238 and Uranium-235. How to separate the two and enrich the concentration of Uranium-235 was a world-class difficult problem. Nowadays, popular science books and memoirs of a few members of the original "fifty-eight squadron" talk about this kind of stuff. It should be fine that I describe some simple ideas here. The Chinese effort used the "gaseous diffusion method". It was based on the principle that molecules of uranium hexafluoride containing Uranium-235 are slightly smaller than those with Uranium-238, and by forcing them through a type of semi-permeable membrane repeatedly, the concentration of Uranium-235 will increase a little bit after each pass. Such a semi-permeable membrane must be resistant to corrosion and high-pressure difference. In fact, I was only seventeen at that time, and did not know anything. I became involved unexpectedly in a top-secret project that was classified at the national level.

The fifteen of us studied during the day, and worked in the evenings, and we were not permitted to speak to anyone about what we were doing, including teachers, schoolmates, and family members. Soon, we assumed an aura of mystery, and became isolated among our schoolmates. The "zero" class became the mystery class, and the white building where we worked became the most mysterious place at Fudan University.

In 1960, China entered a period of great famine that lasted three years. We, the students of the "zero" class who studied and worked day and night, could get neither enough to eat nor enough sleep. We became jaundiced and thin one by one, with our academic performance declining continually. Many students gradually could not keep up with the studies. At that time, driven by a sense of honor, mission, and "specialness," I really exerted myself to keep up my grades, but they were not perfect anymore. I became thinner, too.

Not far from Fudan University, there was a village called Wujiaochang. During that difficult period, many state regulations were relaxed, and a variety of free markets began to flourish. Hawkers set up many stands at Wujiaochang. I can never forget something called the "fried rib with rice cake." One thin piece of rib, with two thin pieces of rice cake, fried in oil, speckled with allspice, gave out a fragrance that could be smelled from far away. That was a stand that I would certainly go to once a week. It would take fifty cents to buy a portion, almost half a day's wage for many people. However, the monthly food ration at that time was thirty-two catties (a catty is half a kilogram) of rice, half a catty of oil and meat, several catties of vegetables, and less than half a catty of pastries, so the taste of this "fried rib with rice cake" would be relished for a whole week. Each time I finished a portion, I would lick clean the dish that came with it. We were most scared of the fourth-period class, because at that time, our stomach would growl with hunger, and we just could not concentrate on what the teachers were saying. The president of Fudan University, Wangdao Chen, wrote to Chairman Mao, asking that the food supply level be raised for the students. Mao ordered the standard to be increased to fifteen yuan per month from thirteen. Vegetables were planted in a lawn in front of the Denghui Hall. The lawn used to be a source of pride for Fudan University. Human waste was collected to feed pigs for food. Every night we went to bed hungry. The Chinese marshal Yi Chen talked about pawning off our pants to make the atom bomb. From what I experienced, that was no exaggeration. Later I found out that the situation with Fudan was by no means the worst. Many people starved to death in other places around China. In a country where rice seeds were eaten up, a famine was sure to follow. A year later, we completed the research on the semi-permeable membrane, and our "zero" class formed with students designated for studying in the Soviet Union was officially disbanded. We were dispersed among the four regular classes. I was assigned to the third class, majoring in nuclear physics.

With the passage of time, a lot of information became declassified. I learned later that in the whole of China over ten thousand people from tens of research institutions and several hundreds of factories were involved in the research, production, and testing of the first atom bomb of China. The research project conducted at Fudan University with our "fifty-eight squadron" on the enrichment of weapon grade uranium was just one of a thousand links in the whole effort. Nevertheless, on October 16, 1964, when I heard about the news of the successful test of the first atom bomb of China, I felt that I had contributed my personal effort, although I was just a seventeen-year-old student at that time.

3.5 Delayed judgment

It was revealed that the three years of famine and natural disasters were not natural at all, but basically man-made. Had the ten thousand-word letter of Peng Dehuai regarding the so-called three red flags of "general line, great leap forward, and people's commune" received serious attention in the communist party, and had the personality cult for Chairman Mao been stopped in time, modern Chinese history would have been re-written.

I was asked the question repeatedly: "Is the communist party good or bad?" I always had to reply that the question was not well-defined. The associate secretary of the communist party committee of Fudan University, Chuangang Chen, was a person whom I loved and respected. Whenever he was making a speech, no matter how hungry I was, I still would listen attentively. One of my schoolmates could no longer tolerate the hunger, so she stole some pastry ration tickets from her fellow student. Chen said in one of his speeches that the most precious quality of a person was "self-discipline without supervision," that was about self-management. When one did something good, it was not to show off to others, but for oneself. His words, I will remember for a life time. However, there was another cadre of the communist party, whose role was to supervise students like us. I will call him "Mr. He." He was the first communist party member that I resented. The slogans at that time were "to be a willing tool for the party," and "to be a screw for serving the people." The job of this Mr. He was to transform each of us students into a docile tool or a screw for the party. In my opinion, such a position should never have existed in universities. Regrettably, such positions still appear to be there to this day, although less powerful.

Since I left the "fifty-eight squadron" and joined the third class, I was subject to the management of this Mr. He, and my conflicts with him never stopped. He constantly asked for me to submit to his will, to become a "docile tool of the party," and to smooth out all my "sharp edges" in my personality. I tried to keep my own characters, so this Mr. He incessantly criticized me for my "liberalism," "bourgeois ideology" and such. In 1964, it was about time to graduate. This Mr. He wielded enormous power over the students, and it was his decision to assign jobs to the students after graduation. The obedient students would go to universities and research institutes; the disobedient would go to the countryside, mining towns and frontier villages. At that time, there was a movie whose story line I have forgotten, but I remember the title: "The Delayed Judgment." If my job was to be assigned by this Mr. He, I would be able to work neither at a university, nor at a research institute. I realized that I must apply to graduate school, to let the "judgment" to be delayed. As I expected, this Mr. He did not give me permission to apply, using "poor political performance" as an excuse. Nowadays, it was difficult to imagine the circumstances of that time. Such an excuse was sufficient to stop a student from applying for a graduate school. However, such was the situation at the time.

I appealed directly to the associate secretary of the party committee of Fudan University, Chuangang Chen, and he gave me personal approval for taking part in the entrance examination for graduate school. However, we were soon sent to the countryside for the so-called "Four Clears" campaign. It was located at Baoshan County, not far from the sea. None of my classmates had seen the sea. I proposed to Mr. He that we should organize a trip to the beach. He gave me a harsh look, saying that I did not have the correct political attitude. I said nothing more. One morning, I got up before dawn, and ran for an hour to go to the beach. I saw the sunrise, and ran another hour to return to where we stayed before everybody else got up. I wrote a poem as follows:

Friend,
Did you ever see the sun rise?
Did you see the darkness before dawn?
That's the transition from darkness to light, from yesterday to today,
That's the melting of water and fire, and the unity of the sky and the sea.

Oh, the fireball that is the sun rising from the east,
a sure proof that the earth rotates on its own axis.
Let us open our arms, against the sunlight,
to welcome our bright tomorrow!

Besides writing the poem, I also thought of using the time for the sun rise to calculate the distance between the earth and the sun. However, all this became issues in the eyes of Mr. He. In addition to the labels with "liberalism," "bourgeois ideology," he heaped other criticisms like "disrespect for organization," and "no discipline." He wanted to discipline me. I talked back: "Where can you find bourgeois ideology?" He said dryly: "How could the poor and middle peasants find such leisurely mood?" It was hard to imagine what would result to have this kind of functionaries managing the students.

Soon, it was about time for the entrance examination for graduate schools. We were still stuck in the countryside to do the "Four Clears." I asked for a leave to return to Shanghai to study and to take part in the examination, but Mr. He denied my request. With just one week till the examination, I got very worried. At that time, the entrance examination included a test for current affairs. I had read neither books nor newspapers for a long time, how could I handle such a test? At this key point, I sought out the leader of the "Four Clears" group at Yanghang Commune, Baoshan County, Liying Mi, who was the secretary of the communist youth at Baoshan County. Her husband was the party secretary of Baoshan County. I explained my situation to her, and she supported me wholeheartedly. She said, "You can return to Shanghai to prepare for the examination, and I will talk things out with the management of Fudan University." Thus, I made it back to Shanghai, and would sleep only three to four hours per day to study. I understood that it was a struggle with fate. If I could not make it, then this Mr. He would banish me to a frontier village or a mining town. I must let the "judgment" be delayed by becoming a graduate student. At that time, the difficulty level for passing the entrance examination to a graduate school was almost as hard as becoming the number one scholar in ancient times. It was quite different from the current situation with an abundance in the number of gradate students. A graduate degree at that time was equivalent to an associate doctor degree of the Soviet

Union. A doctoral candidate in the Soviet Union was equivalent to a postdoctoral position in the USA. A supervisor for a graduate student was appointed by the state council, and there were only a very limited number in the whole country. The guideline at that time was "quality over quantity." Only a few people were admitted to graduate schools. According to statistics, the total number of graduate students for all subjects was only five thousand for the whole country during the seventeen year period from 1949 to 1965. It simply could not be compared with the situation nowadays when there are over ten thousand graduate students each year. Again, the statistics show that there were 4.2 millions Masters degree and half a million PhD degree holders in the 35 years from 1978 to 2013 in China. I could not help feeling the dramatic change of times.

I applied to do my graduate study with Professor Gengou Xu. In December of 1947, Xu went to the University London in UK to do graduate study under the famous physicist Harrie Messey. He studied theoretical physics there, and obtained a PhD degree. In August of 1950, Dr. Xu returned to China, declining the invitation of his supervisor to stay and work in Great Britain. Xu was a noted expert in nuclear physics in China at that time. Due to the deterioration of Sino-Soviet relations, most of the Chinese scientists who worked at the Joint Institute for Nuclear Physics Research at Dubna went to Lanzhou, a so-called third-tier city in China. Lanzhou, located in the northwest of China, became the research center for nuclear science in the whole country. High security measures were taken at the examination place. There were five or six teachers supervising the examination in a room which held only a dozen students. The examination papers were sealed in red paint, which were opened after a supervising teacher and a candidate entered their signatures at the same time. Such was the tense mood that it was almost unbearably oppressive. I remember that one candidate fainted on the spot and was promptly taken to a hospital, never to be seen back at the examination place. At that time, I had just turned twenty, but I already knew that a man could get ahead only through struggling with fate. Hesitation and cowardice were not permitted in this fight. What were needed were self-confidence, self-strength, and self-reliance. Success often came with persistence in the most difficult hours. Finally, the examination was over, and I returned to the "Four Clears" group at Yanghang Commune of Baoshan County to express my sincere thanks to the team leader Liying Mi. Mi was a woman. However, it was not just my luck with ladies. It had more to do with the fact that the communist party had cadres who helped the people as well as oppressive officials like Mr. He.

The day for graduation assignment was a sunny day with a light breeze. I had a hunch about being victorious. I had watched some movies with scenes where students wore graduate caps and threw them high into the sky, shouting excitedly. However, it was quite different from what we experienced. It was more like waiting for the verdict of the judges. I had never been to a criminal court, and did not know how a suspect felt while waiting for the judge to pass the verdict. Those graduation assignments were like verdicts that would send one to a research institute, or a factory or mine. A couple in love might be separated by long distances in different corners of the country. Single children might have to say good-bye to elderly parents, to go to a far away place. The amphitheater of the white building of the atomic energy department was a veritable courtroom. We were waiting for our judgment there, and the crossroads of life started from here. When it was read: "Weimin Wu, graduate student at the Department of Modern Physics, Lanzhou University," the classroom erupted into applause, and tears suddenly flooded my eyes. I really wanted to cry, pouring out the grievances and bitterness that I felt in my heart. My adolescent years, marked by my acceptance as a graduate student, came to a happy ending. From the illiterate generation of my grandparents, to the self-made generation of my parents who worked hard to bring up their children, to my generation who obtained the highest degree in China, the Wu family had a new successful generation.

3.6 Reflection

I was often asked, what was the biggest difference between Chinese and Western education? What was most in need of improvement in Chinese education? Here are several ideas based on my own life's experience. First, there must be freedom of thought. I regard freedom of thought as the soul of cultivating true talents. Positions held by the likes of Mr. He for minding the "political thinking" of students, or for "training docile tools of the party" should never have existed in universities. Despite my immense popularity in high school, I lost my luster after I entered Fudan University. My uninhibited, outspoken personality put me in conflict with communist cadres like Mr. He. Under Mr. He, Chairman Mao's "Combat liberalism" was to be the article that I must read every day. He would interfere if I discussed the limits in the dimensions of the universe; he would also meddle if students were in love with each other. For years, the policy of the communist party towards intellectuals was the political barometer for China. Intellectuals should be treated as precious treasures of the nation. Such a policy should have been in force for all times. It would not be right to put such a policy into practice only when the nation was encountering a difficult time, and then overturn it when the economic situation improved. It was really stupid to limit the freedom of thought with an artificial political frame. I remember that the happiest time that I had with my family was the evening of every Saturday. Six brothers and sisters gathered merrily under one roof after returning from Fudan University, Shanghai High School, and Shanghai Sports School to the home at 64 Julu Road. Mother would always make a few dishes extra, and everyone talked about just any subject. This family cell must have had the most democratic, most free, and most relaxed party. There, one could say anything without worrying about being informed upon, or labeled anything. My parents would not assume the air of authority, and everyone felt uninhibited, spoke freely, and often filled the room with laughter. When a sensitive topic was touched, my parents would get worried, and interject quickly, "lower your voice!" My parents were timid persons, and my brothers and sisters would often see a social problem sharply, but none of us had the determination to dedicate everything to a cause, and to make the real changes needed. That was the reason why I would often say, the Wu family would produce talented people, but no historical figures larger.

Regarding the importance of freedom of thought, Albert Einstein made one emotionally charged comment:

> It is, in fact, nothing short of a miracle that the modern methods of instruction have not yet entirely strangled the holy curiosity of inquiry; for this delicate plant, aside from stimulation, stands mainly in need of freedom; without this it goes to wrack and ruin without fail. It is a very grave mistake to think that the enjoyment of seeing and searching can be promoted by means of coercion and a sense of duty.

Even to this day, I felt inspired by what Einstein said many decades ago.

Secondly, academic democracy must thrive. Fudan had many world-class professors, including those who taught me, such as Xidei Xie and Zhongyi Hua. There were also many very accomplished teachers, such as Guangjun Ni. The "inspirational" series of talks held by Fudan had a glorious tradition. I was a faithful member of the audience of those talks while at Fudan, almost never missing a single session. Those talks included many subjects, various opinions, and all kinds of keynote speakers. In 2001, I, a former member of the audience, gave a talk of my own. However, there were many problems with academic democracy at that time. I will elaborate with an article that I wrote in 1961 titled "On Zi and Dian." In this article, I proposed that any particles in the world were made up of two different kinds of particles: one was to be called "Zi", which had mass but no charge, and the other called "Dian", which had a charge but no mass. Thus, using these two kinds of particles as "building blocks", one could build up all the particles known at the time. I showed this article to the teacher Guangjun Ni and another respected teacher. After reading my article, Ni told me that it was a creative effort, but lacked a theoretical framework and quantitative calculations. It needed further research. The other teacher returned my article with just a glance at the title, with an expression of disdain that showed that he did not care for it at all. In fact, this article put forward a very important new idea, namely that all the known articles at that time were not the most fundamental. They had a deeper level of structure. In an environment where there was a lack of international exchanges, the teachers should have given encouragement to an eighteen year old who proposed such an idea. Half a century went by, I published over two hundred articles in first tier academic journals of the world, including five for which I was the first author. In my opinion, all the two hundred articles combined were not nearly as important as my unpublished article "On Zi and Dian". In 1964, Murray Gell-Mann and others proposed that all particles in the world were made up of three types of fundamental particles, with each carrying a certain amount of mass and charge. That was the quark model for physics. Gell-Mann won the Nobel Prize in physics in 1969. Therefore, I would now make the point everywhere: "Do not look down on young people. Their thoughts are the most uninhibited, most creative. Even their wildest dreams may contain unexpected sparks of genius." Guangjun Ni was one of the most influential teachers in my life. It was he who suggested that I should apply to be a graduate student of Professor Gongou Xu. Half a century later, when I gave a talk at an international conference on high energy physics at Uppsala, Sweden, I met Ni by chance. After I finished my talk, applause that lasted a few minutes erupted in the hall. It moved him very much. He wrote afterwards: "I have had a career in education for decades, with over one thousand students, and Weimin Wu was among the very few truly outstanding." I am not sure if he remembers the article that I wrote "On Zi and Dian." That was one article worthy of publication but regrettably never made it. An ancient Chinese saying goes that "any mountain can be famous with the presence of an immortal, and any river can be holy with the residence of a dragon." I would say that publications do not have to be long, nor have to be numerous in number, but will be treasured for their creativities.

Thirdly, mistakes must be permitted. Academic research is different from production, and mistakes must be allowed. As a proverb goes, "failure is the mother of success." Where failure is not allowed, there would not be great success either. I recall that once in an optics experiment, I unexpectedly shook a photon-multiplier tube while trying to insert it into a board, causing it to leak gas. This was a tube imported from Great Britain. I was not only scolded by a teacher in charge, but also had to sign an agreement that I would pay for the damage from my salary after graduation, six hundred yuan in total. That was equal to a whole year of salary at that time. From then on, I would no longer carry out experiments with my hands. I would just do data analysis. It could be the reason why I was not handy with physical equipment even though I worked as an experimental physicist. It was often asked, "So far why is there nobody winning the Nobel Prize with their work done in mainland China?" I think that poor performance in these three areas is part of the reason.

Chapter Four
The Shadow of First Love

4.1 Returning to my *alma mater*

It was April 1988 in Southern China, when spring was in full bloom, and the sun shone warm and bright. My Institute sent me on a trip to find candidates for graduate schools from Fudan University.

That was the first time I had returned to the university since I graduated from it twenty three years earlier. Almost a quarter of a century had gone by! I had been back to Shanghai many times, but this was the first time to my *alma mater*...

Things went very smoothly. I got the green light from an old classmate of mine Mr. L, and Prof. Ni personally arranged for me to interview a few students with excellent academic results and great characters. It seemed about time to pack up for the return trip. All of a sudden, my classmate asked: "Weimin, you rarely come back to your *alma mater*. Why don't you meet some of your old classmates? Mr. Z is a director at a research institute in Shanghai. Mr. W still teaches, but he is an associate professor now. And Mr. C.... Ha, there is also Xiao Mei, (pseudonym), that unfortunate lady..."

Mei, Mei, I suddenly felt dizzy, and my memory went blank...

"What about her?" I asked Mr. L after pulling myself together with some difficulty.

"Oh, you don't know? She is terminally ill with breast cancer, and it has spread to her heart."

"How is that possible? Terminally ill? Spreading cancer? ... Only minutes left to live? No, that's impossible..." I murmured to myself.

4.2 Falling in love with Mei

Mei and I were classmates at Fudan University. I was seventeen when I got to know her.

Mei was not a pretty girl — not exactly attractive, but not bad-looking either. She had narrow eyes, becoming a line whenever she smiled. On her wide forehead there were two conspicuous scars, probably as a result of a fall when she was a child. She was rather fat, with short cropped hair. Whichever way you looked at her, Mei just did not have the looks to enthrall a guy at first sight.

It was after an examination on theoretical mechanics that Mei caught my attention. I had entered Fudan University with a certain pride, almost some kind of superiority complex. That examination was particularly difficult. Apart from the regular test questions, there was an optional question. It was about the trace made by an insect climbing a ring, as far as I recall. Furthermore, the ring was attached to a revolving door that kept oscillating.

I finished off the regular test questions with ease, and then tackled the optional question, too.

I handed in my papers. In those kind of examinations, I was often the first to finish. The exhilaration of being the first to hand in my papers felt better than drinking a cup of iced soda water in summer, and better than jumping into a hot spring in winter. However, when I handed in the examination papers, I found that the teacher already had another test paper in hand.

"Whose is that?" I had to ask.

"It's from Xiao Mei." The teacher answered with a smile.

Xiao Mei! That name rang in my ears. I looked towards where Mei was sitting, only to see an empty chair. From that moment on, that name and the person associated with it stayed in my mind, with many stories to follow that were unforgettable.

Mei and I almost always took the number one place in test scores in our class for our own genders, respectively. However, when our test papers were on public display for perfect answers, the contrast between her papers and mine became a source of shame for me. Her test papers were tidily written with handsome regular script, like a beautiful picture.

Her math formula derivations and operations were shaped like a series of musical scores. It was such a contrast with my illegible handwriting, wildly arranged math formulations and deductions.

Mei was a member of the university chorus. She could sing as well as dance. On weekends, she often performed in the university musical hall. In the past I seldom got to see the performances, because I would go back to my parents' house on weekends. Since that theoretical mechanics test, I became a regular spectator at the musical hall. Mei's alto solo and duet often got warm rounds of applause from the audience in the hall. That applause had a hypnotic effect on me, conjuring up poetic associations in my mind.

Mei was a cadre for the communist youth league. She became the first party member in the whole class soon after. A big red poster proclaiming her acceptance into the party was hung up near the entrance to the department building. Somehow, I felt jealous at the news. I also applied for party membership at the time. However, she succeeded, but I failed. We were well matched in test scores. She was active in social activities, but I was no idler, either. She could sing and dance, but I joined the university photography team. My photographic work won a prize in a competition held in Shanghai. Furthermore, I was a high jumper. I often jumped over high bars in a chic scissors style, attracting warm applause from viewers all around. In the eyes of my classmates, especially the female ones, I was a "child prodigy" with all-round talents, because I was the youngest member in the class. However, she joined the party ahead of me, so I lost in the undeclared competition. At that time, my inner frustration was beyond words.

One day in the afternoon, I was roaming on the big lawn before the musical hall. A path opened up among withering grass, and red maple trees crimsoned the entire forest. It was fall time. Withered leaves were scattered all over the lawn, making a crackling sound when I walked on them. Somehow, I felt sad and dreary. All of a sudden, I saw Xiao Mei, excitedly walking out of the department office. I turned around and tried to get away, but she stopped me.

"Weimin, Weimin, how come I did not get to see you in the last few days?"

I avoided eye contact with Mei on purpose, gazing at the blood-colored setting sun instead. "Where could I have gone? I'm not like you, a new party member, a busybody in the department…" I said with a tone of irony.

Mei let out a laugh, lowering her head, and said sheepishly: "What are you talking about?…" I felt embarrassed. Unexpectedly, she assumed a serious air: "Weimin, I have been looking for you about some serious business matters. Just now, the party branch made some considerations, and they have asked me to be your liaison to the party. … "

"Liaison, what kind of liaison?" I was caught off guard.

She blushed. Her face shone with some mysterious color, reflecting the light from the setting sun.

"Liaison, so to speak, is just about getting together to exchange ideas…"

So in this way we got hooked up.

Nevertheless, it was a pleasure talking with Mei. We rambled on about many things: astronomy, geography, just about anything. I loved literature, composing essays and poems now and then, whereas she had a lot of knowledge about music. She would talk to me about Mozart's untimely death, Chopin's yearning for his motherland, Beethoven's bumpy career… When Mei got excited, she would often recite sometimes sorrowful, other times melancholy melodies, beating out a rhythmic rattle with her feet.

"You talk so eloquently, it is like you are playing the piano!" I remarked playfully.

"I can try the piano if that is what you like." Mei responded casually. She then invited me to her home, offering me a private audience to hear her play the piano.

Having a piano in the house! What kind of family is hers? I felt somewhat uneasy, but made my way to a contemporary style house according to the address she gave me.

Mei's house was located on a quiet portion of a busy street, in a neighborhood mostly lived in by some senior intellectuals. Walking up some wide wooden stairs, Mei led me to her own room. This room gave a sense of surreal tranquility; even the air felt peaceful and warm. On top of an elegant desk, there were several English books, an inkwell made of marble, an exquisite calendar, and a half-length picture of Mei herself inside a gray-bordered bronze frame. However, even more striking was an ebony-colored piano, placed near the north corner of the room. All these items seemed to reflect the taste and temperaments of the owner.

Mei asked me to sit down. She opened the cover, placed a music sheet on top of the piano, and started to play. Beethoven's cheerful melody "Für Elise" filled the air around the street.

I was mesmerized by the music! I knew that Mei had conquered my proud heart. My mind was like virgin Mount Everest snow, marked by the footsteps of a girl for the first time.

Our contacts became more frequent. The whole thing had an official reason: we were "exchanging thoughts", and she was my party "liaison".

That was a hot summer, hotter than past years. I was celebrating my twentieth birthday. Many friends came to my house, bringing a lot of gifts for me.

Mei came too, giving me a white envelope. My hearted thumped, and I intended to savor it in privacy later. However, another classmate grabbed it from me. I tried to take it back, but he already opened up the envelope. A piece of card fell out.

It was an exquisite birthday card made by Mei herself. She had drawn the lovely smiling face of Princess Snow White, on top of which was an inserted page with a drawing of a palace with "doors and windows" cut out with scissors. The "doors and windows" were covered with semi-transparent papers, making the picture of the Princess behind look hazy and mysterious.

Four slogans in vogue at the time were attached to this imaginative drawing for my birthday greetings:

"To comrades, be warm as the spring;
to work, be hot as the summer;
to individualism, be merciless as the autumn wind sweeping away fallen
   leaves;
to enemies, be cold and ruthless as winter."

Yes, indeed! Exactly four months before, Chairman Mao had made a call to learn from Lei Feng — a dedicated soldier. What else could a communist member wish for an "activist" who was applying for party membership?

Nevertheless, I thought I made a new discovery: she could draw so well.

My heart was conquered and intoxicated. Her image suddenly lifted a cloud off my heart, spouting brilliant and happy sparks. I had never experienced such stirring emotions that filled the whole body, such intoxicating happiness, such excitement from the bottom of my heart. I believed that was love. Her casual glances, when met with my focused gazing, were like collisions of beams of positrons and electrons in the vacuum, producing a fireball that awakened me for the first time. It was she who made me feel for the first time that I was no longer a boy, but a real man.

That night, the moon was dim. After finishing our homework, Mei and I sat on that big lawn to "exchange thoughts". It was quiet all around, so quiet that we could hear each other's heartbeats. Looking at her misty round face, suddenly a poem by Shelley came to mind:

"Look at me — do not move your eyes,
Let them feast upon the love in my eyes.
Indeed, this love is nothing but the light
as reflection of your beauty in my soul."

My heart was moved, and my gaze was fixed upon her face. She realized something, and took her eyes off me.

I was just about to stretch out my hand to reach her hand that was supporting her on the grass. She stood up, and said to me in a muted hoarse voice: "It is too late, let's see about it tomorrow…"

Tomorrow… Tomorrow… I returned to my dormitory, but could no longer fall asleep. I just sat up and, illuminated by torchlight, transcribed a poem from the Hungarian poet Sandor Petofl, using my most elegant handwriting style:

"This world is so large,
but you are so small, my love;
But, when you belong to me,
I would not exchange the whole world for you."

Unexpectedly, those four short lines of verse almost changed — oh no! — they completely changed the course of our lives.

When I plucked up enough courage, and delivered Mei a letter containing the poem, she was first surprised, and then she turned around and went away. I had expected that she would write me something in return. On the contrary, she started to avoid me on purpose. I felt at a loss. Why? Agony started to gnaw at my heart. I suddenly felt an uneasy foreboding. I felt betrayed by the love that had robbed me of my judgment, the love that had made my heart bleed. I had expected her to love me just as naturally as I loved her. However, I was wrong.

I found her.

"Why don't you talk to me anymore?" I asked innocently.

"I have reported the poem that you wrote to the political instructor." She replied, her face paling rapidly.

"What?" My brain was about to explode. "Why?" Feeling the blood boiling all over my body, I looked at her angrily.

Mei got scared. I had never been so angry, and I had never looked at someone with such spite, almost hate.

"You can't. You know, as college students, we are not allowed…" She murmured.

"Not allowed what?" I interrupted her hastily.

"Not allowed that… not allowed love. The party organization has its rules. You know that. I'm your party liaison, and I'm a new party member. You cannot let your imagination go wild, much less let your petty bourgeois sentiments go unchecked…" She finally let out what was on her mind.

"So if you know that college students are not allowed to have love relationships, then why did you have to make the report?"

"I'm a party member, and I must tell what is in my heart to the party. I cannot hide anything from the party." She felt certain of what she did, almost religiously.

"To whom did you make the report?" I somehow felt betrayed.

"Teacher He (pseudonym), the political instructor" She lowered her voice even further.

"Shit!" I cursed rudely. A terrible jealousy, coupled with a feeling of betrayal, made me lose my sense like an angry lion. Teacher He! It was he who talked with her all the time, who introduced her to the party! It was he who criticized me for my vain pride, and for my petty bourgeois sentiments. On hearing that Mei had reported us to He, I simply felt like she was using a sharp knife to bleed all the blood from my body in order to please another man who was chasing her.

I left Mei hurriedly without bothering to look back. The matter did not end there.

One day, my sister found me. She was also studying at Fudan University, in the Journalism Department. She lived in the same dormitory building as my female classmates. Almost all of them knew her.

"I heard you were starting a relationship with Xiao Mei?" My sister asked with concern.

"Who gave you that idea?" I snappily replied.

"Teacher He told me." She said. "He asked me to talk to you. Having a love relationship is not allowed in college. It may hinder your progress."

So it was about joining the party. Perhaps, because I was not a party member, Mei looked down on me.

I decided to avoid Mei from now on. However, this was almost impossible. It was on a Friday when I gave her the poem that brought me bad luck. I regarded her as heinous as a Judah. I hated her. However, it was so hard to hate.

4.3 Going separate ways

It is said that in order to improve his sculpting skill, the French sculptor Auguste Rodin went to a Gothic church on numerous occasions, just to observe the movements of the shadows cast by objects in the church under the sun at various positions of the sky. With the sunrise and the sunset the ever-changing shadows of the church stirred up creative passions in Rodin's heart. Later when Rodin raised his hammer against a large chunk of stone, the stone seemed to take on a life of its own under the glistening sunlight: the bright side bulging and moving, and the shadowy side speaking in whispers. He broke up the stone hammer by hammer, as though being instructed by the gods themselves, resulting in a great life-like masterpiece.

Shadow was important to the great Rodin. However, I just did not need it. I wished to live under a shadowless light, with all dimensions of space and time brightened up. Who would have expected that the shadow of first love would be inescapable for me, becoming longer and longer as the late afternoon sun set in the west? The shadow that encompasses past successes, brewing new successes and failures, holds in its clutch joyful private indulgences and sorrowful love. At that moment, all that the shadow brought me was just a total blackout of my mind. After our last talk, I suddenly had a wicked idea: I wanted my revenge! The best way to have my revenge was to find a girlfriend right now, and she must be a party member.

A man may be forced by anger into a farcical way of thinking. At that moment I was just such a person, losing my reason. It was all understandable though. The "Sorrows of Young Werther" really were many.

In Fudan University, there were few female party members, Miss. Y (pseudonym) was one of them. It was all too easy for a female party member to fall deeply in love with me. My pride was hugely satisfied. Miss. Y and I never even bothered to cover up the relationship between us, perhaps in defiance of Teacher He, or to make Mei jealous. Communist party members were supposed to be made of special material, but nevertheless with bodies of flesh and blood. Unfortunately, how come the party member with feelings was not Xiao Mei? As fate would have it, the party branch reassigned Miss Y to be my party liaison. She was a qualified "liaison" for sure. When Miss Y talked with me, she would either try to indoctrinate or criticize me. She never once truly stirred up my passion. It was all so far from being in love. Only when I met Xiao Mei by chance, did I get a strange feeling of having my "revenge." Only God knows on whom I really did have revenge.

I completely lost hope of joining the party, and my remaining worry was about the job assignment after graduation. For the first time, I realized that I was at a disadvantage! Teacher He, as the political instructor, held the power to decide on my job assignment. I decided that I should apply for graduate school. Once I made it, Teacher He would no longer be able to determine my fate. I wanted "the judgment to be delayed." I thought hard and fast.

I threw myself completely into the preparation for the entrance examination for graduate school. At that time, being a graduate student was a rarity, and the odds were truly one in a hundred. I bought a lot of coffee, which was considered a luxury item then, and I drank several cups in a row. Every day I slept only two to three hours. And I succeeded! When it was announced that I had passed the entrance examination for the graduate school at Lanzhou University, a warm round of applause erupted in my classroom. My face became numb. Was I crying, or laughing? Were they tears of joy, or of released sorrows? I was not sure. All this, however, added to my faith that as long as I held my fate in my own hands, I was sure to succeed. My only failure in life was with her! Although I loved her so much, my fate was not in my hands, but rather in hers, or perhaps in his.

One hot summer day, I embarked on a journey that started my eventful life. Many people came to see me off. Shortly before, I had ended my insincere love affair with Miss Y. She was just a shadow of a "party member." A shadow would disappear automatically once the light source was removed. While a tearful Miss Y was bidding goodbye to me, I kept searching the crowd for Mei... I boarded a west-bound train only when the bell rang for the last time, and I had to leave with a sorrowful heart...

The train finally started to move, *chug chug choo choo*, monotonous and bothersome. I suddenly realized that my first love was born at a time when there was no spring, and ended permanently before the arrival of winter.

4.4 Searching for new loves in the shadow of first love

Soon after I arrived at Lanzhou city, I received a letter from Xiao Mei, asking me to forgive her for not seeing me off at the train station. She said, "There were so many people who came to see you off. I was perhaps one person too many, I thought." It was a very short letter. However, words like "wishing for your letters," and the intimate signature "Xiao Mei," recalled many unforgettable memories.

I did not write back. Why? I am not sure. Perhaps there was too much to say but I did not know how to start, perhaps I was still taking my "revenge," perhaps I was waiting for her to write again to ask for my forgiveness, perhaps...

However, the wheel of history kept turning, and did not permit too many situations of "perhaps" in one's life. Soon, an unprecedented time of upheaval started.

Graduate students like us were consigned to the mountainous and fragmented loess plateau in north-central China. We stayed in ancient cave houses. My parents were in custody separately, to be "isolated and investigated." My brothers and sisters were also banished to the "wide countryside" to become "all red." My home no longer existed, and family letters naturally ceased, too.

Where was Xiao Mei? I did not know. However, I could guess what fate would await her in such an unprecedented time of political upheaval, given that she was born into a privileged family.

All of a sudden, I became anxious to write to her. However, where should I send the letters? Indeed, I desired more than just to write to her. I was wielding a lash to herd a group of sheep, getting them to feed on a dried-up mountain-side. What I really wanted was to return to normal life as a human being.

As time passed, life turned around. Under the highest directive that "universities are still needed," I returned to Lanzhou city. It was a crazy time with many crazy stories. My personal life was no exception. In my propaganda team, I met a pretty girl. We fell in love so quickly. So fast, it almost proved that love did not need time to mature. However, easy come, easy go. We soon parted and the reason was simple: her father was a general of the nationalist party who switched to the communist side at the last moment before the communist take-over. I was soon to be assigned to work at a place with high security clearance. At that time, to separate from her was the only sensible choice. On the night I made the decision to leave her, I went to the bank of yellow river passing through Lanzhou city by myself. I listened to the sound of the water flowing by, and sank into deep thoughts, until the break of dawn the next day.

It was a time when intellectuals were no longer valued. Graduate students were most conspicuous as members of the "stinking number nine," a label reserved for the well-educated Chinese. As I worked at a secluded work unit with high security clearance, it became difficult to find a mate. Love, this most holy word, became debased. As I got older, my family started to be busy with introducing potential "mates" to me.

Thus, I got to know Miss Chen, a girl with a rosy face, correct facial features and shapely body. She wore a kind smile all the time, and looked somewhat like my elder aunt. I loved my aunt, who had the good heart of a Buddha. On our first date, she appeared to be satisfied with me, too. She invited me to her home to see her mother. She said that her mother's opinions mattered more than her own. This was the first time I had heard that such a view existed in the world, but I went along nevertheless.

It was a farmer's house in the suburbs. The bumpy journey had made me tired, but as soon as I came into her courtyard, the smell of life excited me. The house was so quiet. On the ground was the fresh spring grass, with leaves and flowers of willow trees. The yard area was surrounded by several spacious rooms, all under one tiled roof. The property had been left to the mother and daughter by Miss Chen's deceased father. In one corner in the yard, the green leaves of gourd and pod vines on the fence reflected the warm sunshine, giving a peaceful feeling.

The lunch was abundant.

"Eat! Eat!" Miss Chen's mother amiably fed different dishes to me, scanning me with her eyes from time to time.

On the way to see me off, Miss Chen said:

"From now on, you can give your pay check to my mother, and you can focus on your work at your unit!" The tone she used was just like the one used by Chun Ni in the movie "The Good Earth", It appeared that her mother was happy with me.

I, however, became confused. Was that love? Perhaps it was love, but the kind of love that I felt for my aunt. I suddenly remembered Xiao Mei! Just at that moment, this shadow of love took over my mind. Perhaps with Miss Chen my life would be as leisurely as that of a flock of well-fed chickens in her yard. However, I was no chicken, but a bird that liked to fly free. Miss Chen cried. She thought that I was inscrutable. She could be a desirable wife and good mother beyond criticism. So many young men were either rejected by her or by her mother. It was not easy to come across a man that pleased them both. Yet I politely refused her.

"Mate" can be a complicated and mysterious word. I did not check a thesaurus, and I did not know how it was defined by scholars. Never mind the definition, a mate to me was very concrete, because I had a living idol. This idol that I could not have, as it had been raised to the level of perfection, almost like a goddess, by the ever-increasing distance between us, so much so that other girls in real life were under the shadow of this idol, to the point of non-existence. There was a girl named Gao whom I met by chance in a library. She almost fell in love with me at first sight. Wherever I went, her love letters would follow. She would write more than ten pages at a time with her tidy Song-style Chinese characters. Her love, almost tantamount to worship, was revealed in her fluent writing. We would often exchange ideas using laws of physics and mathematics formulas. I almost believed that she could perhaps pull me out of the shadow, making me return to real life. On my birthday, she sent me a handsome jacket as a birthday gift. What she did was really quite normal, but it cracked a nerve in my sensitive mind. I considered her tasteless. Why could not she understand that being unkempt was the hallmark of a talented person like myself? Why could not she send me a painting she drew herself? Or simply a few words in her pretty Song-style calligraphy? A pity she did neither. From that moment on, I could no longer love her. She cried. What could I do? I let her cry, shedding all the tears she wanted to. I cried too, but not so openly. I cried in my heart, and it was the blood of my heart that came out of my eyes.

Love was not meant to be sweet. Love was like an unripe persimmon. Yet my first love, even worse, was a raw persimmon that had been plucked prematurely, bitter and astringent.

4.5 A chance meeting with my first love

A person's stubbornness is sometimes hard to overcome. However, when the right pivot point is found, a light touch can raise up the entire earth.

It was a Sunday. I had a business trip to Shanghai. It was about time that I returned to my work unit. I spent a little time by myself on Nanjing Street, to do some shopping. Suddenly, she appeared before me. It all happened so unexpectedly. I was confounded, not knowing how to react. I could not imagine that it was all true. Yet it was she indeed. However, she had changed so much, almost beyond recognition.

Her steps were no longer brisk. Her body had become round because of her bulging belly, as she was chubby to start with. Her pale face was dotted with unsightly spots. Only her two slightly narrowed eyes were still shining with that quiet, bright light…

"Mei…" I was about to greet her, but reason, like an unseen hand, pulled me back. She passed by me immediately.

Yes, she had made a home with her own man, and their love was soon to produce a child. It looked as though her life was quite smooth. "Did she ever love me? Did she ever reveal her heart? Perhaps she never loved me," I told myself. I did not really have any reason to feel sorry, no reason to feel sad at all.

I hesitated on the street, watching the stream of people passing me by. My eyes strained to follow her. She realized something, stopped in her path, and looked back…

I turned around quickly, saying in my mind: "See you later! …" By the time I looked in her direction again she had disappeared without trace…

"See you later" — what ludicrous words! How could two very "elementary particles" see each other again among a population of one billion, spread out in a land that was nine million six hundred thousand square kilometers deep and wide? The probability of two particles colliding with each other was infinitesimal, next to nothing in such vast four-dimensional coordinates of space and time. However, it was this infinitesimal quantity that raised up the entire earth: the earth appeared to be pushed out of its normal orbit, resulting in a solar eclipse, making the entire world pitch dark, no more bright spots, no more shadows either. A few minutes later, when the bright sun shone upon a happy world again, time was reset to its initial value, zero hour. Life started a new rhythm, and the world recovered. All this appeared to show me that everyone should have his or her own destiny! Never mind what that destiny is.

4.6 Occasional contacts

I at last got transferred from the remote mountain region to Beijing, and later often worked abroad. For more than six months a year, I was absent from China. The earth is like a closed dynamics system, whereas human beings are like countless particles in Brownian movement. They collide with one another every second, producing countless accidental events. However, a totally random accident may have a decisive meaning for a particular particle. Countless necessary results are born in those accidental collisions. However, nothing can change the big picture of this enclosed system. Fate is so different for each particular particle, and one's fate is mostly unimportant to others. I got used to living in Brownian movement.

One day, I returned from abroad. Because of jet lag, I was still sleepy and confused at eight or nine o'clock in the morning. The phone rang, and I picked it up unwillingly, straining to keep my eyes open: "Who is this?"

"This is Xiao Mei..." A remote-sounding voice came over the phone, and yet it was so clear. The voice appeared to have passed through a long century, through countless light years of distance.

I woke up immediately: "Where are you?"

"I'm at the Capital Airport..."

"The Capital Airport?" I was perplexed.

"Yes indeed..." The voice over the phone sounded sad: "I looked you up three times in Beijing. They said you were abroad. Yesterday I went to your research institute. They told me you had returned at midnight. I have already purchased an air-ticket for Shanghai. I... I wanted to see you..."

I held the phone tightly against my ear. It was so quiet that I could almost hear her breathing and her beating heart. I shut my eyes, trying hard to imagine her mood and looks. After a long, long time, I finally asked the question that was on my mind for twenty five years: "Xiao Mei, did you actually love me or not at the time?"

Her breathing became heavy, and after a long while her voice came through the phone: "It was not a question of love or no love. I... I never said that I did not love you. I just said that it was not appropriate, especially at that time..." After a long pause, she asked: "Weimin, must we talk about this on the phone?"

Now it was my turn to be silent. Yes, she was right. She never talked about not loving me, not even about it being inappropriate. Really, we did not even get to discuss our love... A young person who lived in the eighties could never understand the life of college students in the sixties...

All of a sudden, her voice came over the phone again, it sounded like it poured out from the deeply repressed center of the earth: "Weimin, is your life OK? I really miss you..." Then the phone was cut off.

My heart trembled, and my hand held the phone tightly for a very long time.

4.7 Visiting Mei in hospital

I was not sure how I found the hospital. The hospital was building new rooms for in-house patients. It was a messy place with sand, gravel, and steel rods scattered everywhere. The humming of machines was annoying. I went to the small building where Xiao Mei was supposed to be, climbed up the stairs and found room 240, breathing hard. I found her bed empty. I was dumbfounded. Had I come too late? Had she already passed away?...

Mei's roommate asked me: "Did you come to see Xiao Mei? She is now in the intensive care unit."

Before I had time to think, my feet carried me to the intensive care unit at the other end of the corridor. I pushed the door open and saw a woman lying there with an oxygen tube inserted into her nose, and a needle for saline water attached to her arm. A man was sitting beside her.

"Oh, you came." She recognized me immediately. She forced a smile onto her pained face. She tried to sit up, but fell back helplessly. She closed her eyes again because of exhaustion, and breathed heavily. Her head dropped back onto the pillow.

Was this really her? Was this the Xiao Mei who had been on my mind for a quarter of a century? Her face was pale like a piece of white paper. Her slightly plump face had become saggy and thin. Her small straight nose was bulging with the inserted oxygen tube. Her once moist lips were dry and chapped. Only her slightly narrowed eyes still shone with a light that intoxicated and captivated me when opened up wide.

I stood still beside the sick bed, my thoughts racing in my brain:

Not long ago, my mother had passed away after a long time of torture by disease. Modern medicine often shows its horrible manifestation in the last moment of a person's life: artificial breathing pipe, inserted food tube, needle holes all over the bottom, blood vessels swollen and bruised by needles that carried liquids through the body... However, death still came. At last, I achieved some enlightenment. What are the beautiful things in life? Talents, beauty, love, fame, riches... They all are, but may not be. The most beautiful thing in life is peace of mind. Especially in the last moment of her life, nothing was any longer important, except for peace of mind. It was so beautiful to remember the happier moments of life, even those of childhood.

Why not let her have peace for a moment? The words of a wise man resonated in my mind: "Pile up gifts of the world at the feet of a fool, and let me enjoy a peaceful mind." What she needed was not oxygen through a tube, liquid through a needle, feeding with an inserted tube, or crowds of visitors coming and going. I knew that she needed to be by herself for a while.

"Please sit down." The man called out to me.

"This is my classmate, Weimin. You know him!" Xiao Mei said to the man.

"I saw you at Fudan University. You were one year my senior." The man forced a smile on his face. It looked as though he was her husband.

Now I examined him carefully. He was not tall, but somewhat thin and small. Wearing a dark gray polyester tunic, matched by a disheveled beard, he appeared rather old. Perhaps because he had been caring for a patient continually for many days, his eyes appeared slow-witted. I just could not imagine that he was her husband.

Really, what kind of a person should her husband be? I could not say exactly. In my imagination, he should be talented and handsome, truly outstanding. However, the man before me... History and fate made a joke of life. He said that he had seen me at Fudan University, but I had never noticed him. Was such an inconspicuous person with no fame, no outstanding talents and no great looks actually qualified to be her husband?

I sat down beside her.

"Mei, what's happening?" Actually, I already knew about her sickness.

"She had an abscess on her breast." Her husband responded immediately.

"It is not an abscess. Why don't you tell him the truth! I know. They all know..." She interrupted what her husband was saying. As she spoke, tears fell from her eyes. It was the first time that I had seen her in tears.

I held her hands, the pair of hands swollen because of the needles supplying her liquids. Her hands were almost icy cold, and their pale skin had become somewhat transparent because of swelling, as if it could easily be broken by poking. Her hands trembled a little, but then rested in my palm in peace...

Holding hands is such a commonplace action. It happens thousands of times every day, every minute. However, in my memory, it was the first time that I had held hands with Xiao Mei…

Using the little moment when her husband had left the room, she murmured:

"I'm sorry. That's the only thing I could do for you today. Please forgive me."

I felt warm at heart. Looking at her bloodless face, blackened hands because of poor blood circulation, mouth and nose covered with traces of sticking tape, and the rubber tube that sustained her life, what could I say? "No need to talk like that, Mei." I stroked her swollen and bruised hands for the first time.

Another old classmate of mine, Lin Wang (pseudonym), happened to be a radiologist at the department of radiology of the hospital. She called me into her office. Lin had an outgoing personality, a people person who liked to work as the liaison among old classmates, so she knew all the gossip. "Poor Xiao Mei, her cancer cells have spread to the heart. Water is accumulating in her heart chambers. Her radiology treatment had to be stopped. However, her husband is really too useless." Lin said in an angry tone.

"Why it has anything to do with her husband?" I was perplexed.

"Oh, it's a long story." Lin Wang sighed and started to chat. "Mei had bad luck. She was very active for nothing. She stayed at the university for one year, and then came the Cultural Revolution. She got delayed for a few years before being assigned to Sichuan. At that time, four guys and two girls went there from Fudan University. Mei had to pick one of the four."

My relationship with Mei perhaps could not count as a love relationship at all according to the standard of the eighties. Almost nobody knew about what happened between us. Lin had no qualms speaking about Mei.

"What did it all mean?" I asked.

"Didn't you see how incompetent he looked? Not much ability, and a lot of male chauvinism. He did not want Mei to do too well in her career. He put a lot of restrictions on Mei's life, besides getting her to do all the housework. In my opinion, the sickness of Mei was caused by suppressed anger and frustration." Lin let out a lot in one breath.

Perhaps Lin was right. There are many theories about the cause of cancer in a human. It could be genetics, faults in chromosomes, or a polluted environment... But really a lot of facts supported a theory of Chinese medicine: the silting up of blood vessels is a direct cause of cancer, whereas the mood of a person is directly related to the smooth flow of blood and tranquility of mind.

I remember a saying from a great person: "A man's character is his fate." It was hard for me to judge if a person's character indeed had such huge power. However, I think that for a person to live free and happy, the first rules must be: to love like crazy; to hate like mad; to laugh loudly and heartily; to cry to one's heart's content! Love is the essence of life. If love must be held back, then what happiness could there be in life?

4.8 Thoughts on relationships

When I left the hospital, it was evening. With the little light remaining, shadows were still everywhere but not so distinct. Such a strange life! When I first knew Xiao Mei, I was in my teens. We spent only four or five years together. At that time, I did not even truly understand what love meant. I did not think of what kind of life would follow love, and had no way of knowing either. To me, love is a virgin land, an endless wilderness just covered with snow, and a vast sea of unfathomable depth. Only when I got involved in it, would I then slowly mature in the crucible of society, realizing that love was so different from marriage; marriage was so different from family; family was so different from life. Since the ups and downs of life are so closely linked with marriage and family, how then to help the good people of the world to make the theoretically best choice?

Had Xiao Mei and I fallen in love with each other, and then married, perhaps I would not be here, and she would not be there. Perhaps today I would have become a timid person, but then she might not have developed cancer. Had we been married, perhaps I would have sacrificed my own ambition to support the career of the woman I worshipped. Perhaps I would not have been able to accomplish what I had. Yet the union of two "strong personalities" might have produced a lot of friction, resulting in more pain in our lives. Perhaps I would have become more reserved like her, and she would been more outgoing, like me... Perhaps... Oh! Life does not permit too many instances of "perhaps." Life is a not a simple mathematical formula; life is a synthesis of countless accidental and necessary events. If life could be modeled according to a computer simulation, then it would no longer have meaning. Without misery, there would be no appreciation of happiness; without imperfection, there would be no appreciation of perfection; it is the whole spectrum of sour, sweet, bitter and spicy hot tastes that make life rich and meaningful. It is the shadows that help one discover the full stature of a true lively person.

4.9 Seeing Mei for the last time

When I went to see Mei again, her whole body was in pain, with sweat drops the size of soybeans seeping through her forehead. She pleaded with the doctor to inject her with pain-killing medication, and to remove the accumulated water from her heart chambers. A trace of left-over luster of beauty was on her pale face, and pain was gnawing at her heart. She reclined on a pillow, turning her conscious eyes in my direction as I pushed the door open. Her disease-worn face suddenly twitched, revealing an expression that was joy mixed with despair, tinged with a scary color that was both gloomy and warm. Suddenly I felt regret at seeing her again. Perhaps I should not have come. Until now the impressions she had left on me were all so beautiful: a smart genius, a truly talented girl. I just could not link the woman before my eyes with the one that I had loved so much before. It was difficult to reconcile the two totally opposite images. However, perhaps it was the two contradictory aspects of life that made a person whole and real.

Wouldn't it be nice if Mei had left me with only the memories a quarter of a century earlier? The American superstar Marilyn Monroe left charming images with millions of her fans. She died suddenly in 1962 at the age of 36. A quarter of a century later, millions of her fans all over the world still regard her as their own love idol.

However, the Mei before me was now a completely different person.

"Mei, have a peaceful mind. Thinking of happier things may perhaps reduce the pain." I said.

"I have thought about it all, but the more I think, the harder it is to have peace of mind." She answered me quietly, "I need to be more muddle-headed. Why have I always been so conscious?"

Indeed! During the brief hours that I visited her, loud crying from relatives were heard twice from neighboring rooms where patients had just died. How could one have peace in such an environment? Death was so unfair. Among so many classmates, Mei, the most talented girl, had been chosen as the first to pass over to the next world. She was just in the prime of her life.

I never asked God to punish her for not accepting my love. It was not her fault. In fact, it was nobody's fault. Perhaps, it was not about fault or no fault. Now I sincerely prayed to God to give her peace.

She had a lot of friends. In the last moments of her life, numerous people came to visit her. People cried and felt pity for her. Many of her old classmates spoke of her in admiration and with regrets. They remembered her with love. A female colleague of hers used her own body as support for her back night after night. She touched Mei's face with her own face, massaging her continually to reduce her pain. My classmate Lin Wang did disco dancing in the intensive care unit for Mei, letting her hear the music beats of youth before death snatched her away.

However, I thought that what she needed most was not all of this. I suddenly remembered a ritual of Christianity — to ask a priest to help the dying person make a last act of repentance. I thought what she needed most was to empty out all the deep dark secrets and painful memories to someone, so that she would not carry all the dirt accumulated in the eventful life of this world to another world.

4.10 The passing of Mei to a better world

A few days later, I left Beijing for Switzerland. Soon I received a letter from her colleague, telling me that Mei had closed her eyes for the last time. She had gained back her peaceful and calm looks. She was now united with the good earth, belonging to the distant horizon to the east. When the sun set on that ancient land, the shadow of first love disappeared forever.

Her colleague wrote to me about Xiao Mei's last days.

In the sickroom, a bunch of flowers that I had sent to Mei, including a red rose, a pink peony, a purple chrysanthemum, and a white Chinese rose, were inserted into a white bottle for saline solution. When her colleague asked Mei what she liked most, she gazed at the flowers for a long time, but would not answer.

"Maybe it was the red rose?" she hinted.

"Let me keep silent! Don't ask me to say it." She made an effort to utter those words.

Keep silent! The silence that was better than words.

On her death-bed, with dreamy eyes, Mei spoke to her colleague: "I was very happy. I saw the two persons that I wanted to see towards the end. One is my brother's son, and the other is he."

"Who is he?" asked her colleague, though perhaps knowingly.

"The classmate who sent me the flowers." She answered hesitantly.

In her hands she held a chocolate-box with three adorable kittens on the cover. I had brought that box of chocolates to her in the hospital. She had drawn a lovely kitten for my last birthday card, I remembered. She thus went to sleep forever with three kittens.

4.11 The shadow of first love lingers on

I went to Shanghai simply because I was assigned to recruit graduate students from Fudan University. Otherwise, I would perhaps have had no chance to see her in Shanghai. Little did I know that I was there to say goodbye to her for the last time. Still less did I realize that seeing me had been her last wish.

If I had not made it to Shanghai, I would have been left with the youthful images and memories of Mei, just as the beautiful images of Marilyn Monroe stayed with millions of her fans. Then I might have regretted that I was not able to say the final goodbye to her. Had I known about her getting cancer before I went to Shanghai, would I have had enough courage to make a special trip to see her? ... All these "ifs" were automatically answered by the subtle arrangement of God.

On the morning I was to return to Beijing, I went again to Fudan University. An indescribable feeling of sadness and loss made me wander around the campus. Spring was beautiful. Whichever direction I looked, I could see fresh and tender green. Two rows of tall London plane trees lined the main street from east to west inside the campus. Before the conference hall, a lawn stretched far and wide, comparable with the lawn in Edinburgh Park in the United Kingdom. This flat smooth lawn was the most prized part of Fudan University campus. At the same time, it carried me back to the years long past. It was on this lawn that Mei and I had often chatted for a long time. It was when I lay on the lawn that I had completed the emotional transformation from a boy to a man, as though sitting on the magic carpet found in the stories of Arabian Nights. In the difficult period of the Great Leap Forward, it was cultivated as farmland, and then laid waste during the Cultural Revolution. Today, it was once again a prime green lawn, laid like a carpet at the heart of Fudan University. Although it was morning, with most students in class, I could still see some students, both male and female, in the shade of the London plane trees, and especially on the lawn, talking, reading, or whispering into one another's ears. Spring was a beautiful time, but at the same time a dangerous season. Seeds sown in spring might turn out to bear bitter fruits in the fall. Then everything would be too late. One must wait out a long frigid winter to reach the next season for new seeding.

I had often wondered how an episode of infatuation occurring in the late teens could be kept alive in my heart for such a long time. Perhaps it was the puppy love that lasted, as we were still kids at the time.

Be careful, boys and girls. The shadows cast in the early morning may accompany you all the way to dusk in your heart.

Walking out the gate of Fudan University, I believed that the last smile Xiao Mei gave me before parting told me something: that death called on her for both of us to start a new episode of happier life, just in different worlds.

August 1965, the middle of a very hot summer, I boarded a westbound train and had to leave without seeing Xiao Mei, but with a sorrowful heart... I suddenly realized that my first love was born at a time when there was no spring, and ended permanently before the arrival of winter — as if giving me a hint that the ten truly disastrous years were about to enter my life.

Chapter Five
Decade of Calamity

5.1 Lanzhou University

In August 1965, I boarded a train to western China. China is a vast country. At that time, the economy and transportation were so underdeveloped; it was commonplace that folks living in the mountains never crossed surrounding valleys, those living in the countryside never went into the city, and city residents never left their city boundaries. I had just turned 22 then, and my previous travel experiences were limited to the trip I made to Beijing when I was 16, and a visit to Suzhou. I had no clue what Lanzhou was like. After the train crossed the Yangtze River, it soon went westward along the Longhai line, coming into a completely strange land that I had never seen before. Although I was still immersed in the joyous mood of being a "champion", short mud houses along the way, barren land and desolate hills forced the question on me repeatedly: "Is this the 9.6 million square kilometers of rich land that I learned about from textbooks?"

After the train entered the territory of Gansu, I was greeted with a view of barren hills with lots of ditches and ridges, but only a few green areas. Everywhere I saw ragged villagers scavenging along the railway. As the train entered a station, I at first expected that it would be like the Beijing-Shanghai line, where one could savor all the local specialties along the way such as the dried tofu of Suzhou, ribs of Wuxi, dried duck of Nanjing, roasted chickens of Fuliji, doggy buns of Tianjin, and preserved fruits of Beijing. Unexpectedly, along the Longhai line there were only the occasional baked cakes and hot buns that did not look very appetizing. Towards the end, even the supply of boiled water became a problem. It was right in the middle of a hot summer, inside the train it was hot and stuffy, and passengers and luggage were packed to the fullest.

To keep the windows closed felt too hot; but on opening the windows, black soot mingled with yellow dust would be all over the face. When the train went through a tunnel, the choking smoke made it hard to breathe. Air conditioning? No kidding, at that time the term "air conditioning" was not even on people's lips yet. Then I remembered God. Was it the same God that created both the picturesque Southern China and this barren Loess Plateau?

At last I arrived in Lanzhou, and found my way to the Department of Modern Physics of Lanzhou University. Because of its involvement in "classified" research, this department was located away from the main campus. The department had a fairly strong reputation in China with commensurate housing conditions. Our office was a two-storey building designed by a Soviet expert. Living quarters for us graduate students were three-bedroom suites including their own kitchens and bathrooms. It was in stark contrast with the student dormitory that I had had at Fudan University — eight students per room with four bunk beds. All this warmed up my heart a little. I went to the department office to register for food and oil stamps, only to find out what a complicated system it was. The food stamps were divided into three categories: rice, wheat flour and coarse grains. Each person received only two catties of rice per month. Now I saw why many people carried bags of rice on the train. The weather was good in Lanzhou. It was already August, but it was not hot at all. From September to October, it was the season for the prynne melon and winter pear to ripen. The aroma of prynne melon, and the honey-like juice of winter pear significantly reduced my dissatisfaction with "coarse grains." On the weekend, I walked among the Yuquan hills along the Yellow River. A clear spring water flowed merrily among the hills and tasted sweet, giving someone like myself from Shanghai unexpected joys. My teacher Professor Gongou Xu was a very respected and kind person. He discussed potential research topics with me, listened attentively to my ideas, and finally decided that my research focus should be about the shell model of nucleus. At that time there was little access to foreign literature, apart from a few Soviet books and journals. The calculation tools were hand-operated calculators and slide rules. It is hard to imagine nowadays how we carried out our research work without electronic computers. Yet the design of the first atom bomb and the first hydrogen bomb of China were completed with the help of hand-operated calculators. The Department of Modern Physics of Lanzhou University had a very strong faculty, with many members coming back from the Dubna Institute of the Soviet Union, and some others who studied in Japan. From them I learned a rigorous scientific attitude. However, the good times did not last long. A new directive from above ordered all the new graduate students to go to the countryside to "do decentralization exercise." I think there was no policy more foolish than this one in this world. Treating intellectuals as the objects of "reform" was fundamentally wrong, and had never succeeded. Of course, the "decentralization exercise" was not without merit entirely. Life is a teacher itself, and it teaches in both tangible and subtle ways. This "decentralization exercise" let me know for the first time that our lovely China had such poverty stricken places. Even today I have the desire to see those places because China can truly leave poverty behind only if those places become well-to-do, too.

Thus under the misguided policy of the time, I had to give up my study and research work and went to the countryside to do "decentralization exercise." Indeed, nobody would have guessed that an unprecedented decade-long calamity started right from that time.

5.2 The Yinjia Mountains

I boarded a freight truck going from Lanzhou to Dingxi, my designated place for the "decentralization exercise." According to the belief that more knowledge makes one more reactionary, several of us fresh graduate students were assigned to the harshest countryside, because we were the most in need of reform. The vehicle went along a rugged mountain road, sharp turns here and there, kicking up thick dry loess dust, mixed with the smell of incompletely combusted gasoline. It was simply suffocating. I soon started to vomit copiously. However, the truck ride went only as far as the county center! From the county to the commune, I could only ride on a mule. The mule walked along steep hill side, up and down all the way, turning my all internal organs around. When I was a kid, I rode a mule in an entertainment park, at the cost of a dime for going around a full circle. It felt romantic to sit high to look down at everything in the surroundings. However, after riding a mule on a mountain as I did, I would never have the inclination to ride a mule in an entertainment park again. The mule ride only reached the commune! From the commune to the production team of Yinjia Mountain, I could only rely on my two legs. Even by today's standards, Dingxi is still China's poorest region, and the Yinjia Mountain production team was also the poorest production team in the Dingxi region. For someone like me from Shanghai, the contrast was like between heaven and hell. The Kun Mountain in the suburbs of Shanghai and the Huqiu Mountain of Suzhou could all be called big mole hills compared with the real mountains here. Yinjia Mountain was situated among a big stretch of desolate mountains and hills. Were I not accompanied by a peasant, I would not have believed that anybody was actually living here. I climbed one mountain, went down a hill, climbed another mountain, and went down again. Some relatively flat hillsides were turned into terraced fields, but there was no telling whether crops or weeds were growing in them. Although my peasant helper carried all my luggage, I still found it difficult to catch my breath. Upon dusk, I finally reached my "home" — a cave house that was said to have a history of 600 years. I tried to see what the cave house looked like with the help of the moonlight, but could not see clearly. I just figured out that it was a cave on a hillside. It was not so different from what I had read about shelters for the apes, except that there was a door covering up the cave. The local guide left me there, asking me to rest early, promising that he would see me again the next day morning. Inside the cave there was a bed made of earth, that was to be my sleeping area. A small oil lamp was burning there, swaying with the slightest movement of the air, changing brightness constantly, like a ghost light. I was tired and weak, but could not sleep. I just prayed to God that the little oil lamp light would not die out, but it did eventually. I stayed up all night. From time to time came the distant howling of wolves, I felt scared, shivering with fear. However, occasionally I heard dogs barking, so I believed this was an inhabited place. Otherwise it was quiet all around. I knew that if a man stayed in a totally silent dark room, he would become insane. That was almost my situation at the time. When I lived in Julu Road in Shanghai, I was somewhat annoyed by the noises of the morning market, but compared with this terrible silence, the noises of the market sounded more like symphony. I want to open the door a little bit wider, so that the moon light could come in more, but I feared that wolves might get in. I could not help asking myself: Why had fate delivered me here?

The next day at dawn, I carefully opened the door; with a squeaking sound, a touch of sun light came into the cave. Only then did I discover that this cave was very deep indeed. The earth bed I slept on was near the door. I did not dare to walk deeper into the cave, but just stood in the yard outside the door, staring blankly at the never ending mountain ridges before me. Soon the peasant guide came. He asked me if I had slept well. I could barely understand his thick Gansu accent. He took me to a nearby valley, where there was a "well" with a diameter less than half a meter. "How deep must the well be to get water?" I asked him. "This is not a real well. It is a pit. It is used to hold all the rain water flowing downhill when it rains," he replied. The wall of the dry well was treated by fire, using techniques used in making ceramics, to minimize water leakage. The guide also told me that only the commune had a few wells that were tens of meters deep. There, the water must be drawn up by a machine. As he spoke, he drew a bucket of water for me, pouring the water into a container inside my cave. He asked me to save water, because the rainy season had passed, so the water in the pit must last until snow fell. Once finished, I would have to fetch water myself from the commune center tens of kilometers away. Later I found out, nobody here brushed their teeth or washed their faces. They would wash themselves twice in a lifetime, after birth and death. The so-called wash up was limited to rubbing the body with wet towels. No wonder everyone here had a strange smell. The peasant guide was actually the production team leader of Yinjia Mountain. Yinjia Mountain had a dozen households. Each family took up a valley, and had a pit of their own. Later, I had my meals in each house in turn, twice a day. The first meal was at about ten o'clock. After the meal I would go to work. The second meal would have to wait until I returned from the field in the evening. The lunch was in a cloth bag, just a couple pieces of dry corn cakes and potatoes. There were no vegetables here, just some wild edible plants, pickled with salt inside a jar, becoming a sort of "sauerkraut" after some time. Each meal, one would eat a few pieces, sometimes drinking a little "syrup" from the pickled plants. That was the basic meal menu all year around. Here, everyone slept on heated earth beds. Otherwise the cold air of the cave houses would make people sick with arthritis. Heated earth beds could not only be slept on, but could also be used for cooking. The chimney of the stove went through the earth bed. Here, there was no coal, no oil, no wood, but just dried hay, manure and mule dung. So, picking up manure and hay was a major chore throughout the year. A few days after my arrival, I began vomiting and having diarrhea. The reason was simple — the water was too dirty. The water in the pit was just rain, snow mixed with dust, feces, insects, or whatever flowed into the pit together. This pit had not been cleaned up for God knows how many years. After the pit water was placed inside a water tank, some alum might be used for purification. When there was no alum available, even urine might be used to sink particles into the bottom of the tank. The folks here were used to the pit water. The "syrup" of the pickled plants was said to have antiseptic power too. However, how could a scholar from Shanghai like myself drink such water? The vomiting and diarrhea caused me to show symptoms of dehydration. Because of that I had to drink more water, resulting in more vomiting and diarrhea. I lay on the earth bed, all desperate, hoping that the cave would collapse and crush me to death. Actually, the cave I lived in might be called a shrine in Shanghai. It was more than ten meters deep, and the deeper, the darker inside. It was hard to see what exactly was there even with the help of an oil lamp. My guide told me that the cave was a holding place for ancestral tablets, with the earlier ancestors deeper in. I lay on the earth bed in a delirious state with racing thoughts, but did not have the strength to write a letter.

    I realised that if I were to close my eyes forever this way, my parents might neither know where I died, nor how I died. I did not belong to the Yinjia clan, so nobody here would erect a tablet for me. There were also only a small number of trees standing within an area of tens of square kilometers, so nobody would even make a coffin for me. Then again, I thought of the hungry wolves … Thus I fell into a deep sleep. Suddenly, I was awakened by an old lady. That day, I was scheduled to have my meals in her house, but I did not make it, so she sought me out in my cave. She found out that I was seriously ill. Shortly afterwards, she came back with a bowl of noodles with eggs. The noodles were made by hands, thin like human hair, called "lamian," a local specialty in Gansu. The principle of making the noodle was very simple: the power of two. When a lump of wheat flour is stretched out, folded and then stretched out again for over ten times, it will become noodles as fine as the human hair. The old lady's egg noodle soup pulled me back from the brink of death. I dare say that this was the best bowl of noodles that I've ever eaten all my life. Later I learned that in my sick days, what I ate was better than what the village folks got for New Year celebrations. When I left Yinjia Mountain, the old lady made thick cloth pads for my socks by densely stitching layers of rags together. She stood for one episode of my "luck with ladies" that I would cherish all my life.

Gansu is one of the poorest provinces in China, and the Dingxi District is the poorest region in Gansu. The reason is simple — lack of water! When scientists search for life anywhere in the universe, they first check if there is water. Water is the source of life. In a place like Dingxi, crops should never have been planted in the first place. It should have been returned to its original state of nature — turf coverage. However, under the "taking grain as the key link" policy, terraces were made everywhere to grow crops. The turf-covered hillside was forcefully split into terraces, and the result was that when rain came, soil would be washed away, and the soil erosion would lead to more loss of vegetation, forming a vicious cycle. Later in the 1980s, I saw a newspaper report about a speech made by the General Secretary Hu Yaobang after inspecting Northwestern China. He said that the arid Northwest did not need to grow grain food crops, but could develop animal husbandry instead. Farmers may also consider organized immigration into more fertile land. At that time I really felt that there was at last someone within the communist party who really knew the needs of the people. Hu Yaobang put it right, the Dingxi District was more suited for animal husbandry. The artificial terrace would take twenty catties of seeds to obtain a yield of thirty catties, just not worth it. The peasants knew this very clearly, so they made the terraced fields with reluctance, just to fulfill the quota provided by their superiors. The production team leader often sent me to herd the sheep, which was the happiest job I had while at Yinjia Mountain. Equipped with a shepherd's whip, a pot of water, and a few pieces of potatoes, followed by a shepherd's dog, I just had to get the sheep out of their enclosure, they would then make their own way. Indeed not so much that I took along the sheep as the sheep led me, especially that lead sheep. The villagers told me sheep did not eat the same grass twice. After they finished with one piece of turf, they would move forward. If one sheep got out of line, the shepherd's dog would bring it back to the herd. I liked lying on the grass, basking in the sun, sometimes teasing the dog with half a potato, sometimes singing aloud, sometimes reading my mother's letters over and over again. Dogs were my faithful friends, but they almost killed me. Once I took part in a meeting at another production team located on another mountain. Before I got into the village, two large dog rushed towards me, then circled around me. I waived a stick and stood my ground for a couple of minutes, but finally lost my nerve and started to run away. That was a big mistake. A large dog caught up with me, biting my leg. Luckily a villager arrived on the scene promptly. I wore a few thick layers of trousers, but the dog bit through them all on my right leg, and blood came out of a row of tidy bite marks. In the absence of any form of medical attention, my leg got well by itself after becoming swollen for two weeks. The villager told me that I should not run when encountering a situation like this one, much less run backwards. Unexpectedly, this experience saved my life later on.

Once, I went to a meeting held in the commune center, which was supposedly not a bad arrangement, because I could have lunch with meat. The problem was that the commune was far away from my production team. A one-way trip would take four to five hours going over the mountains. I had to depart before dawn. That afternoon, the meeting went a bit over time, it became dark half way on my way home. A gray wolf suddenly appeared on the road in front. For a time, I could not tell if it was a wolf or a dog. However, I thought that here was the middle of nowhere, so it could not be a dog.

Scared to death, I held my breath, stopped, and stared at the wolf. Suddenly, it advanced towards me a couple of steps. I hurriedly used my flashlight to shine light in its eyes. The wolf stopped, I stared at it without making any movement, and we held on for two to three minutes. I prayed silently that the flashlight batteries should not die on me by any means. At last, the wolf disappeared into the darkness. Then I found that the flashlight was thoroughly soaked by the sweat on my hand. From then on, I always found some excuse not to go to any meetings held in the commune center, despite the huge temptation of a meal with meat. The experience of the stand off with the gray wolf chilled me to the bone. I was told that I had done the right thing this time. Wolves in general would not attack people unprovoked, but had I chosen to run away, maybe the wolf would have attacked.

During my Yinjia Mountain days, there was one realisation so shocking that I would remember it for the rest of my life. Because I got "assigned meals," I went to each and every of the more than a dozen households in the village. Surprisingly, I often saw villagers sitting on their beds, covered up by a piece of worn out quilt. At first, I thought they were sick. Until one day, the commune asked me to receive "relief cloth" to distribute to the "poor and middle peasants." Then I realized that many people did not have trousers to wear. The whole family would share one pair of trousers for the person going out to wear. The ones left behind without trousers would cover themselves up with quilts when visitors came. Such stories can only be believed if seen with one's own eyes. No wonder Khrushchev of the Soviet Union commented on how could the Chinese make the atom bomb when they did not even have pants to wear. At first, I thought he was spreading a rumor, but it looked like what he said was based on fact, maybe with a little exaggeration. I also recall that in 1960, when I did the uranium enrichment experiment at Fudan University, I often had to go hungry, which happened at a top university in Shanghai. It is said that at the time of the "three years of natural disasters" between 1958 and 1961, Gansu was one of the hardest hit provinces, with countless peasants starving to death. While at Yinjin Mountain, the commune asked the peasants to hold "remembering bitterness and cherishing happiness" meetings to educate the city intellectual youths like myself. It was intended to complain about the bitterness of the "old society" before the communist takeover, but the "bitterness" remembered by the villagers all referred to the hunger and suffering around 1960. As a result, such meetings were called off subsequently.

Despite leaving Yinjia Mountain, I am still emotionally attached to this place. Some emotional scars have also stayed with me ever since. The first one is a phobia of dogs. While abroad, I would be scared of any dog, regardless of its size. Fate also played a kind of joke with me. I work in the US Fermilab, a big accelerator laboratory, covering a very large area, also quite remote, so there are a lot of American coyotes haunting the place. If I worked a little late, I would often encounter a coyote on the road. There neither the coyotes nor the people were scared of one another. The coyotes often crossed the roads at leisure, and I would stop my car to let them pass slowly. One day, I got a little impatient while waiting, so I turned on my headlights on a coyote, and scared it away. It made me laugh for quite a while, realizing that wolves everywhere were scared of lights.

Secondly, I became disinterested in places like the Grand Canyon. In my opinion, the whole North-west China Corridor is a Grand Canyon. It is one thing to visit there, quite another to live there. Mao Zedong wrote a poem: "Northland scenery, a thousand miles locked in ice, ten thousand miles of snow falling, imposing are both sides of the Great Wall ......" This is a good poem, only someone who had actually experienced life in the Loess Plateau could have written such a poem. Unfortunately, although the people in the Loess Plateau were "liberated," they never really stood up. Where people live in poverty not because of exploitation by landlords, but because of the harsh natural conditions, they should not fight with people, but rather fight with nature. Following the theory of class struggle would only get people poorer and poorer. Destitute people can never really stand up. Development is the only royal way.

Thirdly, I often dreamed of Yinjia Mountain, and felt guilty about not re-visiting the place for so many years. Why did I not see that old lady who saved my life again? Is she well? Did they ever receive the clothing and candies that I sent to them by post? In my mind's eyes, I often see that bowl of egg noodle soup, the green eyes of that wolf which confronted me in the dark night, and the shy expression of a girl who sat on the earth bed, covered by a worn out quilt. A couple of years back, I received a delegation from China that was visiting the Fermilab. Although I often entertain Chinese delegations, this time I was perplexed: This was a "China Poverty Alleviation" delegation. Why had they come to the United States? I was very excited that one delegation member actually came from Gansu Province. After they finished their tour, I found the delegate from Gansu, who was a middle-aged woman. "Do you know Dingxi?" I asked her. She said she knew. I asked again: "Do you know Jinjia Mountain?" She did not know. I asked her again: "Do you know if the Dingxi peasants have a good water supply yet? Do they still drink pit water? Do they have schools? What about doctors? Do the villagers still marry their close relatives?

Do they have public roads?" She could not answer any of my questions. She asked me instead where the outlet malls were, and which places in Chicago were the most fun to visit. If I were the Chinese Communist Party's general secretary, the first thing I would do would be to have her expelled from the party. If she embezzled public funds to go abroad to have a vacation, I would have her arrested and tried. If she misappropriated poverty alleviation funds for personal gains, I would see her brought to justice right away.

I used Google to search for Yinjia Mountain, but to no avail. Perhaps the villagers of Yinjia Mountain have immigrated, as Hu Yaobang suggested. I could only find Dingxi, where there are now highways. Ah! My Dingxi forever! My Yinjia Mountain forever! People from the prosperous and merry-making big cities like Beijing and Shanghai, please do not forget that there are still many places in China like Yinjia Mountain. Do not let them become the forgotten corners.

5.3 January revolution

When we were "decentralized" in the mountains, we faintly heard bits of news from the commune: the provincial party secretary was in trouble, and the president of Lanzhou University had committed suicide. What had happened to the world? We really knew nothing. The intellectual youths "decentralized" to the remote countryside appeared to have become a forgotten group of people. However, in the middle of September 1966, an order came from an unknown source that asked us all to go to the commune center. On reaching the commune, a military truck was waiting there to take us to Lanzhou. I looked back at the Dingxi that I left further and further behind, and my heart was hit hard by all sorts of bitter and sweet emotions, mingled with worries about the future. However, I soon started to vomit in a big way due to motion sickness until I fainted. A doctor attached to the People's Hospital in Gansu told the truck driver: "This man has a life-threatening situation. He must be sent to a hospital at once." The doctor was a recent graduate from the Shanghai Medical College. The driver saw that I was unconscious with shriveled fingers and lips, so he diverted the truck to a small town along the Longhai railway line to get me to a hospital. I slowly woke up after some infusion of liquid.

The doctor from Shanghai accompanied me to Lanzhou on a train. Lanzhou looked entirely different. I said goodbye to the doctor in a hurry, and did not even remember his name. I just remembered that my body weight was 50 kilograms when weighed at the hospital. Now I know that my current body weight is 75 kilograms. Just imagine what I would look like if I suddenly lost 25 kilograms: I must have been a skeleton.

The sound of reading aloud used to fill the campus of Lanzhou University, but now the entire campus was covered up by big character posters. A "Cultural Revolution" was under way vigorously. The fact that such a beast like the "Cultural Revolution" could be born at that time had a deep historical background. Mao Zedong said, "if those capitalist roaders sat on top of the people, lording over them, before long, the communist party would become a fascist party. What a dangerous situation!" Those words of Mao actually moved many hearts. Were not party functionaries like Mr. He the kind of "capitalist roaders" who lorded over the people? Then I saw my professor Xu Gongou, when he was cleaning our toilet. I said to him, "Let us clean our own toilet, Teacher Xu." "No, no, do not call me Teacher Xu. Just call me Xu Gongou," he replied. I learned that Professor Xu was labelled a "reactionary academic authority," and that he was subjected to "reforming."

It puzzled me. At that time, the so-called "great liaison" was hot under way. Students could get a free ride on a train to Beijing by simply showing their student IDs. Later the students could choose almost any destination at their own will. After one year of suffering in Gansu, my first idea was to return to my lovely native city — Shanghai. In the face of hunger, sickness, wolves and thirst, atomic structures and cosmological models all lost their meanings. Life was the only thing to be treasured.

Back in Shanghai, I saw that Mr. He of Fudan University was subject to "criticism" by the students. I felt that he got what he deserved. Who let him lord over the students? However, my mother was also being criticized by the students for her role as the leader of a "Four Clears" work team at the Jiangwan Machinery Factory. She was said to have executed the reactionary line of Liu Shaoqi. I told the students that my mother was a good person. Even if the line of Liu Shaoqi was reactionary, what had it to do with my mother? But the students would not listen to me at all. So I decided to go to Beijing, to check out for myself what really happened.

After arriving in Beijing, my first wish was to see the Xiyi Hotel that I lived in when I was sixteen. The hotel was quite different now, crammed with "red guards." Mao Zedong received the red guards at Tiananmen Square. Seeing him from a distance, it felt totally different from seeing him six years earlier. I no longer felt any kind of excitement. As the students were allowed to go anywhere in the country as they wished, I decided to go to Guangzhou to check it out, as I had never been to the south. I squeezed into an overcrowded train, only to find that it was going to Harbin, rather than Guangzhou. So Harbin would have to do! However I found out how cold Harbin was as soon as I got off the train. A red guard reception station gave us a piece of paper, by which we could receive a free cotton coat from a department store. I went to see the Harbin Military Engineering Institute, where my high school had vouched for me to go but I had declined. Quite a few magnificent buildings were arranged tidily in the campus, all very imposing. I also hurriedly took a look at the Songhua River, made famous by the lyrical line "my home was at the northeast Songhua River." The river was frozen solid with ice three feet thick. Several days later, I boarded a south bound train to Shanghai. My mother was already "liberated." The target of the Cultural Revolution was no longer the "Four Clears" work team, but the "capitalist roaders." The so-called "January Revolution" broke out in Shanghai, and the masses took over power from the "capitalist roaders." I thought naively at the time, Mao Zedong was really great, dared to purge his own party, overthrowing those who lorded over the people. I got infected by the enthusiasm shown by the masses. At the same time, I began to worry about many acts of violence that occurred as part of the Revolution.

At the time, there was a new "vogue," called "the great liaison on foot," which was simply a touristic opportunity not seen in a thousand years. Thus I began a "touring the world" journey that lasted several months, in the style of Xu Xiake, a famous traveler in Ancient China. This kind of "great liaison by foot" is hard to imagine today, with free accommodation and food provided everywhere.

I went to Hangzhou, Nanjing, Huangshan, Jingdezhen and other places. In Hangzhou, I lived in the picturesque Zhejiang University, and toured all scenic mountains and rivers around the city. On the way to

Huang Mountain, the verdant hills and clear waters of the Wannan region left an indelible impression on me. The lush Qingyi river had water that was crystal clear. Bamboo rafts floated with the running water, constituting a wonderful landscape painting. Fishermen fished with their ospreys on their rafts. Lush, dense forests and valleys dotted with birds and flowers all intoxicated me. For the first time I felt that the great rivers and mountains of China were so beautiful, full of charms. I reached the Huang mountain, and was accommodated in the North Sea Hotel with free meals. All I had to do was to show my student's ID without spending a single cent. I hiked during the day, and bathed in a hot spring at night, living a fairy tale lifestyle. Then I went to Jingdezhen, where porcelain figurines for Mao Zedong were being produced, whereas all other pretty vases were smashed up. What a crazy age! I walked through a tea tree farm, where the head of the farm was a disabled former soldier who had only one leg. He used a crutch and had some difficulty standing up, but he had to bow down to receive criticism from the masses. What kind of revolution was this? This kind of scenes reminded me that this was the "Cultural Revolution," not a real site-seeing tour. "The great liaison on foot" had long become a forgotten part of history, because it was after all too brief, too absurd. But this was the only tour that I completed in my life using my two legs that lasted a few months, across a few thousand kilometers. Because of the trip I was later labeled an "escapist school" member, but I feel that the trip was an unforgettable lesson of life. After that I went back to Huang Mountain, Hangzhou multiple times, but as those places got more and more crowded, they lost their paradise like appeal.

After the "great liaison on foot," the Central Committee of the Chinese communist party issued an instruction for "going back to school to make the revolution." So I returned to the Lanzhou University. Because of a politics "jet lag," Gansu revolutionaries seized power more than a month later than Shanghai, in an event called the "February Five" power seizure. The army was stationed in schools, factories and other places of importance, and a "military training group" was also stationed in Lanzhou University. They organized seminars for us to study documents from the Central Committee, to make us recognize the importance of the "power seizure." During one seminar, I made a speech. In contrast with many copycat speeches that sounded banal, I covered several topics: from the "Paris

Commune" of France to the "October Revolution" of the Soviet Union, including story lines in the three famous dramas "Lenin in October," "Kremlin Bells" and "A Person with Gun." I quoted classical Marxist teachings, and cited many historical events leading up to the "January Revolution" of Shanghai. I talked about history using lively, eloquent language. At that time, there were two factions, one that supported the "February Five" power seizure, and the other that was against it. I did not comment on the "February Five" power seizure directly, so both sides liked me. Someone copied my speech into a "poster", and it spread far and wide. All of a sudden I became a famous figure, with many work units inviting me to make a speech at their places. It all seemed to be out of control. I gave talks more than twenty times, with audiences numbering from a thousand to ten thousands at a time. I became a household name in Lanzhou, worshiped by many. The Dance and Singing Troupe of Gansu Province organized a publicity team, and invited me to be the lead person. At the beginning of each show, I would make a speech one hour long, then they would start to perform. We traveled to many parts of Gansu Province, as far as Jiayu Pass. I spent entire days with those merry dancers and singers, warmly treated by all the work units receiving us, so I felt very happy. We actually climbed the Qilian Mountains, which have an altitude of five thousand meters. The snow-capped mountains were so spectacular, a real eye opener. Standing on the look out post at Jiayu Pass, I looked to the west as far as I could. The vast expanse of the Gobi Desert brought up memories of the classic story of the Journey to the West. I really wished to go further west, but we had to stop as we were about to cross the boundary to Xinjiang. I was deeply impressed by the vastness of the land of China.

When I returned to Lanzhou University after my publicity team stunt, the "military training group" was busy setting up a "three-pronged" university leadership. The three-pronged organization combined revolutionary cadres, military representatives and representatives of the revolutionary masses. I became an ideal candidate since I was very well known in Lanzhou but did not belong to any particular faction. Finally, I unwittingly became a standing committee member of the "revolutionary committee" of Lanzhou University. In reality, I was not interested, because my family members in Shanghai were suffering huge disasters. At that time, the Cultural Revolution had turned to so-called "cleaning up class ranks." My mother was labeled a "slipped through the net capitalist" because of some stock issues mentioned before. My father was framed as a "traitor" for saving some underground communists arrested by the Nationalist Party. My younger brother Jimin was sent to Chongming Island Farm; my younger sister Xiaomin was dispatched to Lai'an county of Anhui to settle down there; my youngest brother Minmin was sent as far as Lishu County of Jilin Province in North-east China. When Minmin boarded the ship to North-east China, how he wished that my family members would come to see him off. He took the last remaining piece of glass lens to see who was coming. At the last minute when the ship was about to depart, he saw his big brother Jimin, who had come from the Chongming Island Farm. My second younger brother Xinmin also rode a bike to the pier to say goodbye. They waived their hands until the ship disappeared into the horizon. Their silent hand waving embodied thousands of words of best wishes, comforting my youngest brother in his boarding of the north bound ship. At that time, both of our parents were under "isolation review," subjected to cruel torture, leaving two elderly grand-parents behind with nobody to care for them. I was far away in Lanzhou, and could not even find a contact person back in Shanghai. As I was by myself in Lanzhou with no close friends, I often went to the side of the Yellow River to pour my heart out to waves of water rushing by, as if the running water could wash away my sorrows. One night, when I was walking along the river by myself, an old man walked up to me, patting me on the shoulder, saying gently: "Young man, keep an open mind. You still have a long way to go in your life..." Then I realized that the old gentleman had thought I might commit suicide. During that anti-humanity, anti-progress, anti-social Cultural Revolution, many things occurred which were against decent human nature, such as a husband and wife becoming enemies, or a father and son exposing each other. However, most people still cared for others as this kind gentleman had done for me.

I faced another thorny issue. The Central Committee decided that my grade of graduates could only be assigned jobs in the rural areas, factories and mines. It was thought at the time that we, the graduate students, were aces of the capitalist ivory tower, and revisionist "seedlings" in need of reforming. At this critical moment, I had a good opportunity that many people could only dream of: The "military training group" wanted me to stay at Lanzhou University as a member of the governing body. I hesitated, but finally declined. I knew that if I took this route, I would be forever tied up with politics. My life experience told me, how horrible politics could be. It was proven subsequently that I made the right choice at this critical moment of my life. Many years later, in cleaning up problems related to the Cultural Revolution, someone raised the issue that I had once served as a standing member of the revolutionary committee of Lanzhou University. I said: "It was indeed a mistake, because the Cultural Revolution itself was wrong. The January Revolution was of course wrong. Even the October Revolution is controversial among historians. I became a member of the Standing Committee of Lanzhou University Revolutionary Committee with the approval of Zhou Enlai, and circled consent from Mao Zedong. I have not participated in any vandalism, and rarely took part in criticism meetings. All I did was to shout some slogans like others." My remarks sounded well justified, so the issue was settled without much fuss. However, had I joined the governing body of Lanzhou University, it would have been another matter. So, I often tell young people that one can make mistakes, but no mistakes in directions. I felt fortunate that at this turning point in life, I met a respectable and adored communist member — Wang Shaoren. It could be said that Wang changed my life.

5.4 Artificial satellite

The "military training group" at Lanzhou University was made up of members of a special force. It belonged to the "training base" of the National Defense Science and Technology Commission, specializing in the research, development and test of missiles and satellites. It was a top secret force. That force was located in the Gobi Desert, totally isolated. A few years ago, I read a newspaper report that a US military delegation had visited there. It really surprised me, as if the cold war really had ended. Wang Shaoren was the political commissar of the "military training group" at Lanzhou University. He was once a political commissar of the data processing center at the base. He was deeply impressed by my credentials, a physics graduate so insightful in politics, and so eloquent in speech and in writing, a rare talent indeed. Wang asked me: "Do you want to work at our base?" On hearing that they were engaged in missile and satellite research, development and tests, I was of course more than willing. The graduate assignment scheme at Lanzhou University did not have any quota for the military base, so he intended to have me formally assigned to Lanzhou University, then "transfer" me from the university to the base. The biggest hurdle was really the "political examination." At that time my parents were "examined in isolation," Wang Shaoren sent someone to go to Shanghai to conduct an investigation of my background, stressing that problems revealed during the Cultural Revolution did not count. However, I would not be allowed to work at the base because my mother had "exploiting experience," and my father was considered a "senior clerk" before the communist takeover. Wang Shaoren talked to the top leadership at the base. He used the words of Mao Zedong: Wu Weimin was a "good child who could be educated," "family background could not be selected, but one can choose his own road of life," and so on. Finally, he had his way.

The base was founded in 1958. Former staffers have written many memoirs, describing the difficult years building it from scratch. I started from Lanzhou and boarded a west bound train. I got off at Qingshui, a small station that would not attract much attention. Although this station was hard to locate on maps, all passing trains would stop here for over ten minutes. It was thought that trains stopped here to add water and coal, but really Qingshui was a relay station for a dedicated railway line leading to the base. A small train went north slowly on the vast Gobi Desert that showed no sign of life. Nobody talked on the train, and a sense of mystery permeated the entire carriage. Trepidation and uncertainty filled my heart.

When the train reached the final station called Dongfeng, I was dazzled by what I saw: a veritable oasis in the depth of the desert. After getting off the train, we boarded a bus that took us to a building in the style of Beijing's Great Hall of the People. There was a square in front of the building. Along the way there was a paved asphalt road, with lush trees lining up both sides, exactly like a normal city.

This setup removed some sense of mystery for me. As soon as I settled in the base, I was called to do interviews at the various units for their meritorious deeds and exemplary soldiers. My literary talent was fully exploited. During an interview, I had the opportunity to see the data processing center once led by Wang Shaoren. Although I knew nothing about the missiles, I believed that I could do data processing. I submitted my application to work at the data processing center, but the superiors could not appreciate my request. Some felt that I was being silly. I was already working at the command center in daily contact with senior officers. It was a comfortable job with a promising future. At an age where intellectuals became the "stinking number nine," it was hard to imagine someone would give up a fast lane for promotions to do the technical work of data processing. I was considered some kind of naive "oddball." In fact, this might be another choice I made that had changed the course of my life. If I had followed the path initially given to me, I could have been promoted to a senior leader, then all my life would be totally re-written. At this critical moment, I luckily had the support and understanding of Wang Shaoren who really knew me well. However, the affairs of the world went about in a weird way: if I went to the data processing center to work, then I would be considered a fresh graduate assigned to the base, and must first go to a company to get the "decentralization exercise." I agreed to this condition, and went to an engineering company to become a laborer.

As an intellectual who spent two decades in schools, I started to "eat, sleep and work" together with young soldiers in their late teens. During that time, I did just about any types of hard labor. I worked as a loader, carrying cement bags that weighed one hundred kilograms, almost double my body weight, so heavy that I could not stand up straight. In the severe winter, sweat drenched my whole body, becoming ice, but was melted again by body heat under a heavy work load. The process was repeated again and again. Cement dust formed a thin layer of mist together with my sweat, clouding my eyes so that I could only walk in a stumbling, halting way. I lifted bricks for some time, with one brick clipper holding five or six bricks. As a result of the brick lifting, I grew a wrist cyst so thick and painful that it became hard to even hold a cup to drink water. It had to be removed surgically, leaving a scar to this day. I built houses. When climbing on top of some high scaffolding, I trembled with fear, but still had to lay the bricks to make the walls. I also drilled holes on a mountain, smashed rocks for building materials, fed pigs and scooped manure.

I had had problems with neurasthenia, and just as I fell asleep after a lot of fuss, I was awakened by the sounding of the trumpet for emergency assembly. By the time I got up slowly, my dormitory was already empty of people. When I got to the field, the whole company was already assembled in full. My awkward manners often initiated a burst of laughter from the ranks. The food was poor at the company, so I was often hungry, and just did not have enough energy for the heavy labor. Sometimes I asked myself again and again: Why did I ask for it? Instead of keeping to the easy office work, I chose to do data processing, resulting in doing the "decentralization exercise" in the end. Then I thought, the easy path was often the wrong path, and the difficult path was actually the correct path. Druing my days at the engineering company, only one thing made me laugh when I remembered about it. Once, my platoon was sent to build a house in a remote measurement station. It was located a few hundred kilometers away from the nearest living center, surrounded by the endless Gobi Desert. Every drop of water we drank, every grain of rice we ate, all had to be transported from several hundred kilometers away by car. There were no power lines reaching there, so each day we relied on a diesel generator to generate one hour of electricity just before sleep. Besides that it was all dark and silent. We just worked like machines there to build the house. One day when we were working, we suddenly heard the sound of camel bells coming from a distance. As the bells sounded closer and closer, we saw that it was a young Mongolian girl passing by here on a camel. We dropped whatever we were doing to chat with her, a pity that her Chinese was limited. We offered her what treats we had saved like cakes and candies. We formed a circle around her and asked her to sing a song. When she finished singing, our applause resounded through the Gobi Desert. I was reminded of Wang Luobin's song, "In that distant place, there is a good girl." We treated that day like a feast. Even a few days later, we were still talking about the girl. This episode showed that even in that deserted place, people still maintained their born human nature, not only with blood and flesh, but also with emotions.

One day I suddenly received a notice, asking me to leave the engineering company to report to the personnel department. It turned out that preparations for the launch of China's first artificial satellite was being carried out. Under an erroneous policy, intellectuals were like pieces of broken wood, very insignificant, to be tossed around in a vast sea. The result was that there was a shortage of personnel at data processing and other technical positions. The huge task of launching an artificial satellite forced the leadership to transfer us back to the the technical posts from where we were doing our "decentralization exercises." So I was called by my superiors to take part in the launching of the first artificial satellite of China immediately, specializing in processing the telemetry data transmitted by the satellite. Honestly, I knew nothing about missiles, satellite, and telemetry equipment. However, with my mastery of basic skills in mathematics and physics, I quickly learned the basic techniques of data processing. In fact, it was much simpler than studying nuclear physics. The basic techniques of data processing were very simple: I just needed to understand the physical measurement of the data, recording format, as well as calibrations, etc.

On April 24, 1970, China's first artificial satellite was successfully launched. I, the intellectual who behaved awkwardly and suffered greatly in an engineering company, had successfully completed the data processing task at a crucial moment, receiving a "commendation" for my effort. Anyway, my personal contribution to this historic event added a hint of color to my life. In the archive for recording this historic milestone in China, the data processing reports with my signatures were preserved for history, constituting a bright spot in my life.

China exploded her first atomic bomb on October 16, 1964. I made my contribution to the uranium enrichment research when I was just a 17-year-old student. My contribution could be said to be negligible. In contrast, I made my unique contribution to the data processing after the successful launch of China's first artificial satellite. During the data processing work, I found that the error of the final result was mainly caused by the read-out error of the measuring instrument. The read-out system was manufactured in the Soviet Union in the fifties. But in the seventies in China, such an instrument was still very much treasured, placed in a room with constant temperature and humidity. Senior officials repeatedly told us about how much pork it took to exchange for a piece of equipment like this. I soon found that we could use newer technologies to make a more advanced read-out system, which could be semi-automated. I proposed a design scheme, which was quickly approved by the leadership. With this design, I went to the Shanghai Institute of Optics Instruments. Since this was a military project, it was soon classified as a top priority project. From then on I often had to work at Shanghai Institute of Optics Instrument. This project was assigned the code 90J, for which I was the originator and chief designer, and finally turned out to be a complete success. It won the 1978 National Conference on Science Award, which was the highest science award in China after the Cultural Revolution and before the opening up and reform of China. The winning of this award represented another bright spot of my life. This semi-automated read-out system was widely used by various research units in China.

After the successful launch of China's first artificial satellite, the base decided out of strategic concerns to set up another base located in the mountains in north Shanxi province. It involved the transfer of many key personnel, including myself. I came to northwest Shanxi, known as the "barren land." In reality, that place did not have to be poor. It looked somewhat like the Switzerland to me, with steep mountains full of flowers and trees, rushing waters, and clean air. It made for a perfect tourist destination, and needed only good transportation. Under the erroneous policy of "taking grain as the key," the villagers were forced to grow crops where they were not suited, simply anti-natural. If Switzerland also practiced the "taking grain as the key" policy, how it would be ruined as a country. I went there, staying in the village where the locals had immigrated to other locations. Those abandoned cave houses appeared to be about to crumble down. The cave I lived in had small stones falling all the time. Even more frightening was that there were rats scurrying everywhere in the night, and some even climbed up on my bed. Therefore our first job there was to build houses. Because the locals were very poor and had no grains, we exchanged grains for their eggs. On the weekend, we would often go up the mountains to pick mushrooms, and dig up astragalus. On top of the highest peak there was the "Lotus Ping," a piece of flat ground from where we could look out all around at the lush trees and blooming flowers. It was a gorgeous view. Since we were starting from scratch in this solitary valley, we had to build houses ourselves, heat up a boiler, scoop manure, dig a well, fetch water, feed pigs, raise chickens, cook meals and so on. Although life was hard, it was still much better than my days in Yinjia Mountain, so there was really no comparison.

At that time, I was also in charge of the 90J project, so I often went to Shanghai on business trips, during which a few things happened that I would never forget. One was in February 1972, when the US President Richard Nixon visited Shanghai. At that time, I was in Shanghai on business, and stayed at my old home. As I mentioned before, my home was on Julu Road, downstairs was the open-air market in Shanghai, not far from the Jinjiang Hotel where Nixon stayed. Neighborhood committee members sent notices to ask everyone to stay home. Luckily, the windows of my home were facing the street, so I could see the open-air market from home. Soon, some well-dressed "housewives" appeared in the market, leisurely walking around the market with grocery baskets in hands. That day the open-air market had just about everything including poultry, fish, pork, delicacies, fruits and vegetables. I did not think that Nixon went there himself, but I saw members of the entourage of the US president. As soon as the US delegation left, those "housewives" disappeared with everything in the market. Years later, the grand "live performances" conducted by Zhang Yimou must have drawn inspiration from such an event. It was totally unnecessary. In 1982, I worked at the Institute of High-energy Physics, and was about to invite a British friend to visit me at my home. A director in charge of foreign liaisons told me that the institute could lend me a house to receive my guest. I insisted on receiving my friend at my own apartment, otherwise I would rather cancel the visit. Finally I entertained my visitor at my own place. My apartment was small and simple, but it was real. Actually, poverty did not matter, because nothing was more important than the real thing.

The second was the 1972 Anhui flood. At that time, my teenage sister was settled in the Lai'an County of Chuxian region. My father asked me to see my sister on my way to Shanghai, as the train passed by the Chuxian region. When I got off the train at Chuxian, all the public transportation was halted, and all the word of the mouth news got me very worried. I decided to go to Lai'an on foot, but unexpectedly the rain got heavier and heavier. Along the way, I saw many victims taking along their children, carrying a lot of bags and boxes to flee the flood, and to find a way out along the railway. As I walked on, gradually I could no longer see the road, but followed the treetops and telephone poles which were still above the surface of the water, towards the direction of Lai'an county. I finally made it to the production team where my sister stayed. Luckily, her production team was located on high ground, not yet flooded. I found the home of the team leader, and saw a group of chicks on the ground, and a group of children on an earth bed. There was no room for either standing up or sitting down in the house. I asked the team leader to take me to my sister's living place — a thatched cottage built along the side of a cowshed. It was originally intended to be a resting place for the farmers who tended cows. My sister was not home. I immediately recognized a red box that belonged to our home in Shanghai, confirming that this was indeed where my sister lived. However, where was she? I was concerned. However, I knew that she was a good swimmer, and could swim across the Yangtze River, so I believed that she was all right. It became dark, so I had to stay in my sister's cottage. Her bed was made up of some reeds, spread across two stools. As soon as I lay down, the bed crumbled. It was raining hard outside, drizzling non-stop inside. Thus I spent a whole night dripping wet. I felt emotionally disturbed that my dear sister Xiaomin actually lived in such a place.

The third thing was that I saw Xiao Mei on the Nanjing Road in Shanghai by chance. I had never met her again since I left Fudan University, but "the shadow of first love" had been bothering me all the time, so I was not able to pull myself out of my emotional trap. Seven or eight years later, I saw that Xiao Mei already had a bulging belly. Oh! She was soon to become a mother. All sorts of bitter and sweet emotions raged in my heart. I pretended not to see her when we walked past each other. Looking at her back as she gradually walked out my view, I said to myself: "Yes indeed! She is over thirty and should be a mother by now." However, what about me? I could not help asking myself.

5.5 My first marriage

Recently, I saw an interview with a celebrity on TV. She was asked how many times she had fallen in love. Then I also asked myself: "How many times for me?" I thought about it, counting more than seven or eight times! Someone might say that I had a wandering heart. Perhaps that was true. However, in those days, free love was not really free. Last year, I went to Fudan University to give a lecture. Some of my old classmates came. Among them there was a couple, a handsome man and a pretty woman in our university years. Because they were openly in love while in university, at graduation, one was assigned to Qinghai, and the other to Jiangxi by Mr. He. I did not know how they got re-united eventually, now ready to celebrate their "golden marriage." Not many people had such courage. In Lanzhou University, I met a very beautiful girl, born and raised in Tianshui. It was said, Tianshui had particularly good "feng shui," and good soil and water produced good people. Girls from Tianshui were very pretty, and she was a beauty among beauties. However, she was just a junior high school graduate, not quite my match. Then I met a graduate from Lanzhou Medical School, just about to start working. She was also very pretty, could sing and dance too. However, her father was a senior officer of the Nationalist army, although he later switched to the communist side, but I was soon to work at the base, I just could not make it with her troubles on top of my own. I was introduced to a worker, who was the type that would make a good wife and mother. She could play the role of supporting her husband and taking good care of her children, loyal beyond question. She was not bad looking either. However, when we were together, all she could do was to keep passing food to me without saying anything else. It could not really do. I also met a talented engineer who wrote beautiful calligraphy. When I went to Beijing on errand, and read in the library, she would often send me stuff to eat on her own initiative. When I returned from Beijing to Shanghai, her letters would follow as soon as I arrived in person. However, she was from Northeast China, tall and strong, but quite different from the kind of wife in my imagination. Someone said that I was too choosy, and I agree. I realized that the standard set by Xiao Mei was always in my heart. That was really my trouble.

Finally, the right person appeared at the right time. When I returned to Shanxi from my business trip to Shanghai, a fresh graduate from the Changsha Institute of Technology came to work at our data processing center. Her name was Hengbao, and she was assigned to process telemetry data with me. I was good at mathematics, and knew all about calculation formula and error analysis, but did not know how to program, which was her strong point. We worked together quite harmoniously. We processed telemetry data using a Kalman filter, greatly improving the accuracy of the measurement, winning a big prize. On the weekends, we would climb the mountains to pick mushrooms, and dig up astragalus, all very happy. She had regular facial features with big eyes and a slim figure, a very good simple girl. However, her father was one of the five generals in the entire base, who was an old red army member from Jinggang Mountain and had participated in the legendary Long March. My own parents, although "liberated" from detention at that time, nevertheless belonged to a class of people with questionable origins. Could I really be part of this kind of family? It turned out that my worrying was not without reason. On hearing that we were in love, her parents felt concerned. Her mother decided to talk to me in person. It was the summer of 1973, I visited her mother using my opportunity to have a business trip to Beijing. With my first look, I saw a kind, respectable old lady. Although she was a member of the old Eighth Route army, now a senior leader in Beijing, she was very approachable. We gained a lot of mutual understanding through our conversations. So Hengbao and I got married in Beijing on December 27, 1974. Her mother was definitely another respectable and adored communist member that I knew. She knew that I liked to eat fish, so whenever I visited her at her Beijing home, she would take a crowded bus herself to buy a live fish for me at the Dongdan Farmers' Market, without ever bothering her driver or body guard. I will cherish her memory forever. Hengbao's father was also a senior official of the state, with his own assigned car, driver and body guards. He was also a respectable and adored communist member who was very honest. I think that if every communist member in China were clean and simple like them, the prestige and image of the communist party would be much higher and better. In the summer of 1975, her father went to Shanghai to have a meeting. He stayed in the Yan'an Hotel, and paid a visit to my parents in person. At that time, my parents were still subjected to the so-called "examination." The visit by an old red army member moved our whole family deeply. Even now all my family members still remember the visit vividly. Towards the end of 1975, I said something bad about Jiang Qing and Zhang Chunqiao at my work unit. Someone informed on me, and I was branded a "counter-revolutionary." When the incriminating materials were sent up high, my father-in-law made the comment, "Suit yourself." So things dragged out. Soon, with the downfall of "The Gang of Four," I escaped a major disaster narrowly.

By 1976, the ten years of calamity came to a full stop. In 1978, China held a "National Conference on Science," declaring that "science and technology are primary productive forces," "intellectuals are part of the working class" and so on. The spring of science had come to China. Really it was not quite enough. Workers, peasants and soldiers should be better educated to become intellectuals themselves, which is the only way for social development. To solve the food problem of China, it could not rely on "killing the sparrows," nor on "dense seeding," much less on "deep plowing of the land." It depended on the effort of peasant scientists like Yuan Longping. With the spring of science, then came the spring of China. The reform and opening up was first about the liberation of science and thought. However, such ideas have not yet taken root in the heart of the general population. So I think that the "National Conference on Science" should be convened at least once every five years. Be vigilant always to prevent the restoration of a set of fallacies practised in the Cultural Revolution. I am very pleased to see the "scientific concept of development" written up as part of the constitution of the Communist Party of China. The tragedy should not be repeated that a national leader was not ashamed of the practice of the first emperor of Qin dynasty — burning books and burying scholars alive — but rather took pride in it. I wrote the book not to pass judgment on historical figures, but one thing was certain, a national leader who persecuted intellectuals was not a good leader. A nation that does not value science and education will not stand up tall among nations of the world.

Chapter Six

Pinnacle of Life

6.1 Order out of chaos

The Cultural Revolution ended with the downfall of the Gang of Four. The ten years of calamity made the national economy reach the brink of collapse, with poverty widespread and voices of discontent heard everywhere. China is often criticizing Japan for not clearing up militarism, so there is a tendency for militarism to raise its ugly head now and then. Likewise, many consequences of the Cultural Revolution have not been dealt with properly, so there are politicians who take advantage of people's dissatisfaction with corruption and other current social problems to revive some misguided practices of the Cultural Revolution. The so-called "Singing Red and Striking Black" campaign was one such example. Some of the extreme "leftist" slogans were very deceptive, indeed. Early in the Cultural Revolution I was an avid "revolutionary advocate" myself, something that I deeply regret to this day. I truly admire heroes like Zhixin Zhang. She was well placed within the "system," and could have chosen to go with the system, or simply remain a spectator, but she insisted on telling the truth. She exposed the reactionary nature of the Cultural Revolution at an early stage.

Corruption has its deep roots within the social framework of China, and cannot be solved using the methods of the Cultural Revolution. In any case anti-corruption was not the original intention of the Cultural Revolution. Corruption must be eradicated at a level that reforms the whole system, making people fearful of being corrupt, and unable to be corrupt. That is the only way to eradicate corruption. Moreover, to attribute all the the heinous crimes of the Cultural Revolution to the Gang of Four is also a distortion of history. It is a recipe for disaster not to clear up the issues related to the Cultural Revolution. That is why Israel wanted a

World War II Museum, Nanjing needed a Nanjing Massacre Museum, and the famous writer Mr. Ba Jin suggested establishing a museum for the Cultural Revolution.

The practices of "educated urban youth working in the countryside and mountainous areas" and "decentralization" during the Cultural Revolution were also completely wrong, having a devastating effect on the young students. I previously spoke of how life itself was a teacher, and how educated young people had much to gain by learning about society via working in the countryside and mountainous areas. However, I did not mean to support such a policy in the way it was forcibly practiced. In my mind, the Cultural Revolution conjured up memories of many broken families, of a sign hung on my mother's neck claiming "a capitalist slipped through the net," of my father plugging his nose with toilet paper after it was bloodied by senseless beating, and of the banishment of my brothers and sisters to all corners of China. After the downfall of the Gang of Four, my parents were rehabilitated. During the period when they were "examined in isolation," they were given a living allowance of only fifteen Yuan (RMB) per month. After the rehabilitation, my mother was given several thousand Yuans (RMB) as compensation. My mother gave it all to the communist party as party fees, to thank the party for "implementing the rehabilitation policy." The communist party of China should really be proud to have such loyal members. It should also feel ashamed for the decade of calamity, and lawlessness. The communist party and government should eliminate the root causes of such tragedies institutionally and legally, to prevent the repetition of such tragedies.

With the end of the Cultural Revolution, China embarked on the road to recovery. We, the Wu brothers and sisters, took the fast lane on the road of reform and opening up, like runaway horses. My sister Wu Fumin was among the first group of senior reporters in China with outstanding contributions at the national level. She wrote up many surveys and reports that influenced the policy making process related to the economic reform and opening up of China. My younger brother Wu Jiming, with his excellent entrance examination results, was among the first group of students accepted into the Department of Chinese Language and Literature at Fudan University, and later became a prolific writer and television series editor. My second younger brother Wu Xinmin was a top table tennis player. As a representative of Chinese athletes, his picture with the US table tennis player Glenn Cowan in 1971 became a classic in Sino-US diplomatic history. The big Mao badge on my brother's chest was in stark contrast with the hippie-style long hair of Glenn Cowan. My youngest brother Wu Minmin went to Japan to study at Waseda University at his own expense, later becoming Japan's NHK program producer and reporter, and also a prolific writer. My younger sister Wu Xiaomin became a reporter for *Sports Daily* and *Guangming Daily* after graduating from Beijing Sport University. She was the first director for the office of Guangming Daily in Shenzhen, considered one of the pioneers of the Shenzhen Special Economic Zone. In 1988, she was invited by the United States Information Agency to report on the US presidential election. She traveled tens of thousands of miles all over the US to interview politicians and ordinary citizens alike. In the city of Harrison, she was the first Chinese to be recognized by the mayor as an Honorary Citizen and awarded with "permanent residence." Unfortunately, my parents, because their physical and mental health was severely damaged during the Cultural Revolution, passed away after enjoying a very brief happy time.

There was a wonderful and moving story behind the success of each of my brothers and sisters. I cannot go into all the details here but I would like to talk about a few things that had a big impact on me personally.

My elder sister had a keen eye for the positive driving forces of the society. Her articles like "'My heart goes to the first productive force,' "Shanghai rises on reflections," "Standing at the junction of centuries" and other articles, fueled the process of China's reform and its opening up. She had extensive business contacts in Shanghai. She helped me to organize the collaboration with the Shanghai Institute of Optics Instruments and Plastics Research Institute which led to the successful development of the 90J equipment mentioned before, and detectors needed by later international collaborations. My brother Wu Jiming worked in the Shanghai Museum of Literary History. With his unique appreciation of Chinese culture, he got to know many "living archives" of modern Chinese history. He listened to their stories carefully, creating works like "Exotic Love," "Enigmatic Love," "Life and Death Struggle — Zhou Enlai and the Shanghai Family Massacre," "Suffering and Struggle of Chinese Trotskyists." He was very good at telling stories. I read "The Count of

Monte Cristo," "Les Miserables" and other famous novels only after he intrigued my interest by his verbal interpretation of the story lines.

My second brother Wu Xinmin is a very humorous and kind person. He is the first person in my family to go outside of China. He had strong organizational skills, and worked on organizing many international competitions involving China. He met with many national leaders of different countries. At our family gatherings, his laughter always touched everyone. My little brother Wu Minmin often joked to us: "Each of my brothers and sisters is talented, but I am the only one who is a genius." I thought he actually spoke some truth. He went to North-east China to "go up the mountains and down to the countryside" as an educated youth when he had just graduated from junior high school. He did not know a word of Japanese when he made it to Japan. A few years later, when he returned to Shanghai, people often said to him: "Your Chinese is so good!" He was mistaken for a Japanese because he spoke Japanese so well.

He was a literary genius; his tragic trilogy "Bell at the End of the Century," "Sea Wolf Incident," and "Horizon of Lust" was very imaginative, with plots that were complex and fascinating at the same time. They became bestsellers and were made into a TV series. He still wrote in long hand, without the help of a computer, all in one go with no draft. My little sister Wu Xiaomin is even more of a genius. She was an outstanding swimmer, crossing the Huangpu River at the age of nine, and crossing the Yangtze River at ten. She was sent to get "re-educated in the countryside" as soon as she graduated from elementary school, but she managed to become an outstanding reporter, publishing collections of writings titled "Heart Towards the Five Rings of Olympics," "Heart Moves with the Waves" and others. After 1989, she started her own business and became a successful entrepreneur. The successes of my brothers and sisters served as the motivation for my own life.

It is often argued whether the heroes make the times, or if times create heroes. In fact, both are right. We Wu brothers and sisters could "play heroes" only under the circumstances of the reform and opening up. I believe in two very controversial sayings: "There must be some use for the talent heaven granted me," and "rotten wood cannot be carved." It means that not everyone can make headways with the tide of reform and opening up. Like waves sweeping away the sand, some people just could not handle it. Reform and opening up let people's personalities and abilities come into full play, the differences among individuals were thus exposed, being previously hidden by the big-pot practice. In my case, the reform and opening made me turn a big circle to to my major in college: research in particle physics, a profession that has accompanied me to this day.

6.2 Entering the Institute of High Energy Physics

Sometimes, life is composed of many coincidences. After the Gang of Four was crushed, my wife Hengbao went to Beijing for treatment of an illness. I therefore had the opportunity to go to Beijing to see her. Beijing in Spring of 1977 was filled with a strong spirit of "Beijing Spring," namely the fifth modernization: the modernization of politics. I also heard that in November 1977, the CPC Central Committee had approved the "Application for Speeding up the Construction of a High Energy Physics Experiment Center," starting the "87" project. The Institute of High Energy Physics (IHEP) was also established and was recruiting professionals throughout the country. I was not sure if IHEP would want me because I had lived in a totally secluded world since leaving Lanzhou University. I decided to try my luck anyway. On a sunny day in early spring, 1978, when the weather was still chilly, I made it to the Institute of High Energy Physics located in the western suburbs of Beijing. The PLA guards at the entrance of IHEP told me to inquire at the post room, where a lady on duty asked me whom I intended to visit. I said, "the Human Resource department." "Who in the HR department?" She asked again. I said, "I do not know." She laughed, asking "If you do not know who to see, why did you come here?" I said, "I have come here to ask, does the Institute of High Energy Physics need anyone?" She laughed even harder. Nevertheless, she let me fill in the "guest list," and suggested that I go and see Su Yuncheng of the Human Resource group. This Mr. Su turned out to be another communist whom I adored and respected. When I saw Su Yuncheng, after one glance he said that they did not need anyone from the National Defense Science and Technology Commission, without even bothering to ask me to sit down. I told him that I had studied nuclear physics. As I was introducing myself, I took out my excellent score sheets from my high school and college days plus a pile of awards.

Only after he took a look at them did he sit me down seriously. He said, "We only have thirty positions for entering Beijing. Our requirements are strict. Your materials are private. We need formal files." Yes indeed! Most members of the newly formed High Energy Institute were members of Department One of the former atomic energy research institute, plus some recommended by them. To them, I was a total stranger. He told me: "The first thing you should do is to ask your work unit to transfer your files." This was a reasonable request. However, since I belonged to the National Defense Science Commission, which was a top-secret unit, how would they agree to transfer my files? Here I should feel grateful for the understanding and help of Wang Shaoren and my father-in-law, who actually agreed to my request to allow the High Energy Institute to read my files. It was not until I entered the IHEP that Su Yuncheng told me what really happened. It turned out that my score sheets and many awards caught his eye. He thought that if they were the real deal, he would recommend me to the leadership. However, it was very difficult to have me transferred technically. First, I needed to obtain a "quota" for "demobilization," then get the "permission for living in Beijing" from the State Planning Commission. It all had to be "tailored" for me personally, which was far beyond the scope of his work.

His efforts were worth several times more than others in an equivalent position, and they paid off. I said goodbye to the Defense Science Commission, and entered the Institute of High Energy Physics to work, fulfilling my dream of many years. Early in 1982, when I first came back to China after studying abroad, I saw that the Su family was still using a small nine-inch black and white TV. I offered Su a color television as a gift, which he resolutely refused. Only after much persuasion did Su finally take my duty-free "quota," and use his own money to buy it. In contrast, many party officials nowadays abuse their power, and have no qualms with giving or taking bribes. I could not count how many people got accepted to work at the High Energy Institute through Su Yuncheng, but up to 1982, he had only a nine-inch black and white TV, and lived in a poorly-lit, simple building with shared bathrooms and kitchens. What an admirable and respectable communist! Later, I became a laboratory director responsible for international cooperation and foreign affairs, granting permission to scores of people to go abroad to either study or work, but

I never abused my power for personal gains. I think that it had a lot to do with the fine example set by Su.

After I went to the High Energy Institute, I lived in a large room on the fifth floor of the office building. There were more than ten beds there housing the newly hired male workers. Female employees and children stayed in another. To someone like myself who had stayed in cave houses and shared a wide bed with a dozen young soldiers, this was already heaven. Since I had worked on the 90J reading instrument, I was assigned to work on a "bubble chamber." At that time, China was making preparations for constructing a 50GeV proton accelerator. The "bubble chamber" is a measuring device. When charged particles pass through the "bubble chamber," they form traces under certain conditions. A trigger system would then take pictures of the traces just in time, which would be used to measure the momentum, energy, charge, and other physical parameters of charged particles. The whole process was really very similar to what I did with the 90J reading device for processing film data. To familiarize myself faster with my work, I needed to read a lot of foreign literature. At that time, the High Energy Institute invited many foreign experts to visit and to give seminars. All of this required that I become proficient in foreign languages, especially English. After the end of the Culture Revolution, listening to foreign radio channels was no longer regarded "counter-revolutionary," so I became a frequent listener of the "English Nine Hundred sentence" program of the Voice of America, and the "Follow Me" program of the British Broadcasting Corporation (BBC). I returned to the life style of a student: learning a foreign language early in the morning, working during the day and refreshing some of the knowledge learned in college at night by going through my book collection that accompanied me everywhere for more than ten years. I knew that I just could not let go of this opportunity that history presented me with. Since I soon became proficient with my work, my effort earned praises from the leadership.

In the spring of 1979, the Chinese-American physicist and Nobel laureate Tsung-Dao Lee came to Beijing to give a series of lectures, and various renowned universities and research institutes across the country selected more than 300 young and middle aged physicists to participate. Due to my background as a "graduate student," plus my performance with the "bubble chamber" work, I was chosen by IHEP to take Lee's "Intensive

Lecture" class. This class was held in Beijing's Science Hall for between five and six hours per day over seven consecutive weeks. It was called the "Intensive Lecture Series" by TD Lee for a good reason. Lee would lecture on two courses at the same time: "Field Theory and Particle Physics," and "Statistical Mechanics." Lee talked and talked to the point that his voice was hoarse and we all became exhausted. Every evening, there was a lot of home work to be done as well. China was isolated from the rest of the world for over a dozen years, and the topics touched by the two courses such as quantum chromodynamics and quantum statistics were totally new even to former members of the original Institute of Atomic Energy, not to mention myself. When I listened to Lee speaking on the "quark" model, I thought of my essay "On Zi and Dian," which was written at the same time as the conception of the "quark" model. If only I could have worked together with the originators of the model, or if I could have discussed the idea with my teachers at Fudan University more thoroughly and developed it further, it would have been so wonderful! I was deeply moved by Tsung-Dao Lee's lectures. Lee was an internationally renowned physicist, and a professor at the prestigious Columbia University. He faced a group of students who were not really young, but had been isolated for so long, so he tried to present his subjects as accessibly as possible, and with much patience so that we could all understand eventually. He was the best teacher in my life. His "Intensive Lecture Series" filled some gaps in our knowledge and reduced the distance between us and pioneers at the leading edge of the field. After that, I have had a lot of contact with Lee. I believed that among the Chinese living overseas, he was the most concerned about China's scientific and technological development. Lee's contribution was decisive in China's high-energy physics achievements today. Once I had a conversation with a British entrepreneur about why China's reform and opening up had succeeded. The entrepreneur has business dealings with many countries. He said that when he was doing business with people of Chinese origin in those countries, he felt that those people always regarded themselves as Chinese. So it was a matter of course for them to go to China to invest, exchange ideas, and do business. He got no such feelings from people of other national origins. Yes indeed! Whether it was "returning to their roots" or simply "homecoming in style," these kinds of Chinese culture and tradition are deeply rooted in the heart of hundreds of thousands of overseas Chinese. I believe that China will always be the land dear to Lee's heart. He once mentioned that he accomplished what he did because he benefited from the fact that the nationalist government in China wanted to develop the atom bomb in 1946, and provided the fund for Professor Wu Daiyou to take him to America to study physics. Now he wanted to create the same opportunities for the young and middle aged people today. He did what he said. I was among the hundreds of direct beneficiaries of his program.

In my opinion, apart from his academic achievements, there were four things that Professor Lee did that made history. Firstly, on January 31, 1979, Deng Xiaoping signed a "Sino-US Memorandum for Scientific and Technological Cooperation" with the US Administration during his visit to the United States of America. To promote cooperation in the field of high energy physics, the representative of China's National Science and Technology Commission, Fang Yi, and the US Secretary of Energy, James R. Schlesinger, signed the "Executive Agreement for Cooperation between the Science and Technology Commission of the People's Republic of China and the Department of Energy of the United States of America in the Field of High Energy Physics." This was the first executive agreement under the "Memorandum for Scientific and Technological Cooperation." The driving force behind this collaboration was Professor TD Lee. To date, this partnership has lasted 35 years.

Secondly, in order to cultivate experimental talents that the field of high energy physics in China urgently needed, Lee used his personal prestige to make contacts with many world famous high-energy physics laboratories. He selected 33 scientists and engineers through examination from his "Intensive Class" to work and study there. Luckily I was one of those selected. All those people later became key members of the High Energy Institute.

Thirdly, he established the CUSPEA plan for Sino-US joint training of physicists. CUSPEA stands for the China-United States Physics Examination and Application Program. The program was somewhat controversial, because some believed that it led to a "brain drain." However, in my opinion, this program fully demonstrated TD Lee's far-sighted strategic vision. Science knows no borders. No matter whether or not these people later returned to China, they would either directly or indirectly make many contributions to China's scientific development and international cooperation. Lee's CUSPEA plan was a game changer for China's development of contemporary science.

Fourthly, when the program for constructing a 50 GeV proton accelerator plan was about to fall apart, Professor Lee took a broad view of the global high-energy physics field with his unique insight and vision, and together with the US expert Wolfgang K.H. Panofsky, proposed the construction of the 2.2 GeV Electron-Positron Collider in China. This program could do significant research on Physics, while, costing relatively little money, and had greater advantages in many considerations. It won the unanimous support of domestic and foreign experts and the final approval of the Chinese government. This was a strategic change. It was later proved that Professor Lee's proposal laid the foundation for the huge success of the Institute of High Energy Physics. The international collaboration team for the Beijing Spectrometer III (BESIII) experiment announced on March 26, 2013 the discovery of a new resonance structure in the data recently collected, tentatively named Zc (3900). Particles in the charm energy region generally contain charm quarks and anti-charm quarks, Their bound state is called charmonium, which is neutral with no charges. The newly discovered Zc (3900) contains a charm quark and anti-charm quark and has the same or opposite charge of an electron, suggesting that it contains at least four quarks. It may be the unique hadron which scientists had been searching for a long time. This was a strong endorsement of the strategic planning done by Professor T.D. Lee. As one of the hundreds of direct beneficiaries of his various plans, I went abroad for the first time on November 3, 1979, beginning a new chapter in my life.

6.3 Going abroad for the first time

Among the 33 people selected to go abroad to study and work, 28 were assigned to various experimental groups in the United States, and five were assigned to the European Center for Nuclear Research — CERN located in Geneva, Switzerland, including myself. My two colleagues and I were further assigned to the CDHS experimental group led by Professor Jack Steinberger. One of the colleagues working in the same group was a graduate student of the IHEP director Zhang Wenyu. He was two years my senior in class, and designated our "head". The other was a scientist who had graduated from Beijing University as early as 1956. Our department director in China told us, "Professor Steinberger is a famous scientist (he later won the Nobel Prize), and is also a good friend of Professor TD Lee at Columbia University, so the institute decided to send more and better scientists to work with him." What the director said gave us both encouragement and pressure. In retrospect, I really feel lucky, to have worked together with Professor Steinberger was the best gift God has given me. His knowledge and character set a good example for me for life.

To prepare us for going abroad, the Chinese government gave each of us 700 Yuan (RMB), as the "dress up cost". At that time, China was still very poor, and our monthly salary was only 70 Yuan (RMB). To buy a woolen suit required at least 200 Yuan (RMB), the equivalent of two months' wages. At the time, Beijing set up a special shop, called the "Friendship Store," specifically for foreigners and Chinese going overseas. Seven hundred Yuan (RMB) was equivalent to almost a year of my salary! With the money, I ordered a tunic and a suit set to be tailor made, and bought a wool coat. When the tailor was taking my measurement, I thought that I would wear the two sets of clothing in spring and fall, as well as winter, so I told him to make them larger. I reckoned that in winter, I would wear a sweater under the suit, it just would not do if they were too small. Furthermore, if any alterations were needed in the future, it would be possible to make them smaller rather than bigger. Such expensive clothes were better bigger. After reaching Switzerland, I found that my ideas were so anachronistic, still stuck in the era of living in the mountains and caves. In Switzerland, who would wear layers upon layers of clothes just to keep warm? Those tailor made clothes of mine were simply too large to wear in Switzerland. The little episode was really insignificant, but it reflected our total ignorance of the outside world at the time. In the fifties, as a Chinese children's representative, my sister welcomed a delegation from Belgium. A friend gave her a few black and white postcards, which I remember were pictures of the landscape of a Brussels Palace. Decades later, I still keep those images fresh in my mind, really because in that era, I had too little contact with anything foreign. In the fifties, what foreign stuff we could read were mostly Soviet magazines; in the sixties, we could only read and see magazines and movies from North

Korea, and Albania. In 1959, during the visit of Nikita Khrushchev of the Soviet Union to the United States, a newsreel was shown in Chinese cinemas before the start of a film. One episode was about Khrushchev's visit to New York, in which there was a scene with an airplane flying over the city. The fleeting views of the Statue of Liberty and the skyscrapers left an indelible impression on me. People went again and again to see the film, just to see the seconds of scenes of the skyline of New York. We just could not imagine, how human kind could build such tall skyscrapers. Later, the government discovered this phenomenon, and the brief documentary was omitted. Once, Winston Churchill used the term "iron curtain" to describe the barrier of information exchange between the Eastern European countries of the communist block and the rest of the world. In fact, due to the geographical location, social structure and cultural background, China was far more isolated than Eastern European countries in terms of information exchange. If there was an "iron curtain" for the Eastern European countries, it was the "iron wall" for China. At that time, if there was a blond foreigner on the street, a group of Chinese would surround him with curiosity, as though watching an "alien" from a different planet.

  When I boarded the plane to Switzerland, I kept thinking that I was just dreaming. Before that time I had never boarded a plane, much less going abroad. As recently as one year before, I was still working deep in the mountains, but now I was boarding an airline bounded for Zurich. If this was not a dream, then what was it? This was a Trident aircraft of the Chinese Civil Aviation Administration. The cabin could accommodate more than a hundred persons, but it was now only sparsely seated to half capacity at most. At that time, there were still few people going abroad. Each passenger had the room to lie down and sleep, but I could not fall asleep. I knew some aerodynamics from the physics I studied, but I just could not imagine how such a large aircraft could get the lift to fly by relying on the difference between the air flow lines around the wings. On hearing that the airplane had flown over the Pamirs into Pakistan, I was filled with emotion: generations of the Wu family had at last produced a scientist who flew beyond the country border. The airplane made a brief stop at Karachi. I walked around in the departure lounge of the airport, which was more or less like the Beijing airport, just a little brighter. The airplane continued the flight, and then stopped at the Belgrade airport, Yugoslavia. There was a spacious waiting hall, an array of duty-free shops, and crowds of colorfully dressed people, all very eye-catching. The airplane took off again and continued the journey, and finally arrived in Zurich, the last stop of this flight. Once off the plane, I could not believe my eyes. The departure lounge of Zurich airport simply belonged to another planet. My expression and excitement were probably best described as "an old country lady coming upon a grand viewing park." Because of the long flight, jet lag and over excitement, I found myself seriously motion sick. I started to vomit copiously. Reluctantly, I made it to another waiting hall, and boarded a small aircraft to Geneva. Then my mind went blank, and did not remember any details of the subsequent journey.

The first thing we did after arriving in Geneva was to check in with China's representatives at the United Nations Office. They gave us a lecture on discipline in handling foreign affairs and precautions to take, and at the same time, also talked about "watching out for the enemy," which was nothing more than how the "imperialists, revisionists and counter-revolutionaries" do their "recruiting job," so we had to remain vigilant and so on. What I remembered most clearly was: "to go out in a group of three," and "do not stay out overnight alone," "Every weekend, go back to the representatives' office for 'political education'" and so on. The reason I remember so clearly is because soon after, I had several foreign affairs discipline violations for which I was almost deported back to China. I will talk more about them later.

The CDHS experiment group we participated in was led by Steinberger, to research on neutrinos. The probe used in the experiment weighed one thousand two hundred and fifty tons, consisting of a μ particle spectrometer and a hadron energy detector and other components, including nineteen magnet modules, each separated by a drift chamber. Later, a thirty-one cubic meter tank of liquid hydrogen was placed in front of the probe to study the interaction of neutrino with hydrogen. The experiment ran from December of 1976 to1984, and finally obtained data on the CERN experimental study of neutrino beam to produce some significant results, resulting in the publication of 35 research papers, such as the total cross section of neutrinos and anti-neutrinos with nucleons, the upper limits of neutrino oscillation, and so on. When we joined, CDHS was updating its experimental device. My work was to rewrite a Monte Carlo simulation program based on the new experimental device, and carry out physics research using Monte Carlo simulation.

Steinberger sent a Monte Carlo expert, Paolo Palazzi, to supervise my work directly. Soon Paolo and I became very close friends. The first problem we encountered was language. On the first day we met, Paolo talked to me about work and asked repeatedly if I understood. I always answered "Yes." Paolo felt something amiss, asked me pointedly: "You did not really understand, did you?" I also answered "Yes." Paolo laughed. The truth was that I almost did not understand one whole sentence of what he said. I blamed myself for being so slow. I had learned the "English Nine Hundred" from VOA and "Follow Me" from BBC for nothing. CERN is an international organization, with scientists from many countries, so language problems were not a new issue. Thus we were sent to take English lessons. We had four English teachers, but none of them was an Englishman. There were one Yugoslav, one Indian, one German, and one Scotsman. The Scottish English teacher repeatedly corrected us when we called him an Englishman. Only later did I realize that there was a profound historical background as to why a Scotsman did not like to be called an Englishman. The desire of the Scottish people for independence was deep-rooted. On September 18, 2014, a referendum was held to decide on Scotland's independence from Great Britain. Although Scotland did not become independent as a result of the referendum, I still felt for the desire of my Scottish teacher for independence. These teachers later all became my good friends. Now I know that people who do not want to be known as British Scots, have a profound background.

When we reported to the Human Resource department, we needed to fill a form, in which there was an item for my salary at my work unit in China. I wrote down 70 Yuan (RMB). The secretary asked me how much one Yuan was worth in terms of Swiss francs. I said roughly one Swiss franc. Then, the secretary asked, was that seventy per day or per week? I answered per month. That secretary must have thought that my English was not good enough to understand her question. When she verified the fact with several other Chinese scientists, her eyes had opened wider than walnuts, quite speechless. Yes indeed, the minimum wage in

Switzerland was 2,000 Swiss francs per month. How could she comprehend that our salaries were so little! We were sent out by the Chinese government, and our monthly meal allowance was 300 Swiss francs, plus 30 Swiss francs "pocket money". Provision for our housing costs was: about 1,000 Swiss francs per month for the three of us. This was of course very little. However, just think about it, these costs per month per person were equivalent to two years' salary in China. We felt that it was not easy for the motherland to send us overseas, prompting me to work hard and study hard.

I especially want to thank Paolo for helping me in every possible way and for his teachings. He not only told me about the principles behind the Monte Carlo method, but also taught me to write programs on a computer terminal. At the time, China was still so backward that we used perforated paper tapes to input codes before coming to Switzerland. Paolo also taught me Western etiquette and customs, from using a knife and fork to drinking soup, pouring wine and, eating noodles, from opening doors for others to giving tips. He trained me in complete accordance with how the Flower Girl was trained in *My Fair Lady*. Barely a few months later, a real British millionaire was surprised and remarked: "You really behave like you grew up in the home of an English gentleman.

After ten months of hard work, I had written up the new updated Monte Carlo package of the CDHS detector, and it successfully passed the test. Steinberger was very pleased and decided to let me give a talk in October 1980 at the CDHS plenary session held in Warsaw, Poland. However, at that time, the "solidarity" movement was in full swing in Poland. The Chinese representatives' office in Geneva did not give me permission to attend the CDHS conference at first, citing instability of the political situation in Poland. Because of CERN's insistence, however the office referred the matter to the Chinese government, and obtained the permission for me to attend the conference at the last minute, with one condition: all three Chinese scientists must go as a group. Before leaving, the Chinese representatives told us nervously that if the situation became tense, we should enter the Chinese Embassy immediately. After reaching Poland, we found out that the Polish Communist Party had practically ceased to exist. One day, it happened that the Polish archbishop Stefan Wyszynski was making a tour, and thousands of people lined the streets to welcome him. When he approached the crowds, many people knelt down. By contrast, the headquarter of the Communist Party was located not far away, but it looked gloomy, cold, in a semi-paralyzed state. A Polish friend of mine had planned to invite me to his house for dinner, but had to cancel at the last minute. He told me: "Weimin, I'm sorry that my wife did not manage to buy anything other than bread."

My report was quite successful — although I basically read it out verbatim, I managed to make clear the main ideas. It was the first time in my life that I had made a presentation in front of foreigners. Steinberger was very pleased, and he talked for about five or six minutes after I finished my report. He said that this was the first time that a Chinese person had given a talk at CDHS, and the fact that Weimin could complete the update of the Monte Carlo program in a short time showed that Chinese scientists were talented. In reality, my work was limited to updating the program under its original framework, and moreover, it was all completed with the hands-on help from Paolo. I knew that Steinberger was encouraging me.

After staying in Poland, I had a new understanding of socialism. At that time, the Chopin International Piano Competition was held in Warsaw. In the hotel, I met two pianists from Hungary. We chatted while we had our meals together. They told me that in the last few years, Hungary had "relaxed its policies," so people's lives there were much better than here in Poland. Unexpectedly, they used the political phrase "relaxing the policies" which was exactly the same as what China was using. Now that it had been shown that "relaxing the policies" could help economic development and improve people's lives, why did the communist government have to tighten their policies so much?

Really, what is communism, what is a communist party? These questions were subject to much debate, but there were no clear definitions in my opinion. In May 1981, I went to Bologna, Italy, to attend a colloquium. When I walked into a Chinese restaurant, the owner and I knew from each other's accent that we were both from Shanghai. We hit it off right away and started to chat up. He told me that his father was a big landlord from a Shanghai suburb, who fled to Italy before the communist takeover.

Speaking of the Communist Party of China, he naturally felt a lot of hatred. However, it so happened that he had joined the Italian Communist Party. I was very surprised and asked him why. He told me that the

Chinese Communist Party and the Italian Communist Party were alike in name only, being otherwise totally different. The Communist Party of China spoke of dictatorship, whereas the Italian Communist Party spoke of humanity. The Mayor of Bologna was a communist. At the invitation of some scientists at the University of Bologna, I attended a party of the Italian Communist Party, to celebrate the "L'Unita Daily" day, which was a kind of birthday party for the Party. However, this gathering had almost no political overtones, but was rather like a science exhibition, book exhibition, or snack taste party. People could only figure out that it was a gathering of the communist party from the red flags with hammer and sickle hung on the walls and the loud singing of *Internationale*. It also made me realize that why China at that time was making scathing criticism of the former secretary of the Italian Communist Party, Palmiro Togliatti.

During my first trip abroad, I not only learned a lot of scientific knowledge, working experience and the way of thinking of some of the world's first-rate scientists, but also made many friends, whose personalities, charm and role models deeply influenced the later half of my life. Here I would like to mention three individuals.

First was Paolo. Paolo Palazzi gave me hands-on guidance at work, and also introduced me to the subtleties and intricacies of social life in the west. There is one story that is just unforgettable. It happened in May 1981, when we went to a meeting in Bologna, Italy. As I did not understand Italian, Paolo offered to take me along in a car, starting from Geneva. Just as we were about to depart, he received news that his father was terminally sick in Trieste, Italy. He had to arrange to let me go by train, and drove to Trieste to see his father. Just then, Bologna had an earthquake, and the train station was damaged. Unfortunately Paolo's father died. So, Paolo drove from Trieste to Bologna to help me settle down and then went back to Trieste again to handle the funeral for his father. The back and forth trip was over one thousand kilometers. I thanked him profusely, and he said that he had to keep his promise. I remember his words clearly to this day.

Second was Reinhold Hohbach. He was a German and worked as an engineer at CERN, living in a place not far from our apartment. It was a half-hour walk from where we lived to CERN, so I often just took the walk to work, getting some exercise and saving some bus fare at the same time. Hohbach also had the same habit, so we often came across each other on the road. We would walk together and chat, and slowly became good friends. One day, he invited me to spend a weekend at his Jura mountain country house. That country house was located in the French countryside about two hundred kilometers west of Geneva. Some would say, if you want to understand Chinese paintings, you would have to go up the Huangshan (Yellow) Mountain. After coming back from that country house, I would share my strong opinion with others that if you want to understand painters like Van Gogh, Monet, and Renault, you must go to the Jura mountains. Those layers of mountains were all covered with bright green grass, on top of which there were cows grazing leisurely, with bells hanging on their necks. Country cottages were dotted around, with their chimneys blowing thin smoke into the air under the blue sky and white clouds. However, in winter, the mountains were covered with snow, and the roads were difficult to drive through. A few days before Christmas in 1980, we went up the mountains to take a vacation. Halfway on the mountain it snowed hard, with snow flakes as large as bird feathers, and the visibility dropped down to a few meters. Our car slowly crawled along the winding mountain road. Suddenly we saw a car that had broken down in front of us, and Hohbach stopped his car to check the situation. A minute later, Hohbach told us, "You wait in the car. I will leave the engine on so that you will get heat. I will go and help them." He crawled under their car and worked for more than half an hour in the bitter cold. When he came back, his coat was full of ice, face had turned red, hands were frozen stiff, and mouth was lost for words. He picked up a gasoline reserve tank, returned to the other car, and topped it up for them. Only after all this did he say to us; "I'm sorry for keeping you waiting." At that time, I was so moved by what I saw that I was speechless. Later, I asked him: "Why go all this way to help others?" He replied: "It is the Lord." He was a devout Christian. When he visited Beijing, it happened to be a Sunday. As soon as he got off the plane he asked me to take him straight to a church. I am a non-believer. However, many good people that I know are believers. It makes me think, is that the power of belief and religion?

The third person is Sally Alderson. She is an English lady. One day, I was going to a church to attend a free concert. That church was located in

Geneva's Old Town, where the streets have a lot of twists and turns. All the road signs were in French. I lost my way. At this time, I saw a lady holding a concert flyer like mine, so I asked her for directions. She was Sally Alderson, and we thus got to know each other. It turned out that she had been a BBC reporter and was now a freelance writer. Her husband was the president of a big company, who had just returned from a business trip to China. At that time in Switzerland, there were very few people from China, so she invited me to her house, and later we became good friends. Sally and her husband had both graduated from the University of Cambridge. They were the kind of people who had both money and a good education. We talked very congenially, and their whole family liked me. When I told them that I was an listener of the BBC "Follow Me" program, Sally said to me: "Your English is not good, I'll be your English teacher now." So, we met once a week to have the English lesson. They also liked to listen to me talking about China's customs, historical anecdotes and the like. From my interactions with them, I realized that learning a language was not too difficult, the real difficulty was in learning the culture. One must understand British history and culture, in order to truly master the language. She published some stories about me in newspapers and magazines. In 1985, before I went back to China, I held a farewell party with approximately 80 people participating. The party was full of warmth and friendship, which moved Sally deeply. So she wrote up a report, and published it in a famous newspaper, causing a sensation. At that time, China was not so open, so she used my pseudonym in the report. They were the first foreign couple who visited my small and shabby residence in Beijing. It was they who taught me that nothing was more important than the truth. One could have different opinions but should not hide or change the facts. It was the most important thing that I learned from interacting with them. At that time, credit cards were accepted in most parts of the world. Sally's husband told me: "I believe that China will one day have credit cards, too. By then, China would become a great economic power in the world." I truly admire his vision.

In my interactions with Sally, there was one thing that I will remember for a lifetime. My brother Jimin worked at the Shanghai Culture and History Museum, where he met Gu Gaodi, the father of the famous Chinese pianist Gu Shengying. Gu Gaodi got involved in the political case of Pan Hannian, for which he was sent to Xinjiang to do hard labor. After the end of the Cultural Revolution, Gu was rehabilitated back to Shanghai to work at the Culture and History Museum. However, by that time, he was terminally ill. Gu told my brother repeatedly that his last wish was to listen to the piano tune that his daughter Gu Shengying played at the 14th International Music Competition held in Geneva in 1958, for which she won the highest award in the piano category. During the Cultural Revolution, all the relevant records of audio and video materials were destroyed in a frenzy to clean up anything "feudal, bourgeoisie and revisionist." My brother knew that I was in Geneva, so he sought my help to find the recording of this music piece, in order to satisfy the last wish of this terminally sick old man. Gu Shengying was admitted into the Shanghai Symphony Orchestra at the age of 17, held a solo performance at 18, took part in the Sixth World Youth Festival Piano Competition held in Moscow, winning a gold medal, and won another major prize in the International Piano Competition held in Belgium in 1964. However, such a piano genius was cruelly persecuted during the Cultural Revolution. On January 31, 1967, Gu Shengying, then 30, co-signed a suicide note with her 54-year-old mother and 28-year-old brother, and they killed themselves by turning on the gas. It was not until January of 1979 that they were rehabilitated, cleared of all crimes against the people. When the fatal incident happened, Gu Shengying's father was far away in Xinjiang, so he did not know that his whole family had perished. He learned about this huge tragedy when he returned to Shanghai. No wonder he fell critically ill. After hearing the sad story from my brother, I made up my mind to ask Sally to help. She contacted the Geneva radio station. The staff there were all moved by the story. They took pains to go through many tapes accumulated over the years, and finally found a recording of the live performance of the competition. In fact, when Gu Shengying participated in the 14th Geneva International Music Competition in 1958, she won the highest award in women's piano, tying at second place, because there was no first place designated. When these tapes reached Gu Gaodi, he heard the music and the thunderous applause, then finally closed his eyes peacefully for the last time.

Between 4 and 7 May 1981, the Eighty-Seventh Engineering Command of the State Science and Technology Commission and the

Physics and Mathematic Departments of the Chinese Academy of Sciences jointly held a "Yuquan Road High-Energy Physics Research Base Program Adjustment Convention." At the convention, it was decided that we would build a 2.2 GeV electron-positron collider and cancel the plan for the construction of the 50 GeV proton accelerator. More detailed preparatory meetings were scheduled for September 22 to 25, 1982. The convention decided to immediately recall those of us who were studying or working overseas to take part in the work on the electron-positron collider. At that time, my Monte Carlo program for the CDHS was completed, and new experiments were about to start. The Monte Carlo simulation results had to be compared with experimental data, in order to further improve the procedure. Professor Steinberger hoped that I could stay and continue my work, to be paid by CERN. The other two would return on time. This proposal immediately met with vehement opposition from the Chinese Representatives' Office in Geneva. A lot of small reports about me had already been made to the representatives' office, charging me with no respect for the organization, no discipline, going around by myself, and not returning home at night. I was originally intended for early "repatriation," and now that I wanted to be left here "alone," it just could not be allowed. I almost became a suspect for betraying my country at any minute. Steinberger was very upset, and he called up T.D. Lee to explain the situation. Lee talked it over with the authorities in China. Just a couple of days before I was about to go back to China, the representatives' office suddenly notified me that I was allowed to stay for three more months. At the same time, the period of stay of the head of my group was also extended by three months, with expenses paid by the Chinese government. The representatives' office also informed me that regardless of how much CERN was going to pay me, my living allowance would remain the same, and I would have to handle over the excess part to the Chinese government. If I agreed, then I would be allowed to stay; if not, I would have to return to China immediately. I agreed on the spot. I understood the good intentions behind such an arrangement. In fact, the idea of defection did not even come up in my mind. The new issue was with paying the Chinese government the excess money. We were living on a total allowance of about 1,000 Swiss francs per month. CERN colleagues all knew that we earned less, so whenever we had a gathering, they would not ask us to pay. But if I got paid by CERN, which offered 3,500 Swiss francs, I could no longer allow my colleagues to pay my share, yet I would have to hand over 2,500 Swiss francs to China. So I told Steinberger that I did not need so much, just 1,000 Swiss francs would do. Steinberger felt it strange, and questioned me repeatedly, I had to tell him the truth. The result was that I also made the mistake of "leaking inside secrets". At that time, things became very complicated indeed. The CERN accounting made the point that they "do not need to pay taxes to the Chinese," but the minimum wage in Switzerland for summer students was 2,000 francs a month, anything less would violate Swiss laws. Finally, CERN decided to pay me 2,000 francs a month, and I would have to declare to CERN that I would get all this money; however, I also had to promise the Institute of High Energy Physics that I would handover any extra money above my Chinese standard. At that time, under China's economic conditions, Chinese personnel abroad lived frugally, and most of them would buy "eight pieces" of electronic and electric appliances with their saved money when they returned to China. I just bought my beloved camera. The 2,000 Swiss francs, starting from me, became the standard wage paid to Chinese scientists working at CERN. The practice of "handling over excess pay to the state" was implemented for a long time in China, and IHEP was no exception. If a Chinese personnel was paid by a foreign institution, he or she had to give up the excess payment, or the bonus payment for the entire home research group would be taken away as punishment. In the case of a graduate student, he or she would not be allowed to graduate. Such a policy had some bad consequences. My own behavior in violation of the rules and regulations was recorded into my "file," one point being that I made contact with many "non-work-related" persons, in addition to my association with work-related persons. In 1983, when I applied to go abroad for the second time, my "political certification" was not approved for quite some time. Finally, I made inquiries with an old lady, a veteran cadre in charge of the political certification process, who told me the problems with my files. She took up the issues with the Representatives' Office in Geneva, and believed that those were actually trivial issues, showing her reasonable judgment. So I got the permission to go abroad again. Of course, in 1983 China's political climate was quite different from it was in 1979. Now think about it, "going around in group of three," "no going out alone," "no contact with people outside the scope of work" and such regulations all sound ludicrous, but at that time, the violation of these regulations constituted "political problems" for which clandestine reports were made against me! Nowadays, my "secret files" have long become testimonies for the shameful "informer" network and old policies.

Between 1980 and 1982, CERN finalized a plan to build a 90GeV Large Electron-Positron Collider (LEP), and formed the ALEPH experiment group. The ALEPH group was based on the expansion of the CDHS group to which I was previously assigned. During my extended stay, Steinberger and I discussed the possibility of the Beijing Institute of High Energy Physics (IHEP) participating in the ALEPH Group. At that time, I was just a junior scientist in IHEP with little say, but I agreed to try when I got back to China. Steinberger asked Professor Saulan Wu of Wisconsin University to help me. Unexpectedly, the ALEPH collaboration project became the pinnacle work of my career.

6.4 International cooperation

When I returned to the Institute of High Energy Physics, the atmosphere was completely different from what I imagined. The main task of IHEP was constructing Beijing's own electron-positron collider and getting the Beijing spectrometer ready. At that time, I knew of a member of the Chinese Academy of Sciences, Professor Xiao Jian, who was supervising a graduate student in porting a computer program on a Romanian computer. I recommended a CERN computer program to Professor Xiao that could more effectively accomplish the porting work, and also recommended the CERN libraries that could help his student to finish his work faster and quicker. Furthermore, I also helped IHEP to acquire the entire software package. It was actually very simple: with international cooperation, it all became a matter of course. Starting here, I won Professor Xiao's trust and support. In the high-energy physics community in China, the Chinese-American Nobel Laureate Professor Samuel Ting had a pivotal position and influence. Another academy member in IHEP who collaborated closely with Ting was also a "big guy," who also held influential positions in the government and especially in the communist party of China. When I put forward a proposal to IHEP for establishing the ALEPH collaboration, I met fierce opposition from him. He gave three major reasons for his objection. Firstly, IHEP was already planning a L3 collaboration with LEP, so there was no need to have another ALEPH collaboration; secondly, if IHEP was to establish an ALEPH collaboration group, there would be no academic "leader," since Wu Weimin was not qualified, and "not even an associate researcher"; thirdly, Professor Samuel Ting was a Chinese-American, to collaborate with him had "political significance." The IHEP should not start another initiative to compete with Ting. At the time, I could not even attend the decision making meetings, so there was no way for me to speak in defense of my proposal. His three reasons seemed to make sense, and confused the thinking of many people. At the time, the director of IHEP was Zhang Wenyu, but due to his advanced age, the Executive Vice-director Zhang Houying was in charge of the administrative work. Indeed, with more than two years of experience working and living outside China, I no longer took seriously the arguments that because I, Wu Weimin, "was not even an associate researcher," I "was not qualified," and that the self-proclaimed "authority" knew best. When Zhang Houying told me about all the negative reasons of the "big guy," I refuted them one by one. I emphasized that Steinberger was a scientist with tremendous international reputation, who had a very close working relationship with Tsung-Dao Lee. ALEPH included many leading energy research institutes in Europe, and joining the ALEPH collaboration could greatly improve the status of China's high energy research. In the meantime, I enlisted the help of Professor Xiao Jian to speak on my behalf at the meetings of the institute, and asked the Executive Deputy Director Zhang Houying to invite Professor Saulan Wu to visit China. I also wrote a report to the Academy of Sciences directly. I was officially attached to Department Two of Physics at the institute, and the director of Department One of Physics, Professor Ye Minghan found me and we had a chat. His remarks gave me great inspiration. He said: "You have to find a way to combine the ALEPH collaboration with the Beijing Spectrometer, then your pursuit would be considered part of the core activities of IHEP."

Prof. Ye's ideas gave me the correct positioning for the ALEPH collaboration, and pointed out the direction for focusing my efforts. Through unremitting insistence, the Chinese Academy of Sciences finally gave approval for IHEP to participate in the ALEPH collaboration in 1983, with a funding of fifty thousand Yuan (RMB) a year for a total of five years, and designated me as the person in charge. This made IHEP one of the earliest members of ALEPH. In order to establish the ALEPH collaboration group in Beijing, I wrote about a dozen reports to the leadership at all levels, from the Academy of Sciences, down to my own research group. The final success was my best reward.

For this collaboration to be truly international, we had to participate in the construction of the ALEPH detector based in China, contributing both to hardware and software. After careful discussion, it was decided that the hardware effort would be the manufacture of the μ meson plastic strip tube detector. The software effort would be to complete the computer program for the μ muon detector, related to the Monte Carlo simulation, as well as particle trace reconstruction. The 1983 ALEPH technical design report stated: Beijing would have the responsibility for the "middle inner corner, and if possible the outer μ muon detectors." It was obvious that the ALEPH collaborators were not sure if Beijing could manufacture such detectors. It meant both pressure and motivation for me. As a first step, ALEPH decided to let Italy supply plastic profiles, and let us gain experience by pulling wires, coating graphite, producing and testing the products, etc. However, just to accomplish this first step, we had to first make a series of machines, create a "clean dust-free workplace," train staff and so on. While we stepped up our efforts in Beijing, I went to the Shanghai Plastics Research Institute, to see if they could make such high precision plastic profiles. There was a major problem that was difficult to solve: our total funding was 250,000 Yuan (RMB). In Shanghai, I asked my sister for help, telling her that this was a high-tech international cooperation. The Shanghai Institute of Plastic Products should not think about profits, or making money, but if they did succeed, the international impact would be very large, with a great promising future. This would be a huge leap for China's plastics industry, from producing daily necessities to developing scientific instruments. With help from the leadership of Shanghai, my sister convinced the Shanghai Plastics Research Institute of the significance of this task. Through their efforts, they built a fully-qualified plastic profile, charging only the bare minimum of cost. After our Italian colleagues checked it, they showed deep admiration for the Institute for producing such a fine plastic profile in such a short time.

In the end, we completed a total of 4,508 strip tubes with a length of four to seven meters, covering 66 large μ muon detectors. We completed the manufacturing of the μ muon detectors on the outer layer of the ALEPH detector on time and with quality. As far as I know, this is so far the largest scale high-energy detectors that China has built for a foreign institution. The ALEPH collaboration group, and especially our Italian colleagues, wrote letters specifically to the Chinese Academy of Sciences to praise and thank us. When Professor Samuel Ting visited the IHEP, I accompanied him to see our "dust-free clean workshop", and the μ meson detectors built by us. He very much appreciated what we had accomplished. In my presence, Ting said to the leader of the L3 project of IHEP, the "authority" who had once claimed that "Wu Weimin is not qualified": "Look at Wu Weimin, what a great job he has done with ALEPH! How about you?!" At that moment, the face of the "authority" blushed and then paled, and he was speechless. I figured that I had the last laugh. Ting also told me to look him up when I went to CERN. Soon enough, we met at CERN, and he invited me to dinner. I sat by his side, with members of the L3 group to accompany us. He chalked out my name on the blackboard in his office, drew a circle around it, and told his group members not to erase it, as he wanted to keep it up for three days.

In fact, Professor Steinberger was the key reason for the collaboration of the ALEPH group with IHEP to have succeeded. His charisma and prestige, as well as his close relationship with Professor T.D. Lee, played a decisive role. Working with Professor Steinberger has been the greatest honor of my life. Professor Steinberger had a special feeling for Chinese people. Steinberger was born in 1921. When he attended Chicago University in 1945, he studied and did research work under the guidance of Enrico Fermi, together with Tsung-Dao Lee, C. N. Yang and others. He often told me that he saw from Lee and Yang the wisdom and talents of the Chinese. He also told me that the collaboration with IHEP was one of the most pleasant things that he did with his life. He personally wrote me a greeting card every year, and I kept every single one of them.

In May 1986, Professor Steinberger and his family visited Beijing. They also visited Shanghai, and met all my family. His youngest son, John, fell in love with China, studied Chinese and became a professor at

Tsinghua University, China, teaching mathematics. During that visit, I also arranged a meeting between C. N. Yang and Steinberger. Steinberger told me that Yang left a deep impression on him when he studied at University of Chicago. Unfortunately, because of his close relationship with Tsung-Dao Lee who was also working at Columbia University, he and Yang became somewhat estranged for some years. This meeting fulfilled Steinberger's long-cherished wish to make up with Yang. Among many of Steinberger's touching stories, one was particularly memorable. On the night of August 13, 1989, a Chinese engineer from IHEP working at CERN had a heart attack, and was sent to a hospital for emergency care. At the time, the insurance coverage of the engineer was from Italy, so the hospital wanted to transfer him to Italy. Professor Steinberger strongly disagreed, and he talked with the hospital, CERN and the Italian insurance company to work out a satisfactory solution. He visited that Chinese colleague daily, even on the weekends, and left his phone number with the doctors in charge, telling them to contact him directly for anything, until the Chinese colleague returned to China safely. The care Steinberger showed to an ordinary worker moved many people.

The successful collaboration between IHEP and ALEPH had much significance and saw many innovations:

(1) It established a new model of international cooperation. Typically, international cooperation requires that each member provide a certain amount of funding. The total cost of the ALEPH project exceeded more than 60 million Swiss francs. IHEP obtained 250,000 Yuan (RMB), and later, another 250,000 Yuan (RMB) from the Natural Science Foundation of China, for a total of half a million Yuan (RMB), equivalent to half a million Swiss francs. This level of funding can appear trivial compared with the 60 million total. However, our real contribution was far more than the half a million Yuan could reflect. If those μ meson plastic strip tube detectors were built in Italy, how much money would it have cost? At least three million Swiss francs. "In-kind contribution" became a new way for figuring out the contribution of the collaborating parties. Afterwards, this model was used by the Chinese to participate in many international collaborations.

(2) The ALEPH collaboration trained many researchers for China, especially for IHEP. Altogether, close to 100 Chinese personnel studied and worked at ALEPH, many of whom became the backbone of IHEP and many Chinese universities. In the leadership teams at various levels from the Chinese Academy of Sciences, the departments of IHEP, down to individual research groups, there were former members of ALEPH.

(3) The success of the collaboration between IHEP and the ALEPH group in producing μ meson plastic strip tube detectors established reputation for IHEP. In subsequent collaborations with the United States and CERN in the CMS project, IHEP still took on the task of building μ muon detectors as an extension of our previous work. In fact, the success in the research and development of the plastic profiles brought about profit for the involved plastic product research institute later. I heard that an engineer who worked for ALEPH at IHEP made a fortune by founding a plastic instrument factory using techniques acquired in the process.

(4) The collaboration contributed greatly to the construction of the Beijing Spectrometer (BES), especially on the software side. As Prof. Ye pointed out, ALEPH and BES both won.

As a result of collaboration with ALEPH, an e-mail message was generated, certified to be the first of its kind in Chinese Internet history by the official Chinese network administration center — this was the e-mail that I sent to Steinberger on August 25th, 1986, marking the entry of China into the Internet era.

Looking back on what I got involved with in my life, some things sound great, for example, China's first atomic bomb, the first Chinese artificial satellite, the Beijing Spectrometer, etc. However, I was merely a participant in those events. The ALEPH collaboration, though, was not in the same category. I was universally recognized as the initiator, leader, organizer and implementer. In Steinberger's words, I was the "brain and spine" of the collaboration between ALEPH and IHEP. It is fitting to describe this success as the pinnacle of my life.

6.5 The Beijing spectrometer

The China of 1984 was a thriving scene. With Hu Yaobang as the conscience and Zhao Ziyang as the brain of the Communist Party, they acted as the right-hand men of Deng Xiaoping. He is known as the chief architect of reform and opening up. His policies were received favorably by the people. At that time, the non-Communist Professor Ye Minghan was appointed as the director of IHEP, adopting a "director responsibility" system. Professor Ye was a classmate of T.D. Lee in the National Southwest Associated Universities days. He was one of the groundbreaking members for Chinese cosmic rays and high-energy physics research. In addition to his academic achievements, Professor Ye was good at using the right person for the right job. It was a wise decision for Ye to appoint Zheng Zhipeng as the director of the Beijing Spectrometer research group. Zheng Zhipeng came from a scholarly family, was a top graduate from the University of Science and Technology of China. Zheng was selected by Professor Samuel Ting to go to Germany to take part in his Mark J experiment, and he accumulated a wealth of experience. I think that Zheng, at the prime of his life, was the best possible choice for directing the Beijing Spectrometer research group. Ye used Zheng to replace an older person with higher seniority, someone with more political backing. That important decision was made by overcoming secular bias and prejudices. At the time, my position was attached to Department Two of Physics. Professor Ye told me that he wanted to invite me to participate in the Beijing Spectrometer work. At that time, I had some concerns about possible adverse effect on the ALEPH collaboration work, so I did not agree immediately. Later, Ye talked to me again, suggesting that I would still be in charge of the ALEPH collaboration, and at the same time, serve as the Deputy Director of the Beijing Spectrometer Laboratory, combining the two activities. I then agreed. Later, I learned that my appointment as the Deputy Director of the Beijing Spectrometer research laboratory caused a lot of controversy while it was being discussed at a working meeting of the IHEP leadership. Many members of the party committee regarded me as "politically unsound." However, at that time, the "director responsibility" system was in effect, so at the insistence of

Director Ye, I was appointed as Deputy Director. I was very appreciative of Ye's trust in my ability. Additionally, with his strong recommendation, I was promoted to Associate Researcher as an exceptional case. It was by no means an easy step in IHEP, where there were many strong candidates but the positions were limited, and the competition was intense.

It was the first time after the Cultural Revolution that senior academic positions were conferred on practicing scientists, and as a result, I became one of the youngest Associate Researchers in China.

It was my good fortune and the honor of a lifetime to have been able to work with Professor Ye.

Director Zheng Zhipeng assigned to me the responsibility of online/offline systems and international collaboration. Because we combined the ALEPH collaboration with the Beijing Spectrometer, both of which involved collisions between electrons and positrons, we could use the same software package as the framework for both. Much of the experience acquired through ALEPH could be used on the Beijing Spectrometer. Two group leaders for the online/offline systems were very capable, so my job was not really difficult, and our work proceeded smoothly. On October 16, 1988, the Beijing Electron-Positron Collider achieved collisions between electrons and positrons. After some test runs, various components of the Beijing Spectrometer started to work. We first observed Bhabha Scattering, and data acquisition and event reconstruction procedures also worked properly. In this energy region, however, we should have been able to observe J/ψ particles, but the signals just did not occur. Directors Ye Minghan and Zheng Zhipeng were both worried. Director Zheng decided that the director, deputy director and group leaders for the Beijing Spectrometer should work in shifts to identify the problems and find the causes. On the night of June 22, 1989, the online group leader Zhang Changchun and I were on duty. We found no problem with the energy of the accelerator, the measuring procedure, data collection and so on. Where was the problem then? We called Director Zheng into the duty room, asking him to check and adjust the energy of the Electron-Positron Collider once more with the help of the workers on duty at the accelerator. Zhang Changchun was a very experienced physicist, and he knew the trigger system very well. He thought that the crux of the problem was that the shower counter was not working properly, so it was unable to produce the trigger signals for recording the J/ψ particles. The main reason for the shower counter not working properly was that the high electric voltage did not reach a certain working point. I asked him why he did not apply the right high voltage, and he told me that the quality of the shower counter was not good enough, hence, applying high voltage could cause burning of electrical wires. Therefore, the shower counter was never in a normal working status. At that time, an independent research group was responsible for each of the sub-detectors. Nobody wanted any problem with the part for which he or she was responsible. So nobody wanted the responsibility of damaging a detector even if it meant that the signals for the J/ψ particles could not be observed. I said that the Beijing Spectrometer was not built for display purpose. It would simply be a waste of everybody's time if the trigger system did not work properly. I told Zhang Changchun to apply the high voltage needed, and that I would be held responsible for any problem encountered. Zhang carefully increased the voltage to full working point, and the shower counter reached a normal working status. Signals for J/ψ particles began to appear in the on-line display line on the screen, and later, there were more and more signals. Zheng Zhipeng had a lot of experience, and after further discussion with us, confirmed that these were indeed signals for the J/ψ particles. We printed out figures for several events observed. The online data acquisition system recorded the signals for J/ψ particles observed for the first time with the Beijing Spectrometer. I drafted a news report on a big piece of red paper. The second day, the whole of IHEP was jubilant. In the land of China, we had observed J/ψ particle signals for the first time. I wrote up a report that was posted on the IHEP briefing. The experiment log book of the Beijing Spectrometer Laboratory contained my personal note about the first observation of the signals for J/ψ particles, which constituted a highlight in my life.

On October 24, 1988, Deng Xiaoping and other party and state leaders visited the Beijing Electron-Positron Collider site and met with representatives of participants in the collider project. Mr. Deng made an important speech titled "China must have a place in the high-tech field." He then came to see the Beijing Spectrometer, when I was standing by the detector to welcome the visitors.

When Deng Xiaoping came up to me, I was excited and stretched out my hand. Deng smiled and extended his hand, too, and we shook hands firmly. His hands were warm and powerful. Deng had said his health had no major problems. Indeed, it was all true. At that time, I felt very excited and proud. Deng Xiaoping was a great man. He said something that impressed me deeply. Deng said that Mao's mistakes were not all his personal responsibility, and that the party as a whole was also to blame. It was the party that had pushed him into this position. With the restraint of a good system, a bad leader would find it hard to do bad things; and without a good system, a good person might be tempted to do bad things. His remarks poignantly demonstrated the key to understanding how the communist party had committed all sorts of mistakes over the decades. A party should have a good charter, and a state should have a constitution that can be followed. The Party General Secretary Hu Yaobang was forced to resign in a "family meeting," non-existent in the party's charter. That was an example of the party operating without a good system.

Let me cite one of my personal experiences. In 1986, CERN, UNESCO and the Italian International Center for Theoretical Physics jointly organized an international microprocessor school. This school was held once each in Italy and in Sri Lanka. The leaders of the school approached me to ask if it could be held in China. I thought that this was a good idea. It did not need funding from the Chinese government, but it would strengthen international exchanges with the participation of a lot of Chinese students. As a result, I wrote a report to the Chinese Academy of Sciences, and submitted an application. However, I underestimated the complexity of the problem. I reckoned that all the instruments, equipments, faculty and funds were provided by foreign sources, and that the Chinese hosts only needed to provide a place, classrooms, services, and some organizational work. Was it not simple? I contacted many universities in Beijing, but had only lukewarm support. Then, I thought of Professor Fang Lizhi in the Chinese University of Science and Technology. Before that, I did not know Fang personally. When I told him about it, he was very supportive. Together, we organized a very successful session of the third international microprocessor school in Hefei, China. The Director of the computing Division from CERN was the president of the school, and Fang and I served as vice presidents. Really, it was a very ordinary work arrangement, but in 1987, the trouble came.

Starting from the end of 1986, student demonstrations appeared from many universities nationwide. It was regarded as the result of "bourgeois liberalization." Fang Lizhi and others were expelled from the party. The party general secretary, Hu Yaobang, was regarded as ineffective against the "bourgeois liberalization," and was forced to step down. A nationwide campaign was launched against the so-called "bourgeois liberalization" and "spiritual pollution." IHEP was no exception. Some political cadres were jubilant and congratulated themselves. The careers of those party functionaries depended on persecuting people and engaging in "political movements." At a meeting for cadres with ranks above laboratory directors, the party branch secretary exorbitantly asked everyone to make a "statement," which was nothing more than saying something nasty about Hu Yaobang, Fang Lizhi and others. I sat in a corner of the room, keeping silent. The "branch secretary" singled me out, and said: "Wu, you were usually very articulate, why have you become dumb today?" "I have nothing to say," I responded. She would not give up. "You have a special relationship with Fang Lizhi. Can you talk about what kind of relationship it is?" I got angry at what she said. "What kind of relationship? A working relationship! Why don't you go and investigate it?"

I knew that there were ulterior motives in what she said. During the period from 1984 to 1987, I made presentations titled "Revalue Capitalism." The presentations were organized by the Western Returned Scholars Association, and my ideas were based on my personal experiences and observations overseas. Many ideas of Marx and Lenin were formulated decades ago, how could they remain correct forever without any modifications? The rationale behind my presentation was very simple: capitalism underwent development over a couple of hundred years, and is constantly correcting itself. I used several real-life examples and data to introduce the labor system, welfare, taxation, health insurance, retirement, inheritance, social relationships, legislation, social structure, voting and other aspects in various countries in Europe. My presentation found warm reception, and was made into an article and published in the *Economics Daily* in four serials at the recommendation and invitation of many listeners. At a system reform meeting at IHEP, I proposed that at the level of research laboratories, the position of the party branch secretary should be held by an active researcher. There would be no more full-time political officers. The canteens, medical services and nurseries should all be commercialized. Those proposals were all gradually implemented over the years, but at that time, they infringed on the interests of many people. No wonder those people were so happy when they heard about the movement against the "bourgeois liberalism." Asking me to account for my relationship with Fang Lizhi was just an excuse. Later, the party committee specifically asked me to make a written report of my relationship with Fang Lizhi, but fortunately it all came to nothing when the party general secretary Zhao Ziyang issued an instruction that the "anti-bourgeois liberalization" campaign should not be expanded in its scope. However, Zhao Ziyang himself got into even bigger trouble for his stand in the matter. In China, there were a group of political officers whose only specialty was to persecute people and engage in "political movements." In my opinion, if there was such a thing as a "destabilizing factor" in China, it was the existence of such people and such positions. If society were stable, they would have nothing to do. Therefore, it was in their interest to stir things up to justify their own existence. I really like a saying from the party general secretary Hu Jintao: "No toss!" He meant that the party should not create trouble where there wasn't any. When could the communist party learn to have no tosses? There is a huge difference between a full-time party branch secretary and a party branch secretary who is also an active researcher. If they engage in active research work, they would be too busy to stir up unnecessary trouble, and from my observation, things usually went smoothly under their leadership. On the other hand, units with full-time grass-root party branch secretaries tend to be the source of trouble themselves. I am happy to see that nowadays, many grass-root party branch secretaries are active researchers. The party secretary for IHEP was an expert in high-energy physics, which was an important change.

Finally, I would like to end this subsection by talking about the annual meeting of the European High-Energy Physics Society held at the end of June 1987 in Uppsala, Sweden. Uppsala is a university town on the Scandinavian Peninsula. Uppsala University was founded in 1477, and has a long history. The annual meeting of the European High-Energy Physics Society was a major event for researchers in high-energy physics from Europe and perhaps from the entire world. On May 6, 1986, the full installation of the BEPC project started. The meeting invited Director Ye Minghan to talk about the status of the BEPC/BES. Director Ye was at Beijing, far away from Uppsala, and the timeframe to apply for a visa was tight. At the time, I happened to be at CERN, so Prof. Ye asked me to represent him and deliver the presentation. He supplied me with the status and information about BEPC/BES. I felt very nervous. Although I had made many conference presentations before, this time was different. This time, I would have to make a presentation at the plenary session before more than 1,000 people, among whom there were research institute directors, eminent scientists, as well as a number of Nobel Prize winners, and I was there to represent the China Institute of High-Energy Physics. When the chairman of the organizing committee called me on stage, my heart was beating fast and hard. I took to the podium, dressed sharp, with a blue striped tie. My first slide was the Beijing Electron-Positron Collider with a diameter of only two hundred meters. I talked about its basic parameters, and then superimposed a slide of the 27-kilometer circumference of the LEP, highlighted as a large circle on the BES in a 1: 1 ratio. I said that the BES was the LEP's tiny little brother. Later on, I superimposed a picture of the earth reduced many times onto the LEP, such that LEP could hardly be seen. Then I made the remark that we were all members of a global village, coming together for a common goal. Applause erupted in the hall, lasting several minutes. What I talked about afterwards I do not remember anymore. When I stepped off the podium amid enthusiastic applause from the audience, Nobel Laureate Mohammad Abdus Salam, CERN's Director-General Herwig Schopper, the US Fermilab director, Nobel Laureate Leon Lederman and others stood up and shook my hand, congratulating me. My professor from Fudan University, Guang-Jiong Ni, also happened to be present at the meeting. He excitedly told me afterwards: "I took note of the time. The applause you got was longer than anyone else's. Your sense of humor and power of expression conquered the audience." He later wrote me a recommendation letter for membership to the Chinese Center of Advanced

Science and Technology (CCAST), in which he specifically cited that presentation. With the recommendation of Ye, Steinberger, Ni and others, and approval by Professor T.D. Lee, I became one of the first group of members of CCAST. After the meeting, a Scandinavian television station made a special report about my presentation. I think this was the only time in my life that I represented IHEP and gave a presentation at an international conference. I knew that the heartwarming applause was not just for me, but for China, too. With the BEPC/BES, China had officially joined the high-energy club, becoming one of this big family. China no longer claimed to be "the center of world revolution," but had started to merge into this historical trend of globalization, and the world embraced a new, open China that stood tall in the East.

6.6 China's first e-mail

Early in 2000, I was in the United States. I came across an article published in a local Chinese newspaper, titled "All the Firsts in China's Internet." It mentioned that "on September 20, 1987, a Mr. Qian Tianbai had sent an email "through the Great Wall, to the world", from China to Karlsruhe University, Germany." It went on to claim that Mr. Qian Tianbai was the founder of China's e-mail system. Later, I saw more articles declaring that Mr Qian Tianbai was the father of China's Internet. This piece of news made me embark on a tortuous journey to find the facts to recover the historical truth behind the matter. I clearly remember that in the summer of 1986, I had sent an e-mail to Steinberger in Geneva, Switzerland, and that we had used the same line to transmit data for the Beijing ALEPH project. However, I had not realized then that I was the first person in China to send an e-mail. After reading the newspaper article, I thought that if Mr. Qian Tianbai was considered the "first" on September 20, 1987, we were one year earlier, so we must be the true first. However, it was not until recently, on March 12, 2010, that the China Internet Network Information Center (CNNIC) officially confirmed that my email to Steinberger was the first in the history of the development of China's Internet. It was nine years from when I read the newspaper in 2000. The CNNIC was established on June 3, 1997 as a management and service organization, authorized by relevant national authorities to function as the national Internet network information center in China. In its description of the Chinese Internet history, it stated:

(1) At 4:11:24 of Geneva time (11:11:24 of Beijing time) on August 25, 1986, Wu Weimin from Institute of High Energy Physics of Chinese Academy of Sciences used a IBM-PC at Beijing Information Control Institute (No.710 Institute) to remotely log into the account of Wang Shuqin on a machine VXCRNA located in CERN of Geneva via the satellite link, and sent an email to Steinberger located in Geneva.
(2) In September 1987, with the help of the research group led by Professor Werner Zorn from Karlsruhe University of Germany, Professor Wang Yunfeng and Doctor Li Chengjiong, etc., set up an email node at Institute of Computer Application (ICA) in Beijing, and successfully sent an email to Germany on September 20. The content of this email was "Across the Great Wall we can reach every corner in the world"

In 1986 in China, people did not understand the importance of e-mail and the Internet. When we sent the email, we did not expect the whole thing to become so important. After being recognized as the first email user in China a variety of media interviewed me. Many newspapers, magazines, television and other media outlets made reports about it. In particular, the *New Beijing Newspaper* published a lengthy article — "Looking for the first Chinese Internet user" — arousing the interest of many readers. Therefore, I would like to review some of the little-known history.

In 1984, IHEP had no advanced computer. When we designed the Beijing Spectrometer and did the Monte Carlo simulation, we borrowed computing time on an M160 Japanese computer at the Hydropower Academy located at Mushudi, Beijing. That machine was imported from Japan because the Hydropower Academy had a collaboration project with a Japanese institution. The Institute of High-Energy Physics was located on Yuquan Road, quite far away from Mushudi. Regardless of wind and rain, we would walk and then take a bus to reach Mushudi, a journey of at least one hour. It occurred to me that when I worked on a computer, all I needed were a keyboard for input and a display terminal. Where the computer was located was not important. In any case, the computer was connected to the keyboard and display by electrical wires which might be either long or short. What if I used a wireless connection? Would it work if I, the keyboard and display were located at IHEP on Yuquan Road, and the computer itself was located at the Hydropower Academy at Mushudi? It was a simple idea. When I attended T.D. Lee's lectures, one of his sayings left a deep impression on me. He said, "Important things are often simple. The most important thing is often the simplest." To separate man and machine was a most important and simple thing. In 1971, in a windowless room in Cambridge, Massachusetts, a bearded computer scientist, Ray Tomlinson, hunched over two large computers, trying to send the world's first e-mail. He just wanted to send one message from one computer to another. One of the most important but also the simplest of ideas was to link one machine up with another. He did it. Tomlinson's first e-mail only traveled a hundred yards, from a BBN-TENEXB computer to a second computer, BBN-TENEXA. But this was the first time information was transmitted between two completely different computers, giving rise to the Internet's predecessor — the ARPANET. If I had any important innovation to my credit in my life, it would be this most important and simple idea, to link up an input keyboard and a display terminal located at one place to a computer located at another place, through wireless transmission, creating a wireless remote terminal. At the time, the idea was mine alone, since I had not heard of anyone else doing the same thing. Indeed, without the idea of a remote terminal and remote login, there would have been no first e-mail in 1986. If someone asked me what was my life's most creative contribution was, my answer would be: "a wireless remote terminal." This wireless remote terminal allowed the computer to be treated as a separate entity, physically isolated from the human operator. It was an innovation at the time, just like in 1971, when the linking up of two large computers by Ray Tomlinson was an innovation. One of these two innovations set man and machine apart, and the other one connected machine to machine. What appear to be such simple ideas nowadays were innovations at the time.

The 90J project that I led won the National Science Conference Award. However, in my opinion, the 90J project was far less significant than the creation of the remote terminal. Fortunately, the e-mail that I sent through in 1986 using the remote terminal was acknowledged to be the first event in the history of the development of the Chinese Internet officially and in popular media. That was enough credit for the remote terminal project indirectly.

I remain deeply grateful to Mr. Xiao Jian for his role in developing the remote terminal. At the time, I was just an insignificant nobody, with neither the power nor the position to realize my idea.

Without the support of Mr. Xiao, my idea would have remained just an idea. Even my early idea about particles and electricity would have done better, for I wrote an article titled "On Zi and Dian." Luckily, when I told Mr. Xiao my idea, he was very encouraging. Right away, he climbed on top of the IHEP building with me to survey the landscape. At that time, Beijing hardly had any high-rise buildings, and the landscape was flat all the way from IHEP to the Hydropower Academy. It looked like God was on my side.

With the support of Mr. Xiao, we enlisted the help of an engineer who was familiar with communication protocols from the computer division. We also obtained some funding for the project.

Technically speaking, to create a remote terminal was very simple, but the problem was with bureaucracy. To reduce noise, it was best to use microwave communication, and an application for an appropriate wavelength channel must be applied, which needed to be approved by the State Radio Communication Commission. To purchase relevant wireless equipment, we had to seek permission from the Public Security Bureau. I wrote countless applications, and finally everything was ready to go. Then, a completely unexpected complication arose. It turned out that although it was mostly flat land between IHEP and the Hydropower Academy, the signals had to pass through a very sensitive area, with some army headquarters, as well as residences for many senior generals. Thus, we had to prove that the electromagnetic waves generated by our wireless link would not affect their communications, nor compromise their health. They could not go by our word, and we had to prove it via experiments. This in turn caused a few weeks of delay.

On July 1, 1984, the remote terminal was officially ready for work. I reported the event in the IHEP newsletter, published in the 10th issue on July 23, 1984. After I talked about the event with the National Internet

Network Information Center, the original version of their Internet history in China included the wireless remote terminal as the first item. When this event was discussed at subsequent committee meetings, I was asked to supply details of the equipment used, wavelength, communication protocols and so on. The IHEP newsletter did not provide sufficient information. Because I moved to the United States, and nobody at IHEP was interested in pursuing the matter after several years, I had to give up the official credit. After Xiao passed away, I wrote a special commemorative article published in the journal *High-energy Physics*, which gave a detailed account of this matter. Mr. Xiao's support was crucial. Especially memorable was the fact that when we tried to reach the rooftop, the door was closed. Xiao and I had to go through a window to climb to the top. It was a touching action on his part.

The remote terminal solved the problem of accessing the computer, but I had not thought about e-mail and data transmission yet until 1986, when Steinberger said "Weimin, you made a μ muon detector for ALEPH, now is time to seriously consider analyzing the data in China." To this end, it was essential to link the computer network in Beijing with that of CERN. He asked me and Paolo to form a joint working group to solve this problem. Paolo would be responsible for the CERN side, and I for the Chinese side. On June 17, 1986, Dr Fluckiger from the computer center at CERN wrote to Mr. Boesz of the Vienna radio station to inquire about the possibility of renting a satellite communication line between Beijing and Vienna. This line had just become available to users on June 1 of the same year. On June 27, 1986, Dr. Fluckiger wrote us a memo providing two pieces of very important information. Firstly, the Beijing Institute of Information Control (also known as the 710 Institute) was the interface of this line in Beijing. Secondly, the Swiss Bureau of Telecommunication (Swisscom) was interested to supply TELEPAC to users as a server. TELEPAC was already in use by CERN for data transmission. Thus, Paolo and his colleagues in Geneva were making arrangements with Swisscom and the Vienna radio station. In Beijing, Wang Shuqin and I were contacting the 710 Institute. We also bought some necessary equipment. Director Ye Minghan paid close attention to every step of the work, giving us the green light all the way. At that time, our remote terminal interface was still on the M160 computer of the Hydropower Academy located at Mushudi. In order to save time, we decided to use an IBM-PC computer from the 710 Institute to transmit data from Beijing to Vienna via a satellite link through the Vienna radio station, then to Swisscom, and finally to CERN. On August 11, 1986, we began the data transmission test with multi-lines, and multi-interfaces.

If any one part had a problem, the entire contact would fail. After more than two weeks of hard work we finally succeeded. On August 25, 1986, Swiss time 4:11:24, I used the the IBM-PC in the Beijing 710 Institute and was able to login remotely to the account of Wang Shuqin on a VXCRNA computer at CERN in Geneva through several nodes on the ground plus the satellite link. I sent an e-mail to Steinberger in Geneva. Because of the slow connection speed, after I typed in a letter, it took quite a while to show up on the display screen. Due to my excitement and haste because of the high communication cost, the resulting email contained many errors in spelling, line change, usage of cases and grammar. Only now do I know that this message ushered in the Internet age for China, becoming part of recorded history. Here I quote the original message with all its mistakes and no corrections:

> Dear jack, I am very glad to send this letter to you via computing link which I think is first succssful link test between cern and china. I would like to thank you again for your visit which leads this valuable test to be success.
>
> Now I think each collaboration amoung aleph callaboration have computing link which
>
> Is vey important .ofcause we still have problems to use this link effectively
>
> For analizing dst of aleph in beijing, and need to find budget in addition, but most
>
> Important thing is to get start.at the moment, we use the ibm-pc in 710 institute
>
> To connect to you, later we will try to use the microwave communicated equipment
>
> Which we have used for linking m160h before, to link to you dirrectly

From our institute.

Please send my best regards to all of our colleagues and best wishes to you.cynt hia

and your family.

by the way, how about the carpet you bought in shanghai?

weimin

In this e-mail, there was no rhetoric, but a plain statement of the achievement (the first of its kind), issues (with funds), status (of working with the 710 Institute), plan (to use the mobile microwave communication interface), and so on. In order to provide definitive evidence for the CNNIC, we had to find the original copy of the 1986 e-mail. Paolo asked CERN to read out all the hard drive content generated on the VAX computer for the summer of 1986. Since the VAX computer used for the email system was retired, he requested the help of specialists and special equipment for recovering the data. Paolo finally found it! With the help of an ALEPH secretary, we also found the original ALEPH files. The total communication time between Beijing and ALEPH through this communication line was 1,821 minutes. Recording those files from August to the end of 1986, with a transmission of 80,567 units of data, ended up costing a total cost of 7,732.29 yuan RMB. This was the earliest and most detailed written record of the history of Chinese Internet communication. If someone were to ask me what the brightest moment of my life was, I think I would say that this was the moment.

On March 12, 2010, CNNIC informed me that they had listed my e-mail as the first item in the development history of Chinese Internet and that this fact was included in their official documentation. It followed that the original listing, "Across the Great Wall, to the world" was no longer the first event. As the Internet became more and more important, the title of being the "first" was just too important to many people. Since IHEP was not a primary player in mainstream computer networking and because I had migrated to the United States and become a US citizen, a variety of objections emerged. Some said that it was not an e-mail sent from China; others said that what I had was not a network. The leading committee of

CNNIC debated the issues several times, and changed the wording of the drafts describing the event. After almost three years of research and investigation, my e-mail still stood firm in its position as the first event of the Internet in China, and was confirmed by the committee again. It also turned out that Mr. Qian Tianbai had nothing to do with the September 20, 1987 e-mail sent from China to the University of Karlsruhe in Germany ("Across the Great Wall, to the world"). The whole thing was a big lie. There is a saying: "you can tell the same lie a thousand times, but it never gets anymore true." However, Qian Tianbai almost became a household name in China, known as the founder of China's Internet. Even now, if an Internet search is conducted using the search engine Baidu, many items can be found that name Qian Tianbai the father of Chinese Internet. This annoyed the real senders of "Across the Great Wall, to the world," — Professor Werner Zorn, his research team, Professor Wang Yunfeng and Dr Li Chengjion. They were seeking to clarify the issue through many channels. Werner Zorn's student sent me an email representing his professor. They admitted that my 1986 email was earlier than their 1987 email, but added that the two emails belong to two different types. At the same time, they made it clear that Qian Tianbai had nothing to do with their work. Qian Tianbai had not even participated in their activity. They hoped to keep in touch with me. Finally this debate about the "first" was settled, and the truth came out. In fact, I live in the United States, and have not been to any of CNNIC's committee meetings despite repeated invitations. I just let the facts speak for themselves. I want express my deep gratitude to Professor Ye Minghan. CNNIC contacted him many times for verification of the whole matter, and he always encouraged me to get to the bottom of the truth. Of course, I also want to thank my former colleagues at the CERN Computing Center and the ALEPH group, especially Paolo. Without their effort in digging out the relevant data, the truth would be buried forever, and the lie would continue.

I still do not know who Qian Tianbai is, and how his name and this lie became widespread. I checked with CNNIC, but they were reluctant to provide further explanation. In any case, from May 26, 2009, the historical records established by CNNIC have remained unchanged, and the name Qian Tianbai is no longer mentioned.

On March 12, 2010, CNNIC representative Dr. Wang Enhai sent me an official notice: "After our verification, as well as the deliberation of the expert committee for assessing Internet development in China, we have decided to officially list your email of 1986 under the 'China Internet Development Milestones' as the very first item honorably." Ah! What beautiful and precise words: "the very first!"

The last sentence of the official notice was: "Thank you for your contribution to early Chinese Internet!" Ah! Here was the recognition and thanks that I got after a lapse of 24 years.

No wonder, when someone asked Steinberger what the secret behind winning a Nobel Prize was, he answered: "First, do something useful when you are young; second, you have to live long enough." I remember that in 1989, I wrote an application, using the e-mail as the basis, for winning the second prize for technical progress awarded by the Chinese Academy of Sciences. The application was written, and evidence was also provided. The e-mail was listed by the Academy of Sciences as one of the ten major events in the past six decades. Because I left China, and several other parties also went their separate ways — one went abroad, one lost contact, and one passed away, the prize never materialized, and so far nobody has bothered to bring up the subject again. So, winning a prize perhaps needs another ingredient: luck.

In 1986, as I was able to login from Beijing to the computer system at CERN, and log on to their Internet sites, I could not only download files from the CERN Internet websites, but also access any other Internet websites in the world that were linked to CERN. For example, I was able to read many American university Internet websites. So apart from sending China's first email, I was also in fact the first Internet user in China. Today, the number of Chinese Internet users has reached 630 million. The title of being the first Internet user is perhaps the greatest success story of my life.

Lest we forget, we once made personal contact through letters and phone calls. Now, QQ, WeChat, microblogging and other social networking tools allow seamless contact among friends at anytime, anywhere. We used to buy everything by visiting shopping centers or asking someone to do the purchasing for us. Now, Amazon, Alibaba, Taobao and other online shopping sites have all sorts of merchandise on display to be bought at the touch of a button. Earlier, we found our favorite gourmet shops through personal referrals from friends and family members. Nowadays, either locally or in a different city, we can search for the most popular gourmet shops through the Public Comment Network. Previously, when we bought train and air tickets, we needed to go to a station to queue up or use a live travel agent. Now, it just takes a click on a travel agency's website to book a ticket at any time.

Reflecting over the past few decades, we cannot help but feel that the changes brought about by the Internet are really comprehensive, and many of us will find it hard to keep up with its pace of change. However, the Internet is also inclusive, such that nobody can live beyond its reach. The Internet has become the hallmark of the times, and has evolved into a legend of epic proportions.

In 2004, on the 20th anniversary of China's link to the Internet, the CNNIC produced a documentary film about the development process of the internet in China. At the end of the documentary, my 1986 e-mail was displayed in its entirety on the screen, accompanied by an audio statement to sincerely thank the pioneers of the Internet in China. This thanks was enough to warm my heart.

September 19, 2014 was a watershed day for China. The Chinese Internet company Alibaba went public on the New York Stock Exchange. The same day, its shares rose 38 percent, making Alibaba the second-largest Internet company in the world. Global media widely reported the news and the *Wall Street Journal* commented that this day marked China's formal entry into the Internet era. Twenty-eight years had passed from the time I sent my first e-mail, to September 2014. China and the whole world have undergone enormous change.

In 1987, Chen Hesheng and I wrote a report to the President of the Chinese Academy of Sciences, Zhou Guangzhou, suggesting that we upgrade IHEP's computer network to a new network managed by the advanced X25 system, in line with international standards. At the time, Dr. Chen had just returned from abroad. He soon showed his mastery of physics and strong organizational skills. He was from the L3 group, but we had a very pleasant working relationship. Later, he served as the director of IHEP, contributing enormously to the development of high-energy physics in China. We became very good friends, too. Although IHEP was not the main institution for developing the Internet in China, it was at its forefront in many aspects. On August 25, 2006, the CCAST held a seminar — "From a remote terminal to grid computing", to commemorate the 20th anniversary of the first international e-mail from China. At the meeting, I, presented by Prof. Ye, gave a presentation titled "From a remote terminal to China's first e-mail," while Dr. Chen gave a talk entitled "From remote log on to grid computing." Xu Rongsheng made a report on "The first Chinese WEB server," and others spoke too. These amply demonstrate that IHEP has made outstanding contributions to the Internet in China.

When the Chinese Academy of Sciences celebrated the 60th anniversary of its founding, it compiled a list of ten milestones over the past six decades. Among this list was the first e-mail, which was an honor for IHEP. Successive directors at IHEP, from Ye Minghan, Zheng Zhipeng and Chen Hesheng, to the current director, Wang Yifang, all provided solid support for work on computer networks. It was their vision and tireless effort that put IHEP at the forefront of China's Internet development.

At the end of 1986, I went to a meeting at CERN, reporting to Prof. T.D. Lee on the success of computer networking in China. He invited me to lunch and congratulated me on the successful networking, but told me at the same time: "You need to learn from Saulan Wu. Her physics is really great. Your physics level is far below hers." Yes indeed! Not just far below, but too far below! Professor Wu is the most conscientious physicist I know. She also had the most graduate students under her supervision. She made great contributions to high-energy physics, and is one of the most eminent physicists in the world. Her great contribution towards the discovery of the gluon was recognized by European High Energy Physics Society. In a male-dominated physics community, Professor Saulan Wu stood out and was the pride of Chinese women in the world. She is known to have an extremely noble character as well. A small example — in 1991 or thereabouts, Professor Wu came to the Fermilab from CERN. After we chatted for a while in my office, she asked me where she could make a phone call, because she wanted to call her mother in New York. I told her, "My office phone will do. Just dial '9,' then dial the number you want." Unexpectedly, she said, "I want to make a personal call. Please find me a coin-operated pay phone." On hearing this, I felt I realized the meaning of the saying, "see the light of the sun from a drop of water." Decades later, with the widespread use of cell phones, it is no big deal to make a call now. But the character of Professor Saulan Wu — not wanting to misuse the office phone — served as my role model for life.

Recently, I read an article with a controversial title: "Laziness is the driving force of social development." The article argued that due to laziness, people find ways to invent labor-saving machines. Laziness also prompted people to achieve automation, resulting in today's prosperity. True enough, I thought of the idea of the remote terminal because of my laziness in taking a bus to reach the computer. What looks like "sophistry" is often the truth.

6.7 Early fatherhood

In 1982, shortly after I returned to China, my wife Hengbao was pregnant. Her due date was early January the following year. To be safe, she was admitted to hospital in advance. On New Year's Eve, I was alone at home watching TV. I took a picture of the TV screen displaying the time 00:00:00, 1983. I thought 1983 would be an extraordinary year: I would be a father. It so happened that my wife started to have labor pain at midnight. The nurse on duty promptly called in the doctor. On January 1, 1983, at 6:45 in the morning, our daughter was born, weighing six pounds and eight ounces. Six and eight are both lucky numbers for the Chinese. At the time, the use of a phone was not widespread, and the average household did not have a telephone. On New Year's Day, I went to my office to call my sister who worked at *the Guangming Daily*. She slept in the office. I wanted to ask her where to go on New Year's Day, but she offered me her congratulations first. It turned out that the hospital had notified my father-in-law first, who then called up my sister. Only after I went to my office to call my sister did I learn about the birth of my daughter. This is simply difficult to imagine given today's technology. I rushed to the hospital, and used a Polaroid camera to take a picture of both mother and daughter. I had already come up with a name for my child — "Xing," meaning "star", whether male or female. As it happened to be New Year's Day, I added a character, "Yuan", meaning "the first". So my daughter was called "Wu Yuanxing." I also wrote an article explaining the origin of the name. My father copied out this article using his beautiful calligraphy onto a page inside a photo album. It ran as follows:

Yuanxing

She held on. She had been restless in the womb, but still she persisted. She wanted to stay in there until the New Year bells rang. I dreamed up so many nice names for my baby. Before I knew it, 1982 arrived while I was expecting and dreaming. That was the year when the nine planets were in alignment, a lucky coincidence of a hundred years, or perhaps a thousand. In fact her life began when the nine planets were starting to be in conjunction. Perhaps her future is linked to the stars, but then, whose would not be linked to the stars? Isn't each of us living on a rather ordinary planet in the vast universe? A star is great, great without parallel. A star is also small, so small without match. A star is the hottest object in the universe, when it is burning. It is a star that brings warmth to humanity. A star can also be the coldest, so cold that the thermal motion of its molecules tends to be zero. A star can be so far away, but can also be so close. Stars surround us, and we live among stars. They are continuously being born, and dying. This is a cycle of life and death, motion and quietness, past and future. Stars are sometimes shiny and pretty, and at other times, dim and gloomy. Stars evoke so many childhood fantasies, and they provide endless research subjects for those who aspire to devote themselves to the search for the truth. Stars are the most selfless. They often fall from the sky high above, piercing the boundless night sky, disappearing to nowhere. Stars are the last to say goodbye to the dark night, and the first to greet the dawn.

Yuanxing is lucky. Her birth focused the enthusiasm of my friends under the Alps mountains. Because of the timing of the birth, nurses and doctors had to wake up from their sweet dreams, brave the cold, and come to the hospital under the light of the stars. These angels in white coats have hands capable of grasping the moon and the stars. New lives come to the world through their hands one by one. In an instant, the city by the east sea heard the good news from the distant northern land, offering congratulations.

You are lucky, but also unfortunate because you did not get to meet your grandmother. I was once in the arms of your grandmother, counting the number of stars in the sky. If a mother's love is one hundred, then, the love of a grandmother is ten thousand. Grandmother did a lot to welcome the birth of Yuanxing.

Although I have looked up at the night sky many a time, I still do not know how many stars there are in the universe. If the number of stars in the universe is a constant, then it takes the fall of one star for another star to be born. Ah! What a nice name, Xingxing. Since you came to the earth on the first day of the year, you shall be called Yuanxing! "Yuan" means "the first". However, there is no such thing as the first star or second star, just as in the river of space and time, there is no beginning nor end. It is just a unit, an independent body in an endless sequence. She is self-contained. She is just she. She is a pool of water in the sea of stars, a star born in the conjunction of nine planets, rising amid the sound of bells ringing for the new year. Ah! Xingxing, our lovely Xingxing.

Remember this moment right. On New Year's Day, 1983, at a quarter past zero hour, you were awoken by the sound of bells for the new year. At six forty-five, you greeted the first morning of 1983. (Lunar November 18)

Mother: Hengbao, Father: Wu Weimin

Grandpa: Wu Benhao, Grandma: Luo Xi

January 1, 1983 in Shanghai

At that time, our living conditions were not that good. There were only two rooms with a total area of 22 square meters, plus a small toilet and a kitchen. We had a nanny to take care of little Xingxing. The nanny had her own room, and three of us squeezed in one bed. In the middle of the night, if Xingxing began to cry, the whole family had no peace. We were most worried about Xingxing falling sick. It was cold, and the central heating was not good enough. If we used an electric stove, the fuse for the entire building would get burned. So we had to endure the cold. But Xingxing was a little baby. She caught the cold and developed pneumonia. She had a high fever, and was sent to the 401 hospital. There, each ward had more than a dozen beds. There were a full 20 people in the room with patients plus accompanying parents. Xingxing's mother and I took turns watching her. Several days later, Xingxing's fever finally subsided, and we took her home as soon as we could. We would often wrap her up a in cotton coat and stay up all night to fuss over her. We sang lullabies to comfort her. She would eventually fall asleep but we often did not catch any sleep all night long. We would still have to go work the next day. Nevertheless, this little life brought us a lot of joy. Her plump little feet, red, glowing, smiling face and daily changes all told us that she was our star of hope.

My good friend Paolo sent her a gold coin with an image of the head of Queen Victoria, symbolizing a rich and glorious life; Hans gave her a silver spoon, a symbol of a life free from want; Steinberger bought a portable stroller that folded up like a machine gun. At that time, this folding stroller was so unusual in China that it was inspected thoroughly when Hans took it through the customs. Dr. Zhu Chen, a special friend present at the birth of Yuanxing, brought a golden necklace; and Sally sent a set of baby pajamas by post from Switzerland. When I went to collect the pajamas at the customs, I was charged a duty tax of tens of yuan, equivalent to half a month of my salary. Similar pajamas at shops in Beijing cost only a few yuan. I said to the Customs officers: "I do not want it anymore, please keep it for yourselves." They laughed, and let me have the pajamas without paying the tax. Such was the economic status of China in 1983.

Xingxing's maternal grandmother passed away before she was born. My mother personally made many woolen and cotton sweaters and trousers, thick and thin, with sizes going up to three years of age. She also prepared a good supply of diapers. The expression "tender heart of the parents" should be extended to "the caring heart of the grandparents." My daughter was really raised with the love of many people.

Many years later, in 2000, when Yuanxing was just one year away from graduating from high school, she wrote a poem that was chosen to be a special topical winner by the American Poets Society, of which she was a member. From this poem, we could see that our Xingxing had grown up, and that her life was shining brightly in the sky full of stars.

I wonder whether

Will you have me sink down into a profound sleep?

To voiceless regions, like the abyss of a giant leap

While my soul ache like a wild animal searching for lair

Of air

Of our shared roar and heave, once fair and deep?

You are silent and so speechlessly, I keep

The vast beaches or the turbid ebb and flow, drear

Naked shores of a tremulous cadence, slow

My sudden eternal note of sadness flow

The abyss of King Lear

No Fear

My insides stir at the thought of your consent

Let us love because there's no light, no end, nor certainty

Nor peace, nor help for pain

Only you and me

The Key

6.8 Farewell to my parents

1968, in that chaotic era, my dear maternal grandfather passed away. At the time, I could not even receive the news. I learned of his passing months later. A few years later, my dear grandmother left us too. Just around that time, I went to Shanghai on business, and was to return to my work unit the next day.

My maternal grandmother kept groaning all night. My mother complained to my grandmother: "Weimin will be on his way tomorrow. Let him have some sleep." Still, the moaning of my grandmother got worse. The next day, I took the train and left Shanghai. A few days later, my grandmother passed away. Her last moaning often rang in my ears. They were buried together in the burial lots that were reserved a long time back on the Yangmei Mountain in their home town, Ningbo. It was a piece of land with a good geomantic omen, facing the broad Ming Lake and the sun. In the past, when folks from the home town visited us in Shanghai, they would bring along some bayberries produced there. The bayberries were darkish red, sweet with a touch of sour, really delicious. Wines treated with bayberries were really famous. Unfortunately, we gradually lost contact with the people from Ningbo over the years.

On March 26, 1986, my dear father passed away. Four months before he died, I received a letter from him that I have kept to this day. The letter my father wrote:

"Dear Weimin, I feel deeply concerned that little Yuanxing is coughing. Minmin left Shanghai for Japan on the 24th of last month. I am not sure if I will still be here to see him when he finishes his studies. Fumin went to the south this time ... She saw Xiaomin. They had a happy get-together. Xinmin got his promotion. He is doing well. Your mother's illness is under control after taking some Chinese medicine. My own sickness is just as usual. The arrival of winter has made me worried. After Jimin started to work at the TV station, he is happy with his work."

Half a year before this letter, my mother also wrote one that began: "Dear Weimin, my hands are shaking a bit. I cannot write well. Please forgive me." Actually, my mother had a brain tumor, and she did not have full use of her hands and feet anymore. I have kept this last letter of hers with me all the time.

During the Cultural Revolution, both my parents suffered persecutions, physically as well as emotionally. My mother, especially, was depressed at being given the label of an "exploiter" all the time, which might have been an important cause of her brain tumor. After my father passed away, I wrote a memorial article as follows:

In Memory of My Father Wu Benhao

On March 26, 1986, my father passed away. Father was born in the year of the Xinhai Revolution, when a new page was turned in Chinese history. He was born poor, and had a rough childhood. As an epitome of the suffering China, my father grew up stubbornly amid years of war calamities. I still vividly remember a true story he told me. When he was a child, he had boils on his head. A barber used a pair of fire-treated scissors to cut them off. Tempered by hardship, my father became a self-taught man while working as a printing type setter. Today, there are so many writers and reporters among the six brothers and sisters of the Wu family. They all got their first education of culture and history from their father, who never got a formal education himself. His profound knowledge and beautiful handwriting impressed many. My fellow students at Fudan University also asked him to write couplets for them. It is not difficult to imagine that my father must have made many times the effort to accomplish what he did. Today, he has left us, but his fighting spirit shall always be cherished by us.

Father was a well-known, nice person, being careful all his life. Unfortunately, his six children often got themselves involved in some trouble or the other, not allowing the timid father to have much peace of mind. As I said, the Wu family produced a lot of talented people, but no great men or women, something which had a lot to do with this character of my father. However, such an honest man still suffered inhuman treatment during the unprecedented catastrophe. In the face of persecution, my father showed his unbending character and integrity. As a self-taught person, my father became a school principal and the Chief Accountant of Siming Bank at a relatively young age. However, he felt deeply encumbered by the lack of a formal education, so he devoted himself to providing the best possible education to his children. Each of his six children has graduated from college, a fact that could be attributed to their own efforts, but also to the careful education and cultivation by their parents. Father got sick when he was middle-aged, and he spent half of his life fighting his sickness. Due to his strict public morality, none of his children was infected, and he almost never ventured into public places. It took the selfless care and love of my mother over several decades, for him to have lived for as long as he did. It might also have something to do with his materialist outlook on life. I think that having no fear of death may be a powerful weapon against death. He volunteered to donate his body to medical research after his death. He made a will that his ashes would be used to feed a tree, contributing to the greening of his motherland. Part of his ashes would be scattered in the Qiantang River that nurtured him. It was this fearless spirit that enabled him to live to the ripe old age of 75, with less than one functioning lung.

Father was an ordinary man. He died a peaceful death, leaving a legacy of down-to-earth teachings.

The Eldest Son, Weimin, Beijing, March 26, 1986

Shortly after my father died, my mother's illness was diagnosed to be a brain tumor rather than cerebral blood clotting. Since the brain tumor was located very close to the brain stem, the doctors had no confidence in performing a surgery given the medical conditions of the time. Mother soon fell into a coma. The hospital my mother stayed in was originally a Church and was converted into a hospital. Just before her death, whether by coincidence or by the will of God, the place was about to revert to being a church. Soon after my mother passed away, the hospital moved and the building became a well-known church in Shanghai. That was where mother passed onto the next world. The date was November 8, 1986. Shortly before that, I had returned from a visit to Singapore. In Singapore, I ate abalone for the first time. It tasted really delicious. I wanted my mother to try it, too. So I bought two cans of abalone. Unfortunately, my mother passed away before she had a chance to eat the abalone. 1986! That was the best year in China. However, my dear mother did not get to enjoy the good times in China.

After my mother died, her work unit held a big memorial service for her. Many of her colleagues and friends came to say goodbye to her. At the service, I spoke on behalf of my family, the gist of which is as follows:

Today, we are here to mourn an ordinary member of the great party, and a great mother of an ordinary family. Several years ago, when my mother was busy traveling energetically between Shanghai and Hangzhou to create a rehabilitation center for the Handicraft Industry Bureau, cancer cells started to invade her brain silently. However, this cancer-carrying brain was all concerned about the health and welfare of the workers of the whole bureau. A year and a half ago, she wrote me a letter with her trembling hand:

"My hands are shaking a bit. I cannot write well. Please forgive me. I hope that you will focus your mind on your work abroad. Do not think too much about your mother, but about your motherland and the people."

When I read this letter, how could I have known that this was the last letter and words from my mother?

Half a year ago, when my mother found out that she was terminally ill, she asked us again and again not to make any demands on her work unit. She thanked the doctors and nurses for treating and taking care of her. How could we expect that the heart of an ordinary party member and a great mother would stop beating when our party and our country is at her best historically; when her children are at the most successful stage of their careers; when she deserved rest and happiness after a life-long time of hard work. Indeed, our mother passed away too soon. She was too tired.

While in her youth, she joined the great anti-Japanese struggle led by the communist party. Her bridal chamber on her wedding night was used as a cover up for a comrade who was on the way to the New Fourth Army to join the revolution. At the time, she was only 18 years old. Since then, her fate, her career, her family and her suffering were all tied up with the party. Over 30 years, my mother submitted herself to the will of her organization, changing her jobs nine times. In each of the units she worked at, she took a position of responsibility, developing new ideas and new ways of working, and making new friends. She worked hard, full of enthusiasm, while caring nothing about personal gains and losses. All she thought about were the people, the people only.

After she joined the party, the first "treatment" she received was to be labeled a "big tiger" in the "Three-Anti" campaign. She was investigated in isolation, when she was just thirty years old. When she was completely exonerated, she commented to us: "Even a mother sometimes can do wrong to her children. Can you blame the mother?" Yes, my mother used to liken the party to a mother.

In the decade-long calamity of the Cultural Revolution, even my ordinary family could not escape the ill fate of ruins and death. Both my parents were imprisoned at different times. My brothers and sisters were banished to the Northeast, Anhui and Chongming Island. My elder sister was implicated too.

I, a graduate student of atomic physics, practically lost the right to be assigned a job. A family of ten was broken up thoroughly. Sent to the North-western part of China, I did not know where to send my letters to my family members. My maternal grandfather, a member of China's first generation of production workers, got ill with anger and bitterness, and died in misery. I saw with my own eyes that a heavy metal plate was hung on mother's neck. She was subjected to denouncement for more than ten hours a day. Her body was bruised over a large area. Yet when I went to see her, she still kept saying: "Believe in the people, and believe in the party."

Mother suffered many grievances in her life, but she always derived the greatest joy from her work. She was one of the *pioneers of the Chinese watch industry, serving as the deputy director in charge of production at the Shanghai Watch Factory. She was responsible for the creation and trial production of the first brand of watches in China. I clearly remember that when the first brand of Chinese watches was produced, "Shanghai", my mother was ecstatic. It appeared that all the pains taken to set up the Shanghai Watch Factory had all disappeared in a moment.*

Could all the pain really disappear in a moment? No! That's impossible. When she served as the Deputy Director of the Shanghai Watch Factory, my mother had aging parents and six young children. Father spent half of his life sick in bed, so he needed the care of my mother too. All the burdens of the family, the factory and the state were placed on the shoulders of a 40-year-old woman. Only a strong woman who had the traditional virtues of Chinese women as well as the discipline of the communist party could bear such a heavy burden.

Everyday before dawn, she carried a basket to queue up to buy food. In difficult times, her work unit took the care to give her things like soybeans, but she would save it for my father and my siblings. Because of malnutrition and excessive fatigue, she developed hepatomegaly — characterized by a swollen liver. However, while at the factory, my mother was still able to make impassioned, lengthy speeches to all the workers there, encouraging them to work hard.

At that time, I was preparing for the entrance examinations to colleges. I often studied to midnight. Sometimes, I would fall asleep on the sofa. When I was awakened by my mother, who was trying to cover me up with a quilt, I found that the time was often past midnight. When my mother's superiors in her bureau advised her to stop supporting her children in going to school, my mother said: "When I was a child, there was no opportunity to go to college. I cannot let them lose this opportunity." My mother's wish was realized. Each of her six children did well. Each of them graduated from college, and was a top student. When people marvel at the success of the six Wu brothers and sisters, the first question they ask is: "What do your parents do?" My parents were neither writers nor professors, but they created the cradle for writers and professors. My parents' noble sentiment, character, wealth of knowledge and wisdom gave us a subtle but deep influence which was the source of nourishment for our robust growth.

In July this year, at the annual meeting of the European High-Energy Physics Society in Sweden, I gave a talk on behalf of China's Institute of High-Energy Physics. The enthusiastic applause of scientists from various countries in the world brought tears to my eyes. At that moment, the sound of applause in my ears turned into the sound of my mother's voice: "Reform and opening up made the Chinese people stand up for real." Yes indeed, we six siblings had all stood up, together with our nation, on the shoulders of our great mother.

Mother, dear mother, may you rest in peace! You did not leave us any material inheritance, but you left us endless thoughts and memories. Your honesty, integrity, kindness, warmth, enthusiasm, wisdom, competence, indomitable will and perseverance will be kept in our hearts forever. Your well-deserved honor of "People's Representative," and your image of a model public servant and excellent communist party member will inspire us to work hard and overcome all obstacles in our own careers.

Mother, dear mother, you did not relax and enjoy life for a single day, but worked tirelessly all your life for your motherland, for the people, and for your children. You prematurely left a world that is full of joy. You did not enjoy a day of happiness but unreservedly gave happiness to us, and to the people you showed boundless loyalty to. May you rest in peace, mother, our dearest mother. You will always live in our hearts.

The ashes of my mother and part of the ashes of my father were buried on the Phoenix Mountain of Suzhou, facing the sun and lush woods. A Swiss watch that I gave to my mother as a gift was also buried with her remains. Mother, the Chinese watch industry that you helped to create is now among the advanced industries of the world. Do rest in peace, mother!

The passing of our parents left an incomparable mark on the hearts of Wu family's six brothers and sisters. Our parents used to be the core of our unity. Even during the separation of siblings in the 10 turbulent years of Cultural Revolution, we would fight for every chance to reunite at our home on Julu Road as much as possible. I brought back local produce from the Gobi Desert and deep mountains to share with the family; my younger sister often carried home hens, sesame oil, peanuts and such from Anhui village on a carrying pole for our parents and grandparents. Brother Minmin even brought back a bear's paw once for us to try. The siblings who lived in Shanghai took over the responsibility of caring for our aging parents and maternal grandparents. After our parents passed, the unity of the Wu family has not diminished at all. I sincerely hope that Wu family's traditions of filial piety, loving relationships among siblings and care for one other, will carry on across generations to come.

6.9 Extraordinary human abilities

Over this decade, in addition to my work, I have published many essays and travelogues in various magazines and newspapers, such as "Notes on commodity society," "Thoughts on symmetry," "Remembered by history," "How do foreign friends see cliches?", "A Hell as good as Heaven," "Visiting Pisa after the vindication of Galileo," "On the freedom of communication," "Cat," "The new most-loved persons" and so on. There were two articles involving some extraordinary human abilities. One was called "His brain beats the computer — An interview with the amazing Mr. Klein." The other was "To respect science is to respect the facts." I wish to explore the relationships among science, superstition and so-called "pseudo-science."

On May 12, 1981 at ten o'clock, several hundred world-class scientists gathered at the conference hall of CERN, a holy temple of science, to witness a miracle. A mathematician from the Netherlands, Mr. Wim Klein, was to compete against the high-speed computer from CERN's computer center. Members of the audience could use any language to give out digits until they reached to one hundred in total. I put in one in Chinese. Mr. Klein wrote them all down on a blackboard. At the same time, an operator input the one hundred digits into a preprogrammed computer. It was time to witness a miracle. After the one hundred digits were input on the computer, the computer started to execute program, and Mr. Klein also started his mental computation. The purpose was to find the 13th root of the 100-digit number.

After one minute and twenty-six seconds, Mr. Klein began to write down the answer on the blackboard. Over a minute later, the computer also started to output the computing result. The two answers were identical, but Mr. Klein beat the computer by more than one minute.

The audience burst into a thunderous applause. After that, Mr. Klein performed multi-digit multiplications, divisions, and squares. It was said that Mr. Klein's world record was one minute and fifteen seconds for finding the 13th root of a 100-digit number. Mr. Klein, born in 1912, was the son of a doctor. He showed amazing mental arithmetic ability from a young age. From 1958 to 1976, Mr. Klein worked as a "computing person" at CERN. Right after his performance, I interviewed him. Mr. Klein also performed other types of computation. I was no match for him even though I had the help of a calculator. I asked Mr. Klein how he did it, but he could not describe it at all. He would often forget the address of his own home and telephone numbers. However he could remember immediately the number plates of the cars driving by at high speed. After the interview, I wrote an article, "His brain beats the computer — An interview with the amazing Mr. Klein," which was published in many newspapers. What can we call Mr. Klein's performance other than an extraordinary human ability?

I also wrote an article against the trend of talking authoritatively without painstaking research and investigation. In China, there was a so-called "big guy" in anti-pseudo-science. This man played the role of a politician and used political rhetoric before scientists, while playing the role of a scientist before politicians and using scientific terms. He published some scathing articles with sweeping conclusions. Many serious scientists, such as Mr. Zhao Zhongyao, actually showed strong support for studying those extraordinary human abilities. Mr. Klein could take a 100-digit number to the 13th root, but he could not do the same thing with a 99-digit number, nor could he take it to the 12th root. Why? This was a scientific problem. It cannot be confirmed or denied by using empty rhetoric. Indeed, we still know little about human life. The discovery of DNA was only the beginning in studying human life. Genetic testing can now detect genetic defects related to 2,500 kinds of diseases. It takes about $7,000 to do a genetic screening to find out what kinds of diseases you are likely to develop in the future. The Chinese saying, "A dragon begets a dragon, a phoenix begets a phoenix, and the offspring of a mouse does the tunneling," may not be "fatalism." Furthermore, can everything be understood? If the answer is no, then why does the world follow natural laws so faithfully? If the answer is yes, then did God leave a door that cannot be opened by humans? I made my career studying high-energy physics, attempting to understand the ins and outs of the universe. Is this ultimately possible? Does the universe really have a beginning or an end? What about humans themselves? There is a Chinese proverb: "A man's life was foretold in the heavens." Is that right? In life, there are many coincidences. Are they really all by chance? I have encountered several strange circumstances, and often dismissed them as illusions. A few times, I used a camera to record what I saw, and had to be convinced that way. I will have more discussions on these subjects in Chapter 11. I feel it is a kind of superstition because these experiences cannot be repeated. Science is about facts that can be repeatedly verified. At least I still believe it. Otherwise, it can be a very confusing world.

6.10 Marriage crisis

There is probably nothing we talk more about than relationships, love and marriage, in all the books ever published. This is not a book about love stories, but love is an important part of my life. I got married to my ex-wife, Hengbao, at a time when my homeland was full of sad stories. She is a very kind, honest, and simple person. In those years, I belonged to a "black-five" family, whereas she had parents who were considered the "red-five", with power and prestige. The union of marriage between "red and black" was destined to be full of stories, like the novel by Stendhal, "The Red and the Black." She was born in a family of revolutionary cadres, but I was born in a family that I could not classify easily. Anyway, I always wrote "clerks" when I filled out forms for any reason. She grew up in the army barracks, living a life based on the "free supply" system. Even her handkerchiefs were supplied by the government. She did not even know what money was or how to make a purchase. She had grown up wearing military uniforms since she was born. Sure enough, she didn't care to wear makeup. When I first met her, I was in shock for a while, because she used a large-denomination banknote as a bookmark. Maybe she really didn't know how to spend money. I am versatile and sensitive; she is simple and straight. I love to make friends; she prefers to stay by herself. The large difference between our personalities was not so obvious at that age, but it became more and more obvious when China was reformed and opened up. Then, the crisis of our marriage came up.

I like versatile girls. I enjoy being with someone who can fill in my half-finished sentences. My first love Xiao Mei was such a girl. In 1987, I met another such girl in Geneva. I shall call her "Xiao Ju." She was a student from a university in Beijing. She went to Belgium to study for her Master's degree before she graduated, then she came to Switzerland to study for her doctor's degree. She had mastered French, German and English. We met at my friend's party, and hit it off right away. We not only talked about physics, but also about many subjects across all space and time. We just could not stop talking when we got together. In fact, she was much younger than me, but she always regarded herself as my equal in maturity.

Xiao Ju knew that I had a wife and a daughter, and we got along like close friends. She stayed mostly in Zurich, whereas I was busy running between Beijing and Geneva. So she often wrote to me, and I often wrote back with words full of feelings and emotion, like poems. In a letter, she wrote:

> *"At eleven o'clock on November 11, I walked on snow to the side of a castle. I saw people dancing merrily to welcome the arrival of winter. Indeed, songs always came with the snow. We are creatures who like winter so much. Why not? The creativity of spring, the expressiveness of the summer, the bounty of the fall, and the*

restfulness of winter all constitute a piece of perfect symphony of the four seasons. I hope that the white eyelash-like snow flakes will cover the whole world overnight, making contented people sleep serenely and unsatisfied people ponder quietly.... Sending some photos, I hope that you will smile looking at them...."

After reading her letter, I replied with a prose piece, "The dream of fall." It was written after we traveled together to Interlaken, a famous scenic spot in Switzerland.

The spring is a season that makes a lot of dreams....

when flowers bud, releasing the fragrance,

when fresh leaves grow, delicate and shining,

when glaciers melt, forming noisy streams,

when young birds spread wings, learning to fly,

A pity, the spring of my life was in an age without spring,

and my only dream belonging to spring was so short and faded away so fast in the face of reality.

Summer is a season without dreams....

The hot weather makes everything tired.

The monotonous chirping of cicada sounds like a lullaby.

All the edges of the whole world disappear in the harmonious chorus.

My heartbeat is 72 times per minute and my breath is 18, no more, nor less.

Sparse stars bring a daydream by chance,

but my pulse has started to decrease exponentially before it increases to peak value, disappearing into the suffused hot noise.

Fall is a season that has few dreams....

Describing the chrysanthemum in the fall, there is an ancient saying, "The chrysanthemum is not preferred among flowers, but no more flowers appear after the chrysanthemum blossoms."

When someone has never experienced the "sweet dream," it evokes feelings of the poem: "Where goes the spring? A lonely journey without a path. Find the whereabouts of spring, and bring it back to live in it together."

Who does know the steps of spring? Ah, it is a breeze passing through the roses, rippling the surface of the pond suddenly. It is a scene of lotuses floating in the pond, alfalfa covering the mountain, and a red flower swinging among a thicket of greened trees. A dream lost made me lose myself like floating above the clouds.

Ah, the dream of fall. You cannot bring back time gone, but you can extend the future. Looking behind, "the sun was setting west, along with tears of someone at the edge of the world." Looking forward, "the road ends with the cloud, the spring goes with the stream." The former and the latter are so asymmetric, but then space and time are supposed to be asymmetric. Time cannot go back but can be delayed. Space cannot be expanded but can be compressed.

I really hope that the fifth dimension of space really exists. If it is true, how free humans would be, hovering freely between the space of imagination and ideas.

There will be no more flowers blossoming after this flower withers, and there will be no more dreams after this dream fades away. Dream of fall, please stay, stay in my holy land, Interlaken. No matter where I will be in the future, I will cherish my dream of the fall, sweet or bitter.

Thank you for your praises. In fact, I am just a little blade of grass on the top of a snow-covered mountain. When people say that the grass is tall, the little blade says, I'm not tall. It is the mountain that is tall.

Written by Weimin after visiting Interlaken.

My holy land Interlaken, I love you forever.

We talked about our future as well. She said, "it is enough for me to have a close friend like you." After hearing her words, I wrote a poem for her again. It was called "So hard to find a close friend."

I can't remember how many eves of the mid-autumn festival I have spent,

the beauty of the full moon always inspires a poem.

We got together that day, but separated soon after,

with the love of God ever blessing.

Oh, it is so hard to have an understanding friend in a life time,

and it is harder still to have someone connected to me without any extra words.

We could have hundreds and thousands of friends,

but bosom friends are rare to come by.

The old saying goes, one dies for the one who understands,

but I prefer to say, I live for someone who appreciates.

I once asked her, "Do you think our relationship is unfair to you?

She replied, "Your child is still too young, so let time find the answer by itself."

However, an unprecedented political storm soon began. My dream of the fall ended sadly.

Chapter Seven

A Turning Point in History

7.1 A storm is brewing

In the mid-1980s, China thrived under Deng Xiaoping's reform and opening-up policies. The political climate relaxed, ideological diversity was encouraged, the economy took off, and people's living standards rose steadily. In particular, after the lifelong tenure for cadres was abolished, a generation of young cadres stepped up to leadership positions and replaced the "veterans". Like many other political reforms in Chinese history, however, Deng's new policies encroached on some veteran cadres' immediate interests. I remember a speech given by Yaobang Hu, one of the top leaders, that suggested senior cadres do something beneficial to society after their retirement, such as planting trees. I personally witnessed the rage exhibited by the senior cadres who were used to doing nothing but political maneuvering. This occurred even in an organization as small as IHEP. These cadres, not to mention the "political veterans" in the central government, were not resigned to leaving the political scene to make room for new minds. They often self-identified as "uncrowned kings", and provoked Yaobang Hu, Ziyang Zhao's leadership with accusations like "Bourgeois Liberalization" from time to time.

At the same time, thanks to reform and opening-up, people's individualities and abilities were given opportunities to be expressed, such that some people became rich ahead of others. On the other hand, corruption and the abuse of power for personal gains were rampant because of the lack of simultaneous development of political and management reforms. This caused the wealth gap to widen, giving birth to many nouveau-riche upstarts. I remember traveling to Shanghai at the time and seeing many upstarts who obtained wealth through speculation or taking advantage of their family backgrounds. Their language and behavior were vulgar, but they had loads of money to squander. This phenomenon led to many people's dissatisfaction with society.

The most important change that reform and opening-up brought, however, was the unprecedented information revolution. Chinese people ceased to be mute and blind behind the "iron curtain", but governmental media organizations at all levels continued to use old excuses to deceive. This made many people indignant, especially intellectuals and young students. Let me provide an example. I remember that as late as 1989, the *People's Daily* still used a full page to cover a report on how East Germany was better than West Germany. That article infuriated me so much that I could not help but call the author a big liar! In July 1984, I had been to Leipzig, Germany, to attend an international conference for high-energy physics. My German friend suggested driving so that we could visit some places along the way. We set out towards the North from Geneva, drove through the entire country of Switzerland, and visited the Swiss enclave on the border of Switzerland, Germany, and Austria — the famous royal garden. My friend drove a Mercedes-Benz at more than 150 kilometers per hour, taking us to the border between East and West Germany in a very short time. As soon as we got there, however, the situation was completely different. There was a no-man sand belt separating West Germany from East Germany, surrounded by barbed wire and bunkers. On the East German side, driving across the border resembled a scene from wartime. Not only did we have to open the trunk of the car for inspection, the soldier also had to use a reflective mirror to make sure that there was no one hiding underneath the car. For most people, this kind of situation only exists in movies, but I experienced it firsthand. We spent hours at the border until the guards let us pass. However, there was hardly any checking point procedure on the West German side. When the car entered East Germany, the so-called highways were full of bumps and potholes, so the Mercedes-Benz had to crawl along slowly and spiritlessly. In West Germany, we had real orange juice; in East Germany, there was only water with a hint of orange color. The contrast was drastic. For people like me who had actually been to Germany, how would they feel after reading that article in the *People's Daily*? No wonder an American politician once said that granted our system is flawed, but there is no need to lock our people up.

This is similar to China's situation today: Chinese citizens can travel freely to foreign countries, casually and with great confidence. This was not the case in China during the 80s. Because of the reasons mentioned above, calls for political reforms emerged in Chinese society. In December 1986, some student protest activities started in the Chinese University of Technology in Hefei, Anhui Province, and later spread to more than a dozen cities. The students demanded further political reforms and liberal economic policies, anti-corruption and pro-equality. In fact, these student movements were blameless, and they could have become a driving force for reform and opening-up if given the appropriate direction. It was a shame that the conservative forces that were reluctant to retire from the political arena criticized Yaobang Hu for failing to combat "Bourgeois Liberalization" and forced him to resign, abusing the clauses of the Communist Party Constitution.

Deng Xiaoping has always been a great figure in changing the course of Chinese history. I admire him greatly. Like what Deng and other Communist Party leaders said, the lack of a well-functioning system in the Party to restrain strong political figures' power led to some of these strong political figures abusing democracy. The Cultural Revolution was an example of this kind of abuse. Today, the times have changed, and strong political figures can no longer infringe on the rights of the people. Deng Xiaoping's decision to denounce the Cultural Revolution was a significant step in Chinese history. Abolishing lifelong tenure for cadres and economic reforms were great feats of his. China's future lies in continuing on the path of reform and opening-up.

Yaobang Hu passed away on April 15th, 1989. Although it is said that he died of a heart attack, modern medicine has proven that people with cerebrovascular and cardiovascular problems can die from rage. After the Cultural Revolution, Yaobang Hu did a lot of work restoring order and redressed many veteran cadres who suffered in the movement. However, some of these same veteran cadres he helped forced him to resign. It was not surprising that Hu's true cause of death was rage. To make matters worse, someone came up with the terrible idea of mobilizing large numbers of policemen and soldiers to Tiananmen Square on April 22nd, the day of his memorial service. Even the road to Babaoshan Public Cemetery was lined with policemen and soldiers. This arrangement, as if facing dangerous enemies, fueled the fury of indignant masses and caused tensions to skyrocket. That day, after watching the memorial service on TV, I rode my bike to Yuquan Road to wait for Hu's hearse to pass and pay my homage to one who was called the "last great leader of the Communist Party who will be sorely missed by all his people". To my surprise, the road was fully occupied by the police. Police cars with sirens screaming drove along the crowd, pushing people onto the pavement. It was nothing more than common people trying to express their gratitude and sentiment toward Yaobang Hu, why would the government get so nervous? This mindset of the government antagonized its people. The *People's Daily* published "The April 26 Editorial", and the government's use of political accusation and military mobilization towards people's movements planted the seeds for the tragedy of the Tiananmen Square protests. In my view, the key problem was that any economic reform depends on changes in the ownership structure, and changes in the ownership structure always lead to changes in the social structure, calling for necessary political reforms. This editorial in the *People's Daily* avoided these fundamental problems, but attempted to suppress people's dissent by making political accusations. However, Chinese people in 1989 no longer listened to the lies of the "Party's Paper", nor were they afraid of political accusations. Chinese citizens used their rights granted by the Constitution, took to the streets, and started a mighty anti-corruption, pro-democracy mass movement. Some anti-intellectual and aloof old cadres, who were alienated from the masses, became the main targets of this movement. From my point of view, the vast majority of people, myself included, supported Deng Xiaoping. This movement led to the tragedy of Tiananmen Square protest on June 4, for which Chen Xitong and his gang were ultimately responsible. Their arrogant and superior attitude toward the masses and exaggeration of young university students' actions in front of Deng Xiaoping were abominable. It is easy to imagine Deng in his 80s being infuriated when he was shown a caricature drawn by an overly excited student, depicting a metaphor of hanging Deng on a rope. Obviously, Chen Xitong and his gang did this for ulterior motives.

7.2 Videotape

After April 26th, there were people protesting on the streets almost everyday. I am particularly interested in news reporting. Although this is not my specialty, I have a collector's penchant for it. I love keeping newspapers, photographs, and videos from significant historical events. I have a video camera that was brought by a friend from Switzerland. At that time, most people in China did not own video cameras. So I took my camera to Tiananmen Square, and took irreplaceable videos of students' non-violent sit-in hunger strike protests in front of the People's Heroes Monument. The evening of May 19th was a day of darkness in the book of history. Someone on television viciously announced that martial law was to be enforced in Beijing. This was a dangerous and crucial step leading up to the tragedy of June 4th. Newspapers at the time often portrayed this mass movement as being under the influence of "foreign powers". This idea, however, was indeed an overestimation of the so-called "foreign powers". It seems to me that besides the reasons mentioned above, it was none other than those vicious people talking on television who provoked the mass movements.

Once, I saw on television that some reporters were trying to interview a national leader. This national leader held his face in a sulky pout and shooed the journalists away before he said much. What is serving the people? To these so-called leaders, serving the people means the people are serving, while they themselves are the ones being served. I was especially averse to a saying at that time. It said, "this regime was established over hundreds of thousands of dead bodies, and if you want to revolt, you need hundreds of thousands more dead bodies to replace it." This was the real logic of those "princelings": whoever conquers the world, owns the world. After the father owns the world, the son continues to own the world. How could this be the same as the ideals in the *Communist Manifesto*? How could this be "service to the people?" In my view, these people were worse than the capitalist politicians. After the American Independence War, George Washington dismissed his army and said, your mission has been completed; those of you who were farmers, go back to farming, and those of you who were merchants, go back to business. Boasting about achievements and demanding rewards were not a part of that story. Some people had neither ability nor intelligence, and did poorly even as students in school, how could they occupy important leadership positions in the national government? Among the leaders of China today, there are plenty of people who are highly educated as well as experienced in practical work, who walk the talk and can relate to the people. Those vicious "national leaders" talking on television had nothing on the national leaders of China today. I originally had not intended to participate in activities such as street protests, but the provocative messages uttered by those unreasonable people on television changed my mind.

On the morning of May 20th, I joined the crowd to march toward Tiananmen Square, taking my camera with me. The protesters exhibited excitement all along the way, infuriated by the declaration of martial law. I recorded the reality of this historical scene with my video camera. We arrived at Tiananmen Square; the sound of the government's radio broadcasting was mixed with that of student protesters' radio. The government repeatedly announced martial law enforcement, warning the students that they would be responsible for serious consequences unless they left Tiananmen Square immediately. At the same time, the protesters were calling for unity among the masses to continue to fight. I had never seen anything like that. At 10 am sharp that morning, the big clock on the building of the Bank of China chimed 10 times, and I recorded this historical moment with my camera focused on the clock: at 10 am on May 20th, 1989, I witnessed martial law enforcement for the first time in my life. Students were chanting under the People's Heroes Monument, singing *"L'Internationale"* at the top of their voices. There was an imitation of the Statue of Liberty, a popular background for pictures, so I took many photos there. I also saw a middle-aged man giving a speech there, claiming that he had been a classmate of a high-ranking officer in central government when they were studying in USSR, and what a bad student the high-ranking officer had been. Regardless of how much truth there was in his statement, people's dismay at some high officials in the Party was apparent at the time. That day, the roads were full of military police, and their helicopters flew in circles above our heads. When I focused my camera on a helicopter in the sky, someone patted me on the shoulder and asked, "Which organization are you from?" I took a look at the man and decided that he was most likely a plainclothes policeman. I replied: "I belong to no organization." He then asked: "What do you mean by no organization?" I scurried away and disappeared into the crowd. However, all public transportation, including subway lines, was down. Staying there was obviously too dangerous an option. If I walked several miles home in a white shirt with a video camera on the shoulder, I would become an easy target for other plainclothes police. Right when I was stuck in limbo, I saw a male colleague from IHEP. He suggested staying over at his relatives' place in town for one day. I agreed. So we settled down at his relatives' place. I was afraid that my family would worry, but we did not have a phone at home. I had to call the office. A female colleague picked up the phone. I asked her to tell my family that I was safe, stuck at a friend's house and could not return home. I also told her not to tell anyone else about it. At that time, the Party leaders had already announced that employees of IHEP were forbidden to go to Tiananmen Square. However, after talking to my family, this female colleague told everyone, "Weimin Wu went to Tiananmen Square and couldn't go home." Her spreading the word created many troubles for me afterwards, including serving as evidence of my involvement in the "unrest". The male colleague I met at Tiananmen Square that day later immigrated to the United States as well. Unfortunately, he passed away in a car accident. He had severe shortsightedness and was not young — a complete nerd who was not fit for starting life from scratch in the US. If those people on television had not provoked national outrage, maybe he would never have ended up in the US, maybe he would never have died. I was deeply sorry to learn about his passing. Fate always renders us helpless.

In the following days, the tension in Beijing kept rising. The roads were in chaos. One moment, some said that protesters blocked the army trucks from entering the city at the west entrance; the next moment, rumor spread that the army was mobilizing troops to Beijing. Despite this, I still used my camera every day to take videos. I saw defenseless masses using their bodies to block armed trucks, helicopters circling above, and thousands of people handing water to the soldiers on army trucks, telling them not to point their guns at unarmed people. I garnered courage to record this scene. One day, when I was concentrated on filming a video, another middle-aged man asked me: "Why are you taking videos?" I said: "Personal hobby." He asked again: "Which organization?" I answered: "Academy of Science." Sensing a mistake, I corrected myself: "Academy of Agricultural Science." I slipped away in the crowd. By the end of May, the situation became increasingly tense. I began to worry that continuing filming would be too dangerous, and also worried about what I would do with the existing videotape. Though I wanted to keep it, there was no safe place. Coincidentally, an Italian physicist was visiting IHEP and was planning to return early due to the political unrest. I was in charge of hosting him. On a sunny, breezy morning, I took him to visit the Beijing Botanical Garden. Early summer in Beijing is the best time for going outdoors and admiring the beauty of nature. However, there was barely any visitor at the blooming Botanical Garden. I led him to an open space and said, "I have a favor to ask you. If you agree, we could discuss the best way to do this. If you are reluctant, please do not feel obliged, just act as if I never said it. Here, only the flowers, the birds, you, and I are present. Nobody else knows." He said: "Please feel free to ask anything." So I told him that I wanted to ask him to take the videotape out of China. He agreed right away, but started to worry about the consequences if the customs were to find out. I said: "I will try to come up with a proof that claims the tape is the data cartridge for the cooperation with ALEPH. If the customs confiscate it, you can just act like you are angry and destroy the tape." He said that this was a good idea. I knew that if customs were to set their mind on seizing it, there was no way to prevent them from doing so. On the other hand, leaving it in China was too dangerous: almost everyone knew that Weimin Wu filmed many videos of the "unrest", but it would be a shame to destroy it. I also told him not to show the tape to anyone when he arrived at CERN. If I could still go abroad, we would watch it together; if I could not, or if something were to happen to me, it would be my last gift to my colleagues at ALEPH. He said: "I know its value. The incident in Hungary was not redressed until 30 years later, and it might take even longer in China. This is a valuable reference for history. I will keep it safe." Although I obtained for him a certificate for the tape from IHEP, he was still extremely nervous. He spent a while in the bathroom looking for different storage places and finally packed it in an envelope. On June 2nd, I accompanied him to the airport in the afternoon. Our car drove by Liubukou, where soldiers in white shirts sat in a bus, surrounded by people and various automatic assault weapons confiscated from cars. Angry masses stood on top of the vehicle, shouting "People's army loves people; people's army would never shoot at people." The driver from IHEP wanted to stop and check out the situation. I thought that we had other priorities, so I told the driver: "We have a plane to catch, so why don't we take a detour." We avoided Liubukou and arrived at the airport via smaller roads. Once we got there, I realized that my worries were unnecessary. The airport was paralyzed, and customs employees had no interest in checking any luggage. The videotape arrived in Geneva safely. My friend kept his word and did not watch it until I arrived in Geneva, where we watched it together. They were impressed by my videos and said: "You should sell the tape to BBC. It is worth millions." I replied: "I would not sell it for the money. There are many close-up shots in my film footage, and it is very easy for the police to arrest people based on this tape. I will never endanger anyone. I will keep the video safe until the day the Tiananmen Square protest is redressed." This tape followed me from Switzerland to America. I have been keeping it in the safe every time I move. I believe that one day, I will be able to show people what really happened in China in the year of 1989.

7.3 The tragedy of the June 4th Tiananmen Square protest

Many young people today do not know what "June 4th" means anymore. The event itself has been referred to by many different names throughout history: from "revolt" to "unrest", then to "crisis", while the West calls it a "massacre". "June 4th", or the Tiananmen Square protest, is not the main subject of this book, but it was a life-changing event for me. Even though a quarter of a century has passed, the days around that fateful event are still vivid in my mind. I have written an unpublished article, "A Hundred Days Before and After June 4". Some of the phrases from my article will be used here. I call the Tiananmen Square Protest a tragedy — that it was a tragedy is an indubitable fact. To quote the poet Shuyan Lei:

> *I dare say: if justice cannot be upheld, the sun will cease to rise from the East.*
> *I dare say: if sins cannot be accounted for, the Earth may lose the hold of gravity.*

It is not only an endless pain in the hearts of those who lost loved ones and those who witnessed the tragedy, but also an eternal wound in the history of the Communist Party. I believe that we are obliged to learn the history as well as the underlying causes of the Tiananmen Square protest in order to learn from this tragedy and not let history repeat. Please allow me to recount some facts from my personal experience.

On the evening of June 3rd, all regular television programming was interrupted to play the announcement of martial law and military mobilization repeatedly, warning people against public protest and stating that they would be responsible for all consequences. Under the circumstances then, this kind of announcement actually rallied people to action. Masses took to the streets after seeing the announcement. After dinner, I rode my bike to the intersection between Yuquan Road and Chang'an Avenue, where crowds had already gathered. Long queues of military vehicles carrying heavily-armed soldiers were surrounded by hundreds of thousands of common citizens. The roads were barricaded with all kinds of roadblocks, including people's own bicycles. Masses marched towards the direction of Tiananmen Square. There were also touching moments in the extremely tense atmosphere. Many ordinary people handed water and popsicles to heavily-armed soldiers. Numerous young people lay down in front of military vehicles in an attempt to block the military's advance with their bodies. Around 10 pm, sparse sounds of gunshots came from the direction of Muxidi. From where I stood on Yuquanlu Road, we had no grasp of the situation. Shortly after, several flatbed trailers hurried over to 401 Hospital, carrying injured people. "The army has opened fire!" Everyone was stunned by those shouted words. Would the Chinese People's Liberation Army really shoot at Chinese people? Right when people were still in shock and doubt, military vehicles on Yuquanlu Road sped toward Tiananmen Square, ignoring the crowds. Soldiers threw down bricks from the trucks, and people on the ground threw them right back. The gunshots from Muxidi became increasingly concentrated while the military vehicle convoy passed by Yuquanlu Road. I counted the vehicles at first, and then realized that there were too many of them to count. Right at that moment, gunshots were heard on Yuquanlu Road, right where I was. "The army has opened fire!" "The army has opened fire!" The shouts spread in the crowds. I realized just then that the Communist Party itself had committed the cruel deeds of Kuomintang warlords and Japanese invaders depicted in the "Revolutionary Memoir", which the Party had condemned. I was definitely not a hero, and most definitely a death-fearing coward. I ran home in a hurry. My wife was worried and scared, and my daughter had already fallen asleep. But I could not rest all night. The gunshots from far and near never ceased. I went to the office and found out that the email communication line still worked. I sent an email to the Italian physicist who helped me carry the tape abroad, telling him what happened tonight in Beijing. "Please remember this day," I said in the email, "the fourth of June." I also told him: "You must know the value of that tape now. If anything happens to me, the tape is my last gift to my friends at ALEPH." From what I know, my email communication line was the only one in China at the time, so I believe that my email to my Italian friend made me the first person to report the tragedy of Tiananmen Square protest to people abroad. This is also one of the reasons that I was terrified of the aftermath and made the decision to leave China. The next morning, it was announced on television that the army "quelled a counter-revolutionary revolt" and "gained a great victory". In the announcement, there was a shot of a row of military tanks flattening tents into pieces and crushing the imitation of the Statue of Liberty. How many lives perished during the Tiananmen Square protest? One has to know how many of the visiting students left and how many of them remained to answer that question. What kind of "great victory" could that be? Organized army forces slaughtering defenseless masses, how was that "great"? I walked from my home toward the direction of Yuquanlu Road and saw that Chang'an Avenue was a bloody mess. I garnered courage to walk down East Chang'an Avenue, which was almost devoid of pedestrians. There were burnt tanks smoldering, military vehicles, bicycles flattened, and bricks all over, rendering the street a battlefield. I turned back immediately when I saw a corpse yet to be cleared off the ground around Wukesong. My heart was bleeding. Could this be China after the reform and opening-up policies? Could this be Beijing ready to enter the 21st Century? A week later, I went to Beijing Concert Hall with a concert ticket. It was clear to me that the concert had been canceled, but I just wanted to use it as an excuse to walk around and see Tiananmen Square. I passed by Gongzhufen, saw bullet marks on buildings along Lishilu Road. There were armed soldiers standing by the side of the street. I did not dare to loiter, nor take any pictures. I felt the closeness of death in front of the bullet marks and the armed soldiers. My friends at CERN asked me what had happened in Beijing through email and whether the news they had seen on television was true. They told me to take care. Our email communication line stopped working before I had a chance to reply. Right and wrong can be debated, but truth and lies are immutable facts. However, a State Council spokesman like Mu Yuan said that the army did not open fire, and claimed that modern technology could fabricate any scene on television. I could not imagine that the State Council of the People's Republic of China had such a shameless liar as a spokesman. Today, even Mu Yuan himself felt embarrassed, saying that the lie was out of necessity, in a helpless state. But his boss still attempts shamelessly to deny his role in suppressing the Tiananmen Square protest. This is absolutely unacceptable. People used many different means to reveal the truth behind the lies. What left the strongest impression on me was a reporter from China Central Television with immense courage who used the People's Heroes Monument's repair as an excuse for a close-up shot of a bullet mark on the Monument. The lie that army did not open fire was exposed by the noiseless dissent. The terror after June 4th was even greater than the fear on the day. The names and photos of people wanted for arrest were circulating in the newspapers. Television stations repeatedly played scenes of police arresting "rebels" — policemen handcuffing these people to trees and brutalizing them. I could hardly believe that these things were taking place in broad daylight on Chinese soil more than a dozen years after the Cultural Revolution had ended. Shortly after, the central government issued documents for investigating so-called "Nineteen Kinds of People". The Communist Party enjoys using numbers to describe political movements, such as "Three Antis Movement", "One Strike and Three Counterings", "The Four Cleans Movement", and "Three Kinds of People". This time, good gracious, was a record breaker. They came up with nineteen kinds of people, numerating all kinds of charges. Some people were adamant in their claims to "eliminate all evil", full of viciousness and spite. Martial law troops published a phone number for a "report" line, and they could arrest anybody with a "report" call from anyone. Fully armed soldiers occupied train stations and airports. The discovery of any photograph or pamphlet related to the Tiananmen Square protest meant immediate arrest. Heaven knows where the authority of law went! I felt the imminence of great danger. Many people knew that I had been to Tiananmen Square to videotape, photograph, and even give speeches like "A Reconsideration of Capitalism". This was irrefutable evidence, clear as day. I checked out the so-called "Nineteen Kinds of People", and found that I fit at least eight or nine of those criteria. Hence, I had to leave the bloody reign of terror at the earliest possible moment. I could not fall into the hands of those people. I had to live, and witness the day when the people achieve victory. My only choice at the time, and the most likely choice, was going to CERN in Geneva, Switzerland.

More than 20 years have gone by. The Tiananmen Square protest was an inevitable historical event. In my view, revelation of the truth, indemnification of the people, and accounting for responsibility are eventually indispensable for society's development, stability, and justice. To this day, we are not yet close to the truth of the Tiananmen Square protest. What were its underlying causes? Were students merely the pawns in a conspiracy game of chess? Accountability means not only investigating those who ordered to fire those shots, but also pursuing those who added fuel to the flames with provocative commentary behind the scenes. At the same time, we need to reflect on the fanaticism involved in "Taking to the squares, taking to the streets, and letting jasmine flowers blossom all over China" many years later, during the Jasmine Revolution. History has proven that China's progress depends on the enlightenment of the people, on the emergence of humanity, freedom, human rights, law, and the gradual melioration of culture. Speaking of reparation, every member of the Communist Party needs to remember: in order to not let the tragedy repeat, monitoring the political party in which a party member believes is an undeniable responsibility and a cause worthy of sacrifice.

7.4 Leaving home

To "eliminate all evils" and prevent so-called "absconding", the government ordered that anyone going abroad must obtain a so-called "exit permit" in addition to a passport and visa. This was to prove that the person leaving was not one of the nineteen kinds of people. I went to the Party branch secretary as soon as possible to ask her for a proof of my lack of involvement in the "counter-revolutionary revolt". The Party branch secretary in the physics department was a nice person, but she was timid and overcautious. She said: "You are a deputy director, so just write one yourself. I won't read what you write, but I can sign it for you. This way, if anyone asks in the future, I will just say that I have no clue what you asked me to sign." I considered it, and her idea made sense. It was true that I did not participate in any "counter-revolutionary revolt". If anyone asked her about it afterwards, she would be blameless. I temporarily passed the so-called "political examination", and received a "political examination card" from IHEP. Since I was the deputy director in charge of foreign affairs, I always kept my passport myself. However, buying a plane ticket and getting a visa took time. I was worried that my wife and daughter might get scared; I did not wish them to know that once I left, it would be hard to say when the next time we could see each other again would be. Thus, I sent my wife and daughter on vacation to Xi'an. Before their departure, we went to the KFC in Beijing to have fried chicken, and took a picture for my daughter. My feelings at that instant were complicated beyond words. The days never ended while I eagerly awaited my visa. Everyday I saw people getting captured on television and every night nightmares visited my sleep. I could not endure that kind of torture, so I thought that if one day I were to be captured, I would rather take my own life. Because the tension kept rising during that time, I decided to hide at my wife's parents' home. When the day came for me to collect my visa, I was unprepared to hear that the issue of exit permits was further restricted and that my political examination card from IHEP had already expired. I had to go back to IHEP to obtain a new card; otherwise I could not get an exit permit. My plane was scheduled to depart at 11:50 pm that day. A successful renewal of the card was unlikely, not to mention that I did not have any time. I went to a friend who worked at the foreign affairs bureau at the Chinese Academy of Sciences and told her about my situation. She was another woman who lent her help at a moment of crisis in my life. She said to the people who issued exit permits at the Academy of Sciences: "Weimin Wu has to go to CERN for a conference tomorrow. If you give him an exit permit, I will go to IHEP to get him a new political examination card, and I will assume all responsibilities if anything happens." So I finally escaped with this crucial exit permit. Had she not saved me, my life would have embarked on a different path. Five hours before takeoff, My IHEP employee's card was still with a colleague from ALEPH. Not long ago, ALEPH had mailed us a data cartridge with my name indicated as the recipient, so I had given this colleague my employee's card so that he could collect the data cartridge from the post office.

Now I had to get the card back from him in case I needed it at the airport. When I saw this colleague, he was taken by great surprise: "Ah! Wu! They didn't take you away?" I pretended to be calm and said: "What taking away? Who would take me away? I didn't break the law!" He said: "last night, six or seven people from IHEP were captured. We didn't see you for several days and thought you had been captured too." I said: "I'm fine." The colleague still wanted to ask me how to set up the data cartridge, but I told him that we would deal with it next time. After that, I went to my closest friend at IHEP and gave him three letters. One was for my wife and daughter, another for my family in Shanghai, and the third for my colleagues. I told my friend: "I am going to the airport immediately. Please wait for my call at the office. When I am about to board the plane, I will call you. That would mean I made it to the plane safely, so please mail these letters. If you don't receive my call, it means that something has happened to me, so please destroy these letters." I also told him to leave my office as it is, and not to clear it out. My friend agreed to help me and told me: "Wu, you are way too nervous. You will most definitely be all right." That's true! If even people like me were "enemies", then there must have been millions of "enemies" in Beijing. However, under the "eliminate all evils" policy, they would wrongfully kill a thousand people rather than miss one man. Even if the Party were to redress victims several years later, I would already be dead.

July 25th, 1989 is a date I would never forget. I finally left for the airport. Fully armed soldiers were all over the roadside. I saw that the soldiers were free to inspect any car, even cars of ambassadors. Maybe it was because I rode in my wife's father's military vehicle that there had been no trouble on the way to the airport. When I arrived at customs, I was surprised that there were no inspections at all. I thought this must be a manifestation of the people's aversion to the government's reactionary policies. So many people wanted by the government were able to leave China successfully thanks to other people's help and sympathy. When I finally made it to the waiting lounge, I was confident that I would be able to depart safely. I called my friend to tell him that I was about to board the plane and asked him to mail the three letters.

When I got on the plane and stowed my luggage, I could finally relax. For over a month, I had not been able to sleep well even once and had lost more than a dozen pounds. The bloody scenes, the beaten-up faces, the students with their hair pulled up and hands cuffed onto trees, gave me nightmares that often woke me in the night. I sat in my seat with my eyes closed and fell asleep before I realized it. All of a sudden, a yell woke me from my slumber. When I opened my eyes, I saw that the plane had not taken off, but six armed policemen were walking around in the cabin, repeating five names and ordering those people to leave with them immediately. At first, no one paid attention to the policemen. The cabin was filled with dead silence. Most Chinese people hung their heads and looked down, and the foreigners stared with their eyes wide open and dumbfounded. My heart was about to jump out of my throat until I made sure that the five names chanted by those policemen did not include mine. When the police announced that they would check everyone's passport if no one came forward, five young people stood up. The police shooed them off board right away. When they were gone, it was as if an earthquake had hit the plane. The passengers lost their composure; everyone looked aghast under the cabin's dim light. The plane's engine resumed. Sleepiness had left me, but I could finally breathe easily. However, the engine stopped again, and more armed policemen walked into the cabin, repeating several different names. One of them also had the last name "Wu", but the given name was different. My body tensed up again. This time, no one stood up. When the police threatened to inspect passports again, our flight captain from Polish Airlines started to complain to the police, who began to inspect passports one by one, starting from the back rows. Right then, two more young people stood up, another young woman stood up as well with tears in her eyes. The police took them away, yelling and shouting. I thought these young people must have boarded the plane with special valid permits. Maybe someone tipped them off with a call to the martial law troops at the last minute that led to their arrests right before departure. At any time, there are always some Lilliputians playing the role of Judas in China.

The plane finally took off. There was no walking or talking in the cabin until we had flown over Pakistan. I did not realize until then that a student from IHEP whom I had hired for ALEPH was also on the plane. He was going to France with a connecting flight at Warsaw. We exchanged greetings with a tacit mutual understanding.

When the plane arrived at the airport in Warsaw, I settled down at the hotel designated by Polish Airlines. I called my Polish friend right away. She was a colleague who used to work with me at CDHS, and her father used to be a Polish ambassador to China. My colleague was out of the house, so her father picked up the call. I knew her father as well. He told me: "You do not have to fear anymore. Chinese police cannot track you down at Warsaw. Although Poland is still a Socialist country, we are not far from freedom." When the plane to Geneva circled above Lemon Lake the next morning, I saw the familiar fountains in the lake, and I could not stop my tears from pouring out like the fountain water.

Out of fear for any last-moment mistake, I had not told anyone about my departure except the close friend at IHEP. I called friends right after I got off the plane. Hans rushed to the airport to see me just after a few minutes. I started crying out loud, all my bitter tears were stopped only by a tight hug.

That day, Steinberger invited me for lunch. He was mostly concerned about whether people from IHEP were hurt or arrested. I replied that I did not hear about any deaths or injuries, but I did hear that some people were arrested. I told Steinberger what I had heard from the ALEPH colleague on the day I left. I also said that I did not know the specifics regarding who was taken away or for what reason. Steinberger took this very seriously. He called Prof. Tsung-Dao Lee immediately, requesting him to negotiate with China for the release of these people. Steinberger said: "I cannot do anything for most people, but I will do all I can for the IHEP personnel." TD Lee replied after contacting China, saying that no one from IHEP was under arrest. Steinberger then found me to ask where I got my information. I told him the name of the colleague who told me about the arrests. Steinberger certainly knew him; so he called TD Lee again, asking him to clarify with the person from ALEPH, telling him it was coming from me. Soon after, TD Lee told Steinberger that there had been a few people from IHEP under arrest, but they were unrelated to Tiananmen Square protests. They were accused of "sexual scandals," and had already been released. Steinberger was infuriated at this news, convinced that it was a monstrous lie. How could this kind old gentleman who had suffered at the hands of Fascists believe that at a crucial moment of political struggle, the police would arrest people for "sexual scandals"? It must be the case that he who has a mind to beat his dog will easily find his stick. I was of the same mind as Steinberger. Five years later, in July 1994, I saw the ALEPH colleague again and asked him whether anyone from IHEP had been arrested. He told me that the Chen Xitong Gang had questioned how so many IHEP people had participated in the protest activities, yet no one was a part of the "mob". How was it that no one was arrested? The Babaoshan police station had no choice but to arrest several people who had a gambling habit, and report them as part of the Tiananmen Square protest "mob" as a "scapegoat". One can see the absurdity of Chen Xitong and his gang, and their notoriety among the people. My colleague did not know what was going on, having heard nothing but rumors. What I knew was certainly mere hearsay. At the time, I did indeed tell Steinberger that I only heard a rumor. Who could have known that this whole incident would become one of my main accusations. Along with "Defection Abroad", "Bourgeois Liberalization", and other accusations, I became the one singled out at the entire Chinese Academy of Sciences. IHEP expunged my name from the faculty list, withdrew my residence, and excluded me from all award considerations I deserved. I knew that the administration at the Academy of Sciences and IHEP did nothing but follow the standard procedures, coping with the Chen Xitong Gang's bidding. Especially now that I was abroad, and "a dead mouse feels no cold," doing everything to me could protect other people. This way, however, I had no choice but to stay abroad temporarily under the circumstances at that time.

7.5 Reunion in Switzerland

To be honest, leaving China had never crossed my mind prior to the event. I had spent several thousand Yuan (RMB) on a set of mahogany furniture shortly before the Tiananmen Square protest, with plans for settling down in Beijing to live and work in peace. It did not occur to me that I would have to flee from China before I opened the packaging; it was truly a "panic flight", with no mental preparation. At the time, I only wanted to avoid the limelight. Who knew the temporary escape would drag on for decades, and this life journey would become irreversible? When I arrived in Geneva, upon careful consideration, I determined that I must move my wife and daughter out of China. I knew that if I was accused of "Defection Abroad", they would be "damned for eternity" in China. My friend extended a helpful hand to me. Paolo's friend obtained an invitation letter from the World Laboratory director for my wife Hengbao, inviting her to be a visiting scholar at CERN. My other great friend, Dr. Chu-chen, a leader of the Overseas Chinese Organization in Switzerland, sent a private invitation letter to my daughter, inviting her to visit Switzerland. At that time, going abroad was very difficult for Chinese people. All kinds of regulations, examinations, and procedures for going abroad were in place and were much more complicated than they are today. I mailed all necessary foreign documents to my wife. However, the organization she worked for, the Graduate School of the Chinese Academy of Sciences, just would not approve. After my good friend at IHEP negotiated with the Graduate School's management, they finally agreed. My friends and I had a tacit understanding that they would do all they could to help during my time of crisis. However, the so-called "political examination" was only delayed, not approved. The problem this time was a Communist Party leader at IHEP. I will call him Mr. "Mu". He was another communist that makes my blood boil. He viciously opposed the reform and opening–up policies. When it came to fighting so-called "Bourgeois Liberalization", he became excited like he was high on opium. I will mention later that it was he who turned my temporary stay abroad into permanent emigration. He did many outrageous things; although I can easily sue him in today's legal system, my friend told me that the reform and opening-up policies became so popular that Mr. Mu fell out of favor. There was no need to kick a dead horse. Mr. Mu used a "political problem" as an excuse to prevent my wife from going abroad. This Mr. Mu brought out the practice of "collective punishment". Since my wife was going to be a "visiting scholar", not traveling to "visit family", my "political problem" should have been irrelevant. But this Mr. Mu was adamant in his disapproval. This issue was eventually reported to a senior administrator at the Chinese Academy of Sciences. This administrator had had an hour-long private talk with me at IHEP in 1987. He knew me well. We had talked about many things, from network communication to administration, all the way to successors. I heard it was he who made the decision to approve of my wife's going abroad. He was a man of education and character. My wife's problem was solved, but my daughter's problem became trickier. Although a private passport was finally made for her, rules of the Public Security Bureau maintained that her passport had to be picked up by parents because she was only six years old. Parents had to have proof of parental relationship, and the first step of obtaining any proof was getting a "certificate from organization". In China at the time, "organization" was an institution of supreme power! A "certificate from organization" was required even for private matters like marriage and childbirth. My wife went to the personnel division of the Graduate School for a certificate of mother-daughter relationship, but the simple request brought trouble. The personnel division said: "the Graduate School only approved of your "visiting scholarship" at CERN, did not agree to send both you and your daughter." In China, after the Tiananmen Square protest, going abroad with children meant "defection". No one wanted to be responsible for letting Weimin Wu's family defect abroad. Here I am immensely grateful for those sensible good people. Not everyone in this world is an extreme leftist like Mr. Mu. With the assistance of some good people, my wife was able to obtain both the certificate and my daughter's passport. When going through customs at the airport, however, another issue arose. My wife had a "business passport", but my daughter's was a "private passport"; they had to walk down different aisles at customs. How can a six-year-old child go through customs by herself? Luckily, through a friend's arrangement, my wife and daughter went through customs in different aisles next to each other. Midnight, February 23rd, 1990, they finally boarded the plane heading for Switzerland. On February 25th, the two of them arrived in Zurich after all the toil and trouble, and my family reunited. My heart was filled with all kinds of feelings. I am deeply thankful for those who offered us help at the risk of their own reputation and safety. Although they were not like the heroes from *Schindler's List*, they are people we forever hold in our hearts. Most of them are members of the Communist Party. They are respectable, lovable elites of the Party; they are an army of justice. In contrast, extreme leftists like Mr. Mu seem like they are helping the Communist Party on the outside, but in reality they antagonize the people against the Party. If I were the General Secretary of the Communist Party, I would purge the Party of those anti-people extreme leftists. In order to be a good Party member, one has to be a good person first. If one cannot be a good person, how can one be a good Communist Party member? To sum up, it is rare for Communist Party members to act like Mr. Mu. This is why the Party is still popular among the Chinese people. I cannot emphasize enough that it is essential to remove persons in leadership positions, and their positions, if they do nothing but persecute others. They are the rebels against the nation, the Party, and the people. They are the biggest destabilizing factor in a civilized society. They "take class struggle as the key", see the people as enemies, and work as goons for the Gang of Four, Chen Xitong, and Bo Xilai. They are like the scums in the movie *Hibiscus Town* who do nothing all day but hope for "revolutions" to take place. The people will most definitely abandon them in the end. Bo Xilai's recent downfall is a typical fate for this kind of people.

Although we were immersed in the fleeting joy of family reunion, many worries and troubles found their ways fast. First and foremost, neither my wife nor my daughter spoke a word of English or French, so I had to take care of everything. My wife's visiting scholarship at CERN was really a favor from a friend. Although she was a competent programmer, language barrier posed challenges in conducting deeper research, making her worried. At the same time, I knew that CERN was only a short transition. As the chance of returning to China was slim, I would have to find a relatively long-term job. Because we were both "visiting scholars" in Geneva, not official employees, our income was not high, while the cost for a home of three was big. We rented a one-room apartment. Although the condition was much better compared to what we had in China, housing a family of three in one room was something people frowned upon in Switzerland. Soon, something happened. My daughter had been playing the piano since she was four. I wanted her to continue it, so I rented a piano for her to practice. The rules for the apartment included no loud music after 8 pm. So my daughter practiced the piano from around 4 pm, when she got out of school, to around 5 pm every day. This was completely legal and reasonable, but our upstairs neighbor was very upset. Whenever my daughter practiced the piano, he would hit the floor with a wooden stick in protest. He turned out to be the son of a local drug store owner. I asked him politely: "So when would you say is a convenient time for us to play the piano?" He said never. I explained that we had not broken the rules. He said: "I know you did not break the rules, but I would still request the landlord to cancel your contract. You should find a single-family home. Don't play the piano in an apartment building." I said, choosing a place to live was our business. I asked the landlord and he said: "You did not break the rules, but it is best not to play the piano in order to avoid conflicts." I disregarded them and continued to let my daughter play the piano. The neighbor continued to hit the floor with a wooden stick in protest. Later, I came up with a solution. I sent an invitation letter to all the neighbors, inviting them to my daughter's piano recital, with Chinese refreshments provided. This way, he no longer protested with the wooden stick. My daughter performed on the piano at a school event and was widely praised. Later, in a school parade, neighbors along the road who knew her called out her name, which made her very proud. It was clear to me that although housing three people in one room broke no rules, not "doing as the Romans do in Rome" was sure to bring criticism. It would not work in the long run. This meant that I had to have a real job, and have a normal income. I needed my family to live normally.

Besides worries about work, there was something else that bothered me. Now that my whole family was in Switzerland, it was completely different from when I was there alone. I had the responsibility of taking care of my family. My daughter attended elementary school in Switzerland. She was unfamiliar with the local language, culture, or customs. Once, some children were playing in the sand together. A Swiss boy made a sand castle. The bell ran right when he finished, so everyone rushed into the classroom. My daughter stepped on his sand castle by accident. A simple little sand castle like that — children in China would build it, destroy it, and rebuild it, and it would not be a problem. But the boy kicked my daughter right in the face and made her eyes swell. My daughter shouted in Chinese: "Down with imperialism!" "Down with Eight Power Allied Forces!" People around her had no clue what she was saying. My daughter chased after the boy, hurling curses in Chinese. Afterwards, Steinberger heard about it and was very angry. He went to the principal for a promise that things like this would never happen again. In fact, this showed that the barrier between different cultures and peoples could not be easily overcome in such a short amount of time. When I heard my daughter yell such ridiculous slogans like "Down with Eight Power Allied Forces", I did not find it funny, but found it so sad that I could not help my tears. From then on, when I dropped my child off at school, I always took a look back at her with each step I took, until I watched her walk into the classroom. Juggling work, job search, and all kinds of things at home exhausted me. There was not much time left until my passport would expire. My future appeared dark and hopeless. When I faced such great difficulty in life, I received help from friends from Switzerland, France, Italy, Germany, Singapore, Japan, and the Netherlands. True friends from IHEP also sent me their care and encouragement, at the risk of being framed or implicated for helping me. Whenever I think of them, my heart is always moved with deep gratitude. It was they who convinced me of my life motto: what the mind can conceive, it can achieve. Miracles often come at difficult times to those who have steadfast faith.

7.6 An old flame withered in the fall

I had another predicament in life at the time. It was my "Xiao Ju", the girl I had met previously in Geneva.

Living in Switzerland, Xiao Ju was deeply concerned about the Tiananmen Square protest in China. She had no information regarding my safety. Before I arrived in Geneva, we had no contact. When I suddenly appeared at CERN, she was pleasantly taken by surprise. Very soon, she was asking me if my family was fine and what I would do with them. I asked her: "What do you think?" She replied: "That's an easy question! You must bring them here as soon as possible. Otherwise they might be implicated in your troubles." My heart trembled at her words. What a selfless soul she was!

We used to take walks in the outskirts of Geneva, and we had seen many small houses unique to Switzerland, called chalets. These chalets were generally used for vacation, but some people lived in them as permanent residences. She told me once: "If we have one of those little houses one day, I will be content for the rest of my life." Afterwards, I wrote a poem for her, titled "Morning Fog" (translated into English):

> *I am willing to be the morning fog*
> *Flowing up the mountains and down the vales*
> *To decorate the scattered chalets*
> *Bringing breaths of life into serene dales*

> *How dull is a picture without perception*
> *How arid is a life devoid of emotions*
> *I am willing to be the morning fog in the sun*
> *Even just to make a moment's memory last a lifetime*

Unfortunately, my poetic words came true. The time came when I became "the morning fog" that only left her a long-lasting memory.

Xiao Ju said to me: "If the Tiananmen Square protest had never taken place, your family could live in China, while I live in Switzerland. I wouldn't mind you going back and forth between us." We could talk about the future when your daughter grows up. Now, everything is different. Your family has come to Switzerland with no means to care for themselves; you must look after them. It would be best if I stay out of this." She was right! I thought so as well at the time. A good friend of mine, however, gave me a different suggestion. He said: "Your wife has a great job in China, and a very strong family background. She and your daughter were not involved with any political activities, so they should be fine. If they come abroad, the language barrier and difference in lifestyles would make their lives difficult. Let alone the fact that you have such a great friend like Xiao Ju."

Ah! That was another "what if". Too bad that people do not live in a hypothesis, and there is no room for experiments. Life is but an irreversible course. Once you set out, it is like treading in a racing current. You cannot step in the same spot for a second time, no second chance for a different choice. Later events proved that my friend's words might have been right. Xiao Ju was working on her doctoral dissertation at the time, and she asked me to revise it. Many feelings arose in me after reading it, so I wrote to her:

> *"Counting from when safflowers flew over chrysanthemum fields, it has been five hundred days. Reading your thesis gave me many feelings. The catching title, thorough calculations, meticulous experiment, rigorous analysis, are all manifestations of your dedication, not to mention your efforts and devotion. The characters of a talented young physicist and a strong woman blend together in this thesis. I have reached the age when I should have established myself, but I am still struggling in the face of fate, I cannot help but regret this tragedy of the times..."*

Life is like Brownian motion. We are microscopic particles moving erratically, colliding with each other. Sometimes it is wide-angled, sometimes small-angled. Some people never experience any wide-angle scattering; now a little towards the north, now a little towards the south, but "the mighty Yangtze river flows eastward" in general. What I encountered, however, was mostly wide-angle scattering. There have been many sharp turns in my life, rendering me a helpless in small raft drifting through rough waters.

"If an old flame eventually withers in the fall, would the winter still bring the fragrance of plum blossom?" I asked myself.

A real turning point in the history of my life had arrived.

Chapter Eight
Immigrating to the United States

8.1 America alone

In the beginning of 1990, I was feeling very sad and hopeless and wrote this poem:

> *"I am a lake empty of water, a river in drought,*
> *the Sun in twilight, the moon in wane.*
> *I am a flower withered, a leaf in the autumn wind,*
> *Flowing ice over spring water, snow beneath summer rays."*

Right when I had hopes of ascending to reach the peak of my career, an unprecedented political tumult knocked me to the ground, forcing me to start anew from what felt like the very beginning. It was clear to me that I foremost had to find a relatively stable place to live, a place where I could possibly reside in the long term. I had no way to predict China's political direction after the Tiananmen Square protest, or how long it would take for things to return to normalcy. Although my friends in France and Italy were able to find me short term jobs, the positions were not ideal in the long run. My best option, then, was to go to America.

As I learned during my days in Geneva, the general population in countries like Switzerland harbors an "unwelcome" attitude toward foreigners. Even in countries like France and Italy, a person with Asian facial features can never be fully accepted as either French or Italian despite obtaining a local passport. However, America is a different story. It is the "home of the brave, land of the free", welcoming people from all over the world to pursue life, liberty, and whatever constitutes their happiness. Once you have US nationality, you are American regardless of your race, creed, or country of origin. After all my years spent abroad, however, most of my friends lived in Europe, and I barely knew any Americans. At this moment of crisis, many of my friends offered a hand in need. Dr. KK Phua, the Chairman of World Scientific Publishing Corporation, was the first.

I met Dr. Phua in 1984, when I participated in a photography competition hosted by CERN. Expert judges from Geneva rated all the photographs anonymously, including 10 of my pictures. My submission, "New Born", won the first place in the colored photographs' group. It was a picture of a newly sprouted leaf, shining with tiny wisps of fine hair. The lens was focused on the leaf, and the background was blurred. Although the photograph has a relatively simple structure, its theme made it stand out from the rest. The organizers of the competition put all 10 of my photographs on exhibition, and I invited my British friend to come see them.

While I was in the exhibition room waiting for my friend to arrive, Dr. Phua came to visit the exhibition. He asked me if I was acquainted with the winning photographer, and I said it was me. And that was how we met. I did not realize that he was the well-known Chairman of World Scientific Publishing Co. until I conversed with him. Counting from that day, we have known each other for about 30 years. How often in a lifetime will 30 years go by?

World Scientific Publishing Co. was founded in a small office, with only five employees. Dr. Phua's story about founding the corporation with his wife left a very strong impression on me. After 30 years of hard work, World Scientific Publishing Co. has become one of the leading scientific publishers in the world. It is the largest publisher in the Pacific area, holding a large share of the market in the field of high-energy physics. I personally witnessed its growth, which would have been impossible without Dr. Phua's charismatic leadership. He invited me to work at their office in New Jersey during some of my hardest times. He told local employees to help me with visa and paperwork and gave me a great deal of encouragement. Dr. Phua and I have become very close friends ever since we met in 1984. I was cordially welcomed to Singapore along with my sister upon his invitation. The book she wrote after that trip, *Memoirs in Singapore*, later became the first book that introduced Singapore to readers in Mainland China.

My other American friend, Professor Saulan Wu, also extended a helping hand to me. She and I became good friends while she was helping

IHEP setting up ALEPH. Not only an outstanding physicist, she is an amazingly kind person and a motherly figure to her students. She has strong connections with many national laboratories in America. She recommended that I move to the United States as soon as possible before my Chinese passport's expiration — Friday, April 13th, 1990. Friday the thirteenth represents a day of bad luck in Western culture. I felt an unprecedented sense of foreboding toward the future upon my arrival that day in the rain.

After I landed in the US, my friend Adam helped me as well. He is a Polish man, my colleague at CDHS. He had been working at Fermi National Accelerator Laboratory in Illinois at that time, and he let me stay at his home temporarily. So, I had had a resting place in America. When I left CERN, I purchased round-trip tickets because I did not know what would happen after I arrived in America. Nor did I clear my office at CERN. Who knew that my stay in the United States would last 25 years! How shocking to think of memories of the past!

With the recommendations from Steinberger and Professor Saulan Wu, Argonne National Laboratory agreed to give me an interview. My interviewers were four physicists headed by Professor Larry Price. They examined my resume carefully and asked me many questions about my work experience and physics. In the end, Larry asked if I had any concerns, and I said that I wished to receive the same benefits as employees of the same qualifications and capabilities. Larry told me not to worry about it. He said that if I were to be employed, I would be treated fairly. The law in the United States is thankfully against discrimination based on skin color or country of origin.

June 6th, 1990 was a lucky day because double six is a lucky number in the Chinese tradition. I received a letter from the personnel division of Argonne National Laboratory that offered me a contract to work as a physicist for one year in the high-energy physics department. I was pleasantly taken by surprise. I was deeply grateful for Professor Larry Price and Professor Tom Kirk's support and Steinberger and Professor Saulan Wu's recommendations. I told the good news to Dr. Phua. He wrote a letter to me saying that he was very happy for me because I could continue to work in the field of scientific research, and he hoped that I would strengthen my working relationship with World Scientific Publishing.

I was very glad to work at Argonne National Laboratory, but also a bit worried because it is a laboratory that deals with many state secrets. China had shouted "Down with American Imperialism" for decades, and it would be difficult to rebuild the trust between these two countries for the first few years after China stopped its anti-US campaign. The officials in charge of security at Argonne National Laboratory often asked my colleagues about me. Once, an agent named Hunt from the FBI called to talk to me, which was quite startling. I had seen many movies about the FBI, but it was my first time interacting with a real person who worked there. After that talk, I realized that FBI agents are truly simply dedicated in their work in the best interest of the US. Portrayals of them as "demons" could not be further from the truth. As long as you abide by the law and avoid actions that harm the national interest, they do not bother you. That agent, Hunt, was a very understanding official. He found out that I was starting life from scratch and often had to buy commodities from second-hand markets. Over a weekend, he took me shopping at a very large marketplace for used goods. This was very different from the stereotypical image of government agents. I remember in an American television series I had watched in China, the protagonist was named Hunt, and he was a very handsome, tall man, with great intellect. The Hunt I had met was of the same features: it seemed to be the fictional Hunt in reality.

Once, Professor Saulan Wu was invited to give a presentation at Argonne National Laboratory. I went to pick her up at the airport. Since the flight was delayed, it was late in the night when she arrived at Argonne National Laboratory. The gatekeeper would not let her in. We showed him the invitation letter and the note for accommodation at Argonne National Laboratory, but he still would not take anything but the pass. Professor Saulan Wu had to call the director of Argonne National Laboratory, but even then the gatekeeper persisted. In the end, the director called the head of Security Department and had him talk to the gatekeeper. We finally got in. This incident made me appreciate the devotion and vigilance of the gatekeeper, but also made me balk at the inconvenience of working at a secretive organization like Argonne National Laboratory. Thus, I went to Fermi Laboratory (Fermilab) right away when I received an offer a year later.

Fermilab is a completely open research institute. Both Fermilab and Argonne Laboratory were participants in the project of building a

Superconducting Super Collider (SSC). Solenoidal Detector Collaboration (SDC) was involved in the project. SSC was a complicated hadron collider, the largest in the world. It was built near Waxahachie, Texas, with a circumference of 54.1 miles and each beam 20 TeV in energy. Because both Fermilab and Argonne National Laboratory participated in building the SSC and the SDC, I had few problems transferring from the latter to the former. On June 1, 1991, I was employed as a physicist at Fermilab with a three-year contract. My immediate supervisor was Dan Green. I did not know then that I would work with him for over 20 years and develop a profound friendship.

Funny story — since Argonne National Laboratory hired me, my plane ticket expense from CERN to the United States could be reimbursed. As I mentioned, I bought round-trip tickets; although they were cheaper than a one-way ticket, I could only get reimbursed for half of the money I paid for the trip to America. If I had known in the beginning, I would have purchased a one-way ticket in the first place. After I arrived in the United States, I realized that some matters of legality here make no sense. This is a country governed by laws: laws and regulations have the supreme power. Whether they are reasonable or not is not the question, and perhaps different people will have different interpretations anyway. This was a lesson of law that life has taught me after I arrived in the United States.

After Fermilab had hired me, my most important task was to familiarize myself with the work. Adam was very hardworking. He arrived at work before 8 am everyday, and stayed until after 6 pm. I did not have a car at the time, so I rode with him everyday to and from work. He also gave me a lot of assistance on my own work. My contract at Argonne National Laboratory was for one year, and the one at Fermilab was for three years — I had to prove my competence at my job to obtain the next contract. Because there was no guarantee, the pressure of work weighed heavily on me.

After I got my first paycheck from Argonne National Laboratory, I bought my first car. It was a second-hand Buick with more than 60,000 miles on it, and it only cost me $800. The seller wanted $1,200 at first, but my friend helped me negotiate until we reached a deal at $800. I experienced bargaining in America for the first time and was surprised at its effectiveness. America is a country on wheels, and not having a car is like not having legs. I often told my children in later years that this $800 car helped me through my most difficult first three years in the United States. In fact, driving in the US was much easier and cheaper than in Switzerland.

When I knew that I was going to America, I started taking driving lessons in Switzerland. My teacher was a German engineer at ALEPH. He had a stereotypically German strict and meticulous style. He taught me to drive scrupulously. For example, I had to use both hands when turning the steering wheel, and never pull with one hand and push with the other. Driving like that was not only elegant but safer as well. The driving test in Switzerland was very strict. I remember that one test item was turning backwards on a slope, and another that forbade sliding more than 20 inches when starting the car on a slope. It was harder because we drove manual shift cars! They required changing gears and stepping on the accelerator at the same time as releasing the hand brake, and a moment of delay meant that the car would slide backwards. The road test was even harder. I remember that the examiner told me to take right turns and left turns, which I executed well. Once I was told to take a right turn, so I did. Who would've known the examiner would order me to stop the car immediately, telling me that I had failed the test! I asked why, and the examiner told me to look at the sign on the road that I turned into: "No Entry". "Did you not ask me to turn?" I asked. The examiner said "Yes, I did tell you to take a right turn, but do you go by my words, or the signs on the road?" I was speechless. I did not have time to retake the test, so I never got a driver's license in Switzerland. When I arrived in the US, the driving test was much easier. The examiner saw my standard driving style and let me pass the road test in five minutes. I firmly believe, however, that regardless of one's success on the Swiss or American road test, no one is prepared to drive on the roads of Beijing or Shanghai. The pedestrians and bicycles there never yield for automobiles. I cannot imagine how the road test for a Chinese driver's license takes place on the roads of Beijing or Shanghai.

Although I had arrived in the US, the shadow of the Tiananmen Square protest still lingered, clouding my mind. There were often road kills on the way from Adam's home to Fermilab. Whenever I saw the dead animals, I was reminded of the bodies flattened by military vehicles during the protest. This kind of memory did not fade until many years later. I always drive very carefully in the US, especially when I encounter small animals, so that I do not kill anything on the road. This is in hopes that those shadows will not come back to haunt me.

These relatively trivial matters taught me basic life skills to live in America. But the real problem was, how would I reunite with my wife and daughter, who were still living in Geneva?

8.2 Reunion in the United States

The application process for a visa to the US was very complicated. Although Argonne National Laboratory secured an H1 visa for me, this type of visa only allowed me to work in the US without bringing my family members. Plus, given the fact that my passport had already expired, it was impossible for me to bring my family over from Switzerland. According to US law, my wife and daughter could apply for H4 visas. When they went to the American Embassy in Switzerland, however, they were told that they had to return to their country of residence, China, to apply for the visa. At the time, I was named as a "defector" in China. If they were to go back, it would be the equivalent of turning themselves in for persecution. This unforeseen problem put them in a difficult situation, to say the least. Luckily, my good American friend, Nancy, gave us a great deal of help. She was a high official at the American United Nations Office in Geneva. She negotiated with the American Embassy in Switzerland, and the Embassy said that if CERN could provide written documentation proving that "CERN welcomes Weimin Wu and family back to Switzerland at any time," then the Embassy could count us as "residents" of Switzerland, and my family members would be able to apply for H4 visas in Switzerland instead of China. After some contact, CERN issued a certificate that called me "a highly valuable scientist", saying "CERN welcomes Weimin Wu back to Switzerland to work at CERN at any time." Thus, my family finally obtained H4 visas and embarked on their journey to America. Now, the problem became a question of where they would live.

Housing has been a hard question all over the world. When I worked at IHEP in Beijing, we lived in a tiny unit smaller than 50 square yards on the second floor. The hallway was always dark and crowded with clusters of junk from all the families in the apartment building. Within a few yards of my window was the kindergarten's roof. The kindergarten's chimney pointed right at us. If we opened the window around lunchtime, the soot would go right into our home, so we could only open the window in the mornings and the evenings. On hot days. without air conditioning, it was pure torture. But even a small unit like this was taken away when I left IHEP. In China, housing was closely connected with the organization for which you worked. The size of your home depended on your status, position, seniority, age, etc., as well as your relationships in the organization. For people like me, living in a small unit was bliss compared to the cavehouse in the mountain. When I was in Geneva, because I was alone and had to give IHEP money out of my meager income, I lived a frugal life. To save money, I only rented one room. I had to be extra careful in the fear of displeasing the landlord who lived right by me.

It was completely different in America. In America, there was the "American dream." Almost every family owns its own house, unrelated to people's employers. Your income is between you and your employer, but it has nothing to do with what house you live in, whether you rent it or own it, big or small, far or near ... completely unrelated to your organization, status, position, seniority, etc. I thought, now that I had a normal job, I should try the "American dream" too, especially when Adam told me that the rent is almost the same amount as the monthly payment to buy a house. So why not give it a shot?

The town Adam lived in was called Wheaton. It was a quiet, middle-class town, about half an hour away from Fermilab. We often went to a nearby Chinese grocery store to buy food on the weekends, passing by a town called Glen Ellyn on the way. Glen Ellyn was lush and lively, close to Morton Arboretum. Whenever I passed by, I always thought "How nice it would be if I owned a house here!" Hence, whenever I thought of buying a house, I would think of Glen Ellyn. Deng Xiaoping once said, following the path of capitalism was often criticized, but true followers of capitalism were rare. It was true. How could I buy a house? How could I contact a real estate agent? How could I apply for a loan? Even for such a supposedly simple "path of capitalism", I had no clue how to follow it. Deng was right. In China, there were not too many people who followed the "path of capitalism", but too few. When I started to learn and practice all this, I immediately encountered many unforeseen "capitalism" problems.

The first one was "credit history". Because I had newly arrived in the US, I had never borrowed money, never used a credit card, nor loaned any money. Therefore, the bank thought my credit history was bad and would not lend money to me. This puzzled me. I had never needed to borrow any money; wouldn't that be a good thing? But the bank did not think so. According to the bank's logic, if you have never borrowed money before, how could I lend money to you without knowing whether you would pay it back? That's right! In China at the time, if you had never borrowed any money, it meant that you were self-sufficient and competent. If your life depended on borrowed money, it meant that you had problems. This drastic contrast was a huge cultural shock to me. It turned out that people who could borrow money were rich and the ones who could not were poor. The second thing was finding a real estate agent. In America, an agent was indispensable in a house purchase. All negotiations with the seller had to go through the agent. This job was nonexistent in China at the time. Why would buying a house require an agent? This also confused me.

In any case, I thought I would learn the drill. So I found a real estate agent, a Polish woman recommended by Adam. I told her I wanted a house in Glen Ellyn. She said the houses there were too expensive and could be out of my affordable range. I said I would try it. She was very helpful and found a house for me in a couple days. The price and location were both desirable. That day, I went to see the house right after work. I had just received the one-year contract at the time. The house was next to the Morton Arboretum, on a boulevard. Going up from a slope, I saw a saucer magnolia tree. Although the pink flowers had already faded, it was still a gorgeous early spring sight. The house had a spacious living room connected to a large garden through a big glass door. The garden was a land of idyllic beauty with a grassy lawn decorated by a dozen pine trees and maple trees, all luxuriantly green. The absence of fences made the backyard seem even bigger. There were soft carpets in bedrooms, independent heating and air conditioning systems in the basement, and independent water treatment systems and hot water systems. The garage with two car spots was connected to the house so that we could drive the car right in and step into the living room. The house was also equipped with two bathrooms. A house like this was no less than heaven for someone like me, who had just arrived from China. Seeing the house was "love at first sight", and I decided to buy it, before I looked around for half an hour. I only lowered the seller's price by five percent. My agent was taken by surprise, having never seen anyone who made a decision so quickly. The seller was also shocked to see a buyer who gave a price so fast. Looking back, what I did was stupid, or at least uninformed and lacking strategy. The fact that I decided to buy the house after looking at it for only half an hour was apparently a ridiculous thing to do. My friends also thought that I was too rash. The seller did not accept my price immediately, but that evening, my agent told me that the seller gave a new price after the reduction. I agreed to it. Who knew the agent was afraid that undue delay may bring trouble, and had me sign the contract at my residence on that same night. From checking out the house to signing the contract, I only took seven hours, breaking the record of closing time among all of this agent's clients. In fact, when I think back, it was correct to make a prompt decision; it was also consistent with my character. Some Chinese people look at so many houses that they are dazzled and miss out on good opportunities. Of course, after several years, I began to notice the flaws of this house, but that was way down the line.

Although the contract was signed, I encountered unexpected trouble getting a loan. Besides the credit history problem I already mentioned, the bank also raised many other questions. First was that my work contract was only for one year, so was my H1 visa; what would I do after that year? The only possible solution the bank provided was that I had to pay a down payment as high as one fourth of the full price. I did not have that much money at the time, and barely covered the fare with money borrowed from friends. However, the bank requested that I provide a certificate to prove that all of the down payment money, especially the money transferred from Swiss bank accounts, was all my own. It is common knowledge that Swiss banks keep their clients' information confidential and would never provide such proofs. Moreover, I had to accept an interest rate one percent higher than that for clients with good credit history. The seller seemed to foresee my difficulty obtaining a loan and set the rate for breach of contract due to the lack of a loan at a very high price. This way, I was likely to suffer a penalty of several thousand dollars, and the contract for buying this house would be scrapped too. Someone told me that I was "trying to reach the sky in a single bound" and there was no need to "ask for trouble myself".

I should have settled down in a rental place and looked for a house to buy later. But I am inclined to rise up to challenges by nature. I enjoy striving for things that are difficult to obtain, but which can be achieved through effort. I decided to seek another agent for the loan. The new agent had opened a small firm himself. He tried many solutions, and finally helped me obtain a loan the day before the sales contract's expiration. At the same time, my family members obtained their visas. At this last moment, however, another issue arose. The seller's lawyer said that according to the law in Illinois, any real estate purchase required the signature of the buyer's spouse if the buyer is married. The expiration date for our real estate sales contract was July 31, 1990; the date of handover of the house appointed by the bank was also that day. As it happened, my family's plane was scheduled to arrive in Chicago in the evening on the same day. What should we do? After discussion, we agreed that I would sign with the seller in the morning first and complete the house handover, and my wife would sign her name on the contract when she arrived in the evening. So on that magical day, my family went straight to the lawyer's office after getting off the plane, and went straight to the new house right after signing the contract. Although the house was empty and it was already late in the night, my daughter was so excited that she ran from this room to that, rolling on the carpet. We slept on the carpet that night. Everyone felt like it was living in a dream. We reunited in a house of our own, and for us that was no less than a dream life.

Physicists like to think that space-time is consistent and continuous, and the consistency remains even after quantization. Life experiences, however, were completely different. My signing of the real estate sales contract and my family's application for American visas were independent quantitative changes; as for the application for the loan and sales contract for the house, although they were related, they were completely independent events. These completely independent events taking place on the same day was a remarkable thing. To me, this day was a discontinuous singularity on the space-time coordinates.

8.3 No alternatives

In fact, my main problem at the time was not housing, but my passport. My passport had already expired by then, so technically I was a stateless person. Living in the US on a visa was only a temporary measure. Once the visa expired, I would have had to renew it with a valid passport. I was already 47 years old. Going to the US was a last resort. On the one hand, the situation in China prevented me from returning; on the other hand, starting from scratch at the age of 47 was truly difficult. The best solution was to renew the Chinese passport and work in the US as a Chinese citizen, waiting until the situation in China cleared up to determine my next step.

Therefore, I sent a letter to the Chinese Consulate in Chicago to apply for a renewal of my passport. The Consulate told me to write a report on my reasons for not returning to China, and required me to provide a copy of the documentation that proved that IHEP had expunged my name. I supplied everything they needed and wrote reports repeatedly. I explained over and over again that my stay in the US was only temporary, only to avoid the limelight, and that I wished to return to the motherland as early as possible because I loved my country. Over a year had passed, and I had written as many as seven or eight reports. Here are some samples of phrases I used in the reports: "The warmth of our motherland is the most telling when her citizens need it in cold winters of despair;" "kindness is unnecessary if it does not come until one has achieved success already;" "the Chinese passport proves the citizenship of Chinese people, and no institution has the power to seize it for any reason other than a legal one."

The Chinese Consulate sympathized with my situation. They explained to me that they were only an abroad office, and that the decision to extend or renew my passport depended on the institutions in China. I believed their words, but my friend at IHEP told me very clearly that they never received any reports from the Consulate about my requests. I trusted my friends at IHEP deeply. I knew them well, and I was convinced that they would never lie to me. They would tell me the truth even if for some reason they could not renew my passport at the time. Under these circumstances, I had to suspend my trust in the Consulate. As a result, the Consulate had to break their rule and tell me the code for the document they sent to IHEP: 1991 (004), regarding the extension or renewal of Weimin Wu's passport. I gave the code to my friends at IHEP and told them to check, and they said that they had yet to receive it. Note that special diplomatic couriers delivered these kinds of documents, and it would be impossible for the document to be lost. All my hopes were crushed.

Prior to this incident, many people had suggested that I apply for permanent residency in the US, the so-called American green card. The US President at the time also issued an Executive Order allowing Chinese students and visiting scholars who fled the country after the Tiananmen Square protest to apply for American green cards. I did not apply. It was not just a show of my "patriotism". On the one hand, I did love my country where I was born and raised. On the other hand, I had always felt that immigrating to America was indeed too late for me. Building up a life from the very beginning at the age of 47 — how exhausting a task! However, I had no other choice. Thanks to my outstanding performance at Fermilab, the director John Peoples gave me a new contract on February 11, 1992. This contract said: "I am very pleased to offer you a Fermilab Applications Physicists II appointment, effective February 15, 1992 ... This is a position without time limit, and recognizes your valuable contributions to the Fermilab effort on SDC."

At the time, most of the SDC department at Fermilab worked on hardware or electronics. I was the only one designing the Monte Carlo simulation for the hadron energy converter. I completed all calculations for the physical parameters and published many analysis articles, receiving praises from supervisors and colleagues. After obtaining a "permanent position", my anxiety was greatly reduced. Hence, I started my application for an American green card. I had my contract with Fermilab, recommendation letters from Steinberger and Saulan Wu, a long list of "accomplishments" and titles such as renowned magazine editor at World Scientific Publishing, member of the 22nd International High Energy Physics Conference organization committee, member of China Center of Advanced Science and Technology, and many articles published during my time at CDHS (CERN, Dortmund, Heidelberg, Saclay) and ALEPH. Fermilab helped me apply for the immigration office's first priority green card, the kind of priority green card reserved to be issued to internationally-renowned scientists. I was called to go to an interview within several months. It was the afternoon of June 3, 1992. I called Yuanxing's school to excuse her for half of the day. The interview went very smoothly and only took 10 minutes or so. When I dropped Yuanxing back at school, her whole class had signed on a large piece of paper in congratulations to her. My daughter was deeply moved. The United States was truly an immigrant country that stands in stark contrast with Switzerland. On August 11, 1992, the immigration office gave me official notification that my family and I had become permanent residents of the United States.

The United States not only welcomed immigrants, but also provided them many unexpected benefits. When my daughter first arrived in Switzerland, she did not know a word of French. She had no assistance except for the help of friends. In America, most public schools have English as Second Language (ESL) classes for immigrants. When my daughter first arrived in the US, she thought all foreigners spoke the same language, so she spoke French. Everybody laughed, but no one made fun of her for not speaking English. People were rather envious of her for knowing French. Within two years, her English was one of the best in her class. Unfortunately, her Chinese reading and writing became rusty although she still speaks the language fluently. Sometimes she uses the wrong words when talking in Chinese and creates misunderstandings, which is truly a shame.

When I entered China again and went back to IHEP in 1994, I found out that the Chinese Consulate in Chicago did send the document coded 1991(044) to IHEP, but a Party leader at IHEP, Mr. "Mu", had broken the rules of the Party and the laws of the country to seize the important diplomatic document. He knew that I was a good friend with everyone at IHEP, from the director to the staff at the Foreign Affairs Office, so he secretly withheld the document from everyone else and left the Consulate no reply. I have every right to sue Mr. "Mu" for this kind of criminal behavior. Deng Xiaoping has given a serious talk on the harms of such extreme leftists: "The deepest roots lie in leftism. Some theorists and politicians who threaten people with accusations are not rightists, but leftists." Take a look at history — which big crisis in China was not caused by extreme leftism?

These people often disguise themselves under the glorious title of revolution, but everything they do is against humanity and they have no talents other than persecuting people. Hu Jintao said: "To govern a country with laws, we have to first govern a country with the Constitution." Administrators like Mr. "Mu" who make the Communist Party notorious deserve nothing but to be brought to justice. In fact, these people are the culprits for provoking the Tiananmen Square protest. Deng Xiaoping wished for further reform and opening-up; he said: "The necessity and importance of political reforms are felt with every step forward of economic reforms." Of course, Deng hoped to carry out the reforms with organization and good leadership. Those extreme leftists, however, dreaded that kind of reform, and instead created chaos everywhere and antagonized everyone. They would not let go of "class struggles" and adamantly opposed the kind of reforms Deng envisioned. At the recent Eighteenth Communist Party of China National Congress, a newly elected national leader said, "Reform and Opening-up require abandoning all selfish interests and upholding the people's interests as the highest objective." People like Mr. "Mu" fear the loss of their immediate interests, so they oppose these policies and resent people like me who support them, especially proponents of political reforms. If I were the General Secretary of the Party, I would most definitely expose all sorts of "leftists" like Bo Xilai and let the people know their harms. Mr. "Mu" and his lawless behaviors put me in a situation where I had no choice. He wanted to persecute me to my grave but ended up forcing me to leave the country. My departure completely resulted from the doings of "leftists" like Mr. "Mu".

After the Tiananmen Square protest, Deng Xiaoping's famous "Speech in the South" outlined the direction for reform and opening-up. It proved that Bo Xilai and his backers' "Eliminating Nineteen Kinds of People" movement and the like stemmed from ulterior motives, contrary to the direction of Deng's policies. China returned to the correct path of reform and opening-up because of Deng's "Speech in the South". Today's China is even more open than before the Tiananmen Square protest. Almost every recommendation I made in "Revalue Capitalism" has been carried out in China. My views back then were only somewhat ahead of their time. People like Mr. "Mu" were the true obstacles on the road to reform and opening-up.

8.4 Starting from scratch

Since we decided to settle down in America permanently, I thought I should give my daughter an English name. Her teacher and friends had never been able to correctly pronounce her Chinese name. Western culture seemed very strange to me, especially when I found out that there are special dictionaries for coming up with children's names. No wonder there are so many people with the same names in America. In China, there are so many Chinese characters, and any arrangement of two characters would make a name, which means there are infinite varieties. Of course, in the age of "revolution", many people named their children with the same "patriotic" characters that have something to do with the East, such as "Xiangdong" and "Weidong". I had named my daughter "Yuanxing", which translates to "the first star". I picked the English name Esther for her because it shared the "star" motif and was the name of Persian King Ahasuerus' Queen, who was a kind and intelligent woman. I made "Esther" my daughter's middle name when we applied for American green cards. The story of Esther was from the traditional Jewish celebration of Purim. It was a popular name.

Although we had established ourselves in America legally and had bought our own house, the house was completely empty and we had to start setting up everything from the very beginning. From kitchen utensils to bedding, from tables and chairs to daily commodities, everything needed to be arranged. Many American friends extended a helping hand to me. I will only mention one person here. One day, a friend of mine asked me if I would be interested in his old couch, and I said "Of course!" But my car was too small to carry it back to my house. He said that his friend would deliver it for me, and I thanked him sincerely.

One evening, a middle-aged man and his son drove up to my house with the futon couch in the trunk of their van. The man said that the couch used to belong to his daughter who left it behind when she moved, and asked if perhaps we needed it. As they were talking, the man and his son carried the futon couch into the house and helped us set it up. They worked so hard moving the couch that I could see drops of sweat racing down their foreheads. I did not know until afterwards that the man was the famous theoretical physicist Bill Bardeen, the Director of the theoretical physics department at Fermilab. His father was the only person in the world who had received the Nobel Prize in Physics twice: John Bardeen. This was the essence of America, Americans, and American culture. It is a memory that I will cherish for a lifetime. His actions showed me the true value of a person and the meaning of humanity. In America, donations and volunteer work like this are highly emphasized. Whether a student has done such activities is a criterion in college admissions. The value of service has become a social consensus.

Although there had been many difficulties, the beginning of my time in America reminded me of a famous poem by Johann Wolfgang von Goethe, "Begin It Now":

Until one is committed,
There is hesitancy, the chance to draw back,
Always ineffectiveness,
Concerning all acts of initiative (and creation).
There is one elementary truth in ignorance
of which kills countless ideas and splendid plans:
That the moment one definitely commits oneself,
Then Providence proves too.
All sorts of things occur to help one
that would never otherwise have occurred.
A whole stream of events issues from the decision,
Raising in one's favor all manner of unforeseen incidents
and meetings and material assistance
which no man could have dreamed would have come his way.
Whatever you can do or dream you can,
Begin it.
Boldness has genius, power and magic in it.
Begin it now.

This poem gave me inspiration and strength. I had to begin my journey with no thought of turning back. I believed that only proceeding forward would grant me hope.

It was this kind of belief that made me feel I had to cut off all means of retreat once I committed to starting a life in America for the long term. It was a different mindset compared to when I bought a used car for merely $800. This time, I bought my daughter a new piano costing $8,000. To celebrate obtaining the American green card, I purchased an expensive gift for myself: a collection of silver gilt "American Dream" stamps. This collection included all famous stamps that represent American values issued since American independence, one per month and twenty-four in total. Although collecting the full set would take two years and several thousand dollars, I thought it was well worth the time and the money. It reminded me of what it means to start from scratch and "begin it now". I also bought my daughter a statue and a necklace of the American eagle. The inscription reads: "Man flies with wings of wisdom." Let all these become permanent memorials for our immigration to America!

July 19, 1993 was my fiftieth birthday. I reflected on my life and thought that if I were to take a sample point of one of the parameters of my life, such as the place I live, every 10 years, my life journey is incredible. When the whole world was aflame with wars in 1943, an infant was born prematurely in an alley house in Shanghai; for when I was 10, I only remember the house with a small garden and two trees, but unfortunately I only lived there for two years; when I was about 20, I lived like a savage in a cave-house at a time that could have been the best time of my life; at the age of 30, I did history-changing work in remote mountains and deserts; 40 years of age was marked with sending the first email from China and living in the apartment with a window facing a chimney; when I reached 50, I was living in a real garden house across the ocean in America and working on the energy frontier. What immense change!

To celebrate the family's immigration to America, we decided to go visit the capital city, Washington D.C., to see the tradition and history of American democracy. We went to New York City to see the world-renowned Statue of Liberty and breathe the air of freedom. We went to the Niagara Falls to admire the beauty and the power of nature and reflect upon the ups and downs of life. Life! You are like a capricious river with calm reflections as well as crushing waves. My eventful 50 years demonstrate to me that life becomes immortal in the constant, effervescent flow.

To end this section, I have to mention two ladies who have been influential to me in my immigration to America. One is Nancy, whom I have mentioned earlier. She gave me a set of four books as a gift. These books introduce one to American society, culture, history, politics and economy. After living in China for so many years, I knew next to nothing about the United States of America. These books opened my mind and enabled me to become not only an American on "paper", but also an American in essence.

Another lady is Paula Cashin, who was the head of the benefits office at Fermilab. I think the best way to get to know this country beyond my work in Physics is talking to ordinary Americans, so I always sit with these kinds of people during lunch break. On the first day that I sat down at a table with a group of ladies for lunch at Fermilab, Paula was there. We all looked at each other with surprise. Why did a scientist want to have lunch with a group of non-scientists? I told them that I wanted to know more about the country and Americans, not just be confined to my field of specialty. When she asked me how I came to this country, she was deeply moved by my stories, and encouraged me to write them down. Actually, the initial thought of writing my autobiography was started at the lunch table.

Paula gave me an America flag when I became an American citizen. This flag reminds me that from now on, the US is indeed my home country. In 1998, we had the 100th day celebration after the birth of Yvonne. I was surprised and laughed when I opened the gift that Paula gave to Yvonne. It was a hat with the Irish good luck charm, a shamrock, on it. Paula and her husband had just returned home from visiting Ireland, the place of her husband's heritage. This showed me that we all have a heritage that we can respect and honor. Despite its flaws, the US is a place of freedom and opportunity. That opportunity has served us all.

8.5 Reputation restored

On April 24, 1992, I met up with Zhipeng Zheng, an old friend who had been promoted to the Director of IHEP, at a conference in Washington D.C. It was the first time we were seeing each other in three years. Words were too bleak to express all the feelings in our chests. He said: "Let the past stay in the past. IHEP has never considered you an outsider, far less an enemy. Your significant contribution to IHEP is widely recognized. You need to keep up the good work in the future and serve as a bridge in China-America cooperation." In August 1992, I met with the Secretary-General of the China Academy of Sciences when he visited the US. I had obtained my American green card by then. He said that the situation in China had changed much and that he felt deeply sorry for the injustices I had suffered. He encouraged me to look forward and contribute to China's cooperation with America in the field of high-energy physics. In October, the Chinese Consulate in Chicago notified me about picking up my new

Chinese passport, apologized for the long delay, and invited me to attend all sorts of events at the Consulate. Since then, the Consulate has invited me to Independence and New Year celebrations every year. It seemed that my reputation in China was restored. I was no longer a "defector". IHEP sent me multiple formal invitations to visit. In fact, all of this mounted to the complete condemnation of Chen Xitong and his gang's "Elimination of Nineteen Kinds of People".

At the same time, the SSC project I worked on at Fermilab was terminated in October 1993 because of funding issues. Although I have mainly worked on the SSC and the SDC team, I had never actually seen the accelerator. I went to the last SSC meeting in September 1992 for my last opportunity to take a look. It was my first time in Texas. My impression of Texas then consisted of cowboys, the Space Center at Houston, and President Kennedy's assassination.

I saw the true meaning of "wasteful" when I arrived there. The 14-mile tunnel had already been dug up; the surface of 17 axes had already been prepared; the total cost had already approached two billion dollars. In fact, another billion dollars would be able to cover what it would take to complete the project, but now the plan was to spend another billion dollars on returning everything back to its original state, filling up the tunnel that had been dug. Such a wasteful situation was related to America's funding system. The current President or Congress had the power to reverse decisions made by the last government. The SSC project had gained support in 1983. Its address was determined in 1987. The construction had just started in 1991, but it had to end in 1993. I witnessed new buildings deserted, papers scattered, office supplies upside down ... All of that came out of the nation's wealth!

I did not like the surrounding areas of the SSC construction site. It was far underdeveloped compared to Chicago and suburbs. I went to a supermarket to shop once, and they did not accept credit cards. Because everything had to be paid in cash, the lines were often very long. Once I went to buy fruits, and there was a cowboy standing in line right behind me. He was bored and started playing with two pistols he had. I was so scared of an accidental discharge when he was juggling the guns that I left immediately. In Texas, almost everyone owned a gun. Weapons could even be purchased at second-hand goods markets. No wonder Fermilab employees were offered a 10 percent raise in salary if they volunteered to go work at the SSC site. Even with the money incentive, not many people were willing to go.

The destiny of our SDC team at Fermilab became a big problem after the termination of SSC. Many factory contracts were cancelled. Many employees were fired. At the same time, CERN's Large Hadron Collider (LHC) was approved in 1994. The LHC was not quite as powerful as SSC, with each beam current at only seven TeV. But as a result of SSC's termination, it became the world's largest hadron collider. It was built about 100 meters underground, across the border between Switzerland and France. Its circumference was about 17 miles. Our department's director Dr. Green led several of our physicists to create an American collaboration team to work with a LHC experiment team, called Compact Muon Solenoid (CMS). Dr. Green emailed seven physicists, including myself, to express his hope that we would work together toward building a CMS team at Fermilab and later an American CMS collaboration team. We were very glad to have the honor of joining Dr. Green in this endeavor. On March 23, 1994, I attended a Fermilab meeting about CMS. The CMS department was soon established formally at Fermilab, and I became one of its first members. The era of working on the energy frontier had arrived.

Chapter Nine
Energy Frontier

9.1 Physics focus

Starting from 1994, I focused on my work with CMS for almost 20 years. This has been the only experiment that I worked on from beginning to end. I only did the renewed Monte Carlo for CDHS; I did not have time to participate in data processing for BES. The same thing happened for ALEPH, I had to leave by the time of data analysis. CMS was different from all of those projects. I was there from the designing and building of the detector, to data analysis, to publishing the article. I personally was involved in the entire process. My important contributions in some areas gained public recognition. Right now, the time frame for completing a research project in high-energy physics is too long. From the project proposal to the demonstration program, to approval and application for funds, building the detector, gathering data, analyzing data, all the way to publication, usually takes more than 20 years. There are only so many years in one man's life! Even after publication, it takes time to evaluate the experimental results and gain true understanding. No wonder young people nowadays are uninterested in learning high-energy physics. It is difficult to make money in this field and even more difficult to find a job. Taking years to study the subject and deciding to devote your life to experimenting with high-energy physics require true passion and dedication. I personally love the research, but to be honest, I treat the work more as a "job" to feed my family rather than a "career" to pursue as a life goal. I have many reasons for this. At first, only a few people were involved in Steinberger's Nobel Prize-winning experiment that discovered the muon neutrino. Only a few dozen people participated in CDHS and BES. A few hundred of people worked on ALEPH, while CMS involved several thousand. On a grand scale experiment like this, my presence does not make much of a difference. Second, I was already 50 years old at the time. Although I was competent in completing specific tasks, I was far from proposing creative insights like I did in my youth, when I was more passionate, inspired, and imaginative. Third, despite my US citizenship, I always thought of myself as more "Chinese" than "American" when speaking at international conferences. The days when I would receive a spectacular standing ovation like the time I gave a presentation at Uppsala, Sweden on behalf of IHEP were long past. These are the differences between a "job" and a "career". When I arrived at Fermilab, I told my self: first, I am a physicist, not a politician, and I shall stay out of all political organizations. Second, I need to forget my titles such as Deputy Director and head of ALEPH and do pragmatic work as an ordinary physicist. Third, I will work to promote collaborations between China and the US, especially between IHEP and Fermilab, and break no rules. I have adhered to all three resolutions over the 20 years. These resolutions have been the basis for my work in physics research in these years.

My first task was the physical design for the CMS Hadron Calorimeter. Fermilab was responsible for building the CMS Hadron Calorimeter. Its physical design determined its properties, cost, and many other related technical details. What material should be used for the absorber? How thick should it be? How many layers? How should the readout system be set up? All of these require physical simulation and a reasonable estimation of the cost based on the simulation. At the same time, we had to research the physical properties of such a Hadron Calorimeter: what is its energy resolution? What is its energy leakage? What about the mass resolution after mass reconstruction? We also had to calculate the results for physical processes. Our department director Dr. Green indicated that the energy resolution by the Hadron Calorimeter mainly depends on the physical process itself, not the Hadron Calorimeter's segmentation. If so, what would be a reasonable segmentation? How much would it influence the physical process? All of these required physical simulation. At the time, I was the only person working on Monte Carlo simulations in the whole of the Fermilab CMS physics group. Time was tight, so I worked overtime, completed all physical designs, published many articles, and finished the task beautifully. We used a looser segmentation. This satisfied the requirements and reduced the cost of building this Hadron Calorimeter.

Thus, more funds could be directed towards the building of the electromagnetic calorimeter with better energy resolution. This decision acted as a key contribution to CMS's discovery of Higgs particles. Thanks to the excellent energy resolution of the electromagnetic calorimeter, we obtained the decisive lepton event in determining the Higgs particle instead of the jet event caused by hadrons.

One of the main objectives of building the LHC and CMS was finding the Higgs particle. In 1977, Fermilab discovered the fifth quark, bottom quark. In 1995, Fermilab discovered the sixth quark, top quark. At that moment, all particles that form matter's standard model had been discovered, except for this crucial Higgs particle that was yet to be found. The Higgs particle was thought to be the explanation for why matter has mass. People did not know how large the mass of Higgs particle itself was at that time. The SSC accelerator was set at as high as 40 TeV to accommodate the potential large mass of the Higgs particle. SSC was canceled, but LHC's accelerator could only reach 14 TeV. However, God gave the LHC a chance. The Higgs particle actually had a small mass, only 125 GeV, so the energy of the LHC was more than enough for discovering the Higgs particle. Fermilab announced the discovery of the Higgs particle in July 2012, and reconfirmed the discovery recently. I was one of the authors of the article.

I deserved the authorship of the article that published the Higgs particle's discovery. From 1995, I led the Monte Carlo simulation research team in one of the particular Higgs discovery channels, publishing more than a dozen notes. The mass range we were looking for went from the minimum set by LEP all the way up to 1 TeV. Even so, I still think that I was no more than a "wage earner" with little creative contribution. As for the newest statistical method, the theoretical calculations of confidence level, specially with small statistics, always bothered me. At the time I did not understand them fully. Even to this day, full comprehension eludes me. Therefore, I cannot say that I had any outstanding decisive contribution.

After 2008, I shifted my research to physics beyond the standard model. Some examples include the little Higgs, mini black holes, Majorana neutrino, etc. I did calculations myself until 2009. After 2009, I started to mentor several American and Chinese PhD candidates and stopped writing programs and doing calculations myself. At the same time, I had developed an "aversion" to the article publishing process. Because of the scale of this international collaboration team, publishing an article in the International Journal of Physics required the agreement of several thousands of "hard to please" people. First, the small professional team had to "approve". When it passed, the large professional team had to "approve". They often had differing opinions from the small team. In fact, most contentions or changes were trivial. In order to obtain the approval of both the small and large teams, I had to patiently revise the article over and over again. The Majorana neutrino article I led took half a year from the beginning to the end before it was approved. When the time came for discussion among the entire collaboration team, another round of "amendments" emerged. After going back and forth for about a year, the article was finally published in the International Journal of Physics. I compared the end result with the first draft, and found no significant difference. It seemed that bureaucracy had penetrated the field of physics. This is the inevitable result of over-staffing! One article includes the names of several thousand people, but only 10 of them did the actual work. The rest were merely finding faults. This was another reason I did not wish to continue this work. Over the course of 20 years, there have been several dozen articles with my name published in internationally-renowned physics journals. Out of these, I was the main author of five of them. There have been more than 30 articles published on CMS research. For a "job", I have done more than enough.

 I will digress to discuss something that is not quite off topic. After the discovery of the Higgs particle, people started to talk about who deserves to receive the Nobel Prize for it. As important as the Higgs particle is, the Nobel Prize cannot be awarded to more than three people. I am certain that it is impossible to find the three most deserving people among the 6,000 who work for CMS and ATLAS. I think one of the reasons the 2012 Nobel Prize was not awarded to the Higgs particle's discovery because of the time needed to confirm the discovery's results. CERN collected all necessary data in 2012 and reconfirmed the accuracy of the Higgs particle's discovery a year later. In addition, the issue of whom to award the Nobel Prize to also posed challenges. Later, a Russian billionaire gave prizes to seven "leaders" of LHC, CMS, and ATLAS, which provoked heated controversies. This set the bad precedent of awarding the "leaders" in recognition of scientific research. Now, within the scientific community, people are holding "elections". Even though they are called "democratic elections", they are essentially a balance of interest and power. If these people become leaders through this method and receive the Nobel Prize, the prize would lose its reputation and value. Whether the rule of awarding the Nobel Prize to no more than three people needs to change, and whether a "group prize" should be created, provoked discussions as well. The 2015 "Breakthrough Award for Fundamental Physics Research" was given to the topic of neutrino oscillations, with seven leaders and five research teams. They will split the prize of the award - total three million US dollars. This is a sort of "group" prize. Can the Nobel Prize adopt this kind of model?

Sometimes, I wonder, what exactly do we wish to know, what exactly do we want to do? Currently, accelerators are being built larger and larger, with higher energy capacity, and longer periods of time. They are being staffed more heavily and cost more too. Just where do we draw the line? Some people have already proposed that LHC's energy is not large enough, is there a deeper level than quarks? Is there a combination of a quark and lepton? To explore many things like the existence of extra dimensions, higher energy is required. If we wanted to know how the universe came to be, we would have to simulate the energy of the big bang, which is absolutely impossible. Even reaching energy levels close to the big bang is impossible. So what do we do? Some people are researching ways to build new accelerators with new technology to reach higher energy levels with less money. There are also people trying to do research with Monte Carlo simulations. The US has already abandoned nuclear explosive testing because it is no longer needed. Monte Carlo simulation can replace nuclear explosive testing completely, given that the theory is clear. Then what about high-energy physics? High-energy physics research has encountered "existential crises" in countries all over the world. Fermilab is the only remaining one of the five major high-energy physics research institutions in the US, and even Fermilab has been long troubled by funding problems. An American colleague once told me that we were lucky to be able to work at a high-energy physics research institution until retirement. High-energy physics research institutions may be closed up before the next generation is ready to retire. What a sad prospect to consider! I feel that the current path will lead to an impasse. We must reform.

I have two suggestions that I have mentioned on multiple occasions. The first is to enhance international collaboration. High-energy physics research is the human pursuit of a better understanding of nature. To some extent, a few high-energy physics research institutions would be enough for the entire world. It would be no great feat to build several accelerators if we can concentrate all the talents of humankind. But this requires politicians to act wisely and collaborate. My second suggestion is that we need to sponsor ourselves, using our knowledge as our wealth. Why not? Even the Internet was our invention. If everyone in the world were to pay CERN every time he or she clicks on a page on the Internet, or if everyone in the world were to pay our research institute every time he or she gets an MRI, would we still have to worry about funding? Receiving funds solely from the government should become a relic of the past. The most ridiculous thing was that due to the lack of funding several years ago, everyone at Fermilab had to go on leave without pay for one week every month. This of course caused many inconveniences in our work. A billionaire donated several million dollars to Fermilab so that we could terminate the one-week leave without pay policy. According to rules, however, Fermilab was forbidden from receiving private donations. As a result, the money had to be donated to University of Chicago first, and then transferred from the university to Fermilab. Is this not self-deception? If American universities can receive private donations, why can't national laboratories? Unfortunately it was not my place to make the decision, and my opinion was too idealistic. But if my ideals are heading in the right direction, then why not do like Goethe said, "Begin it now!"

9.2 International collaboration

Because IHEP also participated in the CMS collaboration, finding effective ways to conduct international collaboration became a central concern at IHEP. In theory, CMS was CERN's experiment, figuring out how to collaborate with CERN was a problem. After my name was cleared, administrators at IHEP discussed with me the best ways to work with CERN. Now my role was different from what it was before. I used to be a member of IHEP, now I worked for Fermilab in the US. All my personal connections in China, however, remained. I was familiar with CERN, Fermilab, and IHEP, so I became the ideal person to serve as a bridge in this international effort. Because Fermilab was responsible for building the Hadron Calorimeter, I suggested that China submit a tender for building the Hadron Calorimeter absorber. IHEP contacted several organizations in China. Unfortunately, the price they offered was not the lowest. On the contrary, it was one of the highest. I talked with the IHEP associate director in charge over phone multiple times, and was told that the price levels in China had changed. Equipment in Chinese factories was often imported now, and the high price decreased the competitiveness of Chinese products in the international market. China had gone through a shift of the economic model and started to consider everything from the perspective of profitability. The political and international influences present when I was developing the muon detector at ALEPH were long gone.

The failure at bidding for the Hadron Calorimeter absorber forced me to find alternatives. I had to find another project. Naturally, I thought of the muon detector. I knew that IHEP was experienced in building muon detectors. They were equipped with the staff, machines, technology, and skills necessary for building a muon detector. However, if the muon detector were to become the focus of this collaboration, Fermilab would be an irrelevant participant. At this time, I met up with an old friend who worked with me at SDC. He was a Russian scientist who had gone to work at Florida State University after the cancellation of SSC. He had participated in the building of a muon detector for CMS. I saw him at Fermilab and talked to him about the collaboration with IHEP. He was very glad to hear about it. Later, I talked to the IHEP associate director responsible for CMS collaboration, and gained his strong support. He thought that teaming up to build the muon detector for CMS was a great idea. IHEP director Zhipeng Zheng also supported this plan. After discussion, the leaders of CMS agreed that it was a reasonable choice, especially because IHEP had a good reputation, having built the muon detector for ALEPH. Soon, the CMS collaboration team approved of this suggestion. That Russian scientist and staff at IHEP exchanged visits and confirmed technical details.

The collaboration went smoothly. IHEP completed the task on time with high quality. Later, CMS assigned the task of installing the muon detector at CERN to IHEP. When CMS leaders visited Fermilab, they specifically thanked me for my contribution in this collaboration. Although the Hadron Calorimeter absorber tender failed, I still managed to have IHEP join in the set up, measurement and calibration of the Hadron Calorimeter. This project provided a good opportunity for personnel training for IHEP. On the other hand, it also saved money for Fermilab and deepened the collaboration and friendship between Chinese and American scientists. IHEP sent staff to work on the Hadron Calorimeter at Fermilab three to four times in total, and their great work was highly recognized by Fermilab. I would like to mention two technicians who came to work at Fermilab in particular. These two technicians used to be members of ALEPH back when I worked in Beijing. At the time, I had promised that every single member of ALEPH in Beijing would have an opportunity to study and work abroad. Working abroad was not only a chance to see the bigger world, but also an opportunity to land a higher paying job. The ALEPH group numbered around 20 people. They have been sent to CERN, Italy, France, and other places. These two technicians were the only people who had never been abroad. Because I left suddenly in 1989, there was no one left to arrange opportunities for these two colleagues to go abroad. I have always felt guilt and regret because of this. A promise is a promise. This is a basic principle of humanity. I cannot break a promise I had already made. Over the years, I had always felt ashamed for not fulfilling my promise to these two colleagues. Then the opportunity finally came. I suggested that IHEP send them to work at Fermilab. However, unexpected problems arose. It turned out that one of them was not a member of the CMS team. It would not be appropriate if IHEP were to send her instead of someone from the CMS team. The other person had an even bigger problem. She had already become an archivist, and it was great trouble to send her abroad. After my repeated negotiations with IHEP, their bosses, and other people on the CMS team, IHEP eventually agreed to send the two of them to Fermilab for my sake. This unfulfilled promise that had weighed heavily on my heart was finally resolved. The two colleagues did not disappoint either. They completed the work successfully and received praise from Fermilab.

Because CMS was a massive international collaboration team, communication was essential. Every physicist had to attend experiment duty. It was a fair way to distribute the work while making everyone more familiar with the experiment and data. No one had special treatment among the thousands of people on the team. Steinberger was a distinguished professor back at CDHS, but he still went on shift. The computer assigned the shift schedule at random. Whether someone was on duty at night or during the day depended on the computer. I remember one time it was my turn to be on night shift with Steinberger. His meticulous work ethic left a very strong impression on me. When he checked if the gas system was leaking, he not only checked on the readings, but also climbed up to the top of the piping systems to check if there was any bubbling. I said I would go in his place, but he said it should be him since he was on main duty. Of course, with the new technology now, nobody has to climb the detector any more. However, I will forever remember his dedication. The problem now is that if every research institution were to send people to be on duty at the site at CERN, it would cost a lot of money and time. Thanks to the Internet, remote operations centers have become a reality. Scientists from Fermilab in America do not have to fly to CERN in Geneva. They can collect data right at Fermilab and check on the experiment when they are on duty. Because CMS participants are scattered all over the globe in different time zones, the remote operations center reduces the need for night shift significantly. For the above reasons, Fermilab first built a remote operations center so that we do not have to physically go to the CMS site at CERN to be on duty from Fermilab. I thought, since China had Internet access too, why not build a remote operations center at IHEP in Beijing? Hamburg, Germany had already built a remote operations center at the time. I suggested this idea to the CMS computer department at Fermilab and soon gained their support. After negotiation with CMS teams at IHEP and Peking University and with the help of Fermilab, IHEP built a remote operations center in 2011. We all cheered in excitement when control rooms at CERN and Fermilab showed up on the information display of the IHEP remote operation center.

Because of my outstanding contribution to the collaboration between IHEP and Fermilab, the leadership at Fermilab always treated me as a consultant for all IHEP, or Chinese-related affairs. The assistant director of Fermilab in charge of foreign affairs always called me to his office every time business with China came up. Whenever representatives or important figures from China came to visit Fermilab, I was always the host. Eventually, even Fermilab's users office, reception office, and education office went to me when dealing with anything related to China. IHEP often consulted me regarding collaborations with Fermilab as well.

On November 29, 2007, the 22nd Sino-US High Energy Meeting was held at Fermilab. The next day, Fermilab's leadership held a banquet for American and Chinese representatives. The assistant director in charge of foreign affairs entrusted me with the task of hosting the Chinese representatives on behalf of Fermilab. The assistant director told me that the standard budget was $25 per person. I said it was too little and that I would be forced to take them to some fast food restaurant. Later, the Fermilab director listened to my suggestion and told me through his secretary that this banquet does not have to conform to the standard budget. I was allowed to treat the Chinese representatives to their satisfaction. I took them to a famous local seafood house. Everyone loved it. The Chinese Consulate in Chicago frequented Fermilab as well. Over the past almost 20 years, there had been many Consul Generals, every single one of them visited Fermilab. I was always the host for visits, pictures, and banquets. On January 2011, Chairman Hu Jintao visited Chicago. Because Fermilab was one of the destination candidates, the Chinese Consulate in Chicago took the matter very seriously. They sent the largest delegation in history to inspect Fermilab. Except for the guards, almost everyone who worked at the consulate came. The Consul General hosted a banquet for the director and assistant directors of Fermilab at his official residence, which was a highest kind of honor. When IHEP director Hesheng Chen visited Fermilab, the Fermilab director hosted Chen at his house, which was also a high honor. I can say that during that time, the relationship between China and the US, between IHEP and Fermilab, was like newlyweds on a honeymoon. There were frequent personnel exchanges and numerous collaboration projects. There was also a new program. In recent years, China has often sent young cadres to American universities to pursue advanced studies. This was a strategic policy. Whether or not they had gone to a developed country to study was a big influence on their job prospects later in life. In my view, Deng Xiaoping's ideas of reform and opening-up were closely related to his experience in France as a youth. Some universities in Chicago often hosted short-term classes. These short-term classes liked to have their students visit Fermilab. Once again, I was assigned as the host. I became a minor celebrity for giving presentations and introductions for them, so those universities ended up inviting me to teach classes on campus. I have organized my presentations under the name of "Fundamental Research is the Culture of Civilized Powers". I have given this presentation at Peking University, Fudan University, Nankai University, the Chinese University of Science and Technology and some business units. My favorite memory was when I received the invitation from Fudan University to speak at the "Inspirational Forum". I was proud and honored to speak at that podium. Back when I was a student, every speech there brought a full house. I felt as if I had traveled back in time to my youth.

Of course, there were a few hiccups in the Sino-US collaborations. For instance, Fermilab's assistant director once requested me to host a Chinese delegation. I guided them on a tour that lasted over two hours. When it was time for their departure they gave me a small gift in gratitude. It was a little box to hold business cards. The little business card holder was delicately made with an engraving of a monkey's picture. The gift was nothing extravagant and completely within reason, so I kept it. Who knew that trouble would soon follow suit? Not long after I returned to my office, the resident "counterintelligence" official at Fermilab called me and said that he had something to ask me. When Fermilab was first founded, its first director Wilson made many rules and guidelines. There was also a rule against having resident agents from FBI and CIA. There are no secrets to hide because all research at Fermilab is open to the public. I had no idea when the resident "counterintelligence" agent started to work at Fermilab. When I came in, I had no idea what the subject of our talk would be. He came into my office and asked if I had received a gift from the Chinese delegation. According to the rules of Fermilab, all expensive gifts must be turned in. I thought he mistook the business card holder for an expensive gift and assumed that I kept it without reporting. I explained to him that the gift was small and worth no more than $20. He said, "No, no, money is not the problem here." I asked him, "Then what's the problem?" He replied with, "May I take a look at it?" So I gave it to him. He then said, "May I take it back to inspect?" I said, "Of course!"

I was infuriated. It was clear as day that I had hosted the Chinese delegation as per Fermilab's request. I had no previous connection with anyone on the delegation, but for some reason the entire visit seemed to be monitored. I complained to the assistant director. He told me that this was just the standard procedure and that I should not take it personally. The next day, that "counterintelligence" official called me and said I could go and collect the business card holder. I said, "You can keep it. It's your souvenir." It felt like a farce to me. If I were a "spy", or if someone on the delegation had been a "spy", we would not have been so stupid as to "exchange intelligence" with a business card holder! Moreover, what "intelligence" did I have to sell? What harm could such a small business card holder do? Did he think it hid a taping device or a bomb? This was ridiculous. I had worked at Fermilab for over 20 years and believed in Wilson's famous saying: "I mean all the things that we really venerate and honor in our country and are patriotic about. It has nothing to do directly with defending our country except to help make it worth defending." which means that we produce nothing but knowledge that we all are proud of. I had not the least idea of any "national secret" held at Fermilab or any motivation to steal any "intelligence" or be a spy. I am an American citizen, and doing anything that would break American law had never crossed my mind. This "joke" was not only inappropriate, but also ludicrous.

An even more inappropriate and ludicrous joke, however, was yet to come.

9.3 Being wronged

At 11:30 am on October 13, 2011, the Fermilab director's secretary told me to go to the director's office. I had been called to the director or assistant director's offices multiple times in the past to discuss important business. This time however, my high spirits were dashed as soon as I noticed the strained atmosphere. The personnel department's director was also sitting in the office with a straight face. I had no idea what had happened. The director told me that I was not Fermilab's ambassador to IHEP and that Fermilab had never sent me to attend any discussion at IHEP. Now that China was a rich country, it should contribute what it can. The collaboration between the leadership of Fermilab and IHEP was none of my business. Fermilab's future developments and plans were internal documents at Fermilab. I was not authorized to send them to IHEP. Even if IHEP needed to know about our future plans, it was something for the Fermilab leadership to do. If I did so... The personnel department's director paused for effect and said, I would lose my job at Fermilab.

I was completely lost at the time. I had not the slightest idea what they were referring to. Everything the director had said was correct; I was indeed not Fermilab's ambassador to IHEP, nor had Fermilab sent me to China to attend any discussion, nor was it in my place to participate in any discussions between directors... but what on earth it all meant was beyond me. I only replied that I knew I was not Fermilab's ambassador to IHEP and I should not send Fermilab's future planning to IHEP. I left the director's office utterly confused. Only when I returned to my own office and cleared my head did I remember something that had happened a few days ago.

The Sino-US high-energy physics cooperation meeting was about to take place in November. This kind of cooperation meeting was the earliest cooperation agreement between China and the US. From their first meeting in June 1979, their cooperation has lasted over 30 years. Every meeting, the two countries found many items to cooperate on. As the annual meeting in 2011 approached, however, the CMS collaboration team only a had few projects left that required cooperation. The detector building was already completed, so I asked about the accelerator. I called the IHEP director and my good friend Hesheng Chen and sent an email to inquire whether there was a cooperation project for the accelerator. Hesheng Chen replied to my email and told me about the situation. It turned out that a Fermilab physicist who went to visit IHEP had told him that India was planning on supplying Fermilab with about a hundred million dollars to collaborate. It was the expectation that China too would supply a hundred million dollars of funds. Hesheng Chen explained that every country had its unique situation. China could not do business exactly like India did. Furthermore, the IHEP director had no power to direct such a massive amount of funds. Only the central government was qualified to discuss such business. The Fermilab project itself was not yet officially approved by the American government. How could they request China to commit to it with so much money? At the same time, Chen forwarded me an email originally sent to the people in charge of this collaboration at IHEP, and added the following words:

"I made an introduction email for the IHEP participants in ADS with the FNAL accelerator physicist. It seems that the two sides cannot cooperate. The possibility of collaboration with FNAL was kidnapped by India."

The main text of Chen's email read:

"After lunch on Monday, Weimin Pan, Jianping Dai, and I discussed the possibility of cooperation with Kephart from Fermilab... he said if IHEP would like to cooperate with Fermilab to develop these two cavities, IHEP would need to pay $2 million. Weimin Pan and I talked with the Fermilab side a month ago, their requested price was $280,000 for co-niobium materials (we can use Chinese materials which could be much cheaper), plus $50,000 proceeding fee, and the two sides will get one cavity each. The renegotiated price of $2 million is too much. It is not acceptable... ."

After receiving Chen's email, I thought that we might be able to save the cooperation if the only disagreement was about pricing. So I called the assistant director at Fermilab, who agreed that we might be able to do something to bring this collaboration project back. He told me to forward Hesheng Chen's email to him. I said that the original was in Chinese, so the assistant director asked me to translate it into English. I felt that the line "the possibility of collaboration with FNAL was kidnapped by India" was worded too strongly, so I deleted this sentence in my first forwarded email. The assistant director read it, and asked me why this sentence was gone. I said I had deleted it, and he told me to forward the original email again, including this sentence. So I did.

This was how the misunderstanding arose. This assistant director at Fermilab had forwarded my email to the director instead of reporting to him in person. Since I was the translator and the sender of the original forwarded email, when he read it, the director thought I had written the email. What was worse, one of the participants of the discussion at IHEP had the same first name as I do, Weimin. The director mistakenly thought that I, Weimin, had participated in the discussion and emailed the assistant director of Fermilab. No wonder the director was so angry that he threatened to fire me, saying "you are not Fermilab's ambassador to IHEP; Fermilab never sent you to any discussion at IHEP."

It seemed to me that it must be a misunderstanding, and if I went to the assistant director and asked him to explain the situation to the director, the problem would be easily solved. However, I was shocked when the assistant director told me that he almost never talked to the director in person and that the only one who could talk to the director was the deputy director at Fermilab. I had worked with that assistant director for over 20 years. We had a good private relationship. Not long ago, he invited me to go to a Chicago Chinese Consulate's reception together with him. I could hardly imagine why he would not help me clarify this simple misunderstanding. I asked him repeatedly to clear up the problem with the director, but he kept telling me, "You did nothing wrong. You have nothing to worry about. I never talk to the director himself." He also said, "You know the deputy director fairly well. You can clarify the situation yourself." Later, I reported this incident to my boss Dan Green. He also told me not to worry about being fired since I had done nothing wrong. After thinking it over, I let it go.

But that was not the end of it. Two weeks later, the FBI called me and said they needed to ask me a few questions. I knew what questions they had in mind. At 1 pm on October 31st, two FBI agents came to my office at Fermilab. They first asked me to explain why I sent Fermilab's 20-year strategic plan to IHEP. I was prepared. This document was no secretive internal documentation. Anyone could have downloaded it from the Internet. I had already printed a copy to give to the FBI agents. I also told them the web address where I found it. They took the document. The second question was why I had so many connections with high officials at IHEP. I said, "This is simple. We are close friends who have known each other for a long time. We talk about collaborations between Fermilab and IHEP. Without these discussions, there would not have been so many collaboration projects. More importantly, all of our discussions are completely open. My boss and the assistant directors are all well-informed and supportive. You are welcome to investigate." I also volunteered the information about the potential misunderstanding in which the Fermilab director had mistaken me for another "Weimin" in Beijing, the Institute of High Energy of Physics. They then asked me about my involvement in developing the nuclear bomb in China. I said, "Yes I did. I was 17 years old, a freshman at Fudan University." I described all of these events in my book *The Beauty of Physics*. It seems like they did some work before they came to talk to me. I thought these two agents were just and professional. They did their job scrupulously, staying objective and equitable with no personal emotions attached. Thus, I hold great respect, and even gratitude toward them. They helped me clarify the truth. I told the assistant director about the FBI agents' visit and expressed my wish to have him clarify the situation with the director. However, he once again told me to do it myself and said "You did nothing wrong." I replied with, "Then would you please tell the director that I have done nothing wrong?'" He promptly fell silent, and my hope that he would help me vanished. In the end, I had to write a clarification letter to the director, deputy director and my department head and send it through email. In my letter, I explained all the details of this event, and asked that all the administrators at Fermilab restore my reputation. My requests were reasonable. I only wanted the director to admit that it was a misunderstanding. Unfortunately, things didn't pan out this way. I was reminded of something an important CMS administrator had once told me, "Weimin, you are too naïve. Even if the director made a mistake, you can never get him to admit it." He gave me a personal anecdote to support his claim. Later, it happened just as he said it would. On November 8th, the director called on me again and handed me a letter. In his letter, he wrote:

> *"You assume in your email that we are confused regarding the Sept. 21st message from the IHEP director that you translated. That is not the case and it is not what has created the issues that I raised in our discussion."*

He gracefully avoided the question of whether or not he mistook me for the "Weimin" in my email. He claimed the misunderstanding was not the problem here, saying "it is not what has created the issues that I raised in our discussion." However, he did not give me the true reason for summoning me to the office that day. If he had not mistaken me for the "Weimin" in my email, why would he tell me that Fermilab never sent me to any discussion in the first place? The Chinese proverb "He who has a mind to beat his dog will easily find his stick," came to mind.

He also said:

> *"As I explained to you in our meeting of October 13th, you act inappropriately when you communicate to the leadership of IHEP on business matters of the laboratory.*

It is my impression that when an individual such as yourself makes frequent contacts with high official in a "sensitive" country such as China, the FBI or the DOE Office of counter intelligence will do their due diligence in investigating the nature of those contacts."

I felt wronged upon receiving this letter. If the IHEP director Hesheng Chen had complained about me forwarding his email to the leadership at Fermilab without permission, it would be completely reasonable and acceptable. However, I was acting from Fermilab's standpoint throughout this incident, thinking that I might be able to help with communication if the only disagreement was about the cost. For over 30 years, the collaboration between Fermilab and IHEP had never ceased. It was my sincere hope that the collaboration project for 2011 would not be blank. Moreover, everything I did was upon the request of the assistant director. I could hardly imagine a relationship between an assistant director and the director with no direct communication. How could this be democracy? It was clearly a misunderstanding arising from mistaking the Fermilab "Weimin" for the IHEP "Weimin"; how could such a simple mistake not be admitted and corrected?

I had lived a peaceful life in the US for over 20 years and I was under the illusion that my life would continue in that matter. However, trouble found me eventually. Fate once again put me on the cusp of life. Later, I made peace with myself. China and the US had been enemies for so many years that it would take a long time to remove the misunderstandings and rebuild a trusting relationship. I was a newly immigrated American who had faced so many obstacles posed by China: being on the blacklist, forbidden from renewing my passport, and having my name removed from IHEP roster. A few years later, I became an important guest of IHEP and the Chicago Chinese consulate. Suspicion and conjectures were sure to arise. In fact, none of this should be a surprise. I was convinced that I was never China's enemy, nor did my country ever treat me as an enemy. I was never America's enemy, nor did the US ever treat me as one. It was due to a deep-rooted "ideological" shadow that some people in these two countries were always looking to persecute people. Unfortunately, they found me as a target. I only hope that the Sino-US relationship is peaceful and collaborative. I love the great citizens of these two great countries. The enormous Pacific Ocean is large enough for them both. I only hope to do my best in contributing to the collaboration and mutual understanding between China and America. The Cold War had ended long ago, but some people still held the Cold War mindset. In truth, collaboration is always a win-win situation. I sincerely admire the first Director of Fermilab, Robert R. Wilson, for uniting scientists from America, USSR, and other countries in joint research. What amazing work it was! Still, I felt greatly wronged by the events that had transpired. My boss Dan Green said to me: "Weimin, you are the lawn beneath two mammoths, constantly being trodden. You are innocent." Many friends advised me to appeal to the leadership, or even the court. I did not think that appealing would end well. I am grateful towards Fermilab and had good relationships with all the directors. Even with that particular director, there was never any other conflict or misunderstanding. The assistant director also gave me great assistance and contributed to the friendship between IHEP and Fermilab. He must have had some reason that he could not tell me for not clarifying with the Director on my behalf. I remembered the saying "Forgiveness is a virtue." Let us learn to forgive! This is a common ground in Chinese and American cultures. The facts and the truth were clear to me. The problem arose from a misunderstanding, which also had something to do with the prevailing mindsets at the time. The friendship and collaboration between China and America, however, are great and irresistible. I also believed that America was a country of laws. As long as I abide by the laws, the FBI would respect the facts. In fact, I never had any conspiracy in mind. All I did, I did it out of the hope of contributing to the collaboration between IHEP and Fermilab. I knew full well that the security department monitored my emails, but I still used my Fermilab work email to communicate with IHEP and the Chicago Chinese Consulate because I had nothing to hide from the public eye.

This incident was a vivid manifestation of "prejudice is further from the truth than ignorance." It also proved that if you thought bureaucracy only existed in China, you should think again. Later, I gradually realized that forgiving others equaled saving oneself. When I felt infuriated and wronged, my blood pressure rocketed and resulted in a minor stroke. When I was finally relieved, my mind and my heart were both at peace. Since my life has never been a smooth journey, why not treat this as another wave that had come my way?

9.4 To love again

In the first few years, I struggled to gain a foothold in the US and overlooked many family issues. My "Xiao Ju" had gotten married and we lost contact. It was not that I had forgotten about her. In fact, I wish to hear from her even today. We did not keep in touch because I was hesitant to reach out, afraid to intrude after she had started a new life. The differences in lifestyles, personalities, and interests between my wife Hengbao and I, however, were becoming more pronounced in our day-to-day life. The root cause was that she had not been mentally prepared to immigrate to America. Sometimes, she would say that she was "abducted" abroad by me. There was some truth to this. Immigrating to the US was not her personal choice. She used to work at the mathematics department at the Graduate School of Chinese Academy of Sciences, and she had a small leadership role. After she came to America, she could not find proper employment because of her English. When she resorted to working at a daycare, the employer thought her English was not proficient enough to interact with children. As a result, she was sent to cook in the kitchen. Her self-esteem suffered a blow. She felt that she had lost her life's purpose in America. This mindset often gave rise to many conflicts. I remember taking the ferry that went around Ellis Island when we went to tour New York City. When the ferry approached the Statue of Liberty, I said: "So many Chinese people struggled to immigrate to America illegally, some risking their lives. We are the lucky ones, getting our own house and green cards without going through too much turmoil. Let's take a picture with the Statue of Liberty!" To my surprise, she replied: "I'm not in the mood for any pictures. I never wanted to be in America." It made me very upset. We had a big fight. Afterwards, I realized that she had a point. Not everyone would choose to leave China for America. For people like her, staying in China may have been a better option. However, under the circumstances then, I had no choice. Later, when I decided to stick with the path I had chosen, I suggested to her: "Let's get divorced." I never would have thought she would reply with, "Sure. Let's divorce." This kind of reply was typical of her character. People often talk about woman's feminine tenderness, but she only had toughness and was never tender.

Although I said divorce out loud, I still felt a lump in my heart. After all, marriage is a sacred bond. We had been married for almost 20 years. Moreover, Hengbao married me when I was going through a very difficult time. Condemnations of unfaithfulness and betrayal plagued my conscience. My heart suffered.

Some people say that it is difficult to be a human, more difficult to be a woman, but even more difficult to be a man. Things like divorce are often blamed on the man, on the Don Juan. To be fair, perhaps being a woman is the hardest. Because women are a disadvantaged group in general, they face more repercussions in their lives after a divorce. Anyway, there is much to be said on either side, and neither the wife nor the husband should always bear the blame. In our situation, I was definitely in the wrong.

Sometimes, internal conflicts can be triggered by an external stimulus that disturbs the equilibrium. I attended social events frequently, and met a middle-aged lady at a conference once. She was a tall and slender engineer with a delicately sculpted face. She was the center of attention. We talked about America, China, her life, work, family, friends. We clicked immediately. She told me that she was getting a divorce. I asked her why, and she told me that when she was young, she met a famous scientist. This scientist was a tenured professor at an Ivy League university before he had even turned 30. She admired his talents and married him, but discovered that he was a strange man afterwards. Although they had a child whose intelligence was nearly "genius", their married life was not happy. She decided to file for divorce after consideration. A woman, initiating a divorce with a professor of high achievements and social status because he was a "mad scientist", intrigued me greatly. In what ways was her husband weird? We started an open and free discussion in response to that question. What should a scientist be like? I wrote an article on the subject. I will include an excerpt here. The article, as follows, was titled "Mad Scientists and Science Giants".

There is a television advertisement promoting a weight-loss product. A slim blonde lady introduces the mechanism and benefits of this weight-loss product eloquently. A handsome young man compliments her, saying: "What a scientist you are!" The blonde lady smiles and says: "I'm not the scientist. He is!" The camera then zooms in on a bony old man wearing thick glasses, withering away among a bundle of books. In this advertisement producer's mind, this is obviously the stereotypical image of a scientist.

Coincidentally, there was a newspaper article at the time called "My Teacher Shenke Qi", who was the authority in the field of forestry chemistry. The article described Shenke Qi with phrases like these: his face is a "long, inverted triangle", "pince-nez glasses", "thinning hair", "celibate for life", "skeptical toward females", "stubby fingers contain traces of chemical erosion"...

I had written an article on my interview with the famous mental arithmetic expert Klein. He had an ugly face and a habit of mumbling like a male "witch". He was able to find the 13th root of a 100-digit number with mental arithmetic, but had no basic life skills or sense of personal hygiene.

There is also a famous mad scientist in China. He was known for proving a conjecture. Rumor has it that he never trusted banks. He kept his cash either under his bed or on his belt. He did not even know what a cinema was.

People would keep away from scientists if I keep listing people like these. The gate to science would seem like a gate to hell. In fact, being mad is only one step beyond being a genius. These people may be accomplished in their fields, but they are also mad scientists. If all scientists were like them, it would be not only tragic for scientists, but tragedy for mankind.

Luckily, that is not how the world is. There are many people with souls in the field of science — the science giants. They exist throughout history, in all parts of the world. Da Vinci was known for his work the "Mona Lisa", but he was also an outstanding physiologist, anatomist, and architect. Qu Yuan was a great poet and politician. His work, "Lament", moved many people. However, few knew that he was also a great scientist. He posed the question "why is the night sky black" in the poem "Questions for Heaven". To this day we have no concrete answer. Ten intelligent people cannot answer the question of a fool. Qu Yuan asked hundreds of difficult questions, and then wrote "Answers of Heaven" in response. Marx was a great philosopher, thinker, and revolutionary. His academic *achievements gained recognition worldwide. His love letters to Jenny could make 'The Sorrows of Young Werther' even more sorrowful. Chen-Ning Yang won the Nobel Prize, but his Yang-Mills Field half a century ago was only just recognized as the most fundamental theory of physics in the 20th century. He was most definitely an eclectic science giant. In 1984, I went to Leipzig, Germany to attend the International Conference of High-Energy Physics. On the day after the conference's closing, I saw Professor Yang at the Museum of Leipzig by accident. We walked through the exhibitions together and chatted along the way. We clicked immediately and spent a whole day together. From the rise and fall of the Third Reich to the reason for which Germany recovered quickly after war, from the comparison and conflicts between Eastern and Western cultures to the evolution and development of Hegel and Marx's philosophy, he seemed to know most of the exhibits at the museum like the palm of his hand. This left a strong impression on me. He enjoyed my photography, and he was an outstanding photographer himself. He took a picture for me at Leipzig in which my smile showed my admiration for him. Fermilab's first director, Wilson, was not only a great physicist and engineer, but also an architect and artist. Everyone who has been to Fermilab is fascinated by his creative design of the main building and modern statues. The second director Lederman's speeches were more entertaining than any late-night show. He made academic reports feel like improvisation theater. Nobel Prize-winner Steinberger can play the flute like a professional. He also had the talents of a professional wine taster..."*

That's the end of the excerpt from my article. I asked that friend why she thought her husband was a mad scientist. She told me that according to her ex-husband, "sex has no purpose other than reproduction. If there is no desire for reproduction, sex consumes unnecessary energy and burdens the body." So after giving birth to a child, they had almost never slept together again. Although they were wealthy, he was too stingy to buy drinks when they go out and would rather suffer from thirst than "waste" money. He had many strange ideas and habits like this. Thus, she decided to divorce him after consideration.

I told her to end it well, but they took the most hurtful and least efficient way, through law and court. Her husband would rather spend a fortune on lawyer fees than concede to his wife on dividing properties. The divorce fight had been dragging on for several years by the time she met me, but had yet to reach a conclusion. She learned from our conversations that my marriage also faced a crisis, and we were sympathetic to each other. However, I was almost 19 years her senior, so I suggested that we just be normal friends. But in her mind, her ideal husband was a scientist like me with eclectic interests and a love for life, and she did not care about our difference in age. After meeting me, she gave me several calls almost every day, encouraging me to start a new life. Her presence disturbed my emotional equilibrium.

I garnered courage and brought up the topic of divorce or separation with Hengbao. I suggested to her that we separate for some time to give each other some space, so that she could consider whether to go back to China and decide on our next steps. Making this decision was very painful for me. Whenever I think of the image of her mother squeezing into a bus to go to Dongdan farmer's market to buy some fish for me, my heart would be filled with guilt and regret. I often said to myself, when people talk about marriage, they often say "a lifetime"; but for me, it was not only "two lifetimes", but almost "three lifetimes"! Of course, this was self-deception. I should be thankful for Hengbao's generosity and sensibility. People had advised her to sue me, but she decided not to do so. The relationship between one individual and another can take so many shapes and forms. After tying the conjugal knot, what good does it do to make each other enemies? I owe her, so I would not have given her trouble in dividing our properties. This peaceful agreement laid the foundation for our friendly relationship in later years.

On January 11, 1997, we signed a "Separation Agreement". I picked the date January 11 because it contains many "ones", a philosophical number that gives rise to life in *Tao Te Ching*, a Taoist classic text. I wished for a good, new beginning for both of us. Because the town we lived in was flat, it was difficult to see a rainbow around my home. The most I saw was a faint shadow of a rainbow on the horizon after a rainy summer night. On that day, however, a full, almost circular rainbow appeared above my house, even though it was sunny and clear. When I went to the driveway to get my car and go to work that morning, I saw the rainbow. I could hardly believe my eyes. I stopped the car and walked around my house, and the rainbow looked like it was hanging on my rooftop. I thought I was dreaming, so I took pictures of that rainbow from every angle. I still have those pictures. I thought to myself, "Oh God, was this a premonition? If so, please tell me what kind of sign it was. Was it bad luck or good luck? Was it disaster or fortune? Was this science or superstition?" I attempted to explain the phenomenon but could not make sense of it. I wanted to just forget about the rainbow, but no matter how hard I tried, it lingered in my mind. Later, I thought, there's no need to take heed of the rainbow as long as I had acted according to my conscience. If you feel that you owe someone, just try to make it up with your actions later.

After we separated, Hengbao considered the possibility of going back to China, but that option also had its problems. First and foremost, going back to China would prevent her from seeing our daughter often. Our daughter was attending secondary school by then. Her ability to speak Chinese had already deteriorated. Staying in the US was obviously the best choice for her in the long run. Hengbao eventually decided to stay in the US as well. With that decision, I started to help her find an appropriate occupation. The CMS team was busy building the Hadron Calorimeter at the time and was in need of help. Hengbao has skilled hands. She could take a watch apart and put it back together. I recommended Hengbao to a friend from the University of Rochester who was in charge of this project. I did not tell him that Hengbao happened to be my ex-wife. After interview and probation, the University of Rochester decided to give her a try and see whether she could excel at the work. When she first started going to work there, you could not imagine her enthusiasm and dedication. She arrived early and left late, learning humbly and never complained. On rainy days and in snowstorms, most people came to work late and left early, but she worked diligently even when she was the only one in the lab. She was no doubt the embodiment of "Lei Feng", someone completely devoted to work. Soon, she gained recognition and praise and retained her position. In following years, she not only worked there as a long-term employee, but received more salary raises than anyone else. Her salary reached the level of an official employee by her third year. Later, she not only worked on the CMS Hadron Calorimeter, but also contributed to the work on the more complicated particle vertex detector. The latter project required a clean room, and Hengbao learned how to use radioactive sources to calibrate and other complex technical jobs. Her work continued on like this for over 10 years. A picture of her hard at work was hung on the walls at Fermilab. Because of her fulfilling work, Hengbao's emotional state also improved. Unfortunately, the lack of new projects after the completion of the CMS detector forced her to retire early. In China, this was called "kicked down the ladder", but in America, it was "market economy". But in the end, Hengbao overcame the most difficult time period in her life.

After I separated from Hengbao, all kinds of people started to concern themselves with my future. That friend of mine was still in the midst of her divorce court marathon. At the same time, another good friend of mine introduced me to a lady who later became my second wife and brought me into love again. Her name is Li Liu.

It was March 20, 1997, when we met for the first time at a restaurant. She gave an impression of youth and energy. She was stylish in dress and passionate in manner, full of confidence. She was a doctor of Chinese medicine who had been divorced for over three years. The first impression usually leaves an imprint. Several weeks after our first meeting, she invited me to dinner at her house. Her main course was a famous soup from Shanghai called "Fresh pickled Benedict", a rich and flavorful broth with fresh and salted pork, mushrooms, and bamboo shoots. Although it had nothing on my mother's cuisine, it was not bad and I appreciated her efforts. I also liked that she was a doctor. I have always been interested in the philosophies of Chinese medicine. I thought perhaps Li Liu would be an ideal partner.

When my sister happened to visit the US, I had her meet that friend of mine and Li Liu. My sister had a good impression of both. That friend of mine also treated us to her signature dish. Because she is Cantonese, she cooked us Cantonese broth. She also invited us to attend an opera at the most famous opera house in Chicago. She spared no effort to host us. My sister told her: "My brother has met a very nice friend; if you have plans in mind, you need act fast," but she seemed to be very self-confident. She thought her youth, her beauty, and her good job meant I would pick her for sure. She did not expect things to take a different turn.

Li Liu sent me a letter in April, saying, *"Love has deeper meaning beyond needing each other. It is about selflessness and sacrifice. I can sacrifice everything for it, including my own life. The only deserving recipient of this love is you."* Her words moved me deeply. People say that a woman's weakness is their vulnerability in the face of sweet talk. It turns out that men are no different. In fact, sweet talk can mature into a loving relationship. In Chinese culture, sweet words like "thank you", "I'm sorry", "that's fantastic", "you are beautiful", and "dear" are not said often enough. Is it not?

In May, Li Liu wrote me another letter, saying, *"You are truly an extraordinary man, the best among all I have met. You not only possess knowledge, intelligence, eclectic interest, kindness, and integrity, but you are responsible and trustworthy. You are the only person in the world deserving of my love for the rest of my life… I will never allow anyone to take you away from me."*

After receiving this letter, I wrote her back on Mothers' Day: *"When you flew to me at hyper speed, I was caught off guard and unable to react. Is this gravel or a gem coming my way? Thanks to God's plan, I picked up a gem and you found a diamond. Even then, all of this needed to be refined by the hands of love to become irreplaceable jewels. Spring is the season for dreams. Let us dream with open hearts, wait for the golden leaves of fall to be sure, and use winter to try things out, leaving the summer to…"* Our relationship escalated with such sweet words, and soon it was time to talk of marriage. I also asked Hengbao for her opinion on which one would be more suitable. Hengbao was adamantly opposed to that young friend. On the one hand, Hengbao thought of her as a "home wrecker" who kept calling me day and night before Hengbao and I separated. In fact, my relationship with that friend was completely platonic. Calling her a "home wrecker" would not be fair. On the other hand, Hengbao thought that she was too young, which may pose challenges in her interactions with our daughter in years to come. I listened to Hengbao's advice. At the time, we were only separated, not yet officially divorced. We were also both Chinese citizens at the time so we asked a friend in China to help complete the divorce paperwork. Soon, I officially married Li Liu. We had a little girl shortly after. Her birth gave me a myriad of feelings. It was an unexpected new life making her entrance into my own.

My daughter was born on March 5th, 1998, the year of the tiger. My last name Wu is pronounced the same way as the word for "do not have" in Chinese, so it was difficult to come up with a nice-sounding name that was meaningful at the same time. If we were to call our daughter by her full name, it would sound like "do not have something", also calling her only by her given name required the name to have a good meaning as well. Finding a name that would work both as part of the full name, and by itself, was hard to do. I came up with the word "Yin". Wu Yin, the full name sounds exactly like the word for "boundless" in Chinese. It happened to be that "Wu Yin" sounds like the word for the year of the tiger as well. My older daughter followed my thought and gave her the English name "Yvonne". Her full name together in English and Chinese becomes "Yvonne Wu Yin", which sounds like a famous Chinese idiom meaning "great promising future, boundless". The name Yvonne originated in France. It means "beautiful girl". Many people congratulated us on my daughter's name: Yvonne Wu Yin.

My sudden marriage to Li Liu and the birth of our daughter shortly after shocked that other friend of mine. She could not accept such reality. In the year after I married Li Liu, she called me at home almost every day. When I picked up the phone, she would be silent. She always mailed cards to me on holidays and on my birthday. On the first Valentine's Day after I remarried, she wanted to see me so she could give me a box of heart-shaped chocolates. I declined her request, so she put the box of chocolates in our mailbox. Later, I heard that she had left Chicago and moved to California. I did not make the effort to find out about her life afterwards. We have no way of challenging fate, if such a thing called "fate" truly exists. Such is life! Such is fate!

However, Hengbao was incredibly generous and forgiving. She sincerely congratulated us on the birth of Yvonne and helped us out a lot. Because Yvonne always slept with her mother, she was breastfed for a year and could not wean. It interfered with Li Liu's work as well as Yvonne's nutrition. Hengbao came up with a good solution. She suggested that Li Liu and I go on vacation for a few days while she would take care of Yvonne. When we come back, Li Liu would not lactate anymore and Yvonne could be weaned. We were moved by her generosity. Our relationship with Hengbao has always been friendly. We visited frequently and thought of each other first when we needed help. We frequently went out to eat and attend events together. In 2005, I went to Beijing for the first time after my divorce with Hengbao. Her father was hospitalized, so I went to visit him. I felt very guilty. Hengbao's father resisted great pressure to consent to our marriage and protected me when the Gang of Four persecuted people. Later, he helped me obtain a position at IHEP, and drove me to the airport to flee to Switzerland in 1989... I will never forget any of this. When I saw him at the hospital, I gave him my apologies. But he said: "Both of you are responsible for the bad marriage. Now that you two are separated but forgive and understand each other, it is better than anything." He even generously sent regards to Li Liu.

On November 9, 1998, Yvonne had a little inflammation under her nose that looked like an allergic reaction. I took her to the doctor, and the doctor told us not to worry about it. Two days later, however, the skin on her body became inflamed. We took her to the emergency room and she was hospitalized immediately. Her symptoms worsened on the second day in the hospital. Her skin started to peel off everywhere on her body. She was only eight months old at the time. The doctor tried to inject antibiotics, but her blood vessels were too thin for injection. The hospital used a helicopter to bring in an expert from Chicago Children's Hospital to give her injections. I could hear Yvonne's cries of pain in the hospital hallways. My heart was shredded to pieces. I slowly walked to a small chapel in the hospital and got on my knees. I said, if I have sinned, please punish me, not my child. I was reminded of that round rainbow. Was it bad luck or good luck? Was it disaster or fortune? Could this be karma? But if it was karma, I should be the one to suffer, not my poor child. I was a mess and had no idea what to do. I held up a picture I had taken of her a few weeks ago under a ginkgo tree in the Morton Arboretum. In that picture, Yvonne sat in the middle of golden ginkgo leaves with a beautiful smile on her face. I said to God, I want Yvonne's beautiful smile come back to me. On the third day of hospitalization, a miracle happened. Yvonne's purulent skin started to fall off, and the old damaged skin was completely peeled off by day four. On the fifth day, new skin began to grow. On the sixth day, new skin covered her entire body. Yvonne came out of the hospital in good health on the seventh day. What a miracle it was! I was once again lost, unable to determine whether salvation had come from religion, science, or superstition.

As we got to know each other better, I discovered that Li Liu was completely different from Hengbao. It would not be an exaggeration to say that they were from different planets. Li Liu was all about "taste". She would insist on driving a Mercedes-Benz, she wanted mink fur coats, her watches had to be Rolexes, and her handbags needed to be Louis Vuittons... She had all kinds of sayings, such as "a woman without taste is a woman without status", or "daughters must be raised with privilege and sons raised with hardship." Allegedly, her notions have theoretical foundations in "fashion therapy". This theory holds that fashion influences a person's emotional state, confidence, and even cognition. In fact, fashion reflects a kind of societal mindset, and only God knows whether it has all the magical powers it purports to have. Li Liu not only has an appreciation for brand names, but also pays attention to delicate details in day-to-day life. Every morning when she wakes up, she always makes the bed perfectly and puts on several decorative pillows, prettying up the bed. She irons all her clothes perfectly, including her intimates and underwear. She spends at least half an hour in front of the mirror to put on makeup every morning before she leaves the house.

Hengbao is the polar opposite of Li Liu. I had bought her fashionable coats from Italy, but I cannot recall her ever wearing them. She has never been to a salon or a luxury goods store. She never uses any makeup. How could people be so different! People like us, grew up with the textbooks of the Communist Party. Hengbao pursues "inner beauty", but fashion falls in the category of "outer beauty", a "capitalist" lifestyle, even. Now, after the policies of reform and opning-up, can we combine the two kinds of beauty into one?

My personal taste also changed in many ways after my marriage to Li Liu. My colleagues have noticed that my shirts, sweaters, and jackets changed brand names. However, I cannot completely agree with this fashion theory even today. Are the branded handbags and clothes that much better? Are they worth that much money? It is only vanity. When we go shopping as a family, I usually sit at the lounge as my wife and daughter run around with great enthusiasm.

There have been four women in my life, besides my family members, who are unforgettable. They are my first love "Xiao Mei", my ex-wife Hengbao, my lost lover "Xiao Ju", and my wife Li Liu. People often use flower metaphors to describe women. In my mind, my first love Xiao Mei is a winter jasmine without the advent of spring; that flower bud withered before blooming. My wife is a rose in midsummer, passionate, energetic, and beautiful. My Xiao Ju is a chrysanthemum in the fall, whose elegance and grace was buried by the early arrival of winter. My ex-wife Hengbao is a wintersweet, bringing me the hope of spring in the world of ice and snow. My friends sometimes ask me to compare these four women, asking me which flower is the favorite? I often reply like this: "How can you compare the beauty of flowers that blossom in different seasons?" I have heard of such a story: One day, Concubine Yang and her maids were admiring the flowers in the royal garden. A maid said, "The Lady is as beautiful as the flowers." She wanted to compliment Yang's beauty by comparing her to the flowers, but Yang only smiled without saying a word. Another maid said, "The flowers are as beautiful as the Lady." Yang still smiled without saying anything. A third maid said: "The Lady is more beautiful than the flowers." Yang only laughed genuinely this time. In fact, it all depends on what you are comparing to, the flower or the Lady. To me, there is no such object of comparison. The four flowers reflect different stages in my life. They cannot be compared against each other. I thank God for giving me the opportunity to get to know each of the four. They made my life colorful.

Not only that, fate has brought me a happy union in the end despite all kinds of turmoil in my love life. Although Hengbao and I have divorced, she has a good relationship with my new family, and we have formed a new caring friendship. My wife Li Liu not only helps her patients at the Chinese medicine clinic, but also takes care of the upkeep of our household. People say that there is always a talented woman behind a successful man. I think Li Liu is such a woman. What makes me even happier is Li Liu's generosity, that enables her to have a good relationship with my ex-wife. There is even more harmony and peace in our life because of it.

Let me conclude this section with a little poem I wrote:

> *How much emotion does it take to love a person?*
> *From one heart to another, how far is the distance?*
> *How long does it take for strangers to become intimate?*
> *How many days until a smile appears on a face of indifference?*
> *In life, intimacy is the hardest thing to find.*
> *In life, true love is the warmest thing one can find.*
> *Everything is forever changing,*
> *True love and true friendship are forever lasting*

9.5 Learning to manage finances

The years in America forced me to adopt a brand new lifestyle. A Swiss friend told me in the past, "Those who earn money with physical strength earn little; those who earn money with mental strength earn a lot; those who earn money with money earn fortunes." At first I did not understand what he was trying to say. But now I realize how true his words are. The US is a capitalist country. All rules are set under capitalist principles. After I arrived in the US, buying my first house made me feel like this was heaven. Thereafter, I started to save up all I could to pay off the loan as early as possible so that the house could really become mine. Because I did not set aside pre-tax retirement funds or tax-deferred annuity, and tried to use every dollar to pay off the loan, I paid it off in just seven years. When I filed taxes at the end of every year, however, the tax I had to pay became higher and higher as the loan interest eligible for tax deduction became lower and lower. The result was that I paid more tax to the government than necessary. How silly this was!

First, tax deferral is a great policy in the US for American people. This is a very simple math problem. The interest can multiply and grow very large. Today's one dollar, at an interest rate of five percent, would be $2.07 in 15 years, and $2.65 in 20 years. How could I not have considered such simple a principle? To be honest, it was because my mindset was stuck in a peasant economy.

Second, let's talk about real estate. If your house is worth a hundred thousand dollars, and the price of your house doubles, you make a profit of a hundred thousand. What about a house worth ten hundred thousand? If the price of that house doubles, you make a profit of ten hundred thousand, but the cost of maintaining that house would not be ten times the cost of maintaining the cheaper house because you receive a tax deduction for the money you pay for loan interest.

Third, there's the matter of stocks. In America, not buying stocks equals giving up the opportunity to take advantage of economic growth. Investing in stocks is no doubt risky, but is choosing not to invest really risk free? Is your wealth not at the risk of inflation? We physicists know that a good sailor can sail a boat against the wind. Why? As long as you sail in zigzag, you can use the force curves of the angles to advance. In the long run, the stock market has an upward trend. It is not easy to see if you examine just the ups and downs in the short term. That's not even considering all the calculations, simulations, confidence levels, the risk index, and all the other mathematical tools in stock investment. It is truly a science! No wonder Wall Street often seeks out physicists. Finding good investment combinations and developing regular investment habits needs research.

The first thing I did after understanding all this was to sell my first house and buy a bigger one. This second house was located in a high-end neighborhood with green trails connecting every household. The trees and lawns made the neighborhood a beautiful green canvas. The new house had high ceilings and a dormer. There was a large fireplace in the living room, and a greenhouse connected all the way to the garden. My lawn was right next to a public garden. The master bedroom had a ceiling height equal to several storeys. Compared to the old house, this new house was almost twice as expensive. I tried to pay as little down payment as possible and loan the rest to get more tax deduction. In fact, after purchasing the house, I kept re-financing the loan to cash out more money and used it to buy cars and pay tuition. This house became our tool to obtain money. Of course, I also benefited from the appreciation of the house's value.

Two years ago, the sub-prime mortgage crisis hit the US, and real estate price levels plummeted to historical lows. We saw a brand new house in a high-end residential area located near a nature reserve and a golf course. That house was magnificent beyond compare. Brazilian redwood floor showed us its elegance, fine granite counters were found in all of the kitchens and bathrooms. In the past, this would be a house that I would be too afraid to dream about, but now the construction companies faced bankruptcy, and the bank had to take the house back and was selling it at a bare minimum. Thus, I sold the second house and bought this big house for a price more than twice as much as that of my second house. All of the down payment was from my investments gain. I believed that this house had great potential to appreciate in the future and that it would become useful by the time my daughter Yvonne needed money for college.

Now I am retired and have no salary income. However, as long as I keep managing my finances well and lead an ordinary lifestyle, living a peaceful life will not be a problem.

9.6 Artistic endeavors

After arriving in America, I experienced several art-related events and interacted with great artists. They left unforgettable impressions on me.

The first event was singing the "Yellow River Cantata" in the Chicago Symphony Hall to celebrate the 60th anniversary of victory against fascism, in 2005. I have always loved to sing. I was a member of the Shanghai Children's Palace Choir in elementary school. This time, I was delighted to have the opportunity to work with the world-class conductor Han Situ and sing the "Yellow River Cantata" at the Chicago Symphony Hall. I invited my daughter Yuan Xing to come along with me. Even though rehearsals took up much of my free time, the pride I felt when I heard the applause resounding in that splendid symphony hall was indescribable.

The second event was meeting the Zhou Brothers. When IHEP Director Zhipeng Zheng visited Chicago in 1995, he introduced me to the Zhou Brothers. Their fame had yet to take off at that time. Zheng's father used to be the Associate President of Guangxi University in China. The Zhou Brothers were in Guangxi then. Zheng's father recognized their talents and supported them to go abroad to pursue their bright futures. The Zhou Brothers came to Chicago and started from scratch. They still lived in a shabby old house at the time we met. Now, they are world-renowned for their modern artworks and unique collaborations. They always communicate about each other's hopes and works in drawing, performing, sculpting, and printing. Their minds, aesthetics, creativity, and understanding of eastern and western philosophies, arts, and literature formed a symbiotic relationship. We clicked immediately and had several great conversations. They invited me to their studio multiple times to visit and dine, in turn I invited them to visit Fermilab. They were especially fond of Wilson's sculptures. They were very interested in the objectives of high-energy physics research and considered it a philosophical inspiration for their artistic endeavors. Once, they invited us to dinner. We saw several paint buckets beneath an unfinished giant painting on their studio's wall. My little daughter was so curious and adventurous that she took up a brush and started to paint on the giant painting. I was flustered and tried to stop her, but the Zhou Brothers said: "It's okay. Perhaps she will become a great artist some day!" My daughter Yvonne is now 18 years old and has won many prizes for her drawings. Could this be fate?

Today, the Zhou Brothers are world famous. They have their own galleries, exhibition spaces, and clubs. Many of their artworks have been collected by national museums. In 2014, the Illinois Governor set up a law to name October 16th as Zhou Brothers' day. On October 16, 2015, the government of the City of Chicago named 35th Street as Zhou Brothers street, to recognize their contributions to world art. I am proud to be the Zhou Brothers' close friend.

The third event was organizing two recitals for the famous Erhu (a Chinese string instrument) performing artist Xiaohui Ma in Chicago. This gave me an opportunity to interact with the Erhu angel and get to know her fascinating music as well as her beautiful personality.

Xiaohui Ma is an Erhu performer and composer from Shanghai, China. She is a first-rate traditional artist in China. The critics call her "an artist who communicates with the world through Erhu" and "a musician who performs with her heart". Her famous duet with the cellist Yo-yo Ma in the movie *Crouching Tiger, Hidden Dragon* won the Best Music prize at the Oscars. The John F. Kennedy Center for the Performing Arts named her 1999 millennial performance one of the top 10 concerts of the year.

Fermilab has an arts event called "Performing Arts Series", held every other month. They invite world-class artists to perform at Fermilab's Ramsay Hall. Ramsay Hall has first-rate acoustics. Even though it is not huge, it allows a thousand people to enjoy music at the same time. Everyone in the hall can hear a person speak at any spot in the hall without a microphone. It is an honor to be able to perform in that space because you must be approved by a committee of world-class professionals. Erhu is a traditional Chinese instrument with little recognition in America. Many people have never even heard of it. How can an Erhu performer have a recital there? Many people were skeptical. Even though I sent videos of Xiaohui Ma's concerts and her performing experience to every member on the committee, there were more people against the idea than for it. I have always had the grit to stick with something to the end. I would not believe that Xiaohui Ma, an artist worthy of performing at the Kennedy Center for the Performing Arts, the Carnegie Hall, Vienna, Paris, and London, could not hold a concert at Ramsay Hall at Fermilab. To deny her would be an act of ignorance by the committee members. I did not lose heart and kept on introducing and recommending Xiaohui Ma to people on the committee. They eventually agreed to have Xiaohui Ma perform, but were only willing to pay a meager fee. They were worried that she was the lone performer of Erhu. If ticket sales were bad, they would not lose too much money. However, Xiaohui Ma's performance also required piano, cello, and percussion accompaniments. I had to find three other musicians willing to play at a low cost. It was a very difficult feat for someone not connected to the music industry. Even then, I had great faith in the success of Ma's concert because I had heard her perform. I organized the event with confidence and high spirits. Ma was originally going to refuse such a low payment, but she was determined to introduce the Erhu to world-class scientists even if it meant losing money. I found the other three musicians, had contracts signed, and organized everything from rehearsals to ticket sales to guest invitations all by myself. The concert was a great success. Fermilab's Director, Deputy Director, and other local leaders attended the recital. Ma received a long standing ovation when she finished her performance. Outside the concert hall, people formed long lines to buy her CDs. People who used to be skeptical about the concert came to congratulate me on its success. Xiaohui Ma's charisma made world-class scientists admire the Erhu. The Erhu used to be an instrument of earthy origin, but Xiaohui Ma made it elegant and beautiful.

After the concert, I wrote a poem for Xiaohui Ma: "Double-Stringed Universe (Erhu Concerto Symphonic Poem)":

> *Overture*
> *What is the universe?*
> *The universe is all.*
> *What is before the universe?*
> *Nothing is before the universe.*
> *The universe is all, all and everything besides all.*
> *No past, present, or future,*
> *No size, mass, or temperature,*
> *Nor happiness, remorse, affluence, or deprivation,*
> *All there is none of nothing,*
> *All there is not is all of all.*
> *Be it beautiful, or miserable,*
> *This is the fundamental universe!*

Big Bang
Twenty billion years ago, big bang,
The Tao that can be explained is not the eternal Tao,
The Tao is the unmanageable transcendent reality.
The Tao provisions unity, unity provisions duality, duality provisions trinity,
Trinity provisions the myriad things.
Conceived of as having no name, it is the originator of heaven and earth.
Conceived of as having a name, it is the mother of all.
Big bang,
All originates from nothing.
No trembles of the earth,
Nor roars of the thunder.
The beginning of chaos,
The opening of clouds,
The radiance of sun,
The rumble of life.
This is all originating from none, the universe,
The universe is all originated from none.

Daughter of the Universe
After one hundred billion million million million million million million one-billionth of a second,
The universe is still at one hundred million one hundred million million million million degrees.
The daughter of the universe is born at this precise moment,
Like a goddess created out of fire.
She dances on two strings,
Playing the sound of the universe.
She gazes at the myriad things,
Spreading the seeds of life and the stars.
The universe expanded rapidly,
While its temperature dropped fast.
The velocity of expansion is proportional to distance,
The universe's temperature is inversely proportional to size.
The daughter of the universe leaps out of the fire,
Hands paint the blueprint to create the world.

Double-Stringed Universe
The basic structure of the universe is flexible entities with lengths,
The world on the strings is unique beyond imagination.
Thick and thin, pluck out notes low and high,
The bow draws a colorful arc.
Notes low and high correspond with string-like particles of energies low and high,
Two strings symbolize the asymmetry and symmetry of the wondrous universe.
Positive and negative particles connect on two ends of the string,
A string can only be extended but never breaks.
Just like notes are born out of vibrations at different frequencies,
Superstring vibrates in different manners to create different particles.
It was no other than the mystery of two strings
That gave rise to the all-encompassing universe!

Coda
Is the universe limited or limitless?
Perhaps only a fool can answer.
Want to discuss the origin and destiny of the universe?
God has opened your door to Hell.
The universe is as it is today,
Because otherwise people would not exist.
Without people, the universe would not be questioned.
The daughter of the universe sent us this revelation on two strings.
The most unknowable knowledge in the universe is why the unknowable is unknowable,
Perhaps, people, only exist in the knowable universe.
People and the universe, inseparable.
The universe needs people, no less than people the universe.

In the end, I would like to share my unforgettable experience conversing with one of the world's most accomplished modern artists, Fan Zeng. On Dr. Phua's invitation, I went to Singapore in 2007 to attend Professor Chen-Ning Yang's 85th birthday celebration and academic conference. At that time, I had the honor of meeting the world-renowned Professor Fan.

Hearing him speak was the privilege of a lifetime. I had always admired Professor Fan, but had never met him in person. The first time we met in Singapore, I was overtaken by his charisma. He is a man of portly build, with eyes bright and piercing. When he talks, it feels like an enlightening experience. When we talked, I felt that the Chinese proverb "A conversation is better than 10 years of education", was true. Every seat was filled at Professor Fan and Professor Yang's public lecture — "Chen-Ning Yang and Fan Zeng on Beauty". Their wisecracks won the audience's applause. I thanked Dr. Phua for the invitation and the opportunity to get to know Professor Fan. On the day of my departure, Professor Fan gave me a calligraphy autograph of which I am grateful and proud. "My first encounter with Dr. Weimin Wu at the Lion City of Singapore resembled a reunion with a longtime friend. Words of profound wisdom flowed at the meeting of great minds. It is a pleasure to have a bosom friend in my life, a precious companion rare to find. Weimin is such a cherished friend indeed. Fan Zeng, fall of the Year Dinghai." He even agreed to write those words with a writing brush, but there was no writing brush to be found at the hotel where we stayed.

9.7 Living in peace

Looking back at my 25 years living in the United States, I thank this immigrant country with all sincerity for giving me the opportunity to do work and research on the energy frontier. I have not experienced any major upheavals in my life here. I have just lived in peace. I encouraged my children to adopt local customs, to integrate into American society, and to develop into well-rounded citizens in addition to being good students at school. The definition of being well-rounded is very different in America compared to China. The differences lie in the American emphases on extra-curricular activities, on volunteer work, on community service, and on summer jobs like waiting on tables in restaurants. In China, letting your children wait on people in a restaurant seems to be a shameful thing, but it is common in the United States. There is no social hierarchy, and this concept of equality is instilled in children since they are young. It is important for children to have some artistic or athletic talents in the US, so I encouraged my two daughters to learn painting, play the piano, play the flute, skate... I know that we first-generation immigrants have no family background or establishment to rely on, so everything depends on our own efforts. We have to work twice as hard as American people who have lived here for generations. It is a shame that my English has not improved much but I have lost some Chinese. Therefore, I try my best to provide the best opportunities for my daughters to excel at English. I take them to all kinds of art performances, concerts, and operas so that they can become familiar with American culture and not be "foreigners". I have to thank my daughters for making me so proud. They are straight-A students at school and have frequently won prizes in drawing contests and piano contests. My younger daughter received the Presidential Education Award from President Obama in 2012. The entire school district used her design for a New Year's card. In the beginning, I used the Chinese parenting style to raise my children. In America however, respecting the child's personal will is more important than carrying out the parent's orders. My older daughter is very good at English. I told her to go to medical school and become a doctor, but she did not want that for herself. In the end, she followed her heart and applied to law school. She became a lawyer and works at the Department of State now. We are all very proud of her. Thus, I am very respectful of my younger daughter's personal opinions and interests. For instance, neither of my daughters enjoyed playing the piano. I made my older daughter keep playing until she finished eleventh grade. After she graduated, she never touched the piano again. My younger daughter had no more interest in the piano than her sister, so I learned the lesson and let her quit when she was in ninth grade.

I want to do something beneficial to the country and the people after I retire, taking into account all aspects of my identity. First and foremost, I am an American citizen now, and I have an obligation to abide by US laws and protect the national interests. At the same time, I am a Chinese expatriate, and I am deeply connected to the land where I was born and raised. There is no conflict between the two because the common interest of US and China is my interest. Contributing to the friendship and collaboration between these two great countries is the basis of the peace in my life.

Some people say that China has adopted "capitalism" now, but there are also people who claim that the US President Obama is trying to practice "socialism" in America. In fact, the path of a country cannot be described by a simple "ism". Just like finding comfortable shoes requires wearing them with one's own feet, finding a political direction for a country requires consulting the people of that country. In all cases, living in peace means that one needs to adapt to the progress of the times. Becoming a proud global citizen by the time I die is my biggest wish in this life.

9.8 Confessions

Personal Philosophies

- Your goal in life
  To leave a legacy.
- Your favorite saying
  Nothing is new under the sun.
- The hardest thing to do
  Where ignorance is bliss, it's folly to be wise.
- Biggest wish
  For all my dreams to come true.
- Favorite personality trait
  Understanding.
- Least favorite personality trait
  Not knowing what one does not know.
- Best quality
  Never being content.
- Worst quality
  Being sentimental.
- Most valuable possession
  Friends around the globe.
- Definition of Happiness
  Being understood and appreciated.
- Happiest moment
  Conversing with intimate friends.
- Person you love the most
  Woman. A man is only complete with a woman.

- Most admired politician
  Washington. He made a quick retreat before glory and power.
- Most despised politician
  People who have neither knowledge nor skill but sit on top of ordinary citizens.
- Is Taiwan a part of China?
  If not, was the Republic of China an invading country in 1949?
- Do you believe in God?
  Yes! But I do not name my God as God. The divine is one and the wise call it by many names.

About Science

- Favorite subject
  Physics. It explains not only the nature but also life.
- Favorite natural law
  Newton's laws: crucial but simple.
- Favorite scientist
  Einstein. His mind was always ahead of his time.
- Least favorite scientist
  Mad scientists.
- Hardest subject
  Human biology.
- Most difficult question
  What is a question?
- The ultimate goal of scientists
  Understand why the universe can be understood.
- The last thing scientists should do
  Invent a robot capable of emotions.
- The biggest enemy of science
  Losing freedom of thought.
- The biggest motivation of scientific research
  Curiosity
- Do geniuses exist?
  Yes. Otherwise no one would be asking this question any more.

- The most innovative thing you have done in your life
  Building a wireless remote terminal for a computer in China in 1984.
- A life experience that changed history
  The first email I sent in 1986 was the first step of Internet development in Chinese history.

Personal Life

- Favorite place to travel
  Pompeii. It tells me how little we have progressed in 2,000 years.
- Favorite city
  Paris. It is the kaleidoscope of life.
- Favorite dish
  The ones I cook myself.
- Favorite hobby
  Photography. It lets one observe, reflect, and record the world.
- Favorite novel
  Jane Eyre. It depicts flawed lives.
- Favorite collection
  Coins. Every single one is a milestone.
  Stones. They are natural artworks.
  Stamps. They are miniature history books.
- Favorite furniture
  Mahogany. It is the extension of life.
- Favorite clock
  Grandfather clock. It has the steadiest beats.
- Favorite animal
  Sheep. I was born in the year of the sheep, an animal that never initiates conflict.
- Least favorite animal
  Wolves, which once showed me the proximity of the gate to hell.
- Favorite composer
  Mozart. His life lends style to his works.
- Favorite instrument
  Piano. It allows actions as rapid as thoughts.

- Favorite sport
  Ping-pong. Opponents approach each other without making harmful contact.
- Favorite dance
  Tango. It calls for all the attention of the lead and the follow.
- Worst illness
  Allergies.
- Luckiest thing
  God gave me a healthy body.
- Your highest self-evaluation
  I have led an ordinary life.
- Favorite line of poetry
  What a wonderful life!
- Most important thing you have done in life
  ALEPH collaboration
- When you felt the most wronged
  I was mistaken for someone else, but the accuser would not admit it.
- Do you care about what others say about you?
  I have led an honest life, and history will evaluate me with justice and fairness. Why would I care about what people say of my shadow when I walk toward the sun?

Chapter Ten
Treasure Island Taiwan

When I had finished most of this book, I felt that something was missing. Ah! It was Taiwan. This is a place that has registered in my consciousness all my life but was accessible to me only in the latter half of my life. If my life were divided into periods of a quarter century, then my first period of life was when the nationalists and communists spoke to each other with big guns. The second period was the Cold War period, and the third period was when both sides tried to mend their relationship again.

Everything related to Taiwan affected the fate and thoughts of our generation. The century-long bloody struggle between the nationalists and communists created a most tragic chapter in the history of modern China. Many epic stories were instilled in our minds, becoming part of our lives in films, plays, songs, novels, newspapers and magazines. They were almost omnipresent. Taiwan was once a synonym for the "devil" to the mainland Chinese. What kind of place is it? What kinds of people live there?

When I was in high school, a teacher taught us how to make an ore radio. When I first heard the sound coming from the ore radio, I jumped up with excitement and amazement. Then one day, I suddenly heard a distinctive female voice coming out of the ore radio, soft and sweet: "This is Radio Free China." I immediately realized that this was the so-called "enemy station" from Taiwan. I quickly changed the frequency and tuned it out, my heart beating fast with fear. However, one of my classmates actually got hooked on the Taiwanese radio broadcast and often tuned to the station in secret by himself. One day he was caught, and then he disappeared. We were told that he was arrested for eavesdropping on an "enemy station," and we never heard of him afterwards.

As mentioned earlier, I met a beautiful young, talented medical student at Lanzhou University. Because her father was a high-ranking nationalist officer, notwithstanding his switching over to the communist side through an uprising, she was still regarded as belonging to a separate class, almost untouchable. Likewise, I had a long delay in passing my political background check when I applied for going abroad for the second time in 1983. Later, I found out this delay was because I got to know a lady from Taiwan when I first went abroad and lived in Geneva. She was a Chinese teacher for the wife of one of my German colleagues at the CDHS group. It was really a totally innocent social relationship, but at the hands of those ultra-leftists, it became a "political issue" for me, recorded in my personal profile kept by my work unit. Luckily the relationship between mainland China and Taiwan warmed up at the time, and the lady involved was really an ordinary teacher, so I finally passed my political background check.

For decades, the stories I heard about people and events related to Taiwan were all one-sided. If I did not have any personal experience with Taiwan to share, it would be as if some pages of my book were left blank. All in good time, an excellent opportunity presented itself. Professor Mao Yajun from Peking University invited me to sit on the review panel for several doctoral dissertations, and I wanted to take the opportunity to visit Taiwan. I am also grateful to Professors Hou Weixu and Xiong Yi of the Physics Department of Taiwan National University for inviting me to visit Taiwan as an individual visitor, rather than as a member of a tourist group. Thus I could freely engage in sightseeing and scholarly exchanges and go almost anywhere I wished. I reckon that as an independent visitor, I might see things differently.

10.1 Political Taiwan

On May 25, 2011, I boarded a China Airlines flight from Beijing to Taiwan Taoyuan International Airport. At the Beijing airport, there were separate exit areas for domestic and international flights, as well as for Hong Kong, Macao, and Taiwan. I had to use the exit area for Hong Kong, Macao and Taiwan. This slightly unusual arrangement immediately reminded me that Taiwan was neither domestic nor international, but was a very special place, a separate political region. The flight attendants on board were all young and beautiful, each of them wearing a big smile.

On the plane, there were three newspapers to choose from: *Freedom Daily*, *United Daily News*, and *China Times*. A passenger sitting next to me was a native of Taiwan. He told me that the Freedom Daily belonged to the Green Camp, the pro-Democratic Progressive Party. The United Daily News was run by the Blue Camp, the pro-Kuomintang faction, and the China Times took a centrist position. Before this trip I had only heard that the major newspaper in Taiwan was the *Central Daily News*. To my surprise, the dignified official newspaper of the nationalist party was actually closed down for financial reasons, which was sufficient to show that in Taiwan, the era of free press had arrived.

On opening the *United Daily News* of the day, an eye-catching title immediately greeted me: "Came to Taiwan to mourn a member of the Black Cat Squadron, family members waited for half a century." The article followed: "Chen Huai died in 1962 in the line of duty, at the age of thirty-two. Nine family members came from the mainland to Taiwan yesterday to pay respect. As soon as the second sister got off the plane, seeing a portrait of her brother, she shed tears of emotion." In the eyes of the nationalists, Chen Huai was definitely a hero. The Black Cat Squadron was established in 1961 to gather military intelligence through aerial reconnaissance over the mainland. Chiang Kai-shek, the leader of the Nationalist government in China from 1928 to 1949, and subsequently head of the Chinese Nationalist government in Taiwan, met Chen Huai and told him not to forget to take a parachute. Chen replied that he absolutely would not use a parachute over the mainland so there would be no way for the communists to capture him alive. On September 9, 1962, his plane was shot down over Nanchang in Jiangxi. In Taiwan, there are many schools, airports, and other places named after him.

Coincidentally, I saw a news report in the United States: On August 25, 2000, there was a picture exhibition in Taipei titled "1950 midsummer in Machangding — reflections on war, human rights and peace." The featured pictures were very shocking, especially those of the portraits of several victims of the notorious "Wu Shi Case" before their executions: former nationalist "Second Chief of General Staff of the Defense Ministry" Wu Shi and his adjutant Nie Xi, former nationalist director of the "fourth depot of the joint forces" Chen Baocang, and special agent of the East China Bureau of the communist party Zhu Kanzhi. They sang

L'Internationale before their heroic martyrdom. Those historical pictures of the mass executions of underground communists in Taiwan after the nationalists retreated to that island shocked everyone present at the exhibition. A period of history during which the underground Communist Party gathered intelligence in Taiwan re-surfaced 50 years later, causing considerable stir on both sides of the Taiwan Strait. Still less known was the fact that it caused emotional tumult in the hearts of two persons over 50 years old: one was Wu Shi's son, Wu Shaocheng, and the other was Zhu Kanzi's daughter, Zhu Xiaofeng. There had been no news whatsoever about their parents since they got separated during the raging civil war 50 years earlier. Little did they expect that 50 years later, their kind and loving parents would appear in such tragic images. After searching for their parents for the better half of their lives, they just did not expect to welcome home their parents in such a gloomy circumstance. The legendary stories of the special agents once active on both sides of the strait came to light with the action of Zhu Kanzi's daughter Zhu Xiaofeng searching for her mother in 2003. It culminated eight years later with the finding of the remains of Zhu Kanzi in 2010. The remains were transferred from Taipei to Beijing soon after. It was a story full of twists, probably the most amazing story in the last decade involving the relationship on both sides of the strait. It had implications for reconciling the nationalists with the communists and for the peaceful co-existence of the Chinese on both sides of the strait, encouraging them to build a new future together. The peaceful return of the remains of Zhu Kanzi to her birthplace was smooth and a matter of course. Interestingly, the nationalists and communists did not have any official procedures in negotiating the body transfer. The whole matter was dealt with according to civil customs, all very low-key. However, it served as an example of good will between people on both sides of the strait, giving expression to the Chinese desire for long lasting peace. Yes, both sides of the Taiwan strait are Chinese. They are brothers; even though bones are broken, the tendons remain attached.

 I have read an article about the son of a Chinese founding marshal, remembering his father. That son said that his father's least favorite movies were about the civil war between the Nationalists and the Communists. The founding marshal asked what there was to eulogize about brothers killing each other. I believe the accuracy of this article and hold the same opinion as that founding marshal. After the American Civil War, Washington treated surrendered Confederacy forces with the highest honor and respect. This paved the foundation for America's national unity today.

Indeed, Chen Huai and Zhu Kanzi were both heroes, sacrificing their lives for their own beliefs. I am not here to argue about whose death served a better cause, but would like to discuss how to avoid such tragedies, and never let them happen again. Even before the aircraft landed in Taiwan, I became aware from the article in the *United Daily News*: Taiwan was veritably a "political Taiwan".

The political center of Taipei is just a few subway stops away from the hotel where I stayed. The presidential palace and the famous Freedom Square were nearby too. The Freedom Square was similar to the Tiananmen Square in Beijing, but much smaller. On both sides were the Concert Hall and the National Theatre, in traditional architectural style. In the middle there was the famous Chiang Kai-shek Memorial Hall, bearing some resemblance to the Beijing Temple of Heaven. Inside the hall, exhibition materials truthfully recorded Chiang's life. The Chiang Kai-shek Memorial Hall looked imposing, but the construction materials were neither granite nor marble, but simply white concrete. Some areas of the temple had fallen into disrepair, with cracks showing up in some places. I cannot help feeling that Chiang Kai-shek, after all, was a defeated leader who retreated to Taiwan. Much of the content in the Chiang Kai-shek Memorial Hall was totally unfamiliar to me, but it was rich, detailed, and arranged in a logical manner. I believed that all the displays were true records, although described with wording that was different from what was used in Mainland China. For example: "After the success of the revolution, there was much domestic unrest. The nationalist party adopted the policy of allying with Soviet Russia and working with the Chinese Communist Party with the goal of achieving domestic stability. The party put Chiang Kai-shek in charge of building an army with the Huangpu Military Academy…" There was also an appropriate description of Chiang's leadership role in the Sino-Japanese War. On the other hand, there was only a brief and neutral description of the Chiang's defeat in the civil war and subsequent retreat to Taiwan, which was understandable. It was all what I expected. However, I was touched by the "monument dedicated to the victims of white terror".

It took much courage and wisdom for the current national leader to admit and apologize for mistakes made by his predecessors, and even to erect a monument on behalf of the victims, although he had nothing to do with the past transgressions personally. As a result, it allowed the people of Taiwan to come to terms with current realities, looking to the future rather than being burdened with historical wrongs and guilt. Of course, this development became possible only after the death of the two generations of President Chiangs, with the disappearance of all parties with personal involvement. Therefore, time may be the best medicine for healing historical trauma.

Just below the statue of Chiang Kai-shek at Chiang's Memorial Hall was a huge carved copy of Chiang Kai-shek's will, said to be in the handwriting of the National Palace Museum director Chin Hsiao-yi. That will was written in classical cursive Chinese style, very difficult to read. One day, I took a taxi to Taoyuan, chatting with the driver on the way. He told me that in 1975, when Chiang Kai-shek died, he was a soldier on Kinmen Island, near the mainland. His superiors told everyone to mourn for a month, and also learn Chiang's will by heart. If a soldier could not recite Chiang's will, he would not only be reprimanded, but also be subject to solitary confinement. The taxi driver said he was illiterate, and there was no way that he could remember Chiang's will written in such a style, so he was locked up for many days. He told me that he just did not understand why mainlanders were so interested in Chiang Kai-shek. The vast majority of the visitors to Chiang Kai-shek Memorial Hall and the Mercy Lake were from the mainland. I told him that the reason was simple, it was because the mainland did not have anything related to Chiang Kai-shek, which made the Memorial Hall very special, whereas the scenic spots, cities, and shops looked more or less the same on both sides of the strait. He also told me, when he was serving at the Kinmen Island, the mainland would often shoot over some "propaganda bombs". When such a bomb exploded, there would be propaganda flyers everywhere. At one point, he picked up a flyer, but was caught by his superior, and put in solitary confinement for a long time. The penalty for listening to radio broadcasts from the mainland was death by shooting. He went on to comment that he could not read the traditional Chinese characters taught in Taiwan, much less the simplified writing from the mainland. He could not understand why his officers would have him put under solitary confinement. From what he said, I could feel his dissatisfaction with Chiang. He was not the only taxi driver who told me such stories. Another taxi driver also shared similar experiences with me. The difference was that the latter revealed his admiration for Chiang Kai-shek's son, Chiang Ching-kuo. Pointing to the highways that we were traveling on, he said that they were all constructed on the initiative of Chiang Ching-kuo. In fact, the most important historical contribution of Chiang Ching-kuo was to take the historical first step in the democratic reform of Taiwan in the 80s by repealing the martial law, allowing the formation of new parties and independent newspapers, promoting exchanges of visitors across the strait and reforming the national congress. In the short term, the nationalists lost power as a result of the reform. However, as the nationalist party persisted in working for the benefit of the majority of the people of Taiwan, it regained the power several years later.

For quite some time, I had known that there was a culture park commemorating the two Chiangs in Taoyuan. Taking advantage of attending academic seminars at the Central University of Taiwan, I skipped one day of conference to visit the Chiang culture park. The Taoyuan Da Xi Creek is a very famous site. Chiang Kai-shek thought this place resembled his hometown of Fenghua, so he ordered the Mercy Lake Mausoleum to be built here in 1975. The Mercy Lake Sculpture Memorial Park was established in 1975 by the city council of Daxi Town. The first statue of Chiang Kai-shek was moved there from Kaohsiung on February 29, 2000. To date, there have been 152 Chiang statues of different sizes placed there. It is the world's only statue memorial park dedicated to a single person.

When I read about the Chiang culture park, my thoughts raced. During the Cultural Revolution in China, there were countless statues of Mao Zedong all over mainland China, but they were cleared away thoroughly after the Cultural Revolution, as if by a gust of wind. In fact, Mao was a historical figure, whose merits and faults are best left for our descendants to pass the final judgment. Perhaps, the mainland should learn from Taiwan about how to treat historical figures. Perhaps it is best to establish a Mao Zedong culture park in Shaoshan, his birthplace. A mausoleum for Mao could be moved out of Tiananmen Square and a place could be rebuilt to house his remains and statues gathered all over the country. I believe that the spirit of Mao would agree with my idea, if it exists. Such an act would show due respect to history without causing too much confusion. After some years pass by, people would look at the whole thing like reading a history book. Is it not wonderful? Recently, I heard a suggestion about building the city of Mao Zedong around Shaoshan. It is in line with what I proposed. Such a proposal deserves further exploration.

Standing before Chiang's mausoleum, I was filled with emotions. Many curses and personal assaults were heaped upon Chiang in mainland China. Perhaps Chiang died with many unfulfilled wishes, especially with his thought of making a comeback in mainland China. However, like the irreversible flow of a river, times have changed and there is no way to go back. Once, Chiang entertained the former American President Nixon in his official residence in Shilin, and they spent time under the same roof. However, it was the same Nixon who opened diplomatic relations with mainland China, letting Chiang suffer the pain of being abandoned politically. It was a deal that polarized the "political Taiwan".

Once, the honorary chairman of the nationalist party Wu Poh-hsiung said: "The two sides cannot go back to the era of exchanging gunfire. Both sides have grown wise enough to stop the violent exchanges once and for all. It was very unfortunate to have internal destruction within one people. We have to be worthy of the expectation of our descendants, and worthy of our great nation." The new party Chairman Yok Mu-ming also pointed out: "Peace is the bottom line, development is a process, and reunification is the goal. There is only one China. Patience can overcome the difference between the two sides." What Yok said fit my own observation of how most people in Taiwan felt about the situation during my Taiwan trip: it spoke out their common aspirations. In my opinion, the least controversial side of Chiang Kai-shek was that he was a patriot. In dealing with Japan, the United States, and Russia, Chiang always adhered to the fundamental principle of safeguarding China's interests and unity. Wang Jingwei, head of the regime established in 1940 to govern the Japanese-conquered territory in China, gave the queen mother of Japan a treasured vase from the collection of China's National Palace Museum as a gift during the last Sino-Japanese war. As soon as the war ended, Chiang immediately took this national treasure back to China, and put it back in the National Palace Museum. I think this reflected the best quality of a leader of the Chinese nation.

History is about past events, and the important thing is how to tell next generation about it. I made a point of asking some 20-year-olds in Taiwan, what kind of person Chiang Kai-shek was in their opinions. The answers were almost identical: Chiang Kai-shek was a warlord, dictator, and anti-Japanese hero. That was what the younger generation learned from Taiwanese textbooks. Still there were also many people who told me that Chiang was far too remote for them, and that they were more concerned about current affairs. Yes indeed! Perhaps only people like myself from the mainland, who have experienced ups and downs of modern Chinese history, would still care about Chiang Kai-shek, whereas the younger generation is no longer interested. Perhaps it is a good thing. The part of history in which Chiang played a larger than life role has already passed. The focus should be about creating the future. History should only teach us how to avoid making the same mistakes.

The Chinese dream should include the dream of the Taiwanese people. It represents the common aspirations of all the Chinese people, including those from Taiwan. This is a fundamental principle that must be followed, whereas the other issues are relatively trivial and easy to solve, such as the names and symbols. As both sides reached the 1992 consensus about one China, respective interpretations, it was a matter of course for the leader of Taiwan to call himself the president. When President Ma Ying-jeou studied at Harvard University, he wrote his doctoral thesis on "the legal basis of the Diaoyu Islands" to show that Diaoyu Islands was part of Taiwan Province. Harvard University passed his doctoral thesis and awarded him the PhD degree. Ma Ying-jeou was at least a patriot.

I am so happy to see that the Chinese President Xi Jinping and Taiwan's President Ma Ying-Jeou met in Singapore on November 7th 2015, referred to each other as "Mister", and shook hands for as long as 81 seconds. This is a historical event which shows the world: Chinese people have the wisdom to solve their own problems. The reason is simple: China has more than 5,000 years of history, and separation is only one small portion. Their eventual unification will be solidly based on their common culture.

At the end of this section, I have a fairly serious proposal for the people and authorities: stop using the Minguo (Republic of China) calendar in Taiwan. I saw the awkward notation in newspaper, reports, forms, and on other occasions. This is really a feudal legacy, much like the year of

Guangxu or Xuantong in the Qing dynasty. Why bother? All over the world, people are using the Gregorian (AD) calendar, with rare exceptions like Japan, using the Showa calendar or the Akihito calendar. Taiwan is still using the Minguo calendar, perhaps to wish for the Republic of China to last ten thousand years? Such a way of thinking is really anachronistic. The year 1911 saw the end of the era of the last emperor of the Qing dynasty. The Republic of China should not have inherited such an archaic way of starting a new calendar.

10.2 Humanistic Taiwan

Thanks to the thoughtful arrangement of Professor Hou Weishu, I stayed in a hotel near the National Taiwan University (NTU), called the Jiesi Taida Zunsian Hotel. The name "Zunsian" is rich in cultural connotation. When I entered the campus of NTU, I saw shady banyan, vigorous cypress, and tall-standing cedar trees. Walking on a magnificent coconut tree-lined road made me feel relaxed and happy. Surrounded by green trees, there was a temple-style building, called the Sinian Hall. Before the hall there is sharp-edged stone tablet with no words, and a fountain. Inside the hall there is the tomb of the Chinese scholar Fu Sinian.

Fu Sinian was a well-known proponent of the New Culture Movement, and one of the leaders of the student movement in 1919. Fu co-founded the *New Wave* magazine, organized and directed the student parade of the May Fourth Movement, and for a time was right on the cusp of history in China. After the end of anti-Japanese war, Fu worked feverishly to restore Peking University to her full glory and function back at its original campus location, in a very confusing political situation. He was proficient in both the arts and sciences, with a thorough understanding of both Western and Chinese thinking and manners. Fu had the breadth of vision to see the big pictures and also keen eyes for details. He had the gentle manners of a traditional Chinese scholar but handled the empirical methods of modern science with confidence. He had emotional dynamics coupled with cool-headed rational analysis, and the strength of integrity coupled with the natural warmth of a humanist. All these qualities combined gave him lasting charm as a master in the field of education nurtured by traditional Chinese culture. At the end of Japanese rule, he took over Taiwan

University and renamed it National Taiwan University, which would become one of Asia's top elite educational institutions. Fu strove to maintain the independence and academic freedom of the university in an era of political repression and cold-war confrontation. He stood out as a pillar for supporting the independence and dignity of the academics. Fu made his indelible mark as an educator in the history of modern education in China with his hard work and self-sacrifice. On December 20th, 1950, he died on the podium of the Provincial Assembly, becoming a legend in the hearts of the teachers and students of NTU. NTU established a bell in Fu's honor, which rang 21 times a day to commemorate his famous saying: "There are only 21 hours available per day because the remaining 3 hours are reserved for self-reflection." This bell is still hanging high to this day, and the only change made was to use electronic equipment to ring the bell rather than it being rung by hand.

I have also adopted Fu Sinian's idea of devoting three hours a day to meditation. I used to wake up early, often just after four o'clock in the morning. I would lie in bed meditating, mulling over what I had done the previous day, what I did right, what I did wrong, and what I plan to do today, really like Zeng Zi said: "I reflect on myself three times daily. Did I show any disloyalty to my friends? Did I break my words with them? Did I practice what my teacher taught me?" I have been following this habit right to this day.

NTU has a very strong faculty. I do not know much about other disciplines, but I know that the department of physics has world-class professors. They joined the CMS experiment group at CERN, playing a key role in constructing a pixel detector. They also participated in the neutrino experiment at Daya Bay in China, with their contribution recognized by the cooperative group. The faculty members of NTU come from all over the world. Since the working language at NTU is English, it is easy for NTU to keep in touch with the rest of the world. At the physics department, there were a variety of academic reports or seminars on a daily basis, making a deep impression on me.

Taiwan attaches great importance to promoting traditional Chinese culture, and in this respect I think they are doing better than the mainland. Chinese calligraphy and painting works are often hung in subway stations. There are fewer and fewer viewers of Chinese opera on the mainland. It is also the case with Taiwan. The Taiwanese found a way to remedy the situation. One day, I turned on the television. It was showing the Chinese opera "Zheng He". The opera describes how the Ming Emperor Zhu Di ordered Admiral Zheng He to set sail on a voyage from Taicang Liu harbor (now Liuhe Town, Taicang City, Jiangsu Province), leading more than two hundred maritime vessels and 27,000 people into the Western Pacific and Indian Ocean. They visited 30 countries, including a plurality on the Indian Ocean, seven times between years 1405 to 1431. The program was different from I saw on Chinese television channels. It combined storytelling by the program hosts with Chinese opera performance. There were four hosts wearing Chinese opera costumes, who told the story of Zheng He with relish, then the program would switch to the Chinese opera performance. After a while, it would be storytelling again, so on and so forth, even I started to enjoy the program in earnest though I was no fan of Chinese opera. I have to respect the work and effort Taiwan puts in this regard. Taiwan's television programs almost had nothing to do with politics. The shows were all about ordinary life, nothing on war or spies. Current affairs programs are mostly about local matters, mostly trivial, virtually no international news. Just as well, Taiwan does not have diplomatic relations with most countries of the world. Whatever happened in those countries basically had nothing to do with the people of Taiwan, why bother to know too much?

Like the people from the mainland, people from Taiwan pay great attention to education and the training of their children. The state pays the costs for children to go to primary and middle schools. However, it is very competitive to get into a good public high school. This is because entering a good public school costs less and the student will have a good chance of entering a good university. Therefore, the entrance examination for high schools in Taiwan is as important as the college entrance examination in China. When I was in Taiwan, it happened to be the entrance examination time for high schools. One day, I went to the Longshan Temple, where there were crowds of people, many of whom were parents who had brought teenagers to pray. The offerings were varied, with fruits, pastries, buns… even napkins. It seemed as though Buddha had also started paying attention to eating manners, and had started to use paper napkins. Copies of permits for taking the entrance examination were placed on top of the offerings. Initially, I was baffled by what I saw. I asked a parent and learned that it was all for getting a better score in the examination. My friend at National Taiwan University told me, Longshan Temple was not the most popular destination for parents of students. There were even more people going to the Confucius Temple, and Wenshu Temple. Some worshipers were very devout, and read out their prepared manuscript in front of the Buddha statue. The university entrance examination was not such an intense experience in Taiwan, because the enrollment rate is high, and many people would not even take the university entrance examination after graduating from high school. Of course, the intensity of the entrance examination for high schools here could not be compared with the entrance examination for universities on the mainland. On the mainland, drums and gongs accompanied the movement of the candidates. In Inner Mongolia, armored vehicles were commandeered to transport candidates on rainy occasions, and parents accompanied their children to the examination venue in the rain... Such extraordinary devotion was commonplace. However, the emphasis placed on education by the people in Taiwan was shown in how seriously the people of Taiwan took the entrance examination for high schools there.

I believe that the average level of knowledge of Chinese classics by the people of Taiwan was much higher than mainland China. On one occasion, Ma Yingjeou visited "Baoxiong Fishing Hall" of Taichung Tanzi District. When talking about the development of agriculture and animal husbandry, Ma quoted a saying from Mencius, and said that it was a dialogue between Mencius and King Xuan of the Qi state. In fact, it was a dialogue between Mencius and King Hui of the Liang State. Unexpectedly, this mistake caused uproar in the audience, showing the familiarity with Chinese classics of the common folks of Taiwan, who were quick to spot an error of this type. Ma Ying-jeou once made the comment that although he could not be said to use "half of the Confucian Analects to rule the world," he did draw a lot of inspiration from Chinese classics. For example, there was a saying Ma quoted from *Mencius and King Liang Hui* Chapter Three: "Only with benevolence could the strong treat the weak on equal terms." It was quite applicable in describing the cross-strait relations, very accurate and appropriate. It was said that Ma Ying-jeou defeated the Democratic Progressive Party (DPP) by his skillful use of Chinese classics.

Compared with DPP politicians who could only use vulgar street language in verbal fighting, the nationalist leaders were much more refined and had real talents. Many primary and secondary schools in Taiwan teach Chinese classics. The speech made by the nationalist honorary chairman Lien Chan at Peking University in 2006 was known to have "a keen sense of history and humanist feeling." Many official documents of the Taiwan government still use classical style writing. I saw the inscriptions of Taiwanese leaders in many places, with their masterful skills of calligraphy all too visible.

I made a special trip to the Taipei Confucius Temple. There, I was deeply affected by the display of Confucian culture. Confucian scholars of the Song dynasty had a saying: "Before Confucius was born, history was dark like the night." It described precisely the influence of Confucius on Chinese cultural development. Confucius's "History of Yao and Shun, charters of civil and military conducts" compiled the essentials of ancient Chinese academic thoughts. In February 2013, Tainan City held an examination for reading Chinese classics in the Confucius Temple. There were 1,300 participants who were certified to be reading champions, with the youngest only two years old, and the oldest 87. Tainan was known as the headquarters of the Democratic Progressive Party. Here for once it seemed that culture triumphed over politics. In the Temple, I saw a free 4D movie about Confucius. I had a real opportunity to experience a humanist Taiwan, first-hand.

In Taiwan, the birthday of Confucius was designated as the Teachers' Day. I think this is a good idea. Confucius's idea and thinking about "universal brotherhood" are valuable assets of human civilization. I recently heard that China was considering setting Confucius's birthday as the Teachers' Day. I like this idea. It would be very significant if compatriots on both sides of the strait have a common Teachers' Day.

Because of Taiwan's lack of natural resources, the Taiwanese put a lot of emphasis on energy saving. I visited Beitou Library, which was located in the lush park of Beitou, and built with "green" ideas. The whole library looked like a tree house. The building had large windows right to the floors, capturing abundant natural light. On top the green roof there were solar panels and a large patch of grass area, quite effective at saving energy and recycling rainwater. I was told that Taiwan had many such buildings. Taibei's National Theatre was far less magnificent than Beijing's National

Grand Theater, but several of its inner walls were covered up with flowers and grass. The green ideas behind its construction are worth emulating.

When I attended the symposium at the Chung Yuan Christian University, the men's room there caught my attention. Its urinal used neither water nor electricity, but still managed to stay clean. The idea was to use a liquid lighter than urine. When urine flowed into the urinal, it would be covered up by the lighter liquid, sealing it from the air, so the smell of the urine would not get out. The urine passed through a filter before going to the sewage system. To maintain the system, only the filter needs to be replaced regularly, and the lighter liquid topped up. I have been to many places in the world, but it was my first time seeing such a men's room. Although still in the pilot phase, this waterless urinal system worked very well in my opinion. A lot of water would be saved if it is widely adopted.

Taiwan also had a street scene that amazed me. It was the motorcycles. Taipei has two million residents and one million motorcycles. The rows of motorcycles before the traffic light reminded me of the bicycles of China some years back. The roads of Taipei were not as wide as those of Shanghai and Beijing, but the traffic situation in Taipei was much better than in Shanghai and Beijing. It could be said that the motorcycles made a lot of difference. One car would occupy the same space as four to six motorcycles. Furthermore, the motorcycles of Taiwan are not like the luxury type found in the United States, but rather the Italian-style scooters. They occupy little space, save gasoline, and are inexpensive. I believe that they should be the preferred vehicles for commuting.

Finally, in this section, I would like to comment on the transfer of several thousand pieces of heritage treasure boxes from the mainland to Taiwan on the order of Chiang Kai-shek. Those artworks formed the bulk of the content of the National Palace Museum in Taipei today. Chiang Kai-shek's action had drawn many people's criticism. In reality, I think what he did had both pros and cons, and the pros outweigh the cons. It preserved the artworks from destruction by war, or simply falling into the hands of the Japanese. From a longer-term perspective, the artworks in today's National Palace Museum serve as the cultural ties between the mainland and Taiwan. Every one of the exhibits at the National Palace Museum in Taiwan helps to remind the audience that they are part of the Chinese civilization, with roots deep in mainland China. They should be proud for several thousand years of Chinese civilization and history. When I visited the National Palace Museum in Taiwan, I saw some students touch the inscription of their family names on a carved map, so they could find out where their family came from on the mainland. I'm glad to hear them exclaim: "Ah! That's where my ancestors were." I really feel that the National Palace Museum plays a role in binding the people on both sides of the strait together more than anything politicians can say. So it has all been a blessing in disguise. It was perhaps more than what Chiang Kai-shek could have himself imagined in the beginning. This cultural tie presented an insurmountable obstacle to the independence-seeking separatist movement in Taiwan.

10.3 Hospitable Taiwan

In Taiwan, when you say "thank you," the other will answer "don't be so polite (不会)", with a smile. That "don't" along with the gentle smile are forever fixed in my mind. This hospitable image of Taiwan is what I miss deeply. In the beginning, I did not quite understand the meaning of "don't." I would rather say, "you are welcome", or "it is my pleasure", etc. However, once I got used to this kind of courtesy reply, I started to miss it — back to Beijing, I actually felt uneasy to hear the kind of replies used on the mainland.

Professor Hou Weishu of the National Taiwan University made a thorough and thoughtful arrangement for my trip to Taiwan. I had the chance to see many teachers and students, as well as get to know Taiwan's customs. He invited me to a Taiwanese specialty restaurant frequented by the locals, dining with his family members. A dish of Shanghai-style "large yellow croaker with pickled vegetable soup" made me feel that I was not in Taiwan, but in Shanghai. Professor Xiong Yi of NTU invited me to have a meal together with some other teachers and students at the Din Tai Fung dumpling house, a well-known restaurant in Taiwan. That dumpling house was famous for its steamed soup dumplings. I could not help comparing it with the Shanghai Nanxiang steamed soup dumplings. In fact, as far as the taste is concerned, the Nanxiang steamed soup dumplings found at the Shanghai Chenghuang Temple are better and much cheaper. But the Nanxiang steamed soup dumpling house in Shanghai Chenghuang Temple district made customers feel much less hospitable: there would be a long queue to get a ticket for the meal, then another queue for a table to sit down, all done with brushing shoulders against other customers constantly. All this time, the waitresses looked intense without saying a word, and would eventually put the steamed soup dumplings on the customers' tables when their turn finally came... During the whole process the customers felt like hungry persons who just needed to be fed, but there was no hospitality to speak of. It was not until the customers started to savor the delicious steamed soup dumplings could they forget their unpleasant experiences. Of course, in some so-called high class restaurants in Shanghai, steamed soup dumplings were also served. But I did not think that they were as tasty as those I ate after queuing for a long time at Chenghuang Temple. Once, my brother took me to the Shanghai Restaurant near the Old Chenghuang Temple. The ambience there was hospitable enough, but the steamed soup dumplings were already shrunk and flat, without the "soupy" taste of dumplings that have just come out of a steam pot. It looked difficult to have both elegant service and a delicious taste at the same time. However, at Din Tai Fung dumpling house in Taiwan, I got both. They required pre-booking so there was no need for queuing on-site. It featured an open kitchen, so the customers could see what they were going to have before they were served. The waitresses wore a smile from start to finish. It is small wonder that since its founding in 1958, Din Tai Fung has opened 82 branches all over the world. In 1993, it was named one of the top 10 gourmet restaurants in the world by the *New York Times*. In my opinion, the restaurant chain won with its hospitality.

Taiwanese are well known for their courtesy, especially in the subway. Those seats reserved for the elderly and children were kept for those in need, even when the subway train was very crowded. A friend of mine at NTU joked with me: "Nobody in the subway would give you a seat because you do not look like an old man." One day, I felt really tired, and the reserved seats were all occupied by mothers and children. I just looked around, and a middle-aged woman quickly stood up to give her seat to me. I said: "You are the first one to see that I'm an old man." She quickly replied: "No, no. I just sensed that you were trying to find a seat." It was heartwarming - a far cry from the situation in Beijing, where my students told me that I should be assertive in the subway, otherwise I would never be able to board. Maybe they exaggerated a bit. It is certainly true that on the Chinese subways, passengers are noisy, laughing and talking aloud on cell phones. Once, I took the subway to Tiantongyuan, and I saw a middle-aged woman shouting and cursing on the phone for half an hour, as if nobody else was present. There is absolutely no way one can see a similar scene in Taiwan.

In order to visit the interior of Taiwan's National Theater, I bought a ticket to the "ultimate modern dancing" from Belgium. I never cared much for modern dance, however, this "body does not remember" style dance was said to challenge the limits of the human body. To me, it actually presented a challenge to my patience to stick to the end of the show. One group of people on the stage kept throwing bricks at one another; a man lay on the stage motionless for several minutes; two persons holding each other sat on a chair motionless for several minutes… If someone were to call this dancing, he or she might as well play the role of the sycophant ministers in the story of *The Emperor's New Clothes*.

I had to suppress my impulse to quit the show several times, because I saw that the Taiwanese audience still sat up straight throughout the show. In fact, I could see that many of them did not enjoy the show either. Nonetheless, the audience gave the show an enthusiastic applause at the end of the show. Once I saw the ballet dance *Jane Eyre* in the Peking University Centennial Hall. Before the show started, the audience received repeated warnings to take no pictures and to turn off their cell phones, but these warnings were completely ignored and there were sounds of the ringing of cell phones and clicking of cameras everywhere inside the hall. On another occasion, I saw Ibsen's play *Peer Gyntin* at China's National Grand Theater. Before entering, the audiences were supposed to check in their cameras, and I thought there would be nobody taking pictures anymore. However, I was wrong, and there were still some people in the audience clicking away with their cameras. At Taiwan's Wulai Gaga Theater, my hosts and I watched a show featuring Taiwan's aboriginal style singing, dancing, and talking. It was a pity that there were only five people in the audience, but eight or nine actors. However, the actors still put on a meticulous and earnest performance. I clapped hard at the end of the show, but to no avail, because there were too few of us to create much applause. After the show, the actors pulled us up on stage to dance; the ebullient scene that followed was heartwarming and unforgettable.

What else constituted a heartwarming scene in Taiwan? It was the triumphant smile of a pair of lovers, with the man riding a bicycle, and the woman standing on the shaft of the back wheel, holding tight to her man; it was a mother riding a scooter, with her child holding tight to her waist, and her long hair waving in the wind; it was the soft whispers of lovers by the Sun Moon Lake; it was on a subway carriage so quiet that everyone could hear the rumbling sound of the wheels on track; it was the spontaneous queuing up even when there were only two customers in a line; it was the belief in helping others as a source happiness for oneself; it was in the night market place of Taiwan, with all sorts of goods and food, a wide variety of vendors and noisy crowd; it was in the open air hot springs in Beitou, where men and women bathed in separate areas, embracing their own intimacy with Mother Nature. In fact, Taiwan is far less prosperous than I imagined, its cities not quite as magnificent as I expected. However, the morning Christian television program *Quiet Hours*, or the Buddhist program showing monks chanting, all represented a kind of warmth comforting to the soul. This is Taiwan, a place that makes people from all over China feel proud.

I would only write so much on my Taiwan trip. I would write a little about my visit to China in recent years. If my visit to Taiwan could be said to be a trip of discovery, then the trips to China were quenching my sense of nostalgia. I was invited to visit Beijing by Peking University, as a member of the doctoral dissertation committee for several PhD candidates. My old friends who worked with me on the ALEPH and BES projects previously gave me a warm invitation to visit the Institute of High Energy Physics. Professor Chen Yuanbai, my old colleague at ALEPH, is now the Director at Dongguan Spallation Neutron Source Center, a branch of IHEP. He invited me to visit his research facility in Dongguan. In just 10 days, I was made to feel that I had achieved some measure of success in handling my relationships with my fellow scientists: though the person had gone, the good will still remained.

On June 17, the director of IHEP, Wang Yifang, and several former directors, Chen Hesheng, Zheng Zhipeng and Ye Minghan, all met with me and we dined together. An official of the Chinese Academy of Sciences, Li Zhigang, also came to the party on hearing of my visit. The Director of the IHEP office, Xu Tongzhou, personally made an arrangement with the former Deputy Director of IHEP, Zhao Weiren, to bring a birthday cake for an early celebration of my 70th birthday. The restaurant specially made me a bowl of longevity noodles, for which I was deeply moved. Later, a student of mine at Peking University took me to an upscale restaurant at Beijing Houhai. The plates of food were shaped like bonsai displays, sure to cost a lot. On my way to IHEP, I came across Zhang Chuangchun by chance, who many years back had made the observation of the J/Psi particles with me on the Beijing Spectrometer. Zhang said to me: "Old Wu, whenever I suffered from back pain, I think of you. I will always remember that it was you who carried me to the hospital when I had back pain for the first time. Thanks again." In fact, I had all but forgotten about the incident. An ALEPH graduate met me in a theater, and insisted on taking me to dinner. Subsequently, he invited many of my old friends to come too. He said to me, "Your work at IHEP changed the lives and career paths for many of us."

I went to take a look at the Seventh Building where I once lived. The kindergarten close by was still there, but the big chimney facing the building was no longer there. When I arrived in Dongguan, I could not believe my eyes. A few years ago, the Spallation Neutron Source Center was still drawings on paper, but now it was taking shape with many almost-completed buildings in a forest of litchi trees. It would be ready for full service a few years from now. The completion date on the progress of the project was put on a plate on the site, accurate to the day. It would not be an exaggeration to call this the "Dongguan speed".

In my last trip to China, I also met Mr. Enhai Wang of the China Internet Network Information Center. It was he who did the painstaking investigation over many years and finally notified me that with verification and deliberation of the expert committee for assessing major developments in China's Internet history, it was confirmed that my 1986/8/25 email was officially listed as the first milestone in the history of China's Internet development. This was in fact the first time that we ever met.

Ah! This is the way human life goes on one day after another. Once more I was reminded of what Zeng Zi said: "I reflect on myself three times daily. Did I show any disloyalty to my friends? Did I break my words with them? Did I practice what my teacher taught me?" I have been practicing Zeng Zi's teaching in the past, and will continue to do so until the end of my life.

Chapter 11
Convergence of Civilizations

11.1 Eastern and Western cultures

In the skyline full of mysteries, there are two kinds of creations of nature that fascinate man: clouds and birds.

The footprints of our ancestors have spread across high mountains and snow lands, rivers, lakes, and seas. Mountains and seas never stopped human exploration, not even when Man was confined to Noah's ark. To fly in the sky has always been a fond dream of mankind, but until the invention of the airplane, man never really flew. The different dreams about flying in Eastern and Western cultures may be the most conspicuous among the cultural differences between the East and the West.

The Chinese liked to fly with the help of the clouds. There are many legends of driving the clouds and steering the mist. Whether it is in the story of Chang E going for the moon, or Gods descending to the mortal world, or heavenly generals and soldiers doing the fighting, each of the heroes or heroines rode on pieces of clouds as their vehicles of flight. By contrast, the goddesses, princes, angels and devils of Western culture all have to have wings put on them in order to fly.

In many poems from ancient China, birds and clouds are comparable. From the famous line of Emperor Hanwu: "White clouds fly with autumn wind, grass and wood pieces drop with the return of the goose south", to Cui Jing at the peak of the Tang dynasty: "Yellow cranes flew away without ever returning, the white clouds felt empty for a thousand years"; from the hot line of Li Bai: "Birds flew away high and far, a lonely cloud is left idling around", to Tao Qian's "The cloud has no mind to go out of the mountains, and a bird tired of flying knows how to return". Each one of those lines gives clouds and birds endless and mysterious personalities and inspirations.

The poems of Rabindranath Tagore are totally different from the Chinese ones. They do not compare clouds with birds, but rather attempt to harmonize such relationships:

> *"A bird wants to become a cloud,*
> *A cloud wants to become a bird."*

However, as to the dreams about flying, there are so many different ways to think about dreams of flight, originating from such different civilizations. However, they can easily be reconciled and harmonized. Let's analyze them from the perspective of physics.

What is a cloud? How can it "fly"? A cloud is a system made up of countless dust particles serving as the nuclei for condensation of water vapor. Its destination is not controlled by itself, and the flow of air can make the cloud curl up or spread out in various shapes. When there is a sharp movement of the atmosphere, especially when cold air meets hot air, the rain drops will become bigger and bigger, until their weight can no longer be supported by the air, then they will fall onto the ground. It could be said that the time for "calling up the wind and rain" is the time for the "disappearance of the cloud". Clouds conjure up poetic associations. When the sun shines upon the thick accumulated clouds, they sometimes look like an endless cotton field, yet at other times like wavy, snow-capped mountains. The ever-changing scenes of clouds above the Yellow Mountain intoxicated so many poets and painters. However, neither those poetic descriptions of the clouds, nor the enchanting scenes of gods steering the clouds in the folk legends, provide any scientific clue to allow humans to fly in reality.

However, it is different with birds. Putting wings on little angels may be said to have been the first scientific attempt at designing a method for human flight. A bird can fly because of the aerodynamics of its wings. Even if it has flown over countless mountains and valleys, gone through numerous clouds and mists, and worn out its wings, if it believes that the beauty of life is in flying, then it is fearless. The Western culture was inspired by the flight of the bird, and the first prototype of an airplane started with putting wings on a human being.

No matter how silly of an idea it was to put wings on "little angels", it was something solid. Especially when compared with a vacuous idea like stepping on a piece of cloud. This solid design was honed by human wisdom, perfected through failures, and at last allowed humans to fly. From the first airplane to the modern space shuttle, the same basic aerodynamic principles are equally applicable, and they all need wings.

As can be seen from the associations with either clouds or birds, the difference between Eastern and Western cultures is obvious. The Eastern culture is into poetic associations and literary imaginations, whereas the Western culture is relying on more solid entities based on scientific principles. This difference is also reflected in other areas of human pursuits.

The Western painting is putting emphasis on precise and detailed scientific study of objects, from the projection of light to the perspective of distance, from dissection of human bodies to the drawing of solid objects, one cannot fail to notice the extremely precise details. By comparison, Eastern arts, especially Chinese paintings, make one enter a hazy mood and enjoy a sense of the abstract. Of course, it is not necessarily desirable for an artistic creation to follow reality too closely. When the famous Chinese painter Zuoren Wu created a painting based on the Beijing Electron-Positron Collider, he just used a thick Chinese brush to put two strokes, one clockwise and the other counter-clockwise on a large piece of paper. Whether a philosopher, physicist, or artist, one cannot fail to feel a sense of having endless room for thought after enjoying this painting. Chinese poems are also characterized by playing with words that are open to interpretations, with the meaning of some poems debated for a couple of thousand years. By contrast, a Western opera invariably has a clear story line. Chinese medicine is about yin and yang, strong and weak, hot and cold, with dialectics that make people want to believe. It is about relationships between different parts of the body, and it is about the whole. What is the science behind it all? It is not really clear. Western medicine is completely different. It depends on various kinds of scientific instruments and clinical measurements. It is about determining what kind of germs or viruses are responsible for the diseases and defining the abnormality with a clear shape. The right medicine can be chosen only after everything is clearly understood. The only shortcoming of this approach is that some problems cannot be treated in isolation without looking at the body as a whole. Even in cooking, the Eastern and Western cultures are quite different. Western cooking is about pageantry, cutlery, wine cups and water cups clearly separated, with each dish distinct in itself. Beef is beef, salad is salad, and potato is just potato by itself. Whereas Chinese cooking is about color, smell and taste as a whole, with matching and mixing of ingredients. There are a lot of choices of ingredients with complicated cooking procedures and masterful discretion used to achieve the final result of satisfying the visual, gustatory and olfactory senses as a whole. Many Chinese dishes have names derived by poetic association.

I can enumerate many other examples of the differences between Eastern and Western cultures. While I feel proud of oriental culture, especially the Chinese civilization, I should also reflect on the weakness of such a cultural tradition.

For example, we invented gunpowder, and used it for firecrackers. So why was China still wallowing in fantasies when the Western powers opened her doors with cannons? We had famous doctors and pharmacists like Li Shizhen and Hua Tuo in ancient China, but even today, why do we still have to put our trust in the "ancient recipes" of white haired "old Chinese traditional medical doctors", neglecting modern science, especially modern biological science, and lacking an understanding of human anatomy and physiology? Japan is far ahead of China in terms of defining the efficacy of components of Chinese herbal medicine as well as extracting them. When we have our meals, we sit around a big table with all family members to enjoy the dishes together. It reflects the traditional Chinese family values, but it is not necessarily the most hygienic practice. Chinese writing, especially Chinese calligraphy, won appreciation around the world as an art form, but has its difficulties as a tool for describing natural sciences. We often have to spend more than 10 years to learn our own language. No wonder it is so difficult to combat illiteracy in China. Relatively speaking, it is much easier to learn an alphabetic language used in the West, which tends to be more precise and accurate. The language and writing of a people influence their way of thinking. Some research showed that our ideographic writing system helps abstract thinking, but when the microscope was invented, and calculus was created in the West, our scholars merely contented themselves with stylistic writing and esoteric calligraphy. Indeed this is a tragedy. There is a misguided nationalistic feeling among the Chinese, a feeling that China was the only ancient civilization. The ancient city of Pompeii that was buried by a volcanic eruption is one example of a great civilization that was not Chinese in origin. The still serviceable three story bridge with aqueducts 278 meters long and 40 meters tall is another example.

Yes indeed, from the association of clouds with birds, we can feel for the cohesive power of the clouds. The cohesive power is so great that myriads of clouds make our earth so beautiful, our sky so vibrant with a rich three-dimensional depth. It appears to symbolize the national cohesion of the Chinese people. However, we cannot be just like hermits living in the fog, immersed in the legendary Peach Garden to enjoy the cloud decorated view of the paradise, relishing in the sweet dream of commandeering the clouds and mists. We should learn from the birds: the swans that stretched their necks to fly high indomitably; the seagulls that brave storms to fly tirelessly towards a set goal; the eagles that dominate the sky across clouds and mists... We should know that only the birds can really fly, because they are truly alive.

Ah! The bird wishes it were a cloud, and the cloud a bird. I hope that Chinese people will have the cohesive power of a cloud, as well as the vitality of a bird. "The cloud does not want to go beyond the mountains, and the bird wishes to return home after a tiring flight." That's how I feel at this stage of my life.

In my decades of career, I observed that the Chinese people need to learn from some other countries in the world. One is the United States. The United States is a nation of immigrants, not a single homogeneous people, but its cohesive power is remarkable, and its vitality is even more astonishing. If there is any disaster anywhere, help comes from all directions. Making donations and contributing to charity have become a habit for American citizens. It is a matter of public consensus to help the weak. America experienced several big depressions, but each time it recovered stronger than before. America is never satisfied, but always strives for continuous innovation. This is a country with the most inventions in the world, always leading the world in science and technology, full of vitality. After 25 years of immigrant life, I deeply feel the honor of being a member of the great family of the United States of America.

There is also another country, Russia. When I visited Russia, something happened that I will never forget. One day, I heard that there was a free open-air concert, so I went to participate. It was a big amphitheater, open in the front part, but covered up towards the rear. When I arrived, the concert had already begun. I sat in the back, where there were a lot of vacancies. Halfway during the concert, it suddenly began to rain heavily. On the stage, the performance continued, and the audience remained motionless. Those who sat close to the back could move out of the rain by switching to the last few rows of seats under cover, but they chose to sit tight, for fear of disturbing the show. At that time I was shocked, and I understood in that minute why the Soviets won the war against fascism by overcoming great odds. Some say that this was discipline. In fact, this showed a kind of national cohesion. It is also this nation that gave birth to the great scientist Konstantin Tsiolkovsky, who laid down the theoretical foundation of space flight. The Russians were the first to send a human to space, going beyond the dream of mere flying, which shows the tremendous vitality of this nation.

Today, China is a vibrant nation, with all ethnic groups united in their effort to realize the Chinese dream. Eastern and Western cultures merge in modern China to complement each other to achieve the best of the two worlds. That is the inspiration given to me by the association of the clouds with the birds.

11.2 Science versus superstition

In real life, there are many individual events that people cannot explain and which are open to a variety of interpretations.

On the day of 9/11, the two buildings of the World Trade Center collapsed, but a small chapel nearby still stood intact. On television, I saw the Mayor of New York City standing by the chapel to make a speech. He proudly declared: "This shows that God is protecting us." In fact, this was just one individual event.

If that chapel had also collapsed, would it have shown that God did not protect us?

On the day I presented the divorce papers to my ex-wife, there was a full rainbow in the sky above my house. These were two completely unrelated events. It would be far-fetched to suggest that God implied anything with the rainbow. However, I had never seen such a rainbow prior to the event, nor anytime after.

In 1988, I went to recruit graduate students from Fudan University. Just as I was about to leave Shanghai, I learned from an old classmate, totally by chance, that my first love, Xiao Mei, was terminally ill. Was her last desire calling me from another dimension? Otherwise how could it be that I had gone to Shanghai to do my recruiting just a few days before I went to Switzerland, and was informed of her terminal sickness in such a casual way, all by pure chance? Although she asked her husband to look me up, in fact, her husband did not even try. It was difficult to even find me because he probably did not know where to start. Had this really been an act of God?

After my mother died, her remains were cremated. We put the casket on a table in our house for a night, around which we also put some apples, cakes and other things as offerings to the spirit. All of this was prepared for burial at a cemetery the next day. I slept in a little bed near the table. During the night I heard a noise made by something like a mouse. I asked my brother if the house was infested with mice. He said never, and told me to forget about it and just sleep. However, after a while I heard the sound of a mouse again, so I turned on the light to check carefully, but I found nothing, so I fell asleep. The next day, a miracle had happened. There were signs that the apples and cakes used for the offerings were nibbled by a mouse. My father was born in the year of the rat, and he had passed away a year ago. Was it the spirit of our father that came back to say goodbye to our mother? This is my brother's house, and food was often kept on top of the dining table, but it was never before bitten by a mouse. In fact, after the incident with the offerings, there has been no sign of a mouse again.

In 1972, at an observation station of cosmic rays located 3,200 meters above sea level in Yunnan, the Atomic Energy Research Institute of the Chinese Academy of Science recorded an event of ultra-high energy action, which might be caused by a new heavy particle. They discovered an event of a particle in cosmic ray passing through a cloud chamber, with its track being recorded on film. According to subsequent analysis, this might be a particle more than 10 times the weight of a proton. Professor T. D. Lee helped the scientists at the Yunnan station to analyze the result of the experiment, concluding that their experimental error was about one percent. The evidence was not strong enough to confirm the existence of a new particle. It might have been a new phenomenon with unknown mechanism. In fact, no such observation was ever made again.

In 1976, Tangshan experienced a big earthquake. Zhou Enlai, Zhu De and Mao Zedong died in the same year one after another…

I talked about so many unrelated matters, and meant to say that statistically insignificant events are not suitable subjects for scientific studies. Science is about events that can be repeatedly confirmed and reproduced. While the events I mentioned left physical evidence, some were not amenable to experimentation, and others cannot be confirmed repeatedly. For example, there was the mystery with the cosmic ray recording. Despite so many accelerator experiments going on in the world, the kind of heavy particle implied in that particular experiment was never observed again, thus no valid scientific conclusion could be drawn. Thus, various superstitious and religious interpretations emerged regarding those statistically insignificant events. People in life will encounter many incredibly rare events, which is why there is superstition. Must there really be an explanation for everything? That in itself is a question that I still can not answer. Many people asked me if I practiced a religion, and I said no. However, I believe that there is a God of everything, otherwise the world would not be so orderly. The goal of science is to understand and discover this order. There are a variety of religions, with a common feature that each has a God with a specific name. This raises a fundamental question: some believe in one religion, thinking their God is the supreme with infinite power; and others believe in another God, who is also supreme with infinite power. Whose God is really supreme? Is not this a most typical spear and shield story? It is not that people cannot follow such a simple logic, but those who believe simply refuse to try. That is the reason why there are so many wars in the world. Indeed, religion is about matters that need not be understood, much less proven.

There is a scientific issue that actually deserves further study and discussion. It is about how to calculate the confidence level of an event with a low probability. To calculate the confidence level for a high probability event is relatively easy, but it is not so simple for a small probability event. Science is about events that must be repeatedly confirmed, but how many times would be considered to be "repeatedly confirmed?" This is an issue about statistical confidence. In the past, an apple falling on the ground could confirm the existence of gravity. Now, science has developed to such a stage: more statistical data requires more time and money, so there must be quantitative means for measurement. In the discovery of the Higgs particles, CMS/ATLAS had recorded many events of the Higgs particles with the data of LHC before 2011, but they had only five sigma significance level. Scientists considered the data credible enough to merit the announcement of a new "discovery". However, the Nobel committee was a lot more conservative. It is still hard to define the confidence level for an isolated event, or a unique historical event. To say that the events had a probability of zero is not correct either, because they did happen. It still requires much scientific study and statistical analysis to eradicate superstition, otherwise reason will not always prevail in each case.

In fact, to calculate the confidence level of a small number of statistical samples is a scientific challenge, and to find rational patterns in a huge amount of statistical data is also a tough issue in science. Due to the amazing development of the Internet, statistical analysis of a huge amount of data becomes possible. For example, research was conducted into the correlation among sales of some commodities. The result of the research revealed unexpected patterns. Very strong correlations were found in the sale volume of two completely unrelated items, which is hard to explain. A new discipline on the analysis of a large amount of statistical data began to emerge.

My life is like the random Brownian motion of a particle, to be tossed around in one storm after another. I felt that I was under the protection of a God, allowing me to have my many narrow escapes, surviving my brushes with death. At each critical moment, there was always someone special who came to my help, making my life follow a legendary path, for which I am filled with gratitude. Of course, this is not a science but a low probability event! It is all because life experience and life itself can never be subjected to repeated trials and verification.

I studied physics for decades, and after much deliberation, I feel that science should leave some room for religion and art. Some questions should be asked, thought over, and carefully explored. However, certain issues cannot be handled properly without deference to religions. Einstein said, "Science without religion is lame, religion without science is blind." Religion requires "belief" rather than proof, which may be the right attitude in handling issues with no clear answer, otherwise such issues can literally drive people insane. For example, which came first, the chicken or the egg? Is it necessary to answer this question? Or does it make sense to even try? Another example is "The moving keeps moving, and motionless remains still." How did anything get moving in the first place? Is there such a thing as the first push? What was there before big bang? Why is the world so orderly? Do these questions have scientific answers?! If one keeps asking these kinds of questions, he or she will surely be driven crazy, possibly becoming so pessimistic so as to commit suicide like Ludwig Boltzmann. I had a very talented student who later became cursed this way. She said to me: "Prof. Wu, we studied so much physics, but we could not even answer some of the most fundamental questions. How could we continue our studies, ah?" So she actually quit physics. Indeed, it may not be a bad thing to leave some room for religion.

Science should also reserve some room for art. The French impressionist master Paul Gauguin created a famous painting titled "Where did we come from? Who are we? Where are we going?" The title of his painting asked questions that even 10 wise men could not answer. He left the comfortable life of Paris behind to seek a life of simplicity in a rural island in South America. The ensuing poverty and ill health made Gauquin attempt suicide in despair, but he was saved and narrowly escaped death. It prompted him to think through the true meaning of life. He created the painting between 1897 and 1898, which was regarded as the most successful work of his life, now a collection at the Boston Museum of Fine Arts.

I certainly do not believe the story that God made man in his own image, but it is fine to enjoy it as a fairy tale. Cloning technology is very mature now, and the technology to clone a person is just around the corner. The main issue that needs to be addressed is ethical rather than technical. However, Darwin's theory of evolution also lacks strong evidence in explaining the origin of man. The existing so-called fossil records just do not tell the whole story. If we leave room for art and let paintings describe the philosophical issues, it will at least give people a space for imagination despite not directly answering the question of humanity's origin. That's not necessarily bad, is it? I always have a feeling that there may not be any scientific answer to the study of human origins. If science is about reproducibility, then human origin is not a suitable subject, since such a process cannot be repeated experimentally. Even if a person is successfully cloned, it still does not explain where human beings came from. Therefore, science should be focused on studying the future of human kind, such as how to improve the treatment of human diseases. The question of human origin is best left to religion and art.

When I was a young student, Chinese textbooks often criticized great scientists such as Newton, saying that they took the road of idealism when they reached old age. Now I realized that such criticisms were directed at the kind of ideas that I have just outlined. However, I do believe that my current thoughts have their merit. In the United States, we have the American Academy of Science and Art for a good reason. Science, art, and religion together form the knowledge base for the development of human civilization. The different branches of knowledge complement one another to make a whole picture.

11.3 Convergence of social systems

I lived 40 years in China, 7 in Europe, and 25 in the United States. If I live another 10 years, then I can say that I have spent the first half of my life in China, and the latter half in Europe and the United States. The questions on how to position myself, my own national identity, how to properly handle the relationship between China and the US, all became critically important. Since I have immigrated to the United States, become a US citizen, and sworn allegiance to this country, I must act accordingly. It is the first priority to abide by the laws of the United States in my career and in my life. However, I also have feelings for China, in the spirit that blood is thicker than water. I have an inescapable feeling of nostalgia for the country I grew up in.

If there should be a conflict between China and the United States, what could I do? My idea is that as long as I use the "principle of convergence", I will find a way to correctly handle all the challenges that I will likely face. It is often said that the United States is a capitalist country, whereas China is a socialist country. They seem totally incompatible. Really, are the two systems that different? Social development follows its own courses. Both China and the United States are constantly discovering problems in their own development processes and making adjustments all the time. What I really stand for is "revisionism". This is a term that has become derogatory in China, without justification. It promotes the modification of existing ideas and policies by nonviolent means. What is wrong with that approach? "Revisionism" is a word often used to describe the realistic modification of Marxism. Is it not the right thing to do? Lenin said that once capitalism reached the stage of monopoly, it became imperialism, ready for the death bed. The truth is that capitalism is also engaged in its own revisionism, often correcting its own problems at different stages of development. Many countries in Europe, and the United States, had antitrust laws as early as a century ago. Even today, a variety of antitrust laws are continually improved and practiced.

Therefore, it is worth advocating the use of "revisionism" in promoting social change through non-violent means. After witnessing the capitalist process of self-improvement in his later years, Engels had a change of mind and wrote: "The thoughtful people of various classes began to see a need to open up a new road, which is a path towards democracy." It is exactly because the two systems are undergoing revisions constantly; the result is that the differences between them become smaller and smaller. Is it not how the history of the two countries played out? I call it the convergence of different systems.

Marx made a call: "Proletarians of all counties, unite!" It turns out that all over the world they have indeed joined up. The Fortune 500 companies of the world are well-known to the Chinese, and many Chinese enterprises have also entered that elite circle of big companies. The link up of big corporations, a variety of economic communities and free trade zones have already integrated the world into one system, in which nobody can play the game alone. Most countries in the world have realized that cooperation is the only royal road, and confrontation leads nowhere.

The Cold War period is long past, and the Cold War mentality has lost its appeal.

It is often said that China is an authoritarian state, whereas the United States is a democratic country. So they are simply incompatible. Let me first cite Sir Winston Churchill's famous quote: "Some people say that democracy is the worst form of government except all the others that have been tried." It means that democracy may not be that good, but if there is nothing better than democracy, then it is a good choice. Churchill did not exclude other possibilities. We should not idealize our one-person-one-vote electoral system. Having lived in the United States for 25 years, I have experienced many elections. Really, even many Americans have their reservation about such an electoral system. One-person–one-vote seemed fair enough, but it is actually not that fair. Clever or illiterate, informed or uninformed, rich or poor, the involved and non-involved, everyone has one vote, but each vote my actually have different levels of significance. This system is based on the principle of equality, but would the election result necessarily represent the interests of the majority of the people? Not always so. I know many Americans who voted according to what their priest said, or listened to what was shown on television, but did not really understand what the candidates stood for, and what the real issues were. A tax reduction always sounded good, but it usually went with the disappearance of many social benefits that a candidate would conveniently keep quiet about. In some areas of the United Sates, the Democratic Party is traditionally favored, so even if you want to choose a Republican candidate, your vote will be wasted. The US election uses the electoral college system, where the winner takes all of a state's votes. I live in a Republican area, and the vote I cast for the Democratic Party is simply wasted. A president's speeches and performance may be quite different before and after the presidential election. The cost for winning a presidential election has reached astronomical levels, becoming a financial burden for the citizens. So many people of insight in the United States are discussing ways to improve the election rules.

It can be said that for a long time in China, democracy has been inadequate. Especially during the Cultural Revolution, civil rights and personal freedom were very much deprived. When the whole country had fallen into a state of chaos and disorder, it was called the time of "great democracy", which is simply a big irony. After the bitter experience, the Chinese government was gradually implementing political reforms along the general direction of the reform and opening-up. In recent years there has been much improvement in the participation of the people in the democratic process of government, a fact for all to see.

In a big country like China with 1.3 billion people, it appears to be far-fetched to expect the one-person-one-vote election system to work smoothly at the moment. Some will criticize my stand on this issue, believing that I dislike democracy and am trying to defend the communist party.

They either fail to understand China's national conditions, or are just trying to show in an exalted way how much they love democracy. If a person who had spent his or her entire life in the Yinjia Mountains and knew nothing about the world cast one vote, and a much more informed social elite also cast one vote, it might look fair, but was it really fair? In physics analysis, the impact of various factors on the final result is certainly not calculated by a simple addition, but rather by a weighted averaging process. That is how science operates. Furthermore, the calculation of the "weight" of each factor requires careful study. The size of the "weight" depends on the targeted factor. For example, in order to calculate mass, various factors that would influence the measurement of mass were assigned "weights" by the "least squares method", then the weighted average value is obtained. This is the only way to achieve the best result, indeed. Those self-proclaimed defenders of human rights may jump out to criticize me again, accusing me of feeling self-important and deserving larger "weight" than average. Such people either have ulterior motives or are simply ignorant.

In reality, development is the key. A one-person-one-vote style election only makes sense if people like the ones living in the Yinjia Mountains really learn about state affairs. This is only possible with economic development and improved standards of living. Once this is achieved, an equally weighed election becomes realistic. To ask a totally illiterate and uninformed citizen to participate in election would usually result in a wasted vote. It is not enough to talk big about the pursuit of democracy. Development and equity are sometimes at odds with each other. Rapid development often entails sacrifice of fairness, whereas pursuit of fairness often impedes development. The US republicans and democrats often argue about which is more important, development or fairness? In fact, only when there is food in a big pot can the individual have his or her own bowl full. As the whole nation develops, resulting in more in the big pot, despite some inequality, even the weak will benefit, is it not true? Even the poorest region in China now enjoys a much higher standard of living than in the past. That is a veritable fact. Those leftists under the banner of "pleading for the common folks" really have better things to do than to criticize me. They should talk less and do more in reality.

Of course, social sciences are much more difficult than the natural sciences. If it were as simple as natural sciences, the state would first select a goal to pursue, and it would be much simpler to make the corresponding policies to reach that goal. The question is, what would be best goal for a whole nation to pursue? It could be the growth rate of the economy, the GDP, or people's happiness indicator. If it is the pursuit of happiness, then how do we define happiness? Once a goal is set, and rules for selecting a government are made, then a weighted election can be held to choose the best government. It all seems too theoretical at this stage, and can only be explored and perfected through practice.

I do not mean to say that China's current level of democracy is already very good. Absolutely not! The identity of the next national leader is usually known a few years before the convening of the National People's Congress, which makes the representatives feel that their votes do not really matter. That is no democracy. To have a competitive election would be the first step in improving the Chinese system. The range of competitive election should be widened, and it should be practiced from grassroots offices all the way to the top positions at the national level. Candidates should be allowed to recommend themselves, making their own presentations, allowing the voters to really know their own representatives. Anyone who has gathered support from a sufficient number of voters should qualify as a candidate. This process can be started at the grassroots, especially from the more developed cities in China, and then promoted to all the way up at the top. In this way, there would be a convergence of the Chinese election system with its American counterpart.

It is also often said that the United States practices the rule of law, whereas China suffers from corruption in a major way. Yes indeed! China's level of corruption has reached a most critical point, and everyone must voice their indignation before it is too late. A Swiss friend told me how he personally witnessed the steady retreat of the Nationalists in Shanghai in 1948, with the aggressive advances of the communists. In his opinion, the nationalists were not defeated by the communists, but rather by their own corruption. Even Chiang Kai-shek would have agreed with him. The kind of corruption that he described for me almost exactly mirrored the current situation with some communist cadres. Now the Chinese Communist Party has a Commission for Discipline Inspection, but that is merely for the party's left hand to restrain the right hand. Really effective discipline inspection must be carried out independently with the help of an independent media.

There is little corruption at the personal level in the United States, but much institutional corruption. To take more than $20 would bring about charges of bribery, which is very explicit indeed, a clear warning to all officials so that they will not break the law. I have heard of a story that a Chinese person who received a ticket from a police officer for a traffic violation tried to "settle the issue personally" by offering the officer $50. The officer put him under arrest immediately with a bribery charge.

However, the institutional corruption of United States may be the most important cause of the debt-ridden economy of this country. There were open bids for successive presidents to invite their big fund contributors to stay in the White House, but the cost for such stays was borne by taxpayers. Is it really fair? The Congressional Audit Office announced their findings that the US Army bought a coffee maker for $400, 10 times higher than the market price, because some military orders were not subjected to the restraint of "public tender". It may help to explain the incredibly high cost of the Iraq war. Since the money did not fall into the hands of an individual person, it is hard to make a case for corruption. There is no doubt that some interest groups made huge profits unfairly. Luckily, freedom of speech in the United States allowed such scandals to be exposed, providing some restraint to such institutional corruption.

If China could really put power into a cage, shake up the entrenched interests of various groups, and give the rights of discipline and inspection back to the people, then China and the US would converge on the ways of handling corruption.

With a scientific issue, there is only one truth. A scientific law applies equally in China as well as in the United States. Otherwise, it is not science. However, the path of social development can be different in different countries, because each country may be in a different stage of social development. Each country has its own national conditions. The Chinese people must find their own way, as did the American people. "Only the feet know if the shoes fit." This old Chinese saying embodies the wisdom of Chinese ancestors. If a country takes a wrong path for a short duration in history, the correction must come from its own people. External pressure is often counterproductive. I believe that for social science as well as for natural science, there is only one truth. No matter how tortuous the path is, it will lead to the same destination.

All roads lead to Rome. That is the gist of my book. It is also the biggest revelation of the 70 years of my life.

Epilogue

When I started to write this memoir, I found that staying in America for over 20 years had not improved my English that much, but had made me forget a lot of my Chinese. Only my Shanghai accent remained unchanged over the years. My accent made it difficult for me to use Pinyin for inputting Chinese on computers. At the beginning, I had so many ideas in my head, but just could not get them out fast enough through the keyboard. I could only put down five or six lines of words in a whole day. It was frustrating: working at this speed, how many years would it take to finish my manuscript? Calming myself down, I realized that the plight that I faced was exactly the story of my life. "Results follow the concentration of mind": this has always been my motto. Where there is a will, there is a way. I worked hard and fast to learn Pinyin, and tried not to let my Shanghai accent stand in the way. In less than one week, my typing speed started to catch up with my thinking. After working round the clock for half a year, my manuscript was completed according to schedule. I am grateful that Professor KK Phua and Professor Minghan Ye wrote the Forewords for the book. Professor Guangjiong Ni wrote about his impressions after reading the manuscript. I also thank my brothers and sisters, my ex-wife Hengbao and my wife Li Liu, for their understanding and assistance. They may hold different opinions on many issues I touched upon in the book, but they always encouraged me to write down my true stories.

Austrian neurologist Sigmund Freud wrote to Arnold Zweig, a German writer, on May 31st 1936: "Anyone turning biographer commits himself to lies, to concealment, to hypocrisy, to flattery, and even to hiding his own lack of understanding, for biographical truth is not to be had, and even if it were it couldn't be used."

Freud wrote this, doubtless, because for him the essence of life was in those secrets he believed all people harbor owing to the distortions of their infancy and the disruptions of their early childhood, which made for the necessary deceits of their later lives. He thinks, "Truth is unobtainable; humanity does not deserve it, and incidentally, wasn't our Prince Hamlet right when he asked whether anyone would escape a whipping if he got what he deserved?"

This kind of idea has almost become the classical golden rule for biographies. However, my thought is different.

As a poem of the famous Chinese poet Du Fu goes: "Wine shops can be found here and there, septuagenarians are hard to come across anywhere." There is also an ancient saying: "A dying person speaks well and true." I may not have reached an age ready for the next world, but this book may be my best chance for expressing my personal beliefs about life gained through my own unique experiences. I wish to present my true self to the readers. Therefore, honesty is a guiding principle for writing this book. Some stories might be omitted for expediency, but what I wrote down had to be true. I would not worry too much about the judiciousness of my selections, knowing that my choices were made in the spirit that recommends one to "live an honest life, and leave judgments to history."

This book includes many pictures. These pictures are the tangible impressions drawn by the hand of history along my life's path. The contrasts among the different pictures are great. They tell many unforgettable stories on their own. I am an amateur photographer. The camera was a luxury item before the Reform and Opening Up of China in the 80s. I had my first camera in 1962. Before that, I borrowed cameras from friends to take my pictures. So far, I have collected over 10,000 pictures. Many of the pictures published here were selected from that collection. I shot the majority of my photo collections, developed and enlarged many of them myself. It is a pity that I did not have any pictures from the Cultural Revolution when I suffered political persecutions. Under those circumstances, I just did not have the inclination to take any pictures. May the readers forgive me for the "missing links".

After completing the last chapter of this book, I felt tremendously relieved, recalling the line of poetry "Believe not that my youth cannot be restored, and allow not a page of history to remain blank."

To borrow from the birthday thoughts of Master Liang Yang at the age of 102: "Once we so longed for changes of fortune, only to discover that the most beautiful scene of life is the calm composure of the heart … We so desired recognition by others, only to find out that your world is yours alone, and has nothing to do with anyone else…"

History is not written by the victors alone. Actually, history is made up of many small stories of ordinary people's lives. "Looking back at past bleak and weary scenes of life", 70 years of tide and wind have come to pass; now I just wish that in the years to come, "no wind and rain, nor too much sunshine, would blind my eyes."

Weimin Wu

Summer 2013, in the Western suburbs of Chicago

Book Reviews
(Chinese Edition)

Explore the Inner Workings of True History

by Professor Guangjiong Ni

I have known Weimin for over half a century, since I first met him at Fudan University in 1963. In my memory, he has always been a young, intelligent, hard-working person who enjoys learning at all times. After reading this autobiography, I can only use one word to describe my impression: "Striking!" His life-long experiences of ups and downs and the strong will that he has demonstrated in fighting with fate are all far beyond my imagination. Certainly, Weimin has his unique natural talents and abilities, but his outstanding accomplishments have a lot to do with an excellent family environment and the school education that he received from the key period of life from primary school to high school. I hope that readers, especially young ones and their parents and teachers, will learn from the environment of his youth. Weimin learned since childhood some basic values of life: honesty, kindness, self-discipline, and the willingness to help others. In addition, there were seeds of life-goals and dreams planted in his childhood. Teachers in his early life also worked really hard to carefully nurture the most precious qualities in youth: curiosity and freethinking, at the same time imparting knowledge. That's why at a time even when material comfort was lacking, the spiritual life was rich, and many well-rounded talented people like Weimin thrived.

Accomplished as he is, Weimin did not hide the mistakes that he made in his life, with the lessons learned along the way. Few people can open themselves up as he has done in such an autobiography. Weimin said in the last part of the Prologue: "I hope that my story will take my readers on a journey to explore the inner workings of true history, helping them achieve a deeper insight that may serve as inspiration for making history of their own." I appreciate his effort. Just as Joseph Needham said: "If we do not understand the past, we will have no hope of grasping the future."

Professor Guangjiong Ni

Professor of Physics at Fudan University

Former Director of the Research Institute of Modern Physics at Fudan University

Adjunct Professor at the Department of Physics, Portland State University, USA

Life on the Energy Frontier
Weimin Wu at Fermilab

By Dr. Dan Green

China at Fermilab

Let me make a few introductory comments. I worked with some of the first Chinese physicists to collaborate with Fermilab. These IHEP Beijing physicists started on a fixed target experiment, E769 looking at hadronic charm production. I later convinced them to participate in the Tevatron collider experiment, D0 where they worked on the muon system which I was responsible for. In these early experiments, the Chinese physicists became very familiar with high energy physics at Fermilab.

SDC

After these first steps it was necessary to participate more fully, and have the Chinese groups take responsibility for some major piece of equipment. The American Supercollider, the SSC, had two major experiments, one of which was called SDC. I was the Deputy Spokesperson for SDC and wanted very much to continue collaboration with my Chinese colleagues. The SSC was begun in 1988 and cancelled in 1993. During that time there was a fruitful collaboration with IHEP which included the tests by IHEP in China of the radiation resistance of plastic scintillators.

Weimin came to Fermilab during this period and immediately made an impact on our research. He and I and a small group became heavily involved in the modelling of several physics processes at the SSC. In this way we could see the impact of design choices for the SDC calorimetry, which Fermilab was largely responsible for, on the ultimate physics goals of SDC. Weimin took a strong lead in the model building, leveraging his prior experience with the ALEPH experiment at CERN.

CMS

With the demise of the SSC, the physicists who were involved in the 50-year search for the Higgs boson needed to find an alternative road to the energy frontier. Fermilab again collaborated with our colleagues at IHEP and Weimin performed invaluable liaison work between our institutes. Both China and the USA joined CMS and I served as the leader of the American effort on CMS. At this point the Chinese physicists took responsibility for a major hardware construction, the muon system assembled at IHEP. This was a big step which followed what Weimin believed was needed as part of full participation by Chinese physicists.

Finally, as Chinese expertise grew in high energy physics, it was a goal to fully participate in all aspects of CMS, including data analysis. Weimin applied his seminal experiences in ALEPH to now expedite data transfer and analysis for CERN and Fermilab to IHEP in China. Physicists at nearby PKU also assumed strong analysis positions. The IHEP computing center, a "Tier2", had its ancestor in the Chinese analysis effort that Weimin set up for ALEPH. With the march of technology, we advanced from the e-mail that Weimin initiated to the "Remote Control Room" which IHEP set up and where Fermilab, IHEP and CERN could videoconference in real time. The concept behind this networking tool can be traced back directly to Weimin's e-mail with ALEPH.

PKU and IHEP became deeply involved in the physics of CMS. I meet with PKU physicists on a weekly basis, by teleconference. They have taken direct responsibility for the analysis of two physics processes. Weimin himself took a leadership role in the search for the Majorana heavy neutrino.

We now have reached the goal that CMS is a truly international band of colleagues, working co-operatively. It is a tribute to the vision that

Weimin had, that physics can be a model for international co-operation. Indeed, the success of our long quest for the Higgs boson became public on July 4, 2012 with simultaneous announcements of the Higgs discovery on all the continents of the world.

Dr. Dan Green

Particle Physics Division, Guest Scientist Retired & Scientist Emeritus Group
Fermilab

Flow of History — A Reading of Weimin Wu's Autobiography

By Professor George W. S. Hou

Weimin Wu contacted me in 2013 through a common friend at Fermilab, and fulfilled his life-long wish to visit Taiwan as he was turning 70. Though ever on his mind, Taiwan had always seemed out of reach. Dr. K.K. Phua of World Scientific asked me to write a review for Weimin's autobiography. As much as I find myself inadequate for the task, I accepted for the reason that maybe I can provide a different perspective. Rather than a book review, however, this is really a digest.

We all live in the flow of history, and the life of one is but a special slice. Weimin Wu's life is a witness to the past 70 years of Chinese history, with sweat, tears and blood, but also with pride and not without groans.

Weimin is older than me by half a generation, with Shanghai parents who originated from Ningbo. My mother, a Shanghainese born in Wuxi, is older than Weimin by half a generation, but younger than his mother by only 7 years. Ningbo people are known to be merchants at heart, and Weimin's father was a self-taught accountant, while his mother had participated in factory management. But both Weimin's parents sympathized with the Communist cause and had supported it financially. As for my mother, she became an active right-wing student before she even turned 20, hence she was shipped away to Taiwan by the KMT (Kuomingtang, or Nationalists) when the civil war turned desperate. Our paths therefore departed before we were even born. But Weimin has worked in China, Europe and the US, while I have worked in the US, Europe and Taiwan (and Japan as well), so we share a similar world view, and could often stimulate each other in discussions.

Though communist sympathizers before the "liberation", during the incessant "movements" under Communist rule, Weimin's parents could not escape being branded as "semi" five-darks (landowners, the rich, counter-revolutionaries, criminals, and rightists). From a weakling start, Weimin metamorphosed during his teen years into an independent and freethinking personality. This brought about trouble when he brushed with party members, causing much grief and frustration, including the first love during his college years at Fudan University. Though unfortunate (I deem it fortunate) that his opportunity to study in the USSR failed to materialize (because of rising tensions), by providence, he left the water country of Jiangnan (lower Yangtze river) and went all the way to the much drier Lanzhou in Western China for graduate studies.

As the Cultural Revolution broke out, he also experienced Up-Mountain (Yinjiashan), cavern stay (in the poor Northern Shaanxi province), Down-Country for "Grand-Connect", etc. Through these, he observed the poverty of the vast Chinese population. Being drawn in, he became a Standing Member of the committee, but (fortunately) for only a brief period. Because of its strategic importance to China as an outpost location, Lanzhou turned out to be his salvation. He was handpicked by the special forces that took over Lanzhou University, which sent him to the "base" that was conducting the Chinese satellite project. It was here that his sharp mind and physics training asserted themselves, and he contributed a semi-automatic readout system to the first satellite launch of China. His life was therefore pushed on to the next stage by the hand of fate.

The "base" expanded into Shanxi province, where Weimin was sent. Here he met the daughter of one of the five generals. One knowing mathematics, the other familiar with programming, the two worked together as partners, eventually becoming husband and wife. His father in-law was an old Red Army member from the formative Jinggangshan period, and both the in-laws were "respectable and lovable" old party members. His father in-law eventually saved his life.

A peculiar twist unfolded as the Cultural Revolution came to an end. Both Enlai Zhou and Mao passed away, and China entered a new period of development, which included the founding of the Institute of High Energy Physics (IHEP). Weimin could not forget the nuclear physics he had learned during college. When his wife was in Beijing for treatment, somehow he was inspired and went to IHEP to volunteer himself. With the help of another sincere and respectable party member, he did actually manage to transfer from the Shanxi base of the Defense Science and Technology Commission, and joined IHEP. He thereby entered the most illustrious period of his life, leading Chinese scientists as one of the first to enter the high energy physics arena of the West.

Selected to join the intensive particle physics course given by the Nobel Laureate Tsung-Dao Lee himself, he was then sent to CERN, the European Center for Nuclear Research, to join the CDHS experiment lead by Jack Steinberger (1988 Nobel Prize for Physics). Once again, he met a person pivotal to his life. When Weimin arrived at Zurich Airport, he "could not believe (his) own eyes", it was as if he had landed on another planet. It was November 1979, Weimin was 37 years old, and it was his first trip ever out of the long-locked gates of China. I can imagine his shock and even exasperation, for I left for Los Angeles myself after graduating from college in 1980. Although Taiwan had expressways already, I still marveled at the massive Los Angeles freeway system.

Weimin delved into learning and work, and in one year he could report in Poland the results of simulation work he was tasked to do. At that time, operating with the Solidarity movement and the deep Catholic faith, the Communist Party in Poland was breathing its last. A few years later, in 1984, he rode in the car of a friend and collaborator to the international HEP conference in Leipzig, and saw for himself the contrast between the two Germanys. These firsthand contacts left a deep impression on Weimin. As Steinberger was developing his next and larger ALEPH experiment, based on his own strong performance, Weimin advocated for IHEP to join and collaborate on ALEPH, and stressed that "to have true international collaboration, one must be able to produce detectors within China, and contribute in both hardware and software." Some 10 years later, I pushed for the same at National Taiwan University.

Weimin was promoted by Minghan Ye, the IHEP director at that time, to the Deputy Division Head for the Beijing Spectrometer effort, which allowed the feedback from experience gained with ALEPH. As for ALEPH participation itself, with a budget of a mere quarter million RMB, Weimin was able to deliver the plastic scintillators required to cover 66 large muon detectors for the experiment at CERN. Even Sam Ting, the

Nobel Laureate leader of the competing L3 experiment, commended Weimin for this achievement in front of others. Weimin's sister turned out to be another of his benefactors, for it was her contacts in Shanghai that helped Weimin reach the Shanghai Institute of Plastic Products.

What Weimin himself considers his greatest achievement, worthy of entry in the annals of history, is the sending of the first electronic mail from Beijing to Steinberger at CERN in Switzerland. This occurred on August 25th, 1986, and through the verification of the China Internet Network Information Center (CNNIC), it has been confirmed as the first ever event of its kind for China. But something does not arise from nothing. Besides the openness gained from international collaboration, there was the intellectual acuity of Weimin himself. He figured out how to link a terminal wirelessly to a computer, which he deems his greatest innovation. With the prodding from Steinberger that "now is the time to seriously consider doing data analysis on Chinese soil", Weimin was encouraged to develop the link with CERN.

Another high point of Weimin's life occurred slightly earlier in June 1986, when Director Minghan Ye was not able to attend the European HEP conference held in Uppsala, Sweden, to report on the status of the Beijing Spectrometer. The task fell on Weimin, who attended from Switzerland. In his presentation, he compared the circumference of the mere 200 meters of the Beijing Electron Positron Collider (BEPC) with the enormous 27 kilometers of the LEP collider at CERN, then drew the perspective onto the global scale, and said "We are all members of Village Earth, and have come together for a common goal", for which he received applause lasting for a few minutes. Professor Guangjiong Ni, one of Weimin's teachers at Fudan and who was also in the audience that day, was very deeply moved. One must recall that though China had opened up with reforms, the Berlin wall had yet to fall. This was the first and only time that Weimin represented IHEP for a talk at an international conference. Indeed, he represented the whole of China, and the applause was also for China!

With applause and achievement, however, Weimin's life reached another turning point. He lost his father in 1986, and his mother in 1987. Unfortunate as these were, they can also be viewed as fortunate. His parents suffered a lot throughout their lives, without ever enjoying much the better life. But their passing also meant that they did not have to endure the trauma that was "June 4th" (Tiananmen Square), nor worry for Weimin's subsequent sojourning.

With a love for photography, at that time Weimin possessed a video camera. Perhaps because he did not foresee how the June 4th events would unfold, he went the day after to the center of action to take videos. But confessing that he is no hero but a coward instead, he took the lower risk path and handed the tapes over to an Italian collaborator to take out of China. When the official "Purge Evil with Thoroughness" slogan put everyone on edge, however, he told himself that he must survive, for to live is witness, but with death all would be lost.

As I read through the near-eyewitness accounts of the June 4th event, I came to tears twice: once for the brave young students and Beijing residents, including those young persons who had already boarded but were pulled off from the planes; the other for Weimin's own departure experience from Beijing, when upon arriving at Geneva airport he embraced his German friend and let out his grief ... In Beijing, besides help from friends at IHEP, the chauffeured car of his father in-law also helped him reach the airport. Reflecting on the human condition, Weimin's observation is that, whether you are a party member (or anyone in position of power!) or not, the paramount thing in life is to be a good person. It cannot be better said. In the long history of China, great tragedies abound, but this cannot be used as an excuse for letting tragedies continue to happen.

Weimin left China, and was able to get his wife and daughter out subsequently, which demonstrates his ability at befriending people (I myself am a case in point). Many people lent him a helping hand, including Dr. K.K. Phua, Professor Sau-Lan Wu and Dr. Steinberger. But, to give up one's career at its prime and become a reluctant immigrant at 46 (turning 47), there were of course many struggles, much soul-searching, and the letting go of many things.

The day his family arrived from Switzerland to the US, Weimin miraculously concluded the transactions for the purchase of a house; soon after, he began to learn the American way of life, becoming "a little capitalist" in the chief camp of Capitalism. He was turning 50 when he received the Green Card, but this came partially as the result of the expulsion act by the party representative at IHEP. Weimin now worked at the topnotch

Fermilab, but he no longer had the passion. It became just a profession, he writes, "be an average physicist, and conduct one's work in a down to earth way". Just reading it breaks my heart. He now appreciated the human-centered core value of the United States, and began to accept himself as a US citizen, although when facing the Statue of Liberty, his emotions were complex. His first marriage unraveled as another victim of the forced emigration: differences were amplified by living in a different country and culture. He remarried soon after, while maintaining excellent relations with his first wife, which is admirable.

Weimin Wu's story fills his book with flesh and blood, bearing witness to his life as well as his era. Compared to the tragic fates of many in China during the past hundred or so years, his midlife roundabout caused by "June 4th" is already much too fortunate. China has progressed tremendously since then, but things are still perilous, with many obstacles to overcome.

I have used words such as fate, providence, benefactor, etc., which may seem "feudalistic" to Chinese-educated people in the PRC. Weimin also found Taiwan's usage of "year of such and such of the Republic" a feudal remnant (compare Japan's continued usage of Imperial Eras to this day). But Weimin himself is well-read in traditional Chinese literature, much better than the post Cultural Revolution generations. Is it really a bad thing to keep some traditions from old times? From family ancestry to even larger bodies, cherishing ones past is a virtue. And it is a beautiful thing, because we all live in the flow of History.

Because of the many remarkable events throughout his life, Weimin does believe in a nameless God. I believe that it is this nameless God, who holds all fate, who has showered favor on him and kept him as a witness. With Weimin's excellent health, I am certain that he can see China restore herself to the past glory, and witness the good relations between his two homelands for sake of mankind. That is my wish also.

Professor George W. S. Hou
Department of Physics
National Taiwan University

Your 1986 Email Listed as the Number One Item of Chinese Internet History

By Dr. Enhai Wang

The language of your autobiography is plain, almost colloquial. Reading it felt like when, on a quiet night, we sit around a bonfire, with me sitting opposite to you and listening attentively to an old man of wisdom speak about his experiences and thoughts. Although this old man experienced the ups and downs of life, he spoke with a measured tone, with not a hint of personal emotion or bitterness, expressing his love of life and his attachment to his motherland.

Dr. Enhai Wang,
China Internet Network Information Center

A Stormy Life of No Return

By Wu Gong

The Nobel Prize in Physics 2013 was awarded jointly to François Englert and Peter W. Higgs for their theoretical discovery of the Higgs mechanism for the origin of mass of subatomic particles. According to the Higgs theory, all subatomic particles that make everything and motion possible have no mass originally, and this is called the "strict symmetry" of the subatomic particles; however, because of their different ways of coupling with the Higgs field, some subatomic particles acquire relatively large or small masses, such as electrons and quarks. Others have no mass, such as photons and gluons, and this is called the spontaneous break-down of symmetry. The universe can display its myriad states and never-ending life cycles, only because it is made of asymmetric subatomic particles. Such is life, too. We all came to this world naked, with no difference in status, possessing strict symmetry, but as a person grows in different social environments, the differences start to show: some become politicians, others become scientists; some achieve a lot, others accomplish nothing; some become wealthy, others remain penniless, and such and so on — the spontaneous break-down of symmetry. People of different characters interact nonlinearly, constituting complex societies and eventful histories.

Take the case of the awarding of Nobel Prize to Higgs and his collaborator. There is a strong asymmetry between my attitude and that of Mr. Weimin Wu. I have no reason to covet this lofty prize in any way, but Mr. Wu would think: Why not add a new category for the Prize that would be awarded to a "collective"? This is because, Higgs and others advanced the theory half a century ago, but the final awarding of the Prize had to wait for experimental confirmation of the Higgs boson particle, which was accomplished by a large team of scientists including Mr. Wu, who played an important role.

Weimin Wu, a famous Chinese American physicist, was born in Shanghai, China, in July of 1943. He is now a researcher at the most well-known Fermi National Laboratory of the United States. From China in the East, to America in the West, from a premature baby who barely hung on to life, to an accomplished physicist, how was a Chinese American physicist made? *Life on the Cusp* depicts for us a legendary and colorful life.

Wu's birth was really a legend. That day his heavily pregnant mother took part in an anti-Japanese demonstration, and her pregnancy came to an abrupt end while escaping from the pursuit of the military police. As a result, a baby was born two months ahead of schedule. This baby bore no "symmetry" with other babies: it would neither cry nor drink any milk from the mother. A doctor gave the baby a shot of medicine, and put it on a new bamboo mattress to live or die on its own. Only after the third day after its birth did the baby establish normal coupling with the environment: it cried loud and fast, making his tearful mother smile instead. This was Weimin Wu. Was this his fate? Forced to be born during a demonstration, and after 46 years, forced to be "born" again in another "demonstration"? I do not really believe in fatalism. An individual is an accident, and the society keeps changing, so when the thread of an individual is woven into the fabric of the society, this indeterminism produces a unique life. When Weimin Wu reached school age, a "new" China was born. The "newness" of this country was shown in the fact that different members of the society, in persons as well as in souls, were suddenly divided into two fundamentally opposing groups — the proletariat and the bourgeoisie, namely, the people or the enemy. Everyone found himself walking on a tight rope shaking. Shaking to left, one was a member of the people; shaking to the right, one became a public enemy. The feeling of living under threat is like being "on the cusp" all the time.

The parents of Mr. Wu should have belonged to the "working class". However, their entrepreneurial spirit actually did harm to themselves. During the time when Wu's father worked as an apprentice in a printing shop and as an intern at a bank, he studied hard by himself after a day's hard work, eventually establishing himself as a senior intellectual, especially in the field of accounting, becoming the chief accountant in a bank and schoolmaster in a vocational school. The factory where his mother worked was on the brink of bankruptcy, and it issued products and shares to employees as salary. His mother started to act like an owner once she acquired some shares, so she worked long and lived in the factory, showing excellent management skills and obtained a loan using the father's bank connection, making the factory financially viable again. However, all these efforts were on the "evil" way from the "working class" to the "exploiting class" in the eyes of the new communist power. It would be one thing if only they kept to themselves after they became rich, yet they belonged to the progressive youth, and used their own financial resources to support the revolution. They not only actively participated in the activities organized by the communist underground organizations, they used their own residence to shelter cadres of the communist party, and used their own jobs and social positions to ship medicine and other much needed materials to the New Fourth Army led by the communists during Anti-Japanese war ... The father's vocational school trained many high ranking officials for the new China. After the liberation, some revolutionary folks questioned: "You were so close to the communist party, why didn't you join yourself?" "You have helped so many people to join the New Fourth Army, why didn't you do it yourself?" In one case in particular, Wu's father used a gold bar to rescue a communist cadre from jail, but this cadre wrote down a "declaration of repentance" while in jail, so the label "traitor and special agent" followed Wu's father for the rest of his life. In each political movement that followed in China, Wu's parents have had to humiliate themselves by writing self-critique for this "shameful" event. This struggling premature baby of ours, Mr. Wu, thus became the child of "bad pedigree". This may be the "negative energy" of the Dirac equation. In any case, if this child is to succeed in such a distorted society, he must try harder than anyone else.

Nevertheless, what the parents gave to Weimin was mostly positive energy — smart genes and a positive character. Social interactions can be very complex, but often produce drama of having blessings in the disguise of misfortune. Weimin was a weak child, and his test scores were not good when he was in primary school and middle school. At that time, only test scores determined the entrance to high schools. Because of his scores, he could only qualify for a "community school" with substandard facilities. However, unexpectedly, this third-rate school actually possessed a whole lot of first-class teachers! Many intellectuals of substantial learning could not teach at "select" high schools because of birth, historical and other political problems, but were "banished' to this third-ranked school. Under the careful guidance of such excellent teachers, Weimin's test scores improved dramatically. In order to prove that he was not just first rank in a third-ranked school, "a giant among dwarfs", he took part in many city-wide scholarly competitions, and won contest after contest. Eventually, he made it into a "delegation of outstanding students from Shanghai" that went to Beijing to have an audience with the then much revered great leader Chairman Mao, getting close to him enough to see clearly the famous mole on his face. On graduation from high school, he succeeded in the entrance examination for the most competitive "Students for Studying in the Soviet Union". Unexpectedly, the China-Soviet relationship broke down, and China shelved the plan for sending students to the Soviet Union. The Chinese authority converted this group of students as the "zero class" of the Department of Atomic Energy at Fudan University in Shanghai, who later took part in the uranium enrichment experiment for the first atom bomb. Thus, this 17-year-old boy unexpectedly became an early contributor to the "two bombs and one satellite" projects.

One important reason for the "spontaneous breakdown of symmetry" among humans is the differences in their natural endowments and abilities, with different individuals excelling in different areas. A good educational and social system should nurture the unique talents and abilities of each individual, rather than impoverishing and restricting them. The educational goal of the university that Mr Wu attended was to produce "submissive tools of the communist party", which was really sad! "The independence of spirit and freedom of thought" were taboos. One was not to discover and develop one's special talents and abilities, but rather to "guard against individualism" constantly, hiding all the distinguishing signs of deviations, molding oneself according to the uniform standard specified by the leadership. After the success of the uranium enrichment experiment, members of the "zero class" were dispersed into some regular classes of the physics department at Fudan University. Once when Wu's class organized by the communist party went to the countryside to do the so-called "Four Clears", which was a kind of political activity, he went to a nearby seaside to see the sunrise after discharging his regular duties, and wrote a poem about it afterwards. The political cadre in charge of their class,

Mr. "He" (not his real name), went as far as threatening to discipline him. It was rude enough for Mr. He to criticize Weimin for "disrespect for the organization and discipline", and it was almost ludicrous for him to label this poem as "smacking of bourgeoisie thinking", thinking that "the working class do not have such leisure and taste". The originator of the quantum mechanics system was the 25-year-old Heisenberg from Germany. The first thing Heisenberg did after he completed the calculations for the quantum system was to go to the seaside to see the sunrise. The rising of the reddish sun with all its glowing glory reflected the excitement of the birth of a new mechanics system. How could one associate social classes to such feelings? The test scores of Weimin were still outstanding at Fudan University, but his free thinking style and frankness offended some political overseers like Mr. He. Weimin was repeatedly asked to study an article by Mao Zedong called "On anti-liberalism" but could never quite get the point, and yet his fate was to be decided by such functionaries. He knew that he was to be banished to a factory or to the countryside, and would not be able to carry on scientific research and teaching that he truly loved.

Apart from political interferences, there was also a lack of scholarly appreciation and encouragement in the system. In 1961, the 18-year-old Weimin Wu wrote an article titled "Hypothesis about Zi and Dian", suggesting that there were two kinds of elementary particles, one was to be called "Zi", having mass but not electric charge, and the other called "Dian", having electric charge but no mass. All the other known elementary particles would be formed by using different combination of the two like fitting a jigsaw puzzle. In the same decade, Murray Gell-Mann in the United States advanced the Quark model, and Peter Higgs in Great Britain proposed the Higgs mechanism for the acquirement of mass. These are all different theoretical models, but the scientific methods used to derive them were very similar. That is to say, at the frontiers of physics exploration at that time, the inside of elementary particle was considered to have structure. Electric charges and mass were originally thought to be the intrinsic properties of particles, but now they were considered separate entities. Weimin said he published over 200 papers in first rate international physics journals, but all of them combined do not quite equal the importance of this single article. He showed the paper to a distinguished teacher, but got only contemptuous disregard. Of course, the stifling of an idea of genius could not be blamed on one teacher alone. The real problem was that there were no competitive and encouraging mechanisms set up for scientists in China at the time like there were in the West. Looking back at the history of quantum mechanics, each step of progress was made possible by the "wild thinking" and "nonsensical ideas" of young physicists.

As a matter of fact, to be in motion or to be still, it all depends on the frame of measurement. If you just chase a wave, you will become part of the wind and wave, becoming a lifeless element of the system. However, if you run against the wind, breaking the wave, the strength of the wind and wave is the measure of the strength of your life. Beethoven said that one must "grasp fate by the throat". Weimin gets his deep insight with life on the cusp while struggling with fate itself. In order to escape the fate of terminating his academic career at college graduation, he was determined to take the examination for graduate school. His effort was almost blocked by Mr. He, except that he finally got help to secure the permission just a few days before the examination started, the suspense of which was not unlike a movie about cops chasing suspects. Thus, we can understand Weimin's extraordinary excitement upon the receipt of the admission letter from Lanzhou University: "My tears just burst out. I really wanted to cry out without restraint, to purge all the sorrows and bitterness in my heart." However, this was not to be the end of his bad luck. In 1965, as a prelude to the coming political storm of the Cultural Revolution, graduate students were asked to go to the countryside "to get real life experience". Wu was assigned to an extremely poor village in the West mountainous region of China. Around the village were tall mountains and deep valleys with very limited road access, wild ridges and poor soils, lacking food and water, and the folks were so poor that they could not afford pants for basic decency. Here, ill acclimatization, vicious dogs of the farmers, and hungry wolves in the mountains all nearly killed him. That year he was only 22.

The changing fortunes of politics were also pretty comical at time. During the Cultural Revolution, Mr. He and other party functionaries like him were humiliated and criticized at mass meetings as toeing the reactionary line of Liu Shaoqi. On the other hand, this so called "liberal element" Weimin Wu, using his deep knowledge of literature and history and remarkable oratory skills, came up with a talk that went across time and space from the "Paris Commune" of France, to the "October Revolution" of Russia, and finally to the "January Revolution" of China (In January of 1967, the red rebels took over power in Shanghai). Wu at one time became a shining star worshiped by hundreds of thousands, and was invited to give speeches everywhere, ultimately landing on a position as a standing member of the Revolutionary Committee of Lanzhou University. Fate appeared to have shown him a broad and smooth road to reach a high social position, and after completing graduate studies he would be able to enter the leadership circle of Lanzhou University, becoming a political overseer in charge of other people's fate like Mr. He of yesterday. However, because of his fear of politics and love for science, he declined the popular position of being a cadre, then went on to work at a research base of the National Defense Engineering Committee, participated in the project for launching the first artificial satellite of China, engaging in the processing of remotely acquired data. He once again became part of the "Two Bombs and One Satellite Project". Impermanence appeared to be the rule, and towards the end of the Cultural Revolution, Weimin Wu once again nearly fell into the category of an "enemy" of the people: he was overheard to have said bad things about "Gang of Four" members, Zhang Chunqiao and Jiang Qing, and was about to be made an "active counter-reactionary". Luckily, the ambiguous attitude of his father-in-law, a former member of the Red Army and one of the five generals at the base, who also happened to be his superior, delayed the case until the "Gang of Four" were ousted from power, and eventually saved Wu from persecution.

A spring thunder was heard in the middle of October, 1977, and there was happiness and joy everywhere. That year started the honeymoon period between Chinese intellectuals and the party and government leadership. People cheered for the arrival of "the second spring of science", and Weimin Wu also felt delighted with high spirit. He was transferred to the Institute of High Energy Physics located in Beijing, and had opportunities to go abroad to participate in and manage international collaborations in high energy physics research. He got to know some world-renowned physicists such as the Nobel Laureates Samuel C.C. Ting, Tsung-Dao Lee, Chen-Ning Franklin Yang, and Jack Steinberger. Weimin formed a close working relationship with Steinberger in particular, a German-American scientist who won the 1988 Nobel Prize in Physics for discovering the second generation of neutrinos. Weimin worked under his supervision in the European Nuclear Research Center (CERN), and collaborated with him to establish an international collaboration between China and CERN, becoming the principal investigator in this fruitful project. In this age of ready access to Internet, few netters know that Weimin Wu is an early pioneer in establishing Internet service in China. In 1986, August 25, Wu established the first wireless remote terminal in China, and used it to send out an email to Steinberger in Switzerland. On March 12, 2010, the official Chinese Internet Information Center formally recognized this email, listing it as the first item in Chinese Internet history.

The honeymoon had to end one day. Towards the end of the 1980s, demonstrations were in vogue in China. Weimin Wu used a video recorder that few people owned at that time to shoot many scenes in Beijing that he was not supposed to record. Before that, as one of the earliest Chinese who went abroad, he saw many street scenes in the West that were the complete opposite of what was impressed in his memory by the Chinese party propaganda since childhood. In contrast, capitalism was not "in deep water and hot fire", and socialism was not so "thriving". As a person who actually traveled in both East Germany and West Germany, Weimin was incensed by an article in *People Daily* that talked about the superiority of East Germany over West Germany. He soon published articles like "Re-learn capitalism", qualifying himself as an element of "bourgeoisie liberalism". When the demonstration movement was suppressed, the communist authority tried to rid the society of all the "evil elements", hunting down "nineteen types of bad persons". Using the government's guidelines, he found himself qualifying for six or seven categories of the wanted list! Because of the international scientific collaborations that he was engaged with, Weimin traveled to Europe rather often. His survival instinct drove him to make a decision to escape the political persecution. The special difficulties in a special time were overcome with the help of close friends and simply kind-hearted persons, including his father-in-law who dispatched a military vehicle to send him to the airport. Many of these scenes appeared to be straight out of intense spy movies. For example, Weimin witnessed that on the airplane bound for Europe with engines already running, eight young people were singled out and pulled out of the airplane by the security force. When I read that "one girl stood up and followed them with tears", my own eyes moistened.

Actually, the generation of Mr Wu has deep feelings about its homeland, and they love the country, even the party. Wu's journey to Europe was just to escape the on-going political storm, rather than "betraying the country to join the enemy". However, the radical authorities in China forced him on a path of no return. Mr Wu's trip was classified as a "treacherous escape", and he was dismissed from his job at the Institute of High Energy Physics. When his passport was about to expire, Weimin Wu asked the Chinese Consulate in Chicago to extend the passport. His passport extension failed because a head of the party committee of the Institute in Beijing, Mr. "Mu", illegally held up the application, making him a stateless refuge. Weimin Wu moved from Europe to the United States, applied for the green card, and eventually became an American citizen. The whole process was part of an international rescue effort for Chinese scholars in exile, reminiscent of Schindler, which moved many a heart inside China and among supporters abroad. The similar international rescue effort happened 50 years ago when Nazi Germany carried out its genocide. The United States was the ideal destination of refuge in both rescue efforts.

Thus, a Chinese physicist was reborn in the West. In the USA, he first worked at the Argonne National Laboratory, then the Fermi National Laboratory. These two laboratories are not only first-rate in the United States, but are also well known in the international physics field. The project of a century that Weimin Wu took part in, discovering the Higgs Bosons, became a high point of his life. In the sixties of last century, the world physics community has established the standard model of particle physics based on quantum mechanics. This Standard Model of particle physics is a theory concerning the electromagnetic, weak, and strong nuclear interactions, as well as classifying all the subatomic particles known. The current formulation was finalized in the mid-1970s upon experimental confirmation of the existence of six types of quarks and leptons, with the last two types, bottom quark and top quark, discovered in the Fermi Laboratory where Mr Wu worked. However, in the standard model there was a particle with some most special properties — the Higgs boson, that did not make its appearance. This particle explains the origin of mass for matter, and is a most elementary particle, so it was dubbed the "God particle". The success of the standard model hinged on the discovery of the Higgs boson. To reach this goal, the physics community organized a large-scale international collaboration, involving a few thousand scientists and engineers. Two main kinds of particle detectors were used to detect the Higgs boson: ATLAS and Compact μ particle Muon Solenoid (CMS). Since 1994, Mr Wu participated in the whole process of CMS from design, construction, data analysis to paper writing, playing an important role in some aspects, recognized by colleagues. The experiment that looked for the boson had some positive initial results in 2011, and was confirmed openly by the European Nuclear Research Center in March of 2013. Soon after, the Nobel Prize for Physics 2013 was awarded jointly to François Englert and Peter W. Higgs, showing the importance attached to this research effort from the international physics community.

After Deng Xiaoping's "Speech in the South" in 1992, the extreme leftist line active in China was contained. As a result, the High Energy Physics Institute cleared the name for Weimin Wu. However, the life path of Wu could no longer be reversed. Wu's mother received several thousand Yuan (RMB) of compensation after being redressed at the end of the Cultural Revolution, a sizable sum at that time, but she donated it all to the party as party fees. Likewise, Mr Wu, who already became an American citizen, still loved his own motherland, was very much concerned with the future and fate of China, and worked a lot for the scientific cooperation between the two countries. Though the economy of China had taken off, the shadow of totalitarian politics still lingered on, threatening every citizen and the course of opening-up and reform policies. A few years back, the "Chongqing Storm" of Xilai Bo made Mr. Wu angry and concerned: some totalitarian political games can thrive again under a new disguise! In reality, if there is no constitutional system that takes the protection of human rights as the primary goal, using power balance and checks as the government's basic structure, the people have no power to stop the coming back of totalitarian rule. One of the acts of "bourgeoisie liberalism" of Mr. Wu was to call for the abolishment of political departments and career politicians in research institutions on various occasions. Even now, this call is still an unrealized dream. The "modern university system" based on freedom of scholarship, self-government, and management by professors has a tradition of 300 years, and has been universally adopted by countries all over the world, but is still not realized in China. This hampers the effective development of the brain resources of the Chinese people, much in the same way as the planned economy practiced in the first 30 years since the founding of People's Republic of China slowed down the development of the economic resources of China. Year by year, almost to a routine, the scientific community of China painfully talks about the same question when it is the time to award the Nobel Prize: "Why can't a Chinese person win the Nobel Prize inside China?"

Mr Wu's life on the cusp represents an epitome of the harsh existence and challenges in personal growth of the individual under the unstable political environment of China, resonating strongly with readers of the same generation, whereas the younger generation can read a piece of true history in the making. Any history has a contemporary dimension. The more we reveal the true history, the more easily we can pick up a correct frame for our future path. Lately, because of the new social problems such as official corruptions and uneven distribution of wealth, there is some pathological nostalgia for the first 30 years of the communist rule. Some denied the "three years of famine", others sang praises for the "Go up the mountains and down the countryside" movement that scarred a whole generation of young people for life, and still others called for the justification of the savage excesses of the "Cultural Revolution". This is sheer ignorance, if not out of ulterior purposes. Mr Wu said, "In my mind, the Cultural Revolution was defined as many families broken up or dead, defined as the plaque with the inscription 'misclassified capitalist' hung over the neck of my mother, defined as my father using tissues to stop a bleeding nose hit during a struggle meeting, and defined as my brothers and sisters banished to all remote areas of China." Blind nostalgia results from hiding the true facts of history.

It was said that because of the historical achievements of establishing a complete and independent national economy system, and "two bombs and one satellite", the first 30 years must not be demonized. This is a fallacy in logic! The totalitarian politics and the extreme leftist line of the first 30 years accounted for a negative contribution to the building of new China. While at college, Weimin Wu had to do "Four Clears", before taking on graduate studies he had to go to the countryside to get the "excise", before working on the project for launching the first artificial satellite he had to go to the company of army engineers to "get excise through labor", with little benefit to his professional accomplishment. In fact, they were a simple waste of precious brain resources of China by the extreme leftist line! The economic and scientific achievements of new China should be credited to millions of common people who used their own conscience and judgment, their strong desire for self-realization, despite the political repressions and diversions. They should certainly not be credited to the totalitarian political players. Without such political interferences, Japan and "Four Little Dragons of Asia" achieved a giant economic takeoff during the same period, serving as negative evidence towards the saying that the first 30 years cannot be negated. The economic miracle of the "Later 30 Years" of China, is also a negative evidence for the "First 30 Years".

Weimin Wu is no scientific freak living a secluded life. He has many talents and a thirst for life. His photography works achieved a high professional standard, winning well-recognized awards, and was in the international amateur photography society's "Hall of Fame". Weimin published a photo album. This autobiography describes his life's struggles, pleasures of success, esoteric science, elegant arts, an eventful career, a colorful personal life, serious thinking, and romantic love. Read it, and benefit from it.

December 30, 2013

Wu Gong

Author, The Elf of the Universe — the Story of Quantum Mechanics

Happiness is Being the Person who Takes it All in

By Dr. Zhang Li

It's been a while since I last stayed up late reading far into the night. This recently published *Life on the Cusp* was written by Prof. Wu, who came to my party with his wife Dr. Li Liu and gave me a signed copy of his autobiography. What grabbed my attention immediately was Prof. Wu's written inscription quoting the famous poem by the well-known Chinese educationalist Youren Yu: "Believe not that my youth cannot be restored, and allow not a page of history remain blank." I could hardly wait to turn to the first page of this book out of great curiosity after all my guests left. It turned out that I never stopped until I finished reading it by dawn.

What an autobiography! It is totally a heart-gripper!

Although I have not been well acquainted with Professor Wu and we only met and talked briefly at weekend family parties, I know that he is quite famous and knowledgeable as a Chinese American physicist. My whole family, especially my daughter, has been attracted by Professor Wu's frankness, optimism and many talents. His intellectual insights and theories about high energy physics are beyond my comprehension since I am just a practicing medical doctor. However, his vivid description of the colorful and eventful life, illustrated by a precious collection of pictures, has been so inspiring and enlightening that reader can almost see this genius physicist walking between pages.

If I do not need to repeat that Professor Wu proudly participated in the "Four Firsts": the making of the first atom bomb, the launching of the first artificial satellite, the first electron-positron collider, and the first Internet link to the world, I will emphasize that this book has touched me in the following humanitarian perspectives:

1. Indomitable Will: He expressed this in many places in the book, and he showed it really well when he described how he started writing his memoirs. Where there is a will, there is a way. We all know many of these famous sayings and proverbs, but it's easier said than done. Without such strong willpower, there would never be such a meaningful and accomplished life. Life treats everyone equally.
2. Persistent and Truthful: the most basic qualities in a scientist. Professor Wu once said: what was recorded must be true to the facts. He was most proud to be a pioneer in establishing Internet service in China. In 1986, Professor Wu established the first wireless Internet terminal in Beijing, China, and sent an email to Jack Steinberger in Geneva, Switzerland. However, media reports later credited another person as the first one to use emails in 1987. Through his own persistent effort in searching for original documents as proof, the Chinese Internet Service Center formally confirmed that the message he sent out in 1986 was the first one listed in the history of Chinese Internet. The reader can find many more such stories in the book.
3. Optimistic Attitude: Professor Wu described not only his accomplished career but also his romantic love life. He depicted his two marriages with poetic and romantic flares and in candid details, presenting readers with his youthful passions and the full spectrum of emotions in his first marriage. Many were so amazed by him maintaining very good terms with his ex-wife after he remarried and it almost became a local legend. I must say that Professor Wu is a lucky guy as his ex-wife is very open-minded and his current wife is such a wise lady of big heart and tolerance, so he could enjoy the rainbow of life after a severe storm. Professor Wu has an eye for both beauty and talent. It's not easy to find a scientist like Professor Wu who experienced the dramatic ups and downs of life, struggled on the cusp of historical events, seized every great opportunity along the way, and managed to handle such a colorful life. Likewise, very few could have had the guts to reveal a true self.

It was Professor Wu's inspiring journey of life that grabbed my attention, as it gives readers an interesting glimpse about my own generation at a time in our history. Many of his stories have echoed my memories of those unforgettable years.

The autobiography used a literary style of mixing factual descriptions with comments. The author opened up his heart and expressed his own opinions truthfully and frankly at the same time as he was telling real life stories. It is really remarkable that he could be so straight forward with his political point of views during a repressive era. Many of his bold views later turned out to be avant garde and correct in time of social transformation.

Prof Wu has written in a simple and plain language, with a touch of humor. This autobiography has shown his skillful mastery of the Chinese language and culture. He handled both storyline and the writing with great ease and flow. The joys and sorrows of his life all come alive in the writing. Professor Wu has been living in Chicago for 20 years. It is in this most famous windy city that he has been breathing the fresh air coming in spite of the gusty winds from different directions, as described by Song Yu's poem: "the wind of the commoner, or the wind of the kings and queens, happy (happiness) is the person who takes it all in."

Lastly I would like to endorse Professor Wu with a motto of Samuel Ullman: "Whether sixty or sixteen, there is in every human being's heart the lure of wonder, the unfailing child-like appetite of what's next, and the joy of the game of living. In the center of your heart and my heart there is a wireless station; so long as it receives messages of beauty, hope, cheer, courage and power from men and from the Infinite, so long are you young." I also hope that the wonderful writing of Professor Wu will inspire and impact many more readers.

Dr. Zhang Li

A Book that I have not Seen for Many a Year

By Prof Zheng Zhipeng

I read through *Life on the Cusp* in one go, and had much to say.

This is a book that I have not seen for many a year, true, rich in content with moving details, deep thinking, a plain literary style, and high readability. I think that readers from different walks of life can all benefit, so I strongly recommend this book.

For an autobiography, it is important to tell a true story. As a scientist, Weimin Wu was truthful, and wrote down his 70 years of personal experiences; no matter if they were successes or failures, experiences or lessons, positives or negatives, he spoke as they were. He was even open about his personal matters of privacy to the readers, which is hard to do without a broad mind.

For someone who has grown to an advanced age of over 70, he is no longer prompted by tangible interests. "Vain praise, exaggeration" do not mean much anymore. He just wanted to open his heart, telling his inner experiences and feelings to the world, that's all. As he put it in the preface: "I wish my story will bring live history to the readers, to make them deeply appreciate history, serving as inspiration for making new history." Such a premise ensures the purity, the truthfulness and the readability of the autobiography.

Secondly, this autobiography provides a rich content with moving details. The author describes what he experienced since the forties of the last century to the present. Because of the ups and downs Weimin experienced, a colorful life made to come alive by his skillful writing, the book grabs the attention of the reader gradually but firmly, resonating with his experiences.

Weimin Wu was born in a professional family in Shanghai, getting a good education since childhood. In middle school, he dabbled in many subjects but did not exert himself. He worked really hard in high school, becoming a top student, and went to Beijing for a conference as a representative of the best students in Shanghai, getting an audience with Mao Zedong. After graduating from high school, he passed the examination for "selected students for studying in the Soviet Union", but transferred to Fudan University, getting involved with top secret information for making the atom bomb in the "classified class", and later studied in the department of nuclear physics. After graduating from college, he became a graduate student to the famous nuclear physicist Professor Gongou Xu, studying at the department of modern physics at Lanzhou University. After finishing his graduate studies, Weimin got assigned to the launch base for the Chinese artificial satellite, getting involved in remote data analysis for launching the first artificial satellite, winning official recognition for his contributions. He entered the European Nuclear Research Center (CERN) in Geneva to study and work under Professor Steinberger (who later won the Nobel Prize for Physics). His talents and effort were appreciated by Steinberger. Upon returning to China, Weimin participated in the building of the Beijing Spectrometer, a detector to be used at the first Electron-Positron Collider of the high energy experimental base of China. He became the Vice Director of the first Physics department. At the same time, as he was responsible for the on-line and off-line data analysis of the Beijing Spectrometer, Weimin was also a member of the ALEPH international collaboration, establishing the first Internet link in China in the Institute of High Energy Physics. The e-mail message that he sent to Steinberger on August 25th, 1986 became the first event in Chinese Internet history. After the successful electron-positron collision experiment in October of 1988, Deng Xiaoping came to offer congratulations, shaking hands with Weimin Wu, as one of the participants of the Beijing Electron-Positron Collider Project. In June of 1989, while on duty at the Beijing Spectrometer, Weimin observed the J/Psi particle for the first time in Beijing, meaning that the Beijing Spectrometer was operating successfully.

Just as Weimin Wu was at his peak performance in the Institute of High Energy Physics, he was forced to leave China for the reasons stated in the book. He first went to Geneva, Switzerland, then worked at the

Fermi National Laboratory of the United States. He settled in Chicago, continuing his favorite particle physics research, winning international recognition. The CMS international collaboration team, of which Wu was a member, played an important role in the discovery of the Higgs particle, prompting the award of the 2013 Nobel Prize for Physics to this particle. The Monte Carlo modeling method Weimin Wu used contributed significantly to the experimental search for the Higgs particle.

The life of Weimin Wu was full of ups and downs, but is glorious. Overall, Weimin was a lucky person, presented with many challenges and rare opportunities. He was able to take those opportunities, achieving one success after another. Weimin also had many setbacks in his life, but he never gave up. He overcame them all, making his life a legend. This autobiography faithfully records such a legendary life, and is quite worth reading. Such a unique life path has few parallels.

I have been a friend of Weimin's for many years. We worked together in the Institute of High Energy Physics of China for nearly 10 years. I have kept in touch with him ever since, and witnessed the unfolding of his personal history described in the book, calling back many lively memories of my own.

Weimin entered the Institute of High Energy Physics in 1978, and we got to know each other soon afterwards. His talents, fast thinking, and warm and lively character impressed me deeply. Since 1986, we worked more closely, as I was the Director of the First Physics Division, and he was the Vice-Director. During the course of work, I got to know him even better. Our task was very demanding. We needed to mobilize the effort of over one hundred persons in the whole laboratory to complete the construction, installation, and operation of a key piece of equipment of the Beijing Electron-Positron Collider — the Beijing Spectrometer. We had to complete the work in a short time, and the collaboration between the Director and the Vice-Director was very important as a matter of course. The Beijing Spectrometer was the first large scale particle detector constructed in China, consisting of thousands of individual parts, highly precise and complicated. It was a monster two storeys tall, weighing 500 tons. Its function was to detect and analyze hundreds of kinds of "particles" that were the basic building blocks of matter, that could neither be seen nor touched. Weimin was responsible for a key component of the spectrometer, the on-line and off-line analysis system. Because we did not have any past experience, everything had to start from scratch. Naturally, we encountered many unimaginable difficulties, but eventually overcame them all to make the construction of the Beijing Spectrometer a huge success. It performed marvelously, won international recognition, and was used to obtain world-class research results. Weimin made his critical contributions. We worked together very smoothly, and I often benefited from his excellent suggestions and ideas.

Weimin had to leave the Institute of High Energy Physics Institute later, but his friends and colleagues did not forget him. They still remembered the good work that he did at the Institute. He was warmly received each time he visited the Institute after returning from the United States some years later.

Weimin did not resent the Institute of High Energy Physics after his name was "removed" from the Institute. Instead, he did what he could for the Institute. During the period when he took part in the CMS collaboration in the Fermi Laboratory, he gave hearty help and warm care to his colleagues coming from the Institute of High Energy Physics in both their work and their personal lives. Weimin acted as the liaison to help the Institute of High Energy Physics take on the task of constructing the m particle detector for the CMS, which turned out to be a success. He also did much work promoting the collaboration between the Institute of High Energy Physics and the Fermi National Laboratory. For his role in one of the meetings on high energy physics between those two parties, he was misunderstood by the leadership at the Fermi National Laboratory, who thought that he had disclosed internal planning secrets, even getting the attention of FBI. He felt wronged, and was not happy about it, resulting in high blood pressure and a minor stroke. However, Weimin did not regret it. All that he had done was open and above the board. He believed that it was a win-win situation for China and America to collaborate in scientific research.

Weimin kept the Institute of High Energy Physics close to his heart, and he loved the motherland that nurtured him.

Weimin enjoyed making friends and treating people sincerely, thus he has many friends, including many famous scientists and artists. Especially notable is Professor Steinberger, a top physicist of international fame, who is not only outstanding in his research field but also very charismatic as a person. Steinberger influenced Wu tremendously, recognizing the abilities and talents of Wu and guiding him in his work, helping him overcome many difficulties. Their relationship is of the "teacher plus friend" type. Such friendship is described in the book, becoming almost a legend.

The autobiography also describes the relationships between Weimin Wu and several Chinese American physicists such as Tsung-Dao Lee, C. N. Yang, and Samuel C.C. Ting, giving the reader intimate access to the academic achievements and legendary lives of those giants in science. The autobiography also records the moving friendships of Weimin with many other people of accomplishments, including physicists, painters, musicians, and friends in his local community.

Weimin Wu grew up in a big family full of love, with his parents and six brothers and sisters. The autobiography also tells their stories of joys and sorrows, reunions and separations. Each sibling is described in some details. They loved each other, and each was accomplished just like Weimin himself. Such a moving story of a talented scholarly family in Shanghai makes the autobiography even more interesting to read.

The third characteristic of this autobiography is the profound ideas that the author shares with readers. When describing the factual details of his own experiences, Weimin also reveals his personal feelings and shared his insightful thoughts and opinions. From the perspective of a scientist, Weimin examines the various political movements critically, especially the Cultural Revolution. He also presents his own views and thoughts on the policies and current status of the education, culture and scientific research in China, comparing Eastern and Western views and practices. He tells the facts using measured reasons, which are highly convincing. One may not agree with some of his positions, but will still be touched by his sincerity.

The autobiography has a simple but emotionally charged style, which forms another characteristic of the book. "The writing reflects the person", and "the book shows the person". Everywhere in the autobiography one can find the style and literary talents of Weimin Wu. One may not find many fancy words, but a simple, true description actually touches the heart of the reader even more.

I read about the tortuous experience with applying for the graduate school, being banished to do hard labor in the North-Western village of the Yinjia Mountains, lying sick in bed in a cave house, when an old lady sent him a big bowl of noodles with eggs … Later, he was bitten by a dog, lying in bed for two weeks with a swollen leg … His love entanglements that bore the mark of the time in history, and his separation with his first love. His harrowing experiences when he was about to leave China in July of 1989, especially the tense moment on a Polish airline bound for abroad … These memories are very realistic, engaging and moving.

Finally, I want to thank the World Scientific Publishing Company, also known as the Octagon Cultural Workshop, for publishing this excellent autobiography, giving the reader access to the legendary life of Weimin Wu to understand the time that he went through, as a reliable source of firsthand history. The younger generations can learn from his personal experiences and inspirations. From the perspective of social development, the book's significance is self-evident.

The Octagon Cultural Workshop has provided us with a high quality, stylishly illustrated masterpiece. There are many precious pictures found in the book, all very memorable. We look forward to more good books coming out like this one.

December, 2013, in Beijing

Dr. Zheng Zhipeng

Former Director

Institute of High Energy Physics, Chinese Academy of Science

Translators' Note

At the request of the author, this translation is based upon the Global Publishing House 2013 Chinese edition with minor revisions and updates by the author. A new Chapter 4 was created based on a short novel written by the author, so the English version has 11 chapters versus 10 in the Chinese version. Some deletions from the Chinese version were suggested by Harry Tong and approved by the author. Harry Tong translated the preface, foreword, prologues, epilogue, and book reviews except the one by Dan Green, which was written in English, as well as Chapters 1 to 6, and 10 to 11. Candice Wang translated Chapters 7, 8, and 9 plus all the captions for the figures and pictures included in the book. The English translation was peer-reviewed by the two translators with some help from Kerry Tong, who reviewed Chapters 1 to 11, and Lane Tong, who reviewed Chapter 8. Yvonne Wu has reviewed whole book and gave several important comments and suggestions. The author has reviewed the entire translation. Ms. Sally Alderson has edited Chapter 4 and the Prologue, Prof. Ye Minghan has reviewed whole book and Dr. Roy Rubinstein has reviewed Chapter 9. They have all given valuable comments and we would like to express our great appreciation.